'IRONOPOLIS'

STANDING UP FOR WOLVERHAMPTON
CORRECTLY DEFINING THE ORIGINAL BLACK COUNTRY
AN ANALYTICAL, EVIDENCE-BASED APPROACH

BY NICK MOSS

YOUCAXTON PUBLICATIONS
OXFORD & SHREWSBURY

Copyright © Nicholas Moss 2018

The Author asserts the moral right to
be identified as the author of this work.

ISBN 978-1-912419-39-5
Printed and bound in Great Britain.
Published by YouCaxton Publications 2018

All rights reserved. No part of this publication may be reproduced, stored in a retrieval system, or transmitted in any form or by any means, electronic, mechanical, photocopying, recording or otherwise, without the prior permission of the author.

This book is sold subject to the condition that it shall not, by way of trade or otherwise, be lent, resold, hired out or otherwise circulated without the author's prior consent in any form of binding or cover other than that in which it is published and without a similar condition including this condition being imposed on the subsequent purchaser.

YouCaxton Publications
enquiries@youcaxton.co.uk

Contents

Foreword vii

CHAPTER ONE 1
Introducing the Issues

CHAPTER TWO 27
Definitions of the Black Country
Assessing 4 Different Theories
Which Was Right?

CHAPTER THREE 103
Wolverhampton – 'in', 'out', or 'of the Black Country'?
Correctly Defining the Original
Geographical Borders of the Black Country and Its Original Capital

CHAPTER FOUR 178
Wolverhampton's Borders Over Time

CHAPTER FIVE 191
A Closer Look at Coal-mining in Wolverhampton
and the Wider Black Country Area

CHAPTER SIX 256
Iron Production in Wolverhampton
and the Wider Black Country Area

CHAPTER SEVEN 357
Wolverhampton Social Conditions
During the Industrial Revolution and Later-on

CHAPTER EIGHT 438
Other Considerations Regards the Black Country
Myths and Modern-day Arguments

CHAPTER NINE 444
Wolverhampton and the Black Country
Ten Overall Conclusions

CHAPTER TEN 450
A New Development and Partial Acknowledgement

CHAPTER ELEVEN 453
Wolverhampton and Black Country Quiz

References 458

Foreword

This work is primarily for educational purposes and as far as possible appropriate credit has been given where reference has been made to the work of others.

This research is entirely my own view, and if there are any inaccuracies or misinterpretations they are entirely unintentional. I have researched, examined, and thereafter highlighted the views of many historians, writers, and famous geologists to express various points, and to demonstrate what I consider to be a required degree of impartiality and credibility in discussing issues. A full list of 'References' is produced at the end of the work.

This research, or work, is split into eleven chapters. At the start of each chapter (except the introductory chapter), a breakdown of sub-topics within that chapter is highlighted in dark grey to help readers to follow the arguments within that chapter.

Nicholas Moss

CHAPTER ONE

Introducing the Issues

'The Black Country' – a term that evolved during the Industrial Revolution of the early-to-mid-1800s, to describe the vast, continuous, industrial area linking a number of towns producing coal and iron, to the north-west of Birmingham. Famously described as 'black by day, red by night', it does not appear officially on any map, and it has seldom been a clearly-defined or precisely-designated geographical area. And that is why even today, when the Black Country no longer really exists as such, it creates so much debate and discussion. In geographical terms, where does it start and where does it end? What defined it? Ownership of the term has become more pertinent only in recent years.

Interestingly, it is little-highlighted that the very first, or earliest written quotes to use the term 'Black Country', including that from Reverend William Gresley, perhaps quite significantly referred to it as an area of South Staffordshire, with no mention of Worcestershire which of course included the town of Dudley. A little more of that later.

To many people these days, it simply incorporates the 4 boroughs of Wolverhampton, Walsall, Dudley, and Sandwell, as depicted overleaf (Figure 1). This area is now around sixteen miles at most from north to south, and around ten miles at most from west to east, and it now contains a population of around 1.1 million people, slightly bigger than mighty Birmingham.

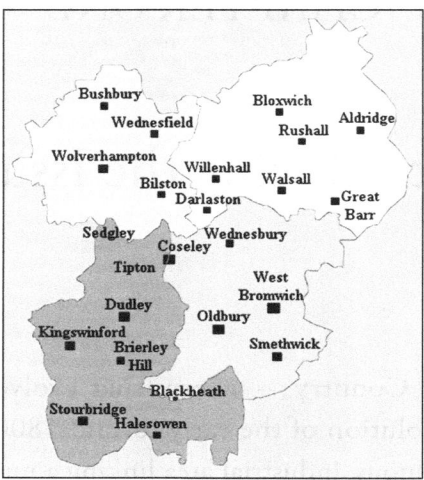

Figure 1 - Diagram of the four modern-day Black Country boroughs

To others, specifically the 'Black Country Society', who are widely perceived as the unofficial but nevertheless authoritative body, it was more restricted in area, defined precisely by geology but lying only where the famous thick coal seam was found, irrespective of the depth of the seam.

This theory was partly-based on the late-1960s 'protectionist stance' of a prominent, founding member of the Black Country Society, and an active member before that of the 'Dudley Canal Tunnel Closure Group', Walsall-born Dr John Malcolm Fletcher. Unquestionably he deserves immense credit for constantly raising the profile of the Black Country, and for highlighting the enormous industrial contribution this region made to the nation, and in fact to the world. Although this work fundamentally questions key parts of his theories, let us never forget or underestimate the immense contribution he and the Black Country Society have made, albeit arguably with a distinctive Dudley-bias.

Within his 1967 statement in the very first edition of 'The Black Countryman' magazine, he specifically excluded the larger towns of the area from the Black Country by suggesting that there were two distinct types of occupational activity ocurring, with the central part of the plateau supplying the raw materials of coal and iron-ore to the outer-lying commercial centres where it was used, thus he made a fundamental, clear-cut distinction between the smaller central villages, and the larger, outlying, commercial towns.

Even more controversially, he suggested that there was 'a very definite belt of open country, or wasteland, between the lower mineral plateau comprising the coal and iron-ore mines, and the elevated commercial centres of Wolverhampton, Walsall, and Birmingham'. In Wolverhampton's case, he suggested that this 'belt of open country' separating the town centre from the mineral-producing plateau was indicated by the names of its eastern districts of Monmore Green and Stow Heath. Yet detailed, archive research reveals that Wolverhampton had coal-mines immediately adjoining its town centre, at Horseley Fields for instance, so this part of his theory was plainly incorrect.

Dudley town too, incidentally, was on high ground, in fact it sat on the highest ground of all, and therefore somewhat separated from the mineral-plateau below it but all around it. As a 'commercial and manufacturing centre' itself, Dudley town was still however admitted into the Black Country fold by the Society, seemingly abandoning the logic applied to Wolverhampton and Walsall, and rightly to Birmingham.

But critically, without any real foundation as far as I can see, the Black Country Society made a landmark decision in the late-1960s, when they subsequently took Dr Fletcher's theory a step further by restricting their geographical definition of the Black Country to specific parts of Dr Fletcher's mineral-plateau, to those districts where only the famous thick coal seam lay, perhaps because they felt that those districts represented some sort of perceived heavily-industrialised, core area of our famous region.

With a reliance solely on the thick coal seam, their Black Country constituted a slightly smaller area perhaps just nine miles in length and eight miles across. Subsequently, it has been rigidly applied in geographical terms, by many of those who popularly and eagerly adopted it.

Many disagreed with and continue to disagree with this definition as it certainly appears at best somewhat idealistic, and at worst contrived. Cynics suggest that this definition was devised to try to exclude Wolverhampton, and to demean its legacy as the 'original Capital of the Black Country'. The theories of Dr Fletcher and the Black Country Society will be fundamentally challenged in this work, as it is arguable that they are quite simply flawed in parts. Although Dr Fletcher's theory appears to make perfect sense at first, the Black Country geographical boundaries that he and then the Black Country Society proposed reflect little resemblance to the way they were evidently perceived throughout the 1800s – when the 'original Black Country' was conceived and truly existed.

Through their definition, it is evident that the Black Country Society over-emphasise the relevance of the thick coal seam, and inevitably as a consequence under-value those areas where thinner coal seams with their adjacent valuable iron-ore existed. The best seams of iron-ore, that were absolutely critical for the developing iron industry, were usually to be found adjacent to the thin seams of coal, and it was the thinner seams of coal in large parts of the Black Country that were principally used in the blast furnaces and for smelting purposes, whilst much of the thick coal, at least in those districts east and north of Dudley and away from Lord Dudley's land, was only suitable for domestic household use, with purpose-built canals constructed specifically to link Wednesbury to Birmingham to fulfill that household demand. So contrary to popular opinion, much of the famous thick coal seam had nothing to do with the industrial development of the Black Country. A fundamental point to remember.

The seams of iron-ore (iron-stone) were of real financial value to prospectors, and it was mined in considerable quantity, notably in the Wolverhampton coal-field, where it often contained eleven valuable bands, more than anywhere else in the region. By 1835, around the time the name 'Black Country' first appeared in writing, around one million tonnes of coal was being mined in the South Staffordshire and East Worcestershire coal-field, and half a million tonnes of iron-ore, producing 150,000 tonnes of iron products. So, the iron-ore in the Wolverhampton coal-field was undoubtedly absolutely-critical for the growth and prosperity of the Black Country, to the point that it was often supplied to the iron works of Dudley as well as to those of its own town, yet the Black Country Society definition by nature excludes such important mineral-producing districts from their Black Country boundary.

Indeed, for many, the Black Country was in fact primarily defined by iron, as highlighted by the famed 19th-Century geologist Joseph Beete Jukes, who expressed that it was specifically the location of this iron-ore tract within the Black Country coal-field that determined where the great iron industry developed, more-so than the location of the thick coal seam, and for him it was the iron-ore tract that therefore defined the Black Country and its borders.

The iron industry itself appears to have been somewhat side-lined through the Black Country Society definition, playing second-fiddle in their version of Black Country history to coal, when in fact iron-production, as suggested by respected people like Jukes, was arguably the key feature of its legacy and the main character of the Black Country story. After all, before and even after the 'Black Country' name first appeared, the region was often referred to as the 'Iron Country', but never the 'Coal Country'. That is how important iron was perceived to be for the region. It was the manufacture of iron products that undoubtedly made the Black Country a great industrial region, bringing the area its living and a level of prosperity, and it was arguably the iron-ore in the ground, rather than the nationally-abundant coal, that really enabled it to take such a prominent role in the Country during the Industrial Revolution.

It is evident, therefore, that there are fundamental issues with the Black Country Society definition once it is scrutinised, and evidence produced within this work will show that quite clearly it was the combination of both coal-mining but perhaps principally iron-production that led to the area being so-called 'The Black Country', and never coal alone, despite it undoubtedly being an important factor.

And concurrently, let me make it clear at this point, that having studied and examined a huge raft of documents, reports, and newspaper articles from the 1800s, it is abundantly clear that the Black Country, at the time it became established and so-named, was never perceived to have been as restricted in geographical area as that designated solely by the existence of the thick coal seam, as suggested by the Black Country Society. They do appear to 'loosely acknowledge' this these days, but it also feels that they would need to abandon or reject parts of Doctor Fletcher's theory, to release them from the stance they adhere to and are strangulated by, to allow them to express and acknowledge the significance of iron and the major iron-producing towns.

There are further issues and contradictions with their definition, which will be scrutinised in due course. No wonder there was, and still is so much debate. There are so many complex considerations. But definitive conclusions can be made. Of course, archived documents that show that the Black Country Society's definition is in-the-main flawed, were in all-fairness much harder to access in the 1960s, when their theory was expressed. But it is still somewhat surprising that few people have challenged their definition over the past fifty years, because evidently there is a great deal to question. On the other hand, perhaps it is not such a surprise, as the small dedicated body that constituted the Black Country Society back at the time of its formation, must have presented as a deeply-passionate, knowledgeable, and even formidable body of people, whose view was difficult to challenge let alone question back then, and even today. But freedom of speech thankfully exists in this Country, so read on. After all, they do not own the Black Country, but they have understandably shaped perceptions.

On a personal level, I was born in the midlands, but brought up in my early years near Crewe, though my ancestors - some English, some Scottish with some Irish genes thrown in somewhere - lived across the industrial West Midlands region, ranging from West Bromwich in the south of the region, to Telford and Brownhills at the northern end. Like many other people, they were attracted to the employment opportunities that the area once offered to ordinary people seeking a living. But I am not a born-and-bred Black Countryman, and I do not pretend to be. Let me make that clear. But, that is not a necessary requirement to be able to assess factual, historic information. So, if that accusation is levelled, that is my simple but relevant response.

As a teenager working in Wolverhampton in the late-1980s however, I initially became interested in Wolverhampton's industrial eastern side when walking to work along the Willenhall Road from the city centre, after the bus from Whitmore Reans, where I lived, dropped me off at the bus station. As I walked this stretch day-after-day, I noted a great concentration of factory buildings just east of the town centre around Horseley Fields, and in recent years I further researched the history of this area and was staggered to discover the sheer number of major iron works that once stood all around. I can still remember Horseley Fields when I first walked through it, recalling the thuds of machinery, and the accompanying acrid, chemical smells, and seeing the sooty appearance of workers covered in grime. Several of my mates from Whitmore Reans worked in foundries there, and I was to be truthful, thankful that I worked in an office as a pen-pusher. But I can only imagine what the sense of sound and smell, and especially the sight, might have been like if I had been able to walk around these streets at the height of the Industrial Revolution. The scene here must have been tremendous, in industrial terms. More of that later.

But I was then also somewhat surprised to discover from old Ordnance Survey (OS) maps from 1901-1903, that there were once collieries spread all-across the town's eastern and southern sides, because I wrongly thought Wolverhampton had very little mining legacy except for the Bilston part, this reflecting the impression often directly or indirectly conveyed in modern times, principally by the Black Country Society or its supporters, who bizarrely continued at least until 2017 to suggest that the coal-seam did not outcrop at Wolverhampton. I had always presumed that they were the knowledgeable body with a responsibility to educate the public accurately. But my research taught me that the coal-seam clearly did outcrop at Wolverhampton, quite widely in fact, so this contradiction-of-fact, unearthed by my own investigation, only served to further increase my level of suspicion regards the attitude towards Wolverhampton, and I began to suspect that there had been some ulterior motives at play. The image of the dirty work only being carried out in the central towns of the Black Country was being widely and readily conveyed. And it is little-known and hence never highlighted, that whilst some Wolverhampton collieries did actually work the thick coal seam, the iron-stone and thin seam miners of the town had to work longer hours in what were arguably worse conditions than their better-paid thick seam compatriots in the Dudley area.

Furthermore, turning the whole Black Country Society theory on its head, it was specifically the 'thin coal seam tract of land' that arguably most typically-characterised the 'original Black Country', described in 1850 in the following way: -

"The appearance of the country around Wolverhampton, Willenhall, and Bilston, where the thin seams principally lie, is strange in the extreme. For miles and miles, the eye ranges over wide-spreading masses of black rubbish, and hills on hills of shale, and masking, as it were, the whole face of nature".

So, if the appearance of the coal-mining area partly led to the district being called 'The Black Country', it seems very likely that it was actually the coal-field between Wolverhampton and Bilston and the process of working the shallow thin seam and iron-stone there that primarily led to that, as the visually damaging effect on the landscape was the probably the greatest. Again, it is hard to find any reference to this in Black Country Society circles or publications, nor at the Black Country Living Museum which focuses strongly on mining of the thick coal seam in the Dudley area.

Moving on, Wolverhampton gained City-status in 2001, but it will be referred to as a town in this work, as that is what it was during the time-period investigated. But Wolverhampton has always been the prominent and largest town in this area. Like Dudley, and smaller neighbours such as Bilston, it was originally a market town, but Wolverhampton retained this role for longer, indeed it still retained a prominent market town role until the mid-1800s due to its position on the north-western edge of the Black Country, easily accessible from Shropshire and Wales, though this is often over-emphasised by some detractors. Metal-work had in fact been the dominant trade in the Wolverhampton economy since the mid-1700s, and in the 1800s the large proportion of its population became more-or-less reliant on coal-mining and the iron industry.

The town itself was built on high ground, occupying a strategically strong and potentially healthy geographical location, on the edge of the Black Country, and arguably 'Of the Black Country, but not in it'. In some respect therefore, it is understandable why Wolverhampton presents a dilemma for some Black Country historians. It was a town of great historic antiquity, with a comparatively grand commercial centre and several attractive high streets typical of a large, commercial town, and therefore the town centre was quite unlike the smaller Black Country towns that evolved from simple high-street villages which had little evidence of commercial wealth. Dudley was in many ways similar, the town centre was also built on high, elevated ground, and like Wolverhampton it too had busy commercial streets. The economies of the two towns were in fact very similar during the Industrial Revolution. But both contained outer-lying residential and industrial districts that were indeed typical of the Black Country.

West Bromwich occupied a similar peripheral geographical location as Wolverhampton, but on the south-western edge of the great mining area, yet like Dudley, its Black Country qualification is seldom questioned. A report from the 'Staffordshire Sentinel' on 26 June 1878, described Sandwell Park at West Bromwich in the following terms: -

"For picturesqueness of scenery, it would be impossible to imagine a more charming resort. Situated just on the fringe of the Black Country, and in marked relief to the gloom which is fairly perceptible in the distant horizon, Sandwell Park commands a charming view of the magnificent landscape, which for many a mile, stretches away into the peaceful country."

Of course, at the end of the Industrial Revolution, in fact around that point in time, Sandwell Park itself became the base of a great mining operation of the much deeper, concealed coal seam, so hence perhaps for this reason, its inclusion is readily accepted. Nevertheless, this area of West Bromwich was clearly not considered part of the 'original Black Country', a point rarely or in fact never expressed by those within the Society. But the land around these later-mining operations was not pitted in the same way that the traditional mining methods affected it, and there was no black smog here due to furnaces and chimneys. It was a million miles away there, from the black, damaged, and smoky Black Country landscape of eastern Wolverhampton.

Wolverhampton was a polarised society during the 1800s, as it always has been in fact, with a large working-class population employed in the factories and mines, and a smaller, prosperous class who controlled local affairs and who resided on its green, western side or in adjacent leafy villages. Where there is muck there is always brass. It has expanded considerably over the past two-hundred years, especially as the 1900s progressed. To compound the issue, many of these newer, western-side residents did not consider themselves to be Black Country folk, and rightly so, they never were part of it. Vast new council estates were built on green-field sites to the north-east of the town during the 1900s, and inevitably these sit outside the 'original Black Country' boundary. Many of the residents there however, originally worked in the town's iron-works, and even in the coal-mines at nearby Essington. So, in looking at modern-Wolverhampton since the mid-1900s, the picture has admittedly become muddled with time.

Despite the delightful scene awaiting travellers approaching its western 'green borderland' of Tettenhall and Penn, as Elihu Burritt described such parts, most of Wolverhampton was as blighted as anywhere in the Black Country back in the 1800s, and well into the 1900s, and the transformation in environment perhaps even more noticeable when travelling in a southerly or easterly direction into Wolverhampton town centre and its railway station, overlooking its grimy eastern prospects. Quite evidently, that is where the northern aspect of the Black Country was considered to have started, not only when you got to Bilston, as is sometimes suggested.

A report from the Birmingham Daily Post succinctly described the polar-opposite environments that the town's eastern and western residents experienced, when it reviewed plans for Wolverhampton's new 'East-end Park' in December 1892: -

"Rarely is there such a striking contrast to be found in the general appearance of any town as there is in the eastern and western sides of Wolverhampton. The western extremity merges into a picturesque agricultural district, while at the opposite end of the town commences that extensive tract of land with its hives of industry, known as 'The Black Country', where chimney stacks, blast furnaces, and pit frames have taken the place of the wide-spreading oak or other trees which in the dim past might have been seen dotted over the landscape. The eastern portion of Wolverhampton presents a desolate sight, with its old pit mounds sparsely covered with dull-coloured herbage, or where a

shrub or a tree is a rarity. But it is here proposed, with the assistance of the landscape gardener, to give the residents of 'darkest Wolverhampton' an attractive park...........an area which is nearly wholly pit-mounds intersected by footpaths and water-courses, with here and there, high masses of blast furnace slag, blackened with the smoke of ages."

Local writer David Clare further highlighted this divergence in perception between western and eastern Wolverhampton residents in modern times, in his 2005 book 'Wolverhampton - Photographic Memories', where he stated: -

"Residents in the leafy western suburbs some years ago were surprised to see new signs on the main roads welcoming them to the Black Country. The inhabitants of the industrial eastern suburbs on the other hand are amazed that anyone could imagine that they were not part of the Black Country."

Of course, it is impossible to say whether ordinary Wolverhampton or Dudley working people back in 1850 for instance, generally saw themselves as 'proud Black Countrymen and women'. I suspect that first and foremost, people did not really care, so long as they put food on their plate each day. It may be a somewhat romantic, modern-day notion to suggest that people argued and counter-argued whether their area should or should not have been considered as part of the Black Country back then. Perhaps we will never know. It is also worth noting that people were, and still are, proud primarily of being from Wolverhampton, Walsall, and West Bromwich as they had and still have a distinctive enough name and history in-their-own-right, with football teams to follow as well, at least from the late-1800s.

Either way, it is largely the written evidence of writers, commentators, travellers, newspaper editors, and even geologists from the period throughout the 1800s that we should arguably rely on to draw an accurate definition of the 'original, true Black Country'. Especially those writers with local knowledge such as the geologist Joseph Beete Jukes, the somewhat-ignored iron-industry expert Samuel Griffiths, and land-owner the Earl of Dartmouth, along with the remarks of local people who expressed their views in local newspapers of course. Their views are compelling, contradicting the definition of the Black Country Society with its sole emphasis on the thick coal seam.

Those detractors who today oppose Wolverhampton's inclusion within the Black Country tend to neglect its immense industrial contribution to the region, and the sheer hard graft of its residents. Between 1841-50, in the middle of the Industrial Revolution, the average age of death for Wolverhampton people was just nineteen years and one month, the third worst, or lowest in the Country. Undoubtedly, this was largely due to the appalling, insanitary housing conditions that were even more prejudicial to health than the dangerous and hazardous occupations in its coal-mines and in its iron and brass foundries. During the Industrial Revolution of the late-1700s and 1800s, there was 'too little brass and too much muck' for the average Wolverhampton worker, when iron works and collieries dominated the town. Swedish Government iron and steel commissioner R.R. Angerstein visited Wolverhampton in 1754, acknowledging its strategic prominance in the metal trade at that time, stating that it was one of three English towns reputed for its iron and steel-ware, but he also noted: -

"On the outskirts of town where most of the artisans live, there are also many wretched hovels, which clearly shows that also in this place the worker is left with the bones, whereas the merchant takes the meat for himself."

Despite the continued existence of numerous empty factories today, there is nothing vaguely comparable to the scene that would have confronted travellers and visitors to the region throughout the Industrial Revolution, with the town's central iron works 'belching-out flame and smoke' through hundred of furnaces and towering chimneys, and numerous shallow coal-mines with black spoil-banks scarring much of the surface, all the way to the horizon.

Hypothetically, if there would have been some sort of emissions-test back then, Wolverhampton, Dudley, and the rest of the Black Country would have been 'closed down'. Especially Wolverhampton and Bilston which were noted to possess the smokiest environments of all the region's towns

The famous 1866 drawing of Wolverhampton depicted at the start of the work, perhaps accurately conveys a striking, visual impression of the Black Country more than any other, even if the London newspaper's editorial-artist crowded all of Wolverhampton's towering chimneys together, to increase the effect. This famous picture once found itself highlighted in the George Pompidou Centre in Paris, and it is now show-pieced in the corridors of the Black Country Living Museum, though perhaps not unsurprisingly, simply titled 'Black Country', if you believe in my 'Dudley-centric conspiracy theory'. No acknowledgement of it being Wolverhampton's eastern environment at all. You can bet your bottom dollar if it had been a drawing of Cradley for instance, it would have been labelled as such. But it certainly conveys the 'strikingly-hellish' environment that existed when the Black Country was truly with us in the 1800s.

A letter written to 'Aris's Birmingham Gazette' on 12 November 1855 by a shell-shocked but unnamed Birmingham-based traveller and writer who spent a day or two in the Black Country, perhaps more than any other written piece, captures in vivid detail the shockingly squalid and morbid existence of the residents of the Black Country: -

"What on earth is to help a people like this? And who will become their friends? Will the Honourable Representatives in the Commons for Wolverhampton, or Dudley, or Walsall, or Birmingham undertake their case? I have for some years been partially acquainted with it, but never till I had visited it for-the-purpose-of ascertaining its condition had I the remotest notion of what the country really is. I think it is impossible for any man with English feelings in his heart even to look

out from a railway carriage upon the utter misery and ruin he is passing through without shame and humiliation. The misery and ruin seen in the houses, reeling like drunken men – the rusty, broken-up machinery – the black wastes over which the blackest smoke is slowly creeping from a thousand different chimneys – represent but too faithfully the human beings who are doomed to live in this horrible district. The first day I spent in it will live in my memory as one of the most dismal days of my life. Everything seemed, or really was dead. If all the dirty stores of rags and bones and old iron to be found in every large town in the Kingdom could be thrown into one heap, it would give anyone a true idea of the squalor and wretchedness so deeply cut in the face of this Black Country. As a member of the national church, I feel humbled that such a place as this Black Country can exist in England, and no attempt, or very feeble attempts be made to make it better. Where hundreds of thousands of people, for the most part fearfully ignorant, who are always dirty, who seldom laugh, who never play, who when they are not working or eating or drinking, are sleeping - are left, for the greater part, uncared for, unthought of, and unbefriended against the tyrannies and avarice of riches on the one hand, and idleness and indifference on the other."

Thankfully, the incredibly-blighted and damaged environment and landscape created by the Industrial Revolution has to a significant degree, now been dramatically addressed, and very few of us live in 'a black country' today. The all-consuming black clouds of smoke and the piles of furnace spoil have disappeared altogether, and consequently the amount of greenery has increased substantially. Even as recently as 1952, in his book 'Black Country', historian Phil Drabble highlighted that: -

"The Black Country was becoming no more than a memory. For one thing, it is no longer black".

But at least the past has been partially 'captured and bottled' by the excellent Black Country Museum - now called the 'Black Country Living Museum', that first opened near Dudley in 1975. It has gone from strength to strength, and it is a wonderful reflection of the industrial legacy of the region, albeit with a Dudley and

Cradley emphasis, especially regards coal-mining. Having said that, the museum does at least highlight the contribution of Wolverhampton, particularly in the 1900s, with a special wall-mural dedicated to the contribution of each of the four boroughs, though like the Black Country Society, it suggests that coal is the key defining feature of the region, and it rightly questions 'all-of-modern-Wolverhampton's' Black Country status, by stating on the mural: -

"There is debate as to how much of this modern borough lies within the real Black Country. Often referred to as lying "off the coal", faultlines limited mining to the south and east. Nevertheless, the exploitation of coal and iron were still backbone industries".

However, those murals don't question 'all-of-Walsall's' qualification, nor 'all-of-Sandwell's' qualification. The eastern part of Walsall borough, and nearly all of Smethwick in Sandwell, surely raise the same question as they also lie 'off the coal-seam'. But apart from its avoidance of Wolverhampton's coal-mining legacy throughout the Industrial Revolution, the Black Country Living Museum does at least acknowledge Wolverhampton's industrial contribution, albeit with an emphasis on the engineering and automobile companies of the 1900s, though it does stress that the town was 'all about iron'. Its immense 1800s contribution is largely ignored.

Perhaps part of any ill-feeling regards the town's under-representation was compounded by the fairly beligerent view in some quarters, especially from some involved in open on-line discussions, including 'some of those within the Black Country Society', that Wolverhampton should not have its place in Black Country history at all, except the Bilston part. The Black Country Society, in my opinion, has allowed this perception to fester unchallenged and unquestioned over a number of years.

The more I investigated and researched, the more I felt uneasy with this dismissive attitude towards Wolverhampton. A distinctive anti-Wolverhampton agenda undoubtedly existed in some quarters in the late-1960s, and it still exists today. Famous writers have even been misquoted by some Black Country historians, perhaps in an attempt to demean Wolverhampton's industrial legacy, whilst the Black Country Society webpage omitted Wolverhampton from that list of towns where coal was mined and came to the surface since the birth of the Society until 2017, further demonstrating that an anti-Wolverhampton agenda existed. Though in relation to this last point, there has very recently been a significant acknowledgement, which is highlighted at the end of the work. This development occurred mid-way through writing this work.

Nevertheless, the level of internal-lobbying for the town to be erased from Black Country history must have been fairly-significant during the late-1960s. I wonder if people from Wolverhampton within the Black Country Society's early membership were included in those it labelled as 'outsiders'? The traditional Black Country Society attitude left me somewhat bemused, but more than anything I thought that some of their views genuinely constituted a 'misrepresentation of history' and a 'miseducation of the general-public'. It was as though Wolverhampton's thousands of miners and metal-workers just didn't contribute, matter, or even exist.

Furthermore, thousands of Wolverhampton school-children (and for that matter children across the region) would perhaps grow-up mis-understanding or misinterpreting the role their own ancestors had played in creating the greatest industrial region that the world has perhaps ever seen. I can only compare the apparent disregard and dismissiveness shown to Wolverhampton by the Black Country Society at times, to the feeling of that of leaving a cinema after watching an American World War Two film where the efforts of the British were under-valued and only reluctantly or very briefly acknowledged. Yes, it almost felt like high-treason.

Let me make it clear, despite the strong sentiments expressed above, the work that the Black Country Living Museum and the Black Country Society have done to create an educational legacy is simply wonderful, it wasn't always popular to admit one lived in the Black Country. And it was historians and passionate lay people from the Dudley area who had the vision to start a society, to build a museum, and to promote the region's industrial legacy through publications, so it is understandable that an over-emphasis on the Dudley area has perhaps inadvertantly evolved since the 1960s. In 'Standing Up for Wolverhampton', I do not wish to dismiss their wonderful work, and I certainly do not wish to appear to question the legacy or the industrial heritage of the Dudley area at all, that is not what this is about. Dudley quite arguably merits the title of 'Capital of the Black Country' simply because it was set in the heart of the region and hence it had coal-mines and iron-works on all sides, and you cannot dismiss the fact that those famous industrial pioneers Abraham Darby and Dud Dudley were both born nearby. But you cannot re-write or change history. There is a significant amount of evidence that is now easily accessible via newspaper archives and through google books, confirming that Wolverhampton was widely considered to be the 'Capital or Metropolis of The Black Country' from the time the phrase 'Black Country' first appeared in writing around 1840, until the mid-1900s - something that is never mentioned by the Black Country Society, and it is a view nowhere to be seen at the Black Country Living Museum, who perhaps wisely avoid the 'Capital' issue altogether, at least from what I saw during my half-day visit.

But there is, or at least was another dilemma for Dudley with its claim to be the unofficial 'Capital of the Black Country', which it does so proudly today. The Black Country was previously divided into two geographical Counties. During the Industrial Revolution of the 1800s, the larger section of the coal-field for instance, was referred to as 'The Great South Staffordshire Coal-field', with Wolverhampton clearly considered its prominent town, whilst the smaller section was the East Worcestershire Coal-field, with Dudley its most important town. Hence, at the time, this left Dudley in a somewhat isolated and difficult position, unable to vie for 'Capital status' of a region that primarily lay in a different County. These days, of course, since 1974, the whole region lies within the unifying West Midlands County boundary, making it easier for some people to meritoriously but non-contemporaneously award the status of 'Capital' to Dudley. But back then, which County you were from mattered to people. So, Dudley was never really considered the 'Capital' during the Industrial Revolution, for that reason.

It doesn't seem unreasonable to question whether the Black Country Society, in adopting its definition of the region based on the revered Dr Fletcher's 'Dudley-centric' views, have always been entirely subjective? So, this research is largely dedicated to highlighting Wolverhampton's industrial contribution to the Black Country throughout the Industrial Revolution. It attempts to dispel any ill-founded notion that its population somehow only benefitted from the hard labour of the inhabitants of neighbouring Black Country towns, which increasingly during the late-1900s and today, seems to be a view 'peddled' by some people. Those same people still believe that 'all of the dirty work' was done by those in the villages of the central part of the Black Country.

I suspect this theory was born out of the fact that after the Industrial Revolution, and from the early-to-mid-1900s particularly, Wolverhampton was no longer so strongly reliant on the primary coal and iron industries. As its natural mineral resources expired and its iron industry declined, a new engineering and construction economy evolved, involving famous companies such as Sunbeam, Villiers Engineering, Clyno, AJS, Guy Motors, Boulton-Paul, and other highly-skilled vehicle, aviation, and bicycle manufacturers, and of course those giant household-names of Wolverhampton industry - Tarmac, and Goodyear. And like Birmingham, though on a smaller scale, Wolverhampton became a centre of great invention and innovation, holding fetes and events to promote the creative diversity of its manufacturing industry – its steel jewelry and toys, its japanned-ware, and its enamels. It held great exhibitions, such as one held in 1902 at its West Park, just within Elihu Burritt's 'green borderland', which promoter's rightly reminded people lay 'just outside the boundary of the Black Country'. At this later point in time, when many Black Country historians and writers of the 20th-Century grew-up, perhaps they perceived part of Wolverhampton's character to be 'too pretentious to be true Black Country'. And at that point the attitude prevailed that 'the Black Country always started in the next town'. But it wasn't simply an attitude of some aloof Wolverhampton people, it was notably an attitude of some aloof and prominent Walsall people, which was noted to have been the most 'aristocratic Black Country town' even back in the 'smoky' late-1800s. For instance, the editor of the 4th edition of the 'Walsall Observer' in September 1862, quite vehemently denied any link of his town to the Black Country in stating: -

"Now I never can or will have it that Walsall is in the Black Country, not a bit of it. The worst that can be said about the worst side of the old town is that it is rather 'whitey-brown'. Now, it is a good thing for you and me dear reader, that Walsall is not in, but out of the Black Country. Surrounded as she is by green fields, country lanes, pleasant nooks and corners, extensive landscapes and charming scenery. Walsall in the Black Country indeed! The nigh-mare on the man who first villified our glorious town by so vile a slander."

Of course, he was not speaking for all Walsall folk, and he may have been exaggerating its beauty somewhat.

There is in fact very little evidence that Wolverhampton people condescended to this view during the Industrial Revolution. In general, the residents and politicians of Wolverhampton acknowledged and even appreciated its very own muck and dirt, and its renowned smoky atmosphere which turned its streets and residents sooty-black, because they knew that coal and iron were inextricably linked to its overall prosperity. And based on available evidence, they clearly felt part and parcel of 'their Black Country', though some people were clearly keen to see the town progress and move forward as the 1900s progressed, and they were perhaps increasingly keen to rid the town of its national reputation of being a dank, dirty, industrial town, and the butt of many people's jokes and slurs. Hence, some were not proud of its Black Country roots.

A word about Bilston. For the purpose of this work, I shall treat Bilston as a separate town, and although it does indeed have a distinctly-proud, individual history, it has had strong Wolverhampton links for hundreds of years, all the way back to 985AD when lands were granted to Lady Wulfruna, except perhaps for a period in the mid-1900s. Willenhall has similar historic links to the town, as does Wednesfield of course.

Moving on to the structure of this work, let me clarify that this is detailed research, it is heavy at times too, especially the following chapter. It is not a novel, it is not about any personal experience of growing up in the region, with amusing experiences and snippetts. No, it is a detailed study of a region, and especially of a town that has arguably been betrayed and misrepresented. All the information is important, and primarily it is reports extracted from newspaper archives that make it an interesting read, and which help readers properly understand Wolverhampton's role in Black Country history. However, there may be sections you wish to skim over.

So, the critical chapter that follows shortly scrutinises three slightly different, often-proposed definitions of the Black Country, including that from the Black Country Society, as well as a little-recognised but very relevant fourth one. To determine which definition is the correct one, this chapter will look at the following key factors - When did the Black Country evolve 'in name' and as 'a physical entity'? Timeframe is critical. And more controversially, which mineral, coal or iron-ore, and which industry, coal or iron, was considered mostly to have defined the 'original Black Country'? Or was it a combination of both? When and where did the vast iron industry develop? Did industry really develop on the thick coal seam, as often inferred by the Black Country Society? And critically, based on historical evidence and popular opinion, where did the 'original Black Country' in geographical terms, really lie?

To define this true, 'original Black Country', it is a fundamentally-critical to catapult-us- back nearly two-hundred years to scrutinise available evidence of that era, as it represented people's views when it first evolved and truly existed. This is an under-valued consideration in my opinion, a strand of thinking that seems to have been fundamentally ignored by many local-historians of the 20th-century, who simply expressed their own thoughts of growing up in the Black Country during the 1900s. The region's economy inevitably evolved and developed as the 1900s progressed, but this does not mean that the Black Country's geographical borders should be shifted-around with subsequent economic change. And if its borders are to be re-appraised in that way, then it raises the question of whether the Black Country exists at all today, because once you start 're-assessing' its boundaries with time, you have adopted an 'ever-changing interpretation' that dictates that you must continually reassess. You cannot simply stop at any given point in time to suit your view. As perhaps happened when the Society formed in the 1960s, when its enthusiasts reconvened to 'thrash it all out' in the pubs of Tipton and Dudley. In doing so, they appear to have perhaps inadvertently, or even unintentionally misrepresented earlier history.

Quite clearly then, all things being considered, there is a strong case that the Black Country lies, and will always lie, where it was first truly considered to have been, at the time it was first so-named. This was the 'original Black Country'.

The following chapter therefore, with all the above considerations, is arguably the key part of the work, the one that scrutinises, discusses, and ultimately proposes and clarifies the correct definition of the 'original Black Country'.

The different definitions of the Black Country have been superficially discussed and disputed repeatedly since the 1960s, but this work is the first as far as I am aware, to look at each of the different theories, and then attempt to analyse and identify the correct one. I believe it is perhaps the first thorough or serious attempt to correctly define the Black Country, reaching beyond the 'chinese-whispers' mentality of local-folklore. A controversial but unintentonally patronising statement, I accept that.

Moving forward from the conclusion of the next 'heavy chapter', chapter three then resolutely clarifies through an evidence-based approach, exactly where the original geographical boundaries of the Black Country lay, particularly with Wolverhampton in mind. The level of evidence produced through the views of writers of the 1800s is truly compelling, and descriptions of Wolverhampton will leave a vivid impression.

Then, in what might be fairly described as 'supplemental chapters', the work first looks at the development of Wolverhampton, examining its borders over the centuries, highlighting a strong community link between Wolverhampton, Bilston, Willenhall, Wednesfield, and Essington over hundreds of years. Separate villages they may have been, but Wolverhampton has not simply 'swallowed them up' following post-1966 boundary re-organisation, a near-mythical view that is today popularly held by some.

Before summarising, the next three chapters look in considerable detail at coal and iron-ore mining, the vast iron-producing industry, and the social conditions of Wolverhampton and the wider Black Country during the Industrial Revolution, sections which may be of less interest to people who are not Wulfrunians. Nevertheless, these informative sections are important, as the fascinating, historic information contained within them, obtained from 'never-before-highlighted' archives in some instances, emphasises the sheer scale of Wolverhampton's industrial heritage and secures its contribution to Black Country history. There are some fascinating articles gleaned from these newspaper archives, items that I hope make these three chapters more interesting, including routine reports of dreadful accidents resulting in horrific injury or death for many young men, women, and indeed children too, in Wolverhampton's coal-mines and iron works. There are also detailed reports highlighting the abject squalor and hardship experienced by those unfortunate people who found themselves resident in Wolverhampton's infamous 19th-Century and early 20th-Century slums. There are also some intriguing but eye-opening reports that reveal the incredibly harsh working-environment, especially for children, in the town's manufactories. Wolverhampton was singled out in a landmark, official mid-1800s Government report as that area of the Country where the treatment of children in industry was of the greatest concern, with their treatment labelled as 'ferocious'. Thank goodness things have improved so dramatically, and that we were born after these incredibly harsh times.

The final short chapters take a light-hearted look at things, include a quiz, and then finally, the important overall conclusions regarding the 'original Black Country' are drawn.

Finally, I must also pay special recognition to the work of others, notably to Bev Parker's immense contribution on the Wolverhampton History website, as much of the detail highlighting Wolverhampton's proud industrial heritage is only presented here due to the research she has clearly painstakingly undertaken. Indeed, critics of this work will with some justification, highlight that it is largely a re-hash of other people's study and full of quotations. The work is not intended to, and indeed nor ever could it highlight any artistic or creative flair on my behalf. And I certainly don't seek the limelight, nor do I have the ability to orally discuss the issues with any great competence.

If having read all the evidence presented, one still feels that it is justifiable to exclude Wolverhampton from the Black Country, perhaps the town could and should adopt and promote the entirely fitting, entirely appropriate, alternative title of 'The Capital of the Iron Country'. The region was often referred to as such, and there are concrete grounds for developing such a status. Wolverhampton was described as 'the central point of the Iron Country' by English journalist William Cobbett during his 1830s tour of the Country, Charles Darwin referred to its great iron furnaces, Queen Victoria amongst many others also referred to it as 'The Iron Country', and the Manchester-press even labelled it 'Ironopolis' during her 1866 visit. Hence, the title of this work. Furthermore, it was 'The Capital of the iron trade in the Black Country' according to local businessman and book-writer Samuel Griffiths, and it was considered by many to be the 'The centre of the iron trade' with regular 'State of Trade' reports from the 'Wolverhampton correspondent' appearing in newspapers across the nation during the 1800s.

If you take the stance that iron was crucial to the legacy of the Black Country, which it quite clearly was, it seems truly inconceivable that Wolverhampton could ever be omitted from it.

Ultimately, of course, people can believe what they choose to believe. It is often said that 'no two people will agree where the Black Country lies'. Long will that continue, undoubtedly. People have concrete mindsets. But I have no doubt that the evidence will ruffle a few feathers to say the least, and perhaps create some fiery debate. Most importantly though, I implore interested people, especially if you question the content and conclusions of this work, to go and undertake your own research, and I suggest that then you too will start to question the standard views expressed by the Black Country Society. But I am simply a lay person, and it is possible of course that I may have slightly misinterpreted some points, and there may be a few inaccuracies and also occasional spelling mistakes within the work, purely unintentional of course.

The work is titled **'Standing up for Wolverhampton' - Correctly defining the original Black Country - an analytical, evidence-based approach**, because I can't help but conclude that there has been some sort of misguided attempt in the last fifty years to misrepresent this grand old town's contribution to the Black Country.

Make no mistake, the Black Country without Wolverhampton would undoubtedly have struggled to thrive and prosper in the way it did. Wolverhampton in isolation, has a long, proud, distinguished history, but it was also a key Black Country component, and its significant contribution towards it helped create an industrial legacy in the region that should be recognised, acknowledged, and indeed celebrated by everyone within it. It should not and does not really need to argue a case for its inclusion within Black Country history, and this work will clarify beyond any doubt, that overall, Wolverhampton was clearly considered to be a key Black Country town, as well as being widely-considered as its historic 'Capital'.

'Ironopolis' was a 'star of the Black Country show', rather than the 'understudy', or even the 'outside-observer' it is scandalously often portrayed to be. Read on, and by the end of the work, I am sure that there is a very good chance that you too will agree that there has been a significant misrepresentation of the 'original Black Country', and particularly of Wolverhampton's role within it. The intention is not paint the town in a dismal light, but in what was a realistic light for so many of its people, an angle which as far as I know has never really before been investigated or revealed.

Take your time in reading it. I hope you will feel better informed, but most of all I hope you enjoy reading all about 'Ironopolis', a wonderful Black Country town.

CHAPTER TWO

Definitions of the Black Country - Assessing 4 Different Theories. Which Was Right?

CHAPTER BREAKDOWN

1) **Introducing four different definitions of the Black Country.**
2) **A Brief History of the Industrial Revolution.**
3) **Assessing the Four Definitions.** Including: - A) When was the term 'Black Country' first recorded? B) When did the Black Country evolve as a physical entity? Examining i) The Region's Economy before the Industrial Revolution. ii) The Rate of Growth During the Industrial Revolution - Coal, Iron, Population. C) What really defined the Black Country? Coal or Iron, or both? Examining i) Statistics in relation to Coal and Iron production. ii) Coal or Iron as the main defining industry? – The views of writers.
4) **Potential Contradictions within the Black Country Society thick coal seam definition?** Including: - A) The 'original Black Country' lay only in Staffordshire and did not include Dudley. B) Wolverhampton, Walsall, and Birmingham were commercial centres separated from the mineral area by very definite belts of open country or wasteland. C) There were two distinct

geographical zones where different occupational activities took place. D) The Black Country was defined by geology - but only one aspect of it - the thick coal seam. E) The 'thick coal seam irrespective of its depth' contradiction – a shifting Black Country boundary. F) Wolverhampton's incorrect ommission from the Black Country adopting the Black Country Society 'thick coal seam' definition. G) The boastful figures within five-miles of Dudley. H) Industry - did the thick coal seam really determine the location of developing Industry? Or was this primarily determined by other factors such as the location of the iron-stone tract or thin seam of the coal-field, or by the location of the canal system?

5) **Conclusions - Correctly defining the Black Country.**

1) INTRODUCING FOUR DIFFERENT DEFINITIONS OF THE BLACK COUNTRY

It is evident that there are four different definitions, each proposing slightly different factors which for them defined the Black Country, and consequently each definition proposes a slightly different geographical boundary for the Black Country.

It is critical to grasp and fully comprehend exactly what each of the definitions propose, because subsequent detailed discussion within this chapter fundamentally revolves around them.

The four definitions now follow: -

DEFINITION ONE- The Black Country Society, formed in 1967 from a local Dudley-based group of activists, produced a definition based entirely on geology, that proposed that: -

"The original Black Country was that area of South Staffordshire and North Worcestershire which was on the famous thirty-foot seam of coal".

Although their website depicts a map that simply includes the 4 Black Country boroughs in their entirety, it states that in their opinion the 'original Black Country was defined by the presence of the thirty-foot (or ten-yard) thick coal seam'. They also acknowledge the existence of the thin coal seam, the seams of iron-ore, and limestone, but for them these areas lie outside the original Black Country boundary.

For fifty years they have specifically named the towns where the coal seam existed on their website, but omitted Wolverhampton, but then they also named additional towns lying on the periphery of the district where the thick coal was mined at a much deeper level at a later date. Inclusion of these additional towns naturally but confusingly extends the boundary of their 'original Black Country'. More of that shortly.

Their website also proudly highlights that 'by 1860, there were 441 pits, 181 blast furnaces, 118 iron works, 79 rolling mills, and 1,500 puddling furnaces within five miles of Dudley', with a clear inference that the iron industry's location was determined by the existence of the thick coal seam. Many of those included in this 'boastful Black Country figure' were in Wolverhampton, the town it finds difficult to acknowledge.

Either way, their rigid definition of the Black Country, based solely on the existence of the thick coal seam, appears to be 'partly-based' on the 1967 statement by the late and popular Walsall-born Dr John Malcolm Fletcher, one of the founder members of the Black Country Society in Dudley. In the first edition of 'The Black Countryman' magazine that year, he indeed theorised that the Black Country was 'solely located on the central mineral area of the plateau', and according to him, and hence the Black Country Society too, this consequently 'excluded Birmingham, Wolverhampton, and Walsall which were each commercial centres lying outside the mineral plateau, separated from it by very definite belts of open country or wasteland'. Furthermore, he used the argument that the names of districts in Wolverhampton such as Monmore Green and Stow Heath were indicative of these belts of open countryside separating the commercial town centres from the mineral-producing area. In doing this, he made a fundamental distinction in proposing that there were 'two types of occupational activities' in the area, 'those supplying the coal and iron from the mineral plateau, and those receiving and using it in the commercial centres'.

This 'protectionist stance' at the time, was perhaps born out of the fact that the Black Country was often described as incorporating Birmingham, or even the equally-black Potteries. It is also true however, that the core group of the Society in its early days had just a handful of members who had emerged from the 'Dudley Canal Tunnel Closure Group'. It seems likely that he must have been influenced by those around him in the closely-knit and evolving Dudley-based Black Country Society. At the end of its first year it had 150 members, including those it labelled as 'outsiders'. Did these include people from Wolverhampton? Either way, his theory certainly set the tone, and 'a clear inference of ownership' of the Black Country was clearly established.

At some later point, the Black Country Society took this 'mineral-plateau' theory a step further by stating that the Black Country lay 'only where the thick coal seam lay', which in turn dictated that those areas where iron-stone and thinner coal seams were mined, lay outside the Black Country. Through this controversial definition, the Black Country becomes considerably restricted geographically, perhaps an area 'nine miles in length and eight miles across'. The thick seam was not consistent throughout, as imagined.

Having excluded certain mineral-producing areas on specific geological grounds from their 'original Black Country', for many years their website then also included Wolverhampton, Stourbridge, and Smethwick 'culturally' as in their view 'they contributed heavily towards the iron and steel industry'. A confusing and muddled theory? This paragraph has now been removed from their website.

We will scrutinise the theories of both Dr Fletcher representing the Black Country Society in 1967, and the newer Black Country Society definition, in due course. Many people continue to strongly disagree with them, but the 'thick seam definition' is the prominent definition adopted by people today, because the Black Country Society is understandably perceived to be the most credible, knowledgeable body.

The map of the Black Country below (Figure 2) from Ian Beach's Sedgleymanor.com website regards the 'Ancient Manor of Sedgley', defined 'only by the presence of the thick coal seam' as opposed to the entire Black Country coal-field, gives a close impression of where its boundaries lay using this definition, though it is debateable whether it extends as far north-eastward, beyond the main A454 Willenhall Road now linking Wolverhampton to Walsall. Despite the much publicised Black Country Society definition, it is actually very difficult or nigh-on impossible to find any map showing exactly where the thick coal seam lay.

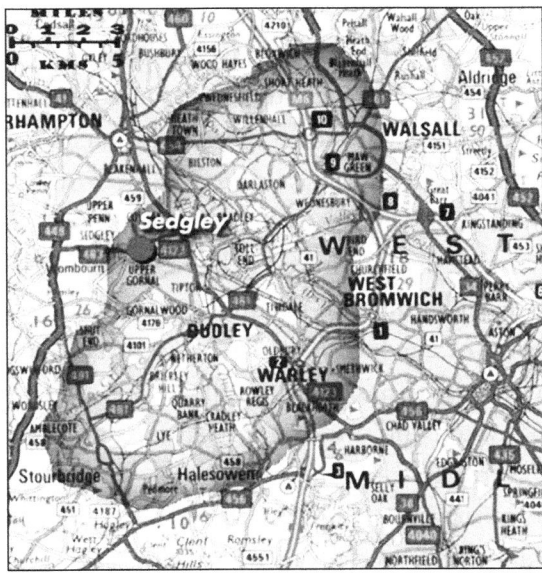

Figure 2. Diagram showing approximate area of thick coal seam, from Ian Beach's Sedgleymanor.com website.

DEFINITION TWO - Many so-called 'traditionalists', including many within the Black Country Society, proposed a slightly different definition, that suggested that: -

'The Black Country was defined by the area where the 'original shallow coal seam' outcropped at or near the surface, creating a black landscape after which the region was named'.

Coal was mined at the surface from around 1273 onwards, and then just beneath it, utilising 'pillar and stall' methods, simple bell-pits and horse-driven gin-pits, which created a black, pitted landscape, albeit on a small scale initially, continuing progressively on a much larger scale during the Industrial Revolution.

The thick and thin coal seams were found near the surface, and 'open-cutting' uniquely took place at Wolverhampton. A map of the entire Black Country coal-district below (Figure 3), is not too disimilar to the map used in the first one, though it expands further into central Wolverhampton, very close to the town centre in fact, as thinner seams of coal out-cropped there, as can be seen by Woodward's 1904 map showing productive coal measures (marked on the map in a dark-grey colour), reproduced by Ian West in 2001. Walsall and West Bromwich occupy similar positions on the edge, with town centres just outside, and Dudley overlies an area of distinct basalt greenstone formation, a zone created chiefly by previous volcanic activity. In colour these small sectiosn are marked in red. The main area of shaded grey highlights the wider mineral-producing coal-field, so it is a good representation of the 'original Black Country coal-field'. It is noteworthy that part of central Dudley did not lie on the 'grey-marked' coal seam, and one might therefore argue that they do not lie within the Black Country.

This definition was thought to reflect the 'original Black Country' quite well, especially its core mining area. The thin seam area between Wolverhampton and Bilston was considered to be that tract of land most damaged by mining activity.

CHAPTER TWO

Figure 3 – Woodward's 1904 map showing productive coal measures (thick and thin seam)

DEFINITION THREE - The famed Birmingham-born geologist Joseph Beete Jukes proposed an alternative and very relevant, but little-highlighted definition of the Black Country in 1858, with an emphasis on a different natural mineral in the ground than the thick coal seam. His definition proposed that: -

'The Black Country was defined by the location of the middle part of the coal-field that specifically contained iron-stone, as this determined where the great iron manufacture of South Staffordshire developed'.

He explained in geographical terms exactly where his Black Country lay: -

"If we take the town of Dudley at its centre, draw a northern boundary line from Wolverhampton through Bloxwich to Walsall, and a southern boundary line from Stourbridge to Halesowen, connecting Stourbridge with Wolverhampton on the west side, and Halesowen with Walsall

on the eastern side, we shall include nearly all of the great iron-making area. This area will approach in form to a parallelogram, ten miles long, and five miles from east to west, containing therefore almost fifty square miles. It is commonly known in the area as the 'Black Country' ".

So, for Jukes, the Black Country was all about iron, and his Black Country was specifically defined by the iron-stone tract of the coal-field (Figure 4), which is a theory that is little highlighted yet potentially extremely relevant, as it largely determined where most of the great iron-works evolved and developed. The coal simply formed the fuel to produce iron products, and so was of secondary significance to iron for Jukes, a view supported by many. For Jukes, the Black Country would rather crudely look like this.

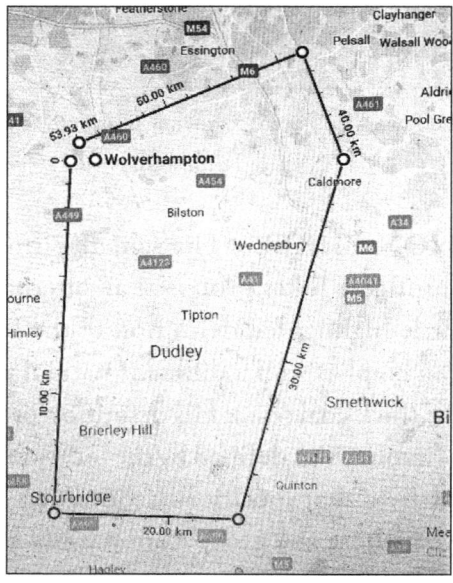

Figure 4 – Approximate area of Joseph Beete Jukes Black Country based chiefly on iron-ore

DEFINITION FOUR - The fourth and final view proposes a slightly wider geographical area, based on both coal-mining and undoubtedly the great iron industry: -

"The original Black Country was defined by those areas of South Staffordshire where the 'shallow seams' of thick or thin coal and iron-ore were mined, which gave the general landscape a pitted appearance, and it was defined at least equally by the adjoining districts where the great iron and brass-manufacturing industries developed with their resultant piles of furnace-slag, spoil, scrap metal, and cinder ash, and with their numerous furnaces and chimneys constantly spewing out dense clouds of smoke that blackened the general atmosphere and everything underneath it".

This definition, based on fully-researched, historical evidence, holds the view that the Black Country clearly emerged both 'in name' and as a 'physical entity' at a specific period in time, which directly correlates and coincides with the establishment of the great iron industry, with resultant widespread emission of smoke from the furnaces and countless chimneys, hindering the growth of vegetation.

It is evident that it was this chiefly, in conjunction of course with the workings of the coal and iron-ore mines, that led to the 'original Black Country' being so-named. And with both iron and coal industries playing important defining roles in the great industrial process, this less-rigid definition dictates that the Black Country would be a little larger in geographical area than that determined by the Black Country Society, or by Joseph Beete Jukes for that matter, perhaps up to twelve miles in length and eight miles across.

Furthermore, with timescale in mind, those areas where the mining of the deeper, concealed section took place at the end of the 1800s and then continued on a large scale well into the 1900s, had little to do with defining this true, 'original Black Country'.

Many writers of the 1800s concur with this slightly larger geographical definition of the Black Country based on both coal and iron, for instance Samuel Griffiths, Samuel Sidney, and

Walter White, whilst Reverend William Gresley potentially, and certainly Elihu Burritt included Birmingham within their wider-manufacturing Black Country, though both recognised that there was a core area where the 'Black Country proper' existed, but like the others, this was based on both iron and coal.

The Earl of Dartmouth, who owned coal-mines around West Bromwich, and Reverand J.H. Isles discussed this very issue of a 'Black Country-proper' in 1869, determining that only 14 of Wolverhampton's 20 parish districts lay within that zone', with those on its western side lying outside. It is poignant that not once, during their long discussion, did they mention the thick coal seam as being a defining feature of the Black Country.

The 1836 map produced on the following page, by William Hawkes Smith (Figure 5), showing 'the mining and manufacturing district of South Staffordshire and North Worcestershire', with an emphasis on both the iron industry and shallow coal and iron-ore mining, therefore accurately reflects whereabouts the 'original Black Country' was perceived to lie when it was first so-named around 1840.

The areas comprising coal mining of the thin seam and thick seam, as well as iron-ore are also the most industrial, and are those darkest-shaded areas on the map (purple in colour). This was perhaps what was sometimes referred to as the 'Black Country proper', where the main coal-field and main concentration of the iron industry lay, with their smoking chimneys and fiery furnaces, but with the 'town centres' of Wolverhampton, Dudley, Walsall, West Bromwich, and Smethwick lying on the edge, just outside, or just above it. The area where limestone was mined heavily are marked by 'striped' zones. The lighter-striped district just south of Dudley town centre is an area of hard basalt-rock, and hence strictly-speaking, could be said to lie outside the Black Country. The north-eastern edge of Birmingham is situated to the bottom right, clearly separate from the Black Country.

This wider definition of the Black Country based on both coal and iron, defines a boundary seemingly-widely adopted by people throughout the 1800s Industrial Revolution, and it is also the Black Country boundary proposed by this fourth definition.

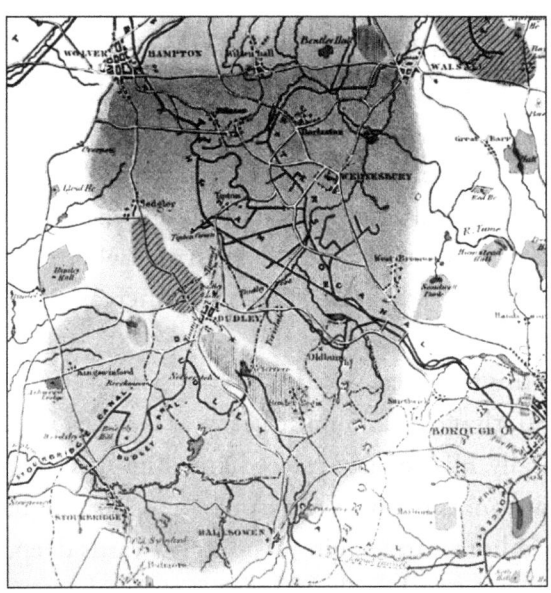

Figure 5 – William Hawkes Smith 1836 map of the mining and manufacturing district of South Staffordshire and North Worcestershire

2) A BRIEF HISTORY OF THE INDUSTRIAL REVOLUTION

Before the merits of the four definitions are analysed, a brief description of the Industrial Revolution is produced, as it is of specific relevance to the arguments and discussion. Although the work and innovation of Dud Dudley in the 1600s, and Abraham Darby at Coalbrookdale in the early-1700s were critical, the region only really transformed from a pastoral, agricultural district, to a smoky, damaged, industrial one as the key era of the 1800s Industrial Revolution progressed, and that is when, as we will show during the course of this chapter, the region became the 'Black Country'.

It is generally agreed that the Industrial Revolution occurred in two phases, from 1760-1840, then from 1840-1870. And it is often conveyed that the Industrial Revolution classically first took place on a large scale in the Black Country.

This time-period reflects the transition where industry progressed from hand-production to machine-manufacture, where new chemical and iron practices occurred, where there was an increase in rotative steam power, and an increase in the general factory system using machine tools.

Prior to this however, Swedish Commissioner R.R. Angerstein highlighted that in 1754 industry was already advancing technologically. His detailed travel diaries highlight that he visited Wolverhampton, Bilston, Wednesbury, and Birmingham, where he witnessed horse-driven gin-pits over 50-yards deep, as well as iron-smelting, charcoal-fuelled furnaces, steel furnaces, rolling mills, welded-tube works, forges, brass works, and galvanising processes using silver soldiered onto iron. But agriculture was still predominant, and the region was still littered with trees and greenery.

Sedgley-born Abraham Darby is widely accredited with creating the first blast furnace fuelled by coal that was first of all coked to produce pig iron, in 1709 at Coalbrookdale, Shropshire. Prior to that date, iron could only be smelted using charcoal-fuelled furnaces. Charcoal of course, was made from wood, and increasing concern was being expressed at the rate of deforestation throughout the Country.

Prior to that, around 1620, Black Country metallurgist Dud Dudley claimed to have mastered the process of smelting iron using pit-coal alone, but he never disclosed his exact method, which was not unusual at the time. It was often argued that Dudley was economical with the truth, and naturally he attracted great hostility from the owners of local, charcoal-fuelled furnaces whom he was in direct competition with. A number of historians rubbished his claims. Robert Plot for instance, argued in 1686, that at that earlier point in time the temperature in existing furnaces was insufficient to ignite raw coal to a high enough temperature to smelt iron. But Dudley built a large blast furnace made of stone and of extra width at its base, near Himley, so it is plausible that he did manage some sort of successful smelting process using coal. Indeed, his relative Abraham Darby managed to do so only twenty years after Plot 'rubbished' Dudley's work, though that was nearly ninety years later than Dudley's claim. Though critically, the coal at his Shropshire mine was fortuitously of a more-suitable, sulphuric content, and well-suited for such purposes.

The Industrial Revolution entered a critical, new phase much due to the work of Cumberland-born John 'iron-mad' Wilkinson, the so-called 'father of the South Staffordshire iron industry'. He undertook extensive experiments at his Bradley iron works, near Bilston, in getting raw coal to substitute coke in the production of cast-iron, around 1767. He also pioneered the use of a 'precision boring machine' that could produce cast-iron cylinders, which in turn could be used on steam-engines or cannons for instance. In effect, this was the first machine-tool.

By a stroke of fortune, another engineering genius, James Watt, became a great friend of Wilkinson, and they developed the first 'blast-engine' at Fiery Holes, Bilston. This was a blowing-device using a steam-engine, which enabled blast-furnaces to work at far higher temperatures, and hence operate far more efficiently. The huge amount of coal available as a local natural resource enabled iron to be produced on an increased scale from that time in the region, and in the early-to-mid-1800s it truly started to become a 'black country'.

3) ASSESSING THE FOUR DEFINITIONS

To fully assess the credibility of the four highlighted definitions of the Black Country, we need to scrutinise, examine, and consider critical points, to reveal exactly 'when and how' the Black Country evolved, and to reveal exactly 'which factors' most-prominently contributed to its incredible levels of industrial growth and primarily led to the naming of this famous region.

Furthermore, after that, this chapter examines potential weaknesses, or contradictions within the widely-accepted Black Country Society definition, based on the thick seam.

Key questions need to be answered first of all: -

a) **When was the term 'Black Country' first recorded?**
b) **When did the Black Country evolve as a physical entity?**
c) **What really defined the Black Country? Coal or iron? Or both?**

A) 'When' was the term 'Black Country' first recorded?

There are a few suggestions that the term 'Black Country' originated from much earlier than the 1800s, perhaps even in the 16th-Century, when the thick coal seam was marked in black on early regional maps. This assumption appears to be based purely on conjecture, and there is no evidence to substantiate the claim. All maps were printed in black and white at that point anyway. It simply does not prove that the term 'Black Country' was used at that point.

Furthermore, the area appears to have first been referred to as 'The Iron Country', highlighting the perceived importance of iron production.

Swedish Commissioner R.R. Angerstein visited the area in 1754 to observe the developing and evolving industry and coal-field, but he did not use the term 'Black Country' in his diaries.

The term 'Black Country' was still not used nearly forty years later, within the nineteen-page 1793 article written by the West Bromwich-based Scot, entrepreneur and Tividale-colliery owner James Keir titled 'The Mineralogy of the South-west part of Staffordshire'. In this famous early document, he did indeed emphasise the 'thick seam' section of the coal-field, by highlighting: -

"The quality of the ten-yard seam at Bilston, Darlaston, Wednesbury, Dudley, Rowley and Oldbury, together with the parishes of these towns, and those of Sedgley, Tipton, Gornal, and Netherton, together with a just a little of the north-west part of the parish of West Bromwich, and, also the several collieries about Dudley Wood, Brettel-lane, Amblecott and the Lye."

But only other people subsequently summarising his work appear to have additionally re-labelled it 'The Mineralogy of the South-west part of Staffordshire - The Geology and Industry of the Black Country'.

This is important as it lends support to the view that the term 'Black Country' in all-likelihood only evolved a little later-on during the early-to-mid-1800s, when significantly-increased levels of iron production occurred in conjunction with increased levels of coal extraction, because as a local colliery owner, Keir failed to use the term 'Black Country' at all. He would surely have referred to it at some point in his work, if it had been known as such in 1793.

Furthermore, William Pitt, in his 1812 'Topographical history of Staffordshire' made no reference of the 'Black Country' despite describing each town of the region in considerable detail.

'The Iron Country' term

Eighteen years later, in 1830, writer William Cobbett in his book 'Rural Rides', also made no mention of the 'Black Country', and labelled the area alternatively, stating: -

"In the Iron Country, which Wolverhampton seems to be some sort of central point."

Indeed, the region was prominently referred to as 'The Iron Country', or as the 'South Staffordshire Iron-producing district' up to this point, and often in fact after the term 'Black Country' evolved.

It is sometimes suggested that inadvertently, Princess Victoria of Kent (later to become Queen Victoria), who was aged just 13 during her 1832 train journey through the region, first referred to the 'blackness' of the district, as her diaries released in 1986 suggest: -

"The men, women, children, country and houses are all black. But I cannot by any description give an idea of its strange and extraordinary appearance. The country is very desolate everywhere, there are coals about, and the grass is quite blasted and black. I just now see an extraordinary building flaming with fire. The country continues black, engines flaming, coals in abundance, everywhere smoking and burning coal heaps, intermingled with wretched huts and carts and little ragged children".

The train journey from Birmingham to Wolverhampton was certainly to leave an impression on the future monarch, as will be further explored within the following chapter. But she too referred to the area as 'The Iron Country' in her later visit to Wolverhampton in 1866, and she only referred to it as 'The Black Country' in 1886.

In local newspapers that same year, 1832, Mr J.P. Roberts issued a prospectus for publishing by subscription, an accurate 'mining map of Staffordshire', which he said included mines and blast furnaces, and hence would include the entire parishes of Kingswinford, Dudley, Sedgley, and Tipton, and parts of the parishes of Wolverhampton, Wednesbury, Walsall, West Bromwich, Halesowen, and Rowley. But he never referred to it as the 'Black Country'.

In the 1834 'History, Gazetteer and Directory of Staffordshire' by William White, he did not make a single reference to the term 'Black Country', despite also describing each town of the district in great-detail.

But in that same year, 1834, it is somewhat tenuously suggested that the first ever reference to, or use of, the term 'black country' was made by Julian Charles Young, within his private journal, according to the 'Oxford English Dictionary.' It is difficult to find any further detail than that.

Yet four years later, in 1838, William Hawkes Smith commented on the coal mining district in his report titled 'The South Staffordshire Mining District since 1780', but still did not use the term 'Black Country' at all.

'Mogg's Handbook for Railway Travellers', written by Edward Mogg in 1840, described each town of the region in significant detail, but he too did not once use the term 'Black Country'.

First references to 'the Black Country'

The first and recently-discovered written reference to the 'Black Country' was found within an edition of the 'Staffordshire Advertiser' from 27 November 1841, where it reported a leading Liberal Reformer's meeting at the Guildhall, Lichfield a few days previously on 24 November 1841. Lichfield Town Clerk Mr C Simpson Esquire, in proposing a toast to the working-class men of the region, stated: -

"No Country in the world possessed such a valuable class of men, as those called the working-class of England, Ireland, and Scotland. Who could go into what was called 'the black country' in Staffordshire............. Wolverhampton, Bilston, Tipton".

This is undoubtedly a significant new discovery, because it pre-dates the previous earliest official written record of the term, and although it is simply a passing reference, it arguably indicates where the 'original Black Country' was thought to lie at that point. It holds credibility as it was written by a local person, living around ten miles distant. Is it poignant to highlight the fact that he said 'who could go into what was called the black country' rather than simply 'who could go into the black country'? He was speaking to a local audience yet had to explain that it was referred to as such, inferring that it might not have been widely-known as such at that point, even locally.

Author and famous 'Chartist' Thomas Cooper wrote his autobiography that was published later in 1872, based on his contemporaneous diaries, and in this he recorded that in 1842: -

"Some of the colliers were on strike in the Potteries, and that the whole body of them had struck in South Staffordshire, or 'The Black Country'".

Of course, he may have added the term 'Black Country' due to his knowledge of the region at the time he wrote the book, or did he simply directly transfer what he wrote at the time from his diary?

The following year, in 1843, in the 'Midland Mining Commission' report by Thomas Tancred, he simply referred to the South Staffordshire Coalfield as 'The Coalfield' as opposed to the 'Black Country Coal-field', stating: -

"The southern portion of this district will form the subject of this report, the more northerly part, or that above the parallel of Wolverhampton, from the nature and position of its minerals, having as yet few mines opened".

The following year, 1844, saw German writer Friedrich Engels refer to the area as: -

"The iron-producing area of South Staffordshire".

But he did not refer to it as the 'Black Country'.

Then on 9 March 1845, the newspaper called 'Bell's Life in London and Sporting Chronicle' reported a boxing match with a twenty-five pounds prize-stake, at Sutton Coldfield, between two colliers named as Tranter from Wolverhampton, described as 'a rough-looking customer', and Jenkins from Dudley, who was seconded by the famous 'Tipton-Slasher'. After twenty rounds the fight descended into chaos, with the ring broken into, though Tranter was deemed to have had the better of the fight with Jenkins 'constantly going down'. The fight was watched by 4,000 spectators, but rather condescendingly the reporter stated: -

"*The quality of the spectators showed they were principally from the 'black country'* ".

This usage of the term was quite important as it highlights that the term at that time, was used to some extent by people outside the region.

And on 12 April 1846, another London publication, the 'Lloyds Weekly Newspaper' also used the term when it headlined a sub-section: -

"*The Iron Trade - Wolverhampton, Tuesday*".

In this report, it concluded: -

"*Nothing can exceed the restless and uneasy state of feeling that now prevails throughout this district on the subject of Sir Robert Peels free trade measures. Trade, in fact, is almost paralysed by the delay and uncertainty that attend them; and unless they become law soon, there will be a season of great distress and feverishness all over the 'black country.'*"

Until very recently, it was presumed that that same year, 1846, saw the first officially-recorded and widely acknowledged written reference to 'The Black Country', by Reverend William Gresley of Lichfield in his book 'Colton Green, a tale of the Black Country', in which he famously described it as: -

"*A dismal region of mines and forges*".

The most relevant and routinely highlighted point in his work however, is that he described the district in the following way: -

"*The scene of this story lies in that part of Staffordshire to which the constant exhumation of its mineral riches has long since given the well-known name of the Black Country*".

This clearly implies that the term was already at that point in time, in routine level of use. It is unclear though, exactly for how long or how widely it had been 'commonly' known as such. Perhaps 10-20 years previously seems a fair estimate, but no one knows exactly for how long the term had been in use locally. More of Gresley's comments later, because he made a significantly-important remark confirming whereabouts in geographical terms, the Black Country was 'commonly' thought to have been, a remark that perhaps somewhat conveniently, seems to have been ignored by the Black Country Society in considering their definition.

It appears that it was from roughly around 1850, that the term 'Black Country' became routinely used by writers or reporters, suggesting that that was the point when the Black Country became more-widely known and established as a phrase to people other than locals, and when it became routinely referred to as such with the use of capital letters.

In 1851, the writer Samuel Sidney described and defined the geographical boundaries of the Black Country in his book 'Rides on Railways', and in this he wrote: -

"In this Black Country, including West Bromwich, Wednesbury, Dudley, Darlaston, Bilston, Wolverhampton and several minor villages, a perpetual twilight reigns during the day, and during the night fires on all sides light up the landscape with a fiery glow".

Digressing for one moment, Sidney is 'brutally derogatory and disparaging' about the Black Country, describing the inhabitants as: -

"Savages without the grace of savages, coarsely clad in filthy garments".

He even stated: -

"Those enthusiasts who gather every May in Exeter to convert aboriginal tribes need not travel so far to find human beings more barbarous. The people of the Black Country are one of the most ignorant, brutal, depraved, drunken, unhealthy populations in the kingdom......... who converse in a language barely recognisable in civilised England".

Another English writer Walter White toured the Country and expressed his thoughts in his 1860 book titled 'All Round the Wrekin'. He described various Black Country towns, including Wolverhampton, in some detail. Clearly for White, as with Sidney, the Black Country was an identifiable, definable, district.

In the 1860s, Bilston celebrated building a new church, and interestingly the 'Wolverhampton Chronicle' reported a small celebration held, where its builder, a Mr Beard forwarded a different proposition as to why the region was referred to as 'The Black Country'. He said: -

"Bilston was not so black as was being painted. It was a Black Country merely for the amount of wealth which it produced".

An interesting, alternative theory, but not one which stands to any scrutiny.

The famous American diplomat Elihu Burritt is often credited with spreading the name 'Black Country' around the globe, through his 1868 book 'Walks in the Black Country and its green borderland', which as most people know, famously described the Black Country as: -

"Black by day, red by night".

He somewhat bizarrely defined a 'Greater Black Country' as existing in a '20-mile radius around Birmingham Town Hall'. He stated: -

"Let us see what wares intervene between the two extremities – between the ribbons of Coventry, the fine carpets of Kidderminster, or between the salt bars of Droitwich or the iron bars of Wolverhampton. Birmingham is the capital manufacturing centre, and growth of the Black Country".

But it should be noted that Burritt did go on to describe what he called the 'Black Country proper', with Dudley at its heart, and including Wolverhampton. It is worth noting therefore, that for him too, as with Gresley, Sidney, and White, the 'Black Country proper' was geographically larger than the area determined as such by the Black Country Society.

Thereafter, to modern times, the 'Black Country' name has become synonymous with 'dirt and grime', and is famous worldwide, with many concluding that 'the Industrial Revolution' evolved there.

Its borders have for some people been rightly extended during the early-1900s to incorporate those border-line districts where the deep, concealed section of the coal seam was mined, but it should still be noted quite clearly, that these districts do not constitute part of the 'original Black Country'.

As recently as in 2009, Peter Jones in his book 'Industrial Enlightenment – Science, technology and culture of Birmingham and the West Midlands' discussed the issues surrounding the identity of the Black Country. He wrote: -

"The notion of the Black Country, that is to say, a rectangle of territory bounded by Wolverhampton and Walsall to the north, and Smethwick, Halesowen and Stourbridge to the south, is an anachronism, since the expression cannot be traced back beyond the 1840s".

In conclusion, despite the uncertainty regards its 'exact birth-date', these points support the notion that the Black Country was first-so-named during the early-to-mid-1800s, probably around 1820-1840, and that the term became commonly used and widely-established nationwide from around 1850. No-one knows exactly 'who' first created the term 'Black Country' to describe the region.

B) When did the Black Country evolve as a physical entity?

The second important, relevant issue to examine so that we can correctly define the Black Country, is to clarify when the 'so-called' Black Country evolved as a physical entity. Clearly the change in environment did not occur overnight, but it transformed rapidly over a short period during the 1800s.

To establish when, we look at: -
i)   The region's economy before the Industrial Revolution.
ii) The rate and scale of industrial development, along with population growth, during the Industrial Revolution.

i) The region's Economy before the Industrial Revolution

Although coal-mining is indeed recorded centuries before the 1700-1800s Industrial Revolution - it was recorded as early as 1273 at Sedgley, 1315 at Bilston, and 1325 at Wednesfield - it was a low key, almost small-scale cottage industry in the main. This early mining inevitably occurred where it cropped near or even at the surface, as it was easy to mine. Much of the surface coal was inevitably the first to be exhausted as it required little or no machinery or equipment, some could literally be hand-picked. In the main it was initially used for domestic purposes. Few records of these early mining operations exist.

Production levels increased in scale progressively through the 1400s, 1500s, and 1600s, increasingly using shallow, pillar-and-stall methods, evolving and developing into a type of gin or bell-pit mining, which was still prevalent in the 1800s across the whole area. Only from the 1770s, and notably from the early-1800s, was coal and iron-ore mined on a larger, commercial scale to meet the ever-increasing demand from the iron-works and from the domestic market.

Metal-manufacture also existed in earlier centuries, but on a small scale, and it was basically the product of the hand-held file.

Robert Plot in his 1686 work titled 'Natural History of Staffordshire' wrote about the region in the 17th-Century, noting that the area was one of 'subsistence and survival', and he does not even refer to the mining or metal trade, referring to it as: -

"A healthy agricultural economy".

He described the regions key towns not accummatively totalling more than 9,000 residents, but he highlighted that there were signs of what he called 'operative industry' even then, with ten or twelve collieries in the region. But he added: -

"There was little smoke then, no tall chimneys, no hissing of the hot steam, no great roaring fires gleaming on the horizon for miles, no clinking of vast machinery shaking the ground at every

throb...............there were no blackened villages swarming with a coal-begrimed population. The cottages were thinly scattered over the whole district, and these were chiefly the dwellings of peasants. True we have Dud Dudley, telling us that there were at this time '20,000 smiths of all sorts and many iron works within a circle of ten miles of Dudley'. But the old iron-master was as prone in this as in other things to exaggerate."

In fact, paintings of Dudley Castle in the 1730s still portrayed a pastoral and agricultural landscape at that point in time. There were no smoking chimneys on either side, as there perhaps were one-hundred years later.

Clearly, the Black Country did not exist as a physical entity in the late-1600s or early-1700s.

To further evidence the low-key description of the area much before this point in time, according to local historian George Barnsby: -

"In the 1600s, coal operations in Bilston were low key and small scale, and in the period 1716-1730 just before the Industrial Revolution, Bilston trades included 240 buckle makers, 61 toy makers, 44 chape makers - all were cottage industries".

The Hearth Tax of 1660 highlighted that there were just 84 hearths in Wolverhampton, and 95 in neighbouring Willenhall. Most of these belonged to locksmiths.

So, it has been well-documented by historians that before 1750 the Black Country was indeed simply 'a collection of industrial villages specialising in making locks and other metal crafts'. Many workers were involved in the production of nails using poor quality iron, and the file was the main tool utilised by workers in what was essentially a cottage industry.

As already highlighted, in 1754, R.R. Angerstein, the Swedish Commissioner, visited the area, but industry was still developing at that point, and he noted some iron and brass-works in the area, and he also visited coal-mines in Wolverhampton, Bilston, and Wednesbury.

But he described what was to become the Black Country's blackest town, Bilston, essentially as a town making toy-ware: -

"Bilston is a town consisting mainly of factories for metal boxes, and other cast and punched work, to paste gems and enamelled work".

And another description of the Wolverhampton area from an unknown observer at that time supports the view that it was still largely agricultural: -

"Until 1760 the land around Wolverhampton, Willenhall, Bilston, Coseley, and Wednesfield was a district abounding in groves and streamlets and occupied by a pastoral population, while the iron and coal lay quietly beneath the surface, undisturbed by the restless cupidity of man".

In 1770, there were 118 lock-makers in Wolverhampton, and 116 buckle-makers. Nearby Willenhall held 148 lock-makers. Most industry was still of a 'cottage-industry' nature. For contrast, by 1855 Willenhall had attained dominance in this industry, with 340 registered locksmiths, whilst Wolverhampton only had 110.

In 1780, there were just 4 blast-furnaces in the region, at least a decade after the smelting of iron using raw coal was first utilised in the region.

Robert Plot, in describing the economy at that time, poignantly highlighted that simply having and exploiting these natural resources was not enough, as the area required an infrastructure and market economy to evolve.

In this respect, the importance of the creation of the canal-network during the period 1760-1780 should not be under-estimated, as for the first time it enabled huge, horse-drawn barges to move the coal, iron-ore, and vast range of other goods around the wider-midlands area and onward, and hence a market-economy was created for the first time. At the peak of the Industrial Revolution, over 40,000 barges per year passed through the Dudley Canal tunnel alone, and immense waterway-traffic jams of up to two weeks occurred. Traffic jams were not simply something from the modern era.

The clusters, or concentrations of newly-built iron-works then developed close to the canal network and its many wharfs, as these linked Shropshire to Wolverhampton, Wolverhampton to Birmingham via Bilston, Tipton, Smethwick, and then onward to other areas of the Country. Not only were the canals crucial for transport of iron-ware and coal, the water it provided was crucial to power and cool the steam-engines, boilers, and steam-hammers. Mechanised steam-power enabled iron production to occur on a much larger scale and become less reliant on water from the canals, but for the most part, their location was already established.

Eventually the railways, which were generally built alongside the canals, out-competed them as they were-able-to move goods more speedily, though the canals still retained an important role for some time after.

The importance of trade with neighbouring Birmingham should also never be under-estimated. Enabled by the creation of the canal network, both were absolutely critical factors for the trade and development of the Black Country that was to follow.

Stuart Russell, in his 2011 thesis at Birmingham University titled 'The Relationship between Agricultural development and Industrial Growth 1660-1880 – A case study of the Black Country', placed considerable emphasis on the 1794 'General and Commercial Directory' developed by the Merchant Taylor's company in Wolverhampton, which was a very important point in time according to Russell, as it was in his words: -

"A genuine attempt to develop business nous in the region – an attempt to spread knowledge and a key point to take society forward. In the Black Country, a collection of economies were brought together by the need to exploit their resources".

Fairly strong evidence that the necessary market economy started to evolve around 1800. Infact, 'Adams and Sketchley' had produced a basic trade directory for Birmingham, Wolverhampton, Walsall, and Dudley as far back as 1770.

In summary, it is certainly hard to perceive that the area would have been developed enough industrially at this pre-1800s point-in-time to 'profoundly affect the landscape' to merit the emergence of the title the 'Black Country'. The coal-field was not yet being mined on a widespread geographical basis, and the vast iron industry which depended upon its iron-ore and coal was still in a relative, early stage of development.

The market economy was in its infancy but evolving rapidly.

ii) The rate and scale of growth during the Industrial Revolution

The scale, and rate of industrial development, and of population growth, also reveal a great deal in chronological terms, and help us determine when the Black Country became established as a visual physical entity, changing from a largely pastoral to an industrial landscape.

Close examination of timeframe, in relation to the development and expansion of the coal and iron industry, is very significant and revealing, as it literally enables us to create an accurate visual impression of how the region's landscape would have been physically affected at specific points in time. And although this does not prove exactly when the Black Country was first so-named, it does help.

Coal production.

In 1665 just 25,000 tonnes of coal were mined in the wider Black Country, then 50,000 tonnes just before the start of the Industrial Revolution in 1750, increasing dramatically by nearly ten times to 845,000 tonnes by 1790, after smelting of iron-ore using coal became a common-place and perfected practice. Finally, this increased to an estimated 4 million to 8 million tonnes of coal being mined at the height of the Industrial Revolution in the 1850-1870 period, after which the shallow coal-field started to expire.

Quite clearly then, the scale of mining 'much-before 1800' would not have impacted the area's landscape significantly. These figures speak for themselves.

We retain few detailed records regards coal extraction from the centuries before the Industrial Revolution, when the thick seam existed at the surface in some parts of Wolverhampton. But we do know that the Black Country's 'obtainable coal' from the shallow seam near the surface, expired around 1870-1880, and hence the associated iron-producing industries also declined greatly during the 'Great Depression' that occurred around that same time. Iron-ore had in fact been brought in from Northamptonshire and elsewhere from the 1850s to supplement what was being mined in the Black Country, as iron-stone mines were some of the first to expire locally.

In a way, the Black Country became a victim of its own land-locked location once its own natural resources expired, and that is why South Wales became the prominent, iron-producing region as the Black Country declined by 1880.

Deeper mining practices of the concealed coal seam indeed then developed at a few key sites around the edge of the Black Country, but it was 'too little too late' to prevent economic collapse of the great iron industry occurring in the region, despite huge amounts of coal being mined throughout most of the 1900s at these geographically-peripheral Black Country operations. By 1900, most of the output from the South Staffordshire coal-field actually came from the adjoining Cannock Chase Coal-field.

Finally, for comparison, nationally, 2.7 million tonnes of coal were being mined in 1700, 4.7 million tonnes in 1750, 10 million tonnes by 1800, 50 million tonnes by 1850, and a huge 250 million tonnes by 1900, which reflects the technological advances enabling the deeper, concealed coal-field to be mined in huge quantity across the nation.

Iron production.

Following the adaption of Abraham Darby's discovery of the smelting of iron using raw coal instead of coke, by John Wilkinson during 1767 at Bradley near Bilston, and due to the increased power and production rates of blast furnaces using steam-engine power, the iron industry consistently evolved in the Black Country.

In 1796, just 13,210 tonnes of iron were being produced in the Black Country, by 1823 this increased to 133,000 tonnes, and then it leapt to an impressive 771,000 tonnes by 1856, mainly due to the demand for armoury for the Crimean War. This meant that production of iron increased by more than 50 times during the first half of the 1800s. By 1870, the Black Country was producing 1.2 million tonnes of iron, which accounted for over 30% of the UK total.

Accordingly, there were just 4 blast furnaces in what we now loosely define as the Black Country in 1780. This figure rose to 14 in 1790, 28 in 1800, 45 in 1810, 66 in 1823, 98 in 1830, then between 1839-1870 the number grew from 106 to 181.

In addition to the 181 blast furnaces, by 1860 there were 118 iron works, 79 rolling mills, and a staggering 1,522 puddling furnaces, comprising 38% of those in the whole Country, shooting their flame into the Black Country sky, within a five-mile radius of Dudley. The distance from Dudley to Wolverhampton is exactly five miles.

So again, this information enables us to see that the landscape and environment would only have started to be profoundly affected by the workings and emmissions of the iron industry from the early-to-mid-1800s, and then progressively so until its peak around 1860-70.

Iron and coal production statistics are inter-connnected, though domestic household demand for coal continued after the iron industry declined.

Population growth

Population growth figures also help to paint a picture of the rate of industrial development in the area during the Industrial Revolution, as people thronged to the great industrial centres where employment in the coal-mines, iron works, and brick works was available.

Wolverhampton's population, according to the Wolverhampton Census, rose from just 7,500 in 1750 to 12,500 in 1801. With the real and continued progression of the Industrial Revolution, it increased greatly, up to 50,000 by 1850, and up to 75,000 by 1880, as coal was mined in quantity and iron production increased on a huge scale, drawing in many workers to the area. This explosive pattern of 'population-boom' was particularly profound in Wolverhampton but repeated across the Black Country and in major towns across the Country during the Industrial Revolution.

By 1850 some 36,000 people in the Black Country area were employed in mines or iron-works, and that increased further still, over the next few decades. By the 1860s, the industrial revolution peak-period, there were 61 collieries and 2,000 miners in the small town of Bilston alone, a stark contrast to those Bilston pre-Industrial Revolution employment figures provided earlier in by George Barnsby.

In summary, these three sets of figures - **'Coal Production', 'Iron Production'**, and **'Population Growth'** - certainly help demonstrate exactly when the area developed as a physical, industrial entity. This dissection, examination, and interpretation of information provides strong evidence in support of the view that the 'physical and environmental effect of industry' would not have significantly changed the landscape of the region until the early-to-mid 1800s, and that is when the Black Country evolved as a physical, industrial entity. Critically, this coincides with the time-period the term 'Black Country' was first used to describe the area – probably between 1820-40.

Although this is pretty much universally accepted, it is an important fact to establish.

So now that we have determined that the Black Country evolved both 'in name' and 'as a physical entity' during the early-to-mid-1800s, probably around 1820-1840, we need to look more closely at 'which industry was most pivotal to its growth', and 'why' the 'original Black Country' became so-named, before concluding how to correctly define the Black Country, geographically.

This is perhaps the most contentious aspect, but arguably the most important one.

C) What mostly defined the Black Country? Coal or iron, or both?

In some respects, it remains a matter purely of personal choice, which of the two, coal or iron, one chooses to adopt as the key defining industry, because both clearly played fundamentally important roles in Black Country life.

But, as we have established, it is a matter of fact that the term 'Black Country' was only first used to describe the region once the iron industry had evolved, around 1820-1840. Coal had been mined in the region for the previous 500 years, albeit in ever-increasing quantities, to meet local domestic-household demand, and that from the iron-works and brick-works.

Both coal and iron were clearly critical defining industries for the Black Country, but it perhaps helps to examine statistics, and then look at the views of historians and writers, to assess if one industry would have been more prominent in Black Country life during the Industrial Revolution, and which of the two was most commonly considered to have created that physical effect that led to the area first being called 'The Black Country'.

i) Statistics in relation to Coal and Iron production

It certainly helps to look closely at the production levels, and man-power figures of both industries in more detail during the Industrial Revolution, to glean some idea which industry was arguably the most dominant of the two, in influencing the lifestyle of Black Country people.

HC Derby, in 'A New Historical Geography of England after 1600' (1973) highlighted the 1851 census of English occupations, which was the first scientific attempt to classify people's occupations, and in this he stated: -

"Of the English regions where coal and iron occur in bulk, the 'coke-iron' industry of the Black Country outstripped all others". The Black Country ranked 1st in the English output of iron ore and pig iron, and 3rd in coal production".

These figures emphasise the importance and dominance of the Black Country's iron industry even compared to coal production, and surely, it might well be argued, the Black Country should be defined by the product for which it was ranked as the top producer in England – iron.

Only South Wales and Scotland produced more iron-ore and pig iron at the peak of the Industrial Revolution, each producing 1.4m tonnes of pig iron per annum, through 200 blast furnaces each respectively, compared to the Black Country's production of 1.2m tonnes of pig iron per annum, using 181 blast furnaces. But when you consider the Black Country was simply a small, individual district of England, the concentration of iron-related industry in the Black Country is self-evident.

Richard Trainor in his 1993 book 'Black Country Elites – The Exercise of Authority in an Industrialised Area 1830-1900' emphasises the districts' prominence of pig-iron production throughout the 1800s: -

"In 1815 the Black Country was producing one-third of Britain's pig-iron. Although the district's share of national pig iron production fell from 1830, in absolute terms Black Country output trebled during the next three decades before peaking in the early-1870s. In 1860 Black Country pig iron production was still more than a sixth of the national total, and the district remained the national leader in manufactured high-grade wrought iron, with a third of British output."

Coal-mining, on the other hand, existed on a large scale throughout the Country, but the main centres were the North-east of England (especially for iron-ore), South Yorkshire, Nottinghamshire, Derbyshire, South Wales, Southern Scotland, North Staffordshire, and South Staffordshire including the Black Country. Of course, the Black Country had the unique thick coal seam.

In terms of man-power, Stuart Russell's thesis at The University of Birmingham in 2011, titled 'The Relationship between Agricultural development and Industrial Growth 1660-1880 – A case study of the Black Country', details the numbers of people employed in various industries within the Black Country.

In 1841, 29,000 people were still employed in agriculture, 19,500 in mining, 18,000 in metal manufacture, 14,500 in brick production, 11,000 in construction, 9,500 in clothing and footwear, 3,000 in textiles, and 2,500 in transport.

Twenty years later, at the peak of the Industrial Revolution in 1861, 46,000 workers were involved in metal manufacture, 43,000 in mining, 37,000 in agriculture, 33,000 in brick production, 25,000 in clothing or footwear, 17,500 in construction, 11,000 in transport, and 9,000 in textiles.

Clearly, the bulk of workers during the peak-period of the Industrial Revolution were employed in some form of metal (chiefly iron) production, coal-mining, and that other great Black Country industry, brick production.

The large numbers still employed in agriculture may come as something of a surprise to some people, at that point in time. But it was the Industrial Revolution itself that transformed the Country from one of self-subsistence, where people lived off the land, to one where thousands of peasants thronged to the new industrial centres in search of work. Many of those farmers who still worked the land, also specialised in some form of metal-craft from their holdings.

So as the Black Country evolved industrially during this period, these figures show that metal manufacture became the prominent industry of the two, when it is measured via manpower, but only just.

Overall, in terms of both production levels and man-power, the iron industry was arguably the greater or more significant industry of the two in the Black Country, though both were clearly pivotal.

ii) Coal or Iron as the main defining industry? – The views of writers

Was the 'Black Country' so-called due to shallow coal-mining that blackened the ground where it outcropped, or was it so-called due to the black clouds of smoke from the many furnaces and countless chimneys that permanently and grimly hung over the towns?

Of course, the Black Country was 'so-named' not because of production figures, but because of the visual impression the workings of industry left upon people. So, it is worth examining the revealing and telling views of writers and early visitors to the region, to see which feature of industry they described, sometimes inadvertently, as being the one that they felt mostly defined the Black Country – the workings of coal-mining, or iron-production?

CHAPTER TWO

Just before the start of the Industrial Revolution, in 1754, Swedish Commissioner **R.R. Angerstein** visited the region because of its pre-eminence in the manufacture of metal, noting: -

"Wolverhampton is one of three major iron and steel-producing centres in England".

He also visited coal-mines in Wolverhampton, Bilston, and Wednesbury, including those where the world-famous thick seam was mined.

Without the coal to fuel the furnace, the iron-ore that was mined could not have been smelted, a key and valid argument of the Black Country Society. As far back as 1793 the geologist **James Keir** stated: -

"Birmingham, Wednesbury, Bilston, Wolverhampton, and Stourbridge owe their foundation and prosperity to the coal seam".

Before the 'Black Country' name emerged, **William Cobbett**, in his 1830 work 'Rural Rides' tellingly referred to the great industrial district he saw, in the following way: -

"In the Iron Country, which Wolverhampton seems to be some sort of central point."

This is clearly a telling description of the region, with the workings of the iron industry, as opposed to those of the coal industry leaving a distinct impression on this neutral, non-local observer of the district.

Similarly, in 1844 the German writer **Friedrich Engels**, in writing about child-labour in the region, described the region as: -

"the iron-producing district of South Staffordshire".

But individual physical descriptions of the Black Country perhaps best show why the region became to be so-called 'The Black Country'.

Reverend William Gresley of Lichfield in 'Colton Green, a tale of the Black Country' (1846) is often portrayed as the first writer to officially use the term 'Black Country'. He highlighted the importance of both the coal and iron industries, but he certainly placed much emphasis on the latter when he stated: -

"The iron-ore of the district was indeed known and valued. It was dug from the bowels of the earth".

And from the elevated view at Dudley Castle, Gresley described the great Black Country scene around and beneath him, placing emphasis on both coal and iron production: -

"A confused mass of chimneys vomiting forth volumes of black smoke, blazing furnaces, glowing coke heaps, heaps of ashes around the pit mouth, steam engines plying their incessant work, and other signs of human drudgery. The whole country is blackened with smoke by day and glowing with fires by night".

Nevertheless, he stated that the Black Country got his name because of: -

"the constant exhumation of its mineral riches".

This of course was in-reference to its coal and iron-ore.

In 1858, the renowned Birmingham geologist **Joseph Beete Jukes**, who specialised in assessing the different coal seams, offered a critical line of thought in placing great emphasis on the iron-ore section of the coal-field as the defining Black Country feature, as that for him specifically determined where the great iron-industry developed thereafter. His article was presented in the Wolverhampton Chronicle on 8 December 1858 in which he placed great emphasis on iron: -

"The Black Country was based on the location of the seat of the great iron manufacture."

As highlighted earlier in the chapter, he explained his reasoning: -

"The seat of the great iron manufacture of South Staffordshire is not co-extensive with the whole of the coalfield, nor is it likely to become so since it is the middle part only of the coalfield which has ever been productive of ironstone. There is hardly perhaps to be found anywhere in the world, another space of fifty square miles so peculiar in character. It is commonly known in the area as the 'Black Country', an epithet the appropriateness of which must be acknowledged by everyone who even passes through it on a railway".

So, this view proposes that both iron-production and iron-stone mining defined it. Jukes was a very knowledgeable and highly-respected geologist.

That same year, 1858, American writer **Henry Adams** highlighted the 'visual impact' of travelling into the region by train: -

"The plunge into darkness lurid with flames, the sense of unknown horror in this weird gloom which then existed nowhere else, and never had before existed, except in volcanic craters, the violent contrast between the dense, smoky, impenetrable darkness, and the soft green charm that one glided into as one emerged".

For him, the sooty atmosphere created by the chimneys and furnaces of the great iron industry was clearly the striking feature.

In 1860, **Walter White** in his book 'All Round the Wrekin' suggested that the Black Country was so-named due to the combined-effect of coal-mining and the smog created by the iron industry: -

"The Black Country of Staffordshire – the name is eminently descriptive, for blackness everywhere prevails. The ground is black, the atmosphere is black. And amid all this are the cottages of artisans and miners, English homes whence sun and stars are seen darkly.".

But he described the Black Country's 'blackest town Bilston as being full of iron-pits', rather than placing emphasis on coal, and he added: -

"And so it continues for 13 miles, all the way from Birmingham to Wolverhampton, but whatever may be the gloom, havoc, and confusion elsewhere, you only see the worst when passing Bilston".

Bilston was generally thought of being the 'blackest part of the Black Country', where a local legend once told 'of a man losing his way while trying to find a blade of grass'.

Queen Victoria also referred to the district as the 'Iron district' when she famously visited the region in 1866, despite the fact the area by then, was fairly-well known as the 'Black Country'. Her fascinating personal diaries were released in recent times. This visit was widely reported by the nation's press, who described the Black Country in vivid detail, emphasising both iron-production and coal-mining working in conjunction.

The blazing furnaces and smoke from the chimneys of the iron industry were certainly the striking feature that most profoundly affected the landscape and the atmosphere of the Black Country for American diplomat **Elihu Burritt**.

His description of his 'Black Country proper' in his 1868 book 'The Black Country and its green borderland' famously describes and emphasises the workings of the iron industry: -

"Black by day and red by night, cannot be matched, for vast and varied production, by any other space of equal radius on the surface of the globe. Nature did for the ironmasters of the Black Country all she could, indeed, everything except literally building the furnaces themselves. She brought together all that was needed to set and keep them in blast. The iron ore, the coal, and lime – the very lining of the furnaces – were all deposited close at hand for the operation. One would be inclined to believe, in seeing the black forest of chimneys smoking over large towns and villages as well as the flayed spaces between, that all the coal and iron mined in the district must be used for it. The furnaces, foundries and manufactories seem almost countless......and all the while the furnaces roar and glow by night and day, the great steam hammers thunder, and hammers from an ounce in weight to a ton, and every kind of machinery invented by man, are ringing, clinking, and whizzing, as if tasked to intercept all this raw material of the mines and impress upon it all the labour and skill which human hands could give it".

Like Gresley, Burritt was determined to view his 'Black Country proper' at night, from the elevated position at Dudley Castle. Though highlighting his own lack of poetic license, he attempted to describe the scene through the eyes of an imaginary poet, comparing the iron industry at work before him to a 'military battle-scene'. He said: -

"In figures beyond my prosaic conception he would describe a scene which cannot be paralleled on the globe. Wolverhampton on the extreme left stood by her black mortars which shot their red volleys into the night. Coseley and Bilston and Wednesbury replied bomb-for-bomb and set the clouds on fire above with their lighted matches. Dudley, Oldbury, Albion and Smethwick, on the right, plied their heavy breachers at the iron works on the other side, while West Bromwich and distant Walsall showed that their men were standing as bravely to their guns. The canals twisting and crossing through the field of battle, showed by patches in the light like bleeding veins".

Clearly, the main defining, visible feature for Burritt was the fire, flame, light, smoke, and dirt from the furnaces and chimneys of the iron works, in combination with the great wall of sound created by the very same source. Not coal-mining, despite its obvious involvement in the process that unravelled in front of him.

Nevertheless, Burritt did highlight that the ten-yard coal seam was the main factor 'underlying the success of the Black Country', again demonstrating that both industries were critical, and demonstrating the complexity in making such an assessment.

A report in the 'Staffordshire Sentinel and Commercial and General Advertiser' on 14 August 1869, on 'Spiritual Destitution in the Black Country' discussed the geographical boundary of the 'Black Country proper', but interestingly **Reverend J.H. Isles** and the **Earl of Dartmouth** determined that the term 'Black Country' was negative and instead it should be referred to as 'The Mining district of South Staffordshire' in their report. Clearly with an emphasis on coal, though no reference at all was made to the thick coal seam.

A fairly-ambiguous report from the **Dundee Courier** in 1901 chose to define the Black Country through the iron industry. It read: -

"The iron and steel trade of South Staffordshire was at one time of great magnitude. Numerous small forges were scattered all round about the towns of Dudley, Wolverhampton, Smethwick, and others. It

was this trade more than any other that gave its specially-characteristic name and appearance of the Black Country."

It is fair to say that virtually all 'local historians' of the 20th-Century recognise that the Black Country was defined in some way by both the coal and iron industries, and their respective workings. There was no obvious, clear consensus from local historians, regards which industry of the two was considered to be the primary defining one. In fact, most seemed to feel it was defined by a combination of both.

W.K.V. Gale, the West-Bromwich-based writer whose highly regarded book 'The Black Country Iron Industry - A technical history' (1979) unsurprisingly highlighted quite definitively, that the Black Country became so-named due to the effect of iron-production, stating: -

"After the rotative steam engine had made industry independent of water power, and the use of mineral power had become common, the iron producing undertakings of South Staffordshire and North Worcestershire were concentrated into a small area. This became known, from its countless chimneys and furnaces, as the Black Country."

Harold Parsons, in his 1986 book 'The Black Country', like most others, adopted a dual-assessment, stating: -

"The Black Country was defined by its great profusion of chimneys belching out smoke from ironworks and furnaces, combined with a general incidence of grime and dirt which typified the region. But that is only part of the reason. The other, perhaps major part of the answer is in the South Staffordshire coal-field itself, shaded grey or black on maps of the time. To be precise, this area is the true Black Country".

But he concludes by stating: -

"The Black Country got its name, by reason of its ironworks, furnaces, as well as its mineral wealth".

A combination of both coal and iron for Parsons therefore, it might well be surmised, despite his somewhat-contradictory statements.

In 1998, local historian **Dave Ogden** placed emphasis on the coal, stating: -

"Its known as the Black Country due to the colour of the ground."

Nevertheless, these conflicting views do perhaps highlight in a nutshell, the difficulty in correctly defining the original Black Country for local historians. Parsons clearly accepts that the Black Country got its name through a combination of the processes of both iron-production and coal-mining but feels that the 'true Black Country' was where the coal-field was situated. A view shared by several other local historians. But then like many others, he also acknowledges that it was the vast iron works that created the pollution, and hence also the immense and striking visual image of the Black Country.

Phil Drabble summarised the conundrum in a simple but poignant way in his 1952 book 'Black Country', where he wrote: -

"But before it is clear how Black Countrymen became townsmen with country minds, it is necessary to see why the Black Country is there at all. There are three main reasons: Coal and Iron and Lime. Three minerals which have made it possible for this area to influence life not only in the Midlands or England, even, but the whole world".

And he went on say: -

"So, there wasn't any difficulty in persuading the peasants from the land to flock to the new-born prosperity, to worship the trilogy of Coal and Lime and mighty Iron".

Perhaps to get a modern-day view, we should refer to **The Black Country Living Museum's** website, which currently opens its description of the region in the following way: -

"Firstly, it is very important that we understand what is the big story of the Black Country? The story of the Black Country is distinctive because of the scale, drama, intensity, and multiplicity of the industrial might that was unleashed. It first emerged in the 1830s, creating the first industrial landscape anywhere in the world. Beneath the smoke and glare from blast furnaces and forges, Black Country innovation, entrepreneurial and manufacturing skill established the region's supremacy for the making of wrought-iron. The Black Country also

possessed important hardware and other manufactures distinctive to itself – structural ironwork, chain-making, locks and keys, tube manufacture, trap-making, and many others – which brought fame to Black Country towns across the globe".

Quite clearly with an emphasis on iron production, and not a single mention of coal.

In summary, having examined all these opinions, it seems improbable that any truly-subjective researchers today would conclude that coal-mining in isolation, would have led to the Black Country becoming so-named.

It is plainly evident that 'both coal and iron' both played pivotal roles in defining the Black Country, but that perhaps the cloak of smoke from the furnaces and chimneys most likely led to the region being so-named.

But before we draw overall conclusions regards the four different Black Country definitions, there are further, specific considerations, and potential weaknesses and contradictions with the Black Country Society definition that need to be looked at, before anyone is in a position to produce a comprehensively sensible and accurate definition of the Black Country.

4) POTENTIAL CONTRADICTIONS WITHIN THE BLACK COUNTRY SOCIETY THICK COAL SEAM DEFINITION

So before moving onto an overall conclusion regards the different definitions of the Black Country, it seems arguable that the most widely accepted one, that proposed by the Black Country Society which in turn was partly based on the theory of **Dr John Malcolm Fletcher**, perhaps has several potential, fundamental flaws, which will be highlighted at points **A, B, C, D, E, F, G and H.**

But before we highlight these alleged flaws, it is worth briefly highlighting the origins and history of the Black Country Society.

The history of the Black Country Society

As we know, the Black Country Society was first formed in late-1966 and became active in 1967. It was formed from members of the 'Dudley Canal Tunnel Closure Group', who had formed a preservation society.

The Black Country Society initially totalled 150 members and was presided over by Walsall-born, Wednesbury-resident Dr John Malcolm Fletcher, with active support from the likes of John Brimble. The first meeting was held in Tipton. They noted that most of the initial members originated from Dudley, Tipton, and Cradley, and they expressed disappointment regards the lack of apparent interest from areas such as Darlaston and Willenhall. Perhaps this was inevitable as the origins of the Society held a strong Dudley-interest in matters. That is not a criticism however.

The Society thereafter produced a quarterly magazine titled 'The Black Countryman'. Its editor from 1968–1988 was another revered Dudley-man named Harold Parsons, and he was succeeded by yet another Dudley-man Stan Hill from 1988-2001, from 2001, Stourbridge-man Dave Cox took over the role, and in recent years Dudley-based Mike Pearson stepped into the breach as Chief Editor and Website administrator.

It does not take much imagination to see that inadvertently at least, the Black Country Society held and still maintain a Dudley-perspective on the regions industrial legacy. Of its current board members, none appear to be from the Wolverhampton area at all. Of course, different people within the Black Country Society will hold different personal opinions, but inevitably it is the Society's 'publicly-declared stance' that is the one that is analysed.

But make no mistake, they have each done a wonderful job, despite holding a view that is perceived by many as an anti-Wolverhampton stance. The depth of knowledge possessed by the many individuals involved, surpasses by some considerable degrees anything that I could hope to develop. They have produced superb publications and worked tirelessly to promote the legacy of the area over many years.

Interestingly and somewhat ironically however, one of these men, Harold Parsons, happened to work in a major Wolverhampton iron-works for most of his working life, and co-incidentally, he concluded that Wolverhampton was within the Black Country, at least in part. Stan Hill too, in fairness, recognised the contribution of Wolverhampton's industrial heritage. He favoured the stance that: -

"*Wolverhampton was 'Of the Black Country but not in it'* ".

This view is perhaps a reflection of its geographical position on the edge of this famous district. But the same would apply to Walsall, West Bromwich, Smethwick, and Stourbridge. But ever since Dr Fletcher's 1967 theory was adopted by the Black Country Society, Wolverhampton found itself increasingly 'edged-out altogether' by some people.

The virtual absence of Wolverhampton-related articles on its website even today, is noticeable, and one can only conclude that the Black Country Society, which is arguably Dudley-centred and focused, is quite sadly no true friend, neighbour, admirer, or respecter of Wolverhampton's significant contribution to the Black Country.

Interestingly perhaps, in contradiction of Dr Fletcher's stance, it is little-highlighted that just two-three years after his landmark statement, the Black Country Society made a proposition through a special report forwarded to the Minister of Housing and Local Government, that was published in the 'Birmingham Daily Post' on 13 January 1970, urging the Black Country not to be split into

4 boroughs, and alternatively to be made a single authority with similar responsibilities as the City of Birmingham. The report recommended the following: -

"The 'artificial division' of the Black Country should be ended and a single authority covering Dudley, Walsall, Warley, West Bromwich, Wolverhampton, Halesowen, Stourbridge, Aldridge-Brownhills, Seisdon and Cannock, should be created".

So, this inclusion of Wolverhampton, and even Cannock, contradicts Dr Fletcher's definition somewhat, and arguably highlights some confusion and a lack of clarity within its ranks even at that time.

They have now, in 2017, published within the excellent 'Black Countryman' publication, my four-page explanation of why Wolverhampton should undoubtedly be considered a key Black Country town. So perhaps Wolverhampton's immense contribution to the Black Country is gradually now being acknowledged. Great credit is due to the editor Mike Pearson for allowing me that opportunity to challenge the status-quo view, highlighting that it is not the closed-shop perceived as such by many these days.

There has subsequently been a vital further development, which will be explained in Chapter Eleven at the end of the work.

Doctor Fletcher's Time-defining post in 1967

Before raising these alleged flaws or contradictions with the Black Country Society definition, it is appropriate to post the highly-respected Dr Fletcher's time-defining article back in 1967, from the first edition of the 'Black Countryman' as it was this more than any other piece of literature, that first defined a restricted-geographical Black Country, and set the tone from the Black Country Society for the next fifty years: -

"Perhaps no area has suffered more misrepresentation than the Black Country. Local people are constantly being annoyed by the fatuous and puerile knowledge of the area shown by national figures and by the national press. The depth was reached by one famous Sunday newspaper which recently spoke of activities in Wednesbury, then headed a photograph which illustrated this particular-article with a caption speaking of the town as being in the Potteries!

To many southerners, the Black Country seems to be a term that is used to describe all-of-this country north of Stratford-upon-Avon. To others, probably avid readers of Arnold Bennett's novels, the Black Country will be forever associated with the area around Stoke-on-Trent. There is really no excuse for this attitude. The borders of the Black Country can be clearly defined, although a true 'Black Country mon' might say that he carries the characteristics of the area with him everywhere.

Historically, the West Midland plateau has not played a significant part in the development of this country until recent times. At the time of the Norman Conquest, Domesday Book shows the plateau as being sparsely populated and economically insignificant. The position remained essentially unaltered during the whole of the medieval period. No major river ran through the area, and at the time when traffic and trade was concentrated on the natural waterways, this meant that the plateau was isolated from developments in the rest of the country.

No major Roman road passed through the region. Activity, therefore, tended to bypass the Midland plateau and concentrate on the river valleys to the north, south and west, or in the booming manufacturing town of Coventry. This situation was changed only when the building of canals opened the plateau to influence from the outside.

The development of the region during the early industrial revolution laid down in outline the boundaries of the region we know as the Black Country. Contemporary writers were careful to differentiate between two types of activity they observed to be appearing on the plateau. In the first plaee, they saw the towns of Walsall, Wolverhampton, and *especially Birmingham appearing as large manufacturing centres with also a commercial element in their population. The central part of the plateau supplied the raw materials, coal and iron, that were used in these large towns. Of course, some manufacturing was also carried out in this central area, but the distinction is on-the-whole a valid one.*

The three towns were themselves also separated from the mineral producing areas by very definite belts of open country or waste-land.

Between Birmingham and West Bromwich lay the country district of Handsworlh Heath. This area known as Soho gets its name, so it is said, from this being the cry of the hunters as they rode over the open fields and waste-land then characteristic of Handsworlh.

Between Walsall and Wednesbury, a belt of waste-land known as the Pleck, a word meaning 'waste,' divided the manufacturing towns from the coal and iron mining area.

To the north, heathland lay beyond Bilston, separating it from Wolverhampton; the modern names Stow Heath and Monmoor Green today indicate where this belt of land was situated.

We have the picture, then, of three busy manufacturing towns on the edge of the plateau divided from the mineral producing region by belts of open country. It is this mineral producing region that should rightly be known as the Black Country, and no other area. It is possible to speak of this as a specific region because the nature of the coalfield in South Staffordshire did produce close and compact development.

To the south and west, the field is limited by faults running approximately from north to south. Only in the later nineteenth century were investigations for coal beyond these faults attempted. To the north, a line of faults known as the Bentley Faults running roughly from east to west, divide the coalfield from the deeper, thinner seams found in the Cannock Chase area. Only in the south is the field not clearly defined; here the seams peter out around Halesowen. The faults in the east, north and west concentrate development of the coalfield within a very closely defined area, and this is rightly the Black Country. In this region until comparatively recently, the exploration of the rich coal seams with their associate deposits of iron, clay, and limestone, provided employment for the-majority-of the inhabitants.

On the coalfield itself, we must distinguish between two types of development. The earliest mining was naturally located in those areas where the seams lay at a very shallow level. This 'outcrop' coal, as it is called, was found particularly in Wednesbury, Darlaston, Willenhall, Bilston, Coseley, Tipton, Dudley, Brierley Hill and the adjacent villages. In these centres the early development of the Black Country was most noticeable. The coal also lay at a greater depth, 'concealed,' in three other areas, West Bromwich, Smethwick, and Oldbury. Here development came somewhat later and lasted a little longer than elsewhere.

These towns, originally small villages and hamlets, on the exposed and concealed coalfield, form the Black Country as it should be defined.

The isolation of the region in medieval times had already laid the basis for the development of a strongly conservative, inward-looking culture on the plateau. The industrial revolution did not seriously change this.

Mining communities are always close-knit, introspective groups, and those of the Black Country were no exception. The development of the region was also slow enough to prevent a sudden influx of immigrants who could radically alter the traditions of the area; the only outside element to come into the Black Country in any quantity was the Irish. Their arrival caused considerable disturbance but does not seem to have seriously affected the culture of the Black Country.

As a prosperous region, compared to many others, the Black Country was also able to retain much of its population which then contributed to stabilise the customs and traditions of the area. All these factors tended to produce a tightly knit community, inward-looking and with peculiar customs associated often with the distant past.

The ending of the dominance of mineral production in the Black Country, the ease of obtaining transport and the spread of housing beyond the boundaries set by the old coalfield has inevitably blurred many of the distinctions noted above between the area and its adjacent regions. However, it would be easy to ignore the effect of this long history on the people of the Black Country. As a prosperous, rich area, the Black Country still retains its population and its stability. The traditions of the past cannot easily be dropped in the space of a few years. Although the character of the region has changed and is still changing rapidly, the sense of belonging to a distinct local community is very strong today.

We can still speak of the Black Country as that area lying on the southern part of the South Staffordshire coalfield, although its boundaries today are not so clearly defined and its activities no longer base themselves on the exploitation of its mineral wealth".

So, having highlighted his defining-post from that first edition of the Black Countryman magazine from 1967, those several alleged potential weaknesses and contradictions are now discussed, at points A – H. Much of what Dr Fletcher stated does make sense, but it also seems that he applied his own thoughts rather selectively at times, making rather simplistic, sweeping generalisations to produce his own, contrived Black Country boundary.

The following points highlight what are intended to constitute thought-provoking concerns with Dr Fletcher's definition of the Black Country reliant solely on the coal-seam, and also with the the slightly-later Black Country Society definition which took his theory a step further by restricting the geographical boundary of the Black Country to that where only the thick coal seam section of the wider-coal-field lay.

A) The 'original Black Country' only lay in Staffordshire, and did not include Dudley

Wait for it……the original Black Country did not include Dudley!

It is relevant, but very rarely-highlighted that the first written references to the 'Black Country' in 1841 and 1846 quite clearly referred to it as only being 'a part of Staffordshire'. Dudley town, at that point in time, lay in a separate enclave of Worcestershire. It stands to reason therefore, that strictly-speaking the term 'Black Country' did not 'originally' include the town of Dudley.

These first two written references to the Black Country were as follows.

In November 1841, the clerk of Lichfield Mr C Simpson Esquire, was quoted in the 'Staffordshire Advertiser', as raising a toast to the working men of the Country, where he stated: -

"Who could go into what was called the 'black Country' in Staffordshire...........Wolverhampton, Bilston, Tipton...........".

Then in 1846, Reverand William Gresley, in his novel 'Colton Green – A Tale of the Black Country', clarified the Staffordshire-only theory, where he introduced the region within his novel: -

"The scene of this story lies in that part of Staffordshire to which the constant exhumation of its mineral riches has long since given the well-known name of 'The Black Country.'"

From around 1850 however, the the term 'Black Country' undoubtedly became routinely used to refer to a slightly-wider area incorporating the north-east Worcestershire coal-field too, with its adjacent iron works and Dudley as well, as highlighted by Samuel Sidney, Joseph Beete Jukes, Elihu Burritt, and Samuel Griffiths during the 1850s, 1860s, and early-1870s. That is abundantly clear.

Nevertheless, it is evident that the 'original Black Country' seemingly only referred to the South Staffordshire section of the region, if the very first references to it, including Gresley's significant and widely-quoted one, are to be believed. The 'Birmingham Evening Mail', for example, still referred to the Black Country as being solely a Staffordshire entity, on 21 November 1851, when it stated: -

"The crowds came from the Black Country of Staffordshire."

And Walter White, in 'All Round the Wrekin' (1860) still described the region as: -

"The Black Country of Staffordshire".

Perhaps most poignantly, this 'Staffordshire-only' view was supported by an 'old Thetfordian' writer named Chas C. Bush, who spent time as an assistant-master at a North Worcestershire elementary school, and who on the 4 March 1905 wrote about the Black Country in his local 'Lowestoft Journal' newspaper: -

"Used in a general sense, the term Black Country includes the whole of South Staffordshire, with adjacent parts of Worcestershire and Warwickshire, although the name was originally given to South Staffordshire alone."

This is a little highlighted line of thought, one which some may portray as being fairly- arbitrary and insignificant. But on the other hand, is it? It is perhaps somewhat ironic that Wolverhampton's claim to lie in the 'original Black Country' is stronger than that of Dudley's.

B) Wolverhampton, Walsall, and Birmingham were commercial centres separated from the mineral area by very definite belts of open country or wasteland

The geographical definition of the Black Country proposed by Black Country founder-member Dr John Malcolm Fletcher suggested that Wolverhampton, Walsall, and Birmingham lay outside the mineral-producing plateau that for him comprised the Black Country, as in his eyes they were simply manufacturing and commercial centres, separated from the mineral plateau by 'very definite belts of open country or wasteland'.

For Fletcher, rather absurdly, further proof of this was present in the fact that these specific districts possessed 'place names indicative of rural origin', such as Monmore Green and Stow Heath in east Wolverhampton. It was a surprisingly shallow argument. What does that say about Brierley Hill, Cradley Heath, Woodside, or Golds Green? Surely the same thinking should apply?

Either way, this theory is fundamentally incorrect, and it raises possibly the most obvious weakness with his geographical definition of the Black Country.

Whilst it was perhaps understandable that he wanted to distinguish the large manufacturing and commercial 'town-centres' of Wolverhampton and Walsall from the mineral producing district he called the Black Country, he was clearly wrong to exclude Wolverhampton and Walsall as 'entire entities', as they both contained obvious mineral-producing districts, that abutted right up to the town centres.

So, his distinction between what he called the 'mineral-producing-plateau', and the 'manufacturing and commercial centres', was in-essence way too simplistic, and wrong.

In relation to Fletcher's theory, Birmingham quite evidently, was indeed a separate commercial and manufacturing centre, distinguishable from the mining and key iron-producing areas, though of course still part of a continuous, industrial, manufacturing region.

In Wolverhampton's case especially, at the point in time the name 'Black Country' first emerged around 1820-40, there was certainly no sort of buffer zone at Stow Heath and Monmore Green, both were typical Black Country districts, and there was no 'belt of open country separating Wolverhampton town centre from the mineral plateau' producing iron-ore and coal, as Fletcher suggested. It was an absurd and spurious notion.

The mineral plateau that Fletcher referred to, ran very close to Wolverhampton town centre, in fact immediately adjacent to it. Coal-mines, such as the foundations of an old pit recently discovered beneath the Midland Metro tram-line at Horseley Fields in November 2014 that significantly delayed the process of laying a new track, prove this to be the case. This old mine was just a stone's throw from the town centre and a hundred metres from the ring-road, with Midland Metro Programme Director Paul Griffiths stating: -

"It was known there may be old workings in the area, but the scale of what was found came as a surprise".

There is further solid evidence that coal-mines existed immediately adjacent to the commercial centre of Wolverhampton. On 18 June 1848, The Editor of the 'Wolverhampton Chronicle and Staffordshire Advertiser', made clear reference to these mines near the town centre, when he described the town's changing landscape: -

"Not a long time ago, in the immediate vicinity of the town on the roads to Willenhall and Bilston was the more active scene of mining operations, and huge mounts of shale and other waste testified to the enormous extent of the operations beneath, while far too often a yawning pit-mouth a yard or two of the turnpike road seemed almost purposely left unprotected as a death-trap to the errant wayfarer. Close to the town these indications of subterranean activity have become less common, and over some spots, exhausted of their coal and iron-stone, the process of 'leveling' has been carried into effect. Rows, indeed streets of small houses, in many cases, occupy the surface of the abandoned mines. A gradual exhaustion - rapid perhaps, would be the correct epithet - of the mines abutting on the south-eastern extremity of the town, where 'The Great fault of the South Staffordshire coalfield' occurs, in-the-course of its devious range, and the necessity of the proximity of their work has led to the migration of a multitude of colliers and miners formely inhabiting a large part of Horsley Fields, Walsall Street, Bilston Street, and adjoining portions of the town."

Concrete proof that coal-mines stood immediately adjacent to the town centre, beyond the districts proposed by Dr Fletcher at Stow Heath for instance, which lies around a mile-and-a-half from the town centre.

There was no 'definite belt of open country' between the two town centres of Wolverhampton and Bilston unless one looks back to pre-Industrial Revolution times, but then there were open belts of countryside across large tracts of the Black Country. Ironically, perhaps one of most obvious tracts of attractive, open country in the region lay all around Dudley Castle, even during the Industrial Revolution.

In summary, Dr Fletcher's simple analogy treated the large towns as if they only had a commercial, manufacturing centre, and he clearly failed to take account of the mineral-producing areas lying adjacent to the town centres but still clearly within their boundary.

If he had argued that only the 'commercial town-centres' of Wolverhampton and Walsall lay just outside, or in Dudley's case, just above the Black Country, his point may have been a valid one. But he failed to do that.

C) There were two distinct geographical zones where different occupational activties took place

Linked to the previous point, Dr Fletcher's implication that the residents of the mineral area, and the manufacturing, commercial centres of Wolverhampton and Walsall undertook distinctly different occupations is also very questionable. This theory is also way too simplistic.

He stated: -

"Contemporary writers noted two very different activities in the commercial centres and on the mineral plateau".

Whilst he accepted that some manufacture using the minerals from the ground inevitably took place in the smaller central towns, which was certainly an under-statement, he failed to acknowledge that the larger areas of Wolverhampton and Walsall also supplied the minerals as well as utilised them. Ironically, the iron-ore from the Wolverhampton coal-field was routinely transported to the iron-works of Dudley for instance, to be smelted. So infact, the reverse of what Dr Fletcher claimed in reality also occurred, in that the minerals from the districts he classed purely as commercial centres were utilised by the manufacturing works of the mineral-plateau towns.

Dr Fletcher implies that the commercial economy of Wolverhampton relied on the central mineral areas outside its borders, but this is wholly untrue as well. Wolverhampton's own coal and iron-ore mines adequately supplied its manufactories, a fact specifically highlighted by Swedish Commissioner R.R. Angerstein.

Furthermore, as far back as 1754, Angerstein had also noted blacksmith's shops lining the whole length of the road from Wolverhampton to Wednesbury, each offering nails, buckles, and other simple metal products, demonstrating similarities between the large commercial centre and the smaller central town.

Official census figures highlighted by George Barnsby in his 1990 book 'Social Conditions in The Black Country', perhaps hammer the final nail in the coffin for this part of Dr Fletcher's theory. They show that Wolverhampton-parish held more miners than any other parish except Bilston, and proportionally about the same for instance as Dudley, within the entire Black Country in 1841, this being the decade in the Industrial Revolution when the term 'Black Country' first evolved. This was at a time when parish populations were more-or-less equal in size. Over the next two decades, the number of miners was to double, and the number of iron workers would increase ten-fold. These figures, from 1841, are shown below: -

"Wolverhampton had a male population of 18,789, of whom 1,886 were miners, and 599 were Iron-workers.

Dudley had a male population of 15,689, of whom 1,606 were miners, and 259 were iron workers.

West Bromwich had a male population of 13,480, of whom 1,340 were miners, and 704 were iron-workers.

Sedgley had a male population of 12,586, of whom 1,818 were miners, and 371 were iron-workers.

Kingswinford had a male population of 11,466, of whom 1,333 were miners, and 578 were iron-workers.

Walsall had an adult male population of 10,967 of whom 718 were miners and 123 were iron-workers.

Bilston had a male population of 10,540, of whom 2,474 were miners, and 643 were iron-workers.

Tipton had a male population of 9,773, of whom 1,151 were miners, and 508 were iron-workers".

These figures were obtained from official parish census records, so should certainly be fairly-reliable. Dr Fletcher's statement is now proving to be a somewhat muddled and over-simplified theory, and arguably one that was designed to suit his stance.

D) The Black Country was defined by geology - but only one aspect of it - the thick coal seam

The Black Country Society definition further restricts the Black Country to a certain section of Dr Fletcher's mineral plateau, to that where the only the thick coal seam lay. Part of this theory was based on the presumption that industry relied on it most of all, and hence developed close-by. The other part was because it was presumed the black thick coal seam near the surface created a notable visual effect.

Consequently, this definition inevitably excludes some areas where thinner coal seams were mined, and where some of the best seams of iron-ore (or iron-stone) and fireclay were mined. And it excludes some of the areas where the greatest concentrations of iron works lay.

Whilst the theory that the Black Country was defined by geology perhaps has some credence, it is evident that the developing great iron industry relied not just on the thick coal seam, but perhaps primarily on the thinner seams of coal, with their excellent, adjacent seams of iron-stone and fireclay.

Much of the thick coal was in fact simply mined to meet the demand for domestic household consumption, as in the greater part of the South Staffordshire coal-field it was more crystalline in character, and hence better-suited for domestic use and for drawing-off gases. It was heavily favoured in Birmingham for domestic household use, so much so that canal supply routes were specifically created from Wednesbury, for instance. The thick seam west of Dudley however, was better suited for smelting, and clearly had been used for that purpose from earlier times.

Overall, those districts where the thin seam and best iron-ore were found, have in-effect been disregarded through the Black Country Society definition, yet these were arguably the districts chiefly responsible for the development of the great iron industry.

The remarks of Birmingham-based geologist Joseph Beete Jukes already explained in this chapter, are clearly then very relevant. They alternatively place great emphasis on the iron-ore tract of the coal-field in determining where the vast iron industry developed, and thus where for him, where the Black Country lay.

These considerations fundamentally conflict with the Black Country Society definition, with its sole emphasis on the thick coal seam.

And finally, it is seldom, or never highlighted by Black Country historians that the most heavily-damaged and hence eye-catching swathe of mining land in the region, was noted to have been situated in the Wolverhampton thin coal seam district. On 3 January 1850, the 'Morning Chronicle' issued a report called 'Labour and the Poor – Manufacturing Districts', in which it highlighted this unique effect on the landscape: -

"The appearance of the country around Wolverhampton, Willenhall, and Bilston, where the thin seams principally lie, is strange in the extreme. For miles and miles, the eye ranges over wide-spreading masses of black rubbish, and hills on hills of shale, and masking, as it were, the whole face of nature".

So, even if one chooses to adopt the theory that the Black Country was so-named because of coal near the surface, it seems that the Wolverhampton coal-field more than any other, may well have led to the evolution of this term.

E) The 'thick coal seam irrespective of its depth' contradiction – a shifting Black Country boundary

The Black Country Society stated that the Black Country should be geographically defined by the presence of: -
"the thick coal seam, irrespective of its depth".
With this statement, there is arguably a fundamental contradiction, as the deeper, concealed section was only mined later-on in time, and hence these areas cannot constitute part of the 'original Black Country', which we know was characterised by shallow coal-mines.

To accommodate these newer, additional areas, the Black Country Society definition, with its wording above, inevitably expands the Black Country boundary at a later point in time, to incorporate those peripheral geographical areas of the district where the coal seam was mined at great depth using newer mining practices.

In some respects, it seems reasonable to adapt or amend the boundary to incorporate these peripheral areas, whilst in other ways, it definitely feels wrong and inappropriate.

There is no definitive answer, but if you accept that the Black Country boundary can be amended, altered, or expanded with change and over time, the counter-argument is that you cannot simply adapt it finitely at any specific point in time chosen to suit your view, as it is thereafter ever-changing. Does it even exist today, at all?

And this, is why geographically defining the Black Country is so difficult and controversial if you allow it to be defined and then redefined by different mining practices that evolved at different points in time in different parts of the region.

It surely makes sense to conclude that there was an 'original geographical boundary of the Black Country', and that that was the finite, correct boundary, as it was first and originally perceived to be.

To support this view, we know that the Black Country evolved both 'in name' and as a 'physical entity' in the early-to-mid-1800s, when shallow coal-mining was widespread in the area. The deeper, concealed section of the coal-field around the edges of the Black Country, such as at Baggeridge, Sandwell Park, Jubilee, Hamstead, Holly Bank, Hilton, and Walsall Wood, first mined around 1880-1900, took place due to technological advances in mining practices at least fifty years after the 'original Black Country' evolved, so the areas where these practices occurred quite clearly had little to do with defining it. They certainly did not scar, shape, nor blacken the landscape in the same way as the many late-1700 and 1800s 'shallow' gin and bell pits. At best, such later mining operations only represent a continuation of the mining industry some time after the Black Country was defined.

Local author Phil Drabble in his 1952 book 'Black Country' concisely highlights this train-of-thought in describing the newer Cannock Chase coal-field, where he stated: -

"The difference in appearance was caused by the mechanical elevation of the dross, while the ancient coalfield was characterised by flatter, lower spoil banks. Hamstead and Jubilee at West Bromwich, and Baggeridge are similar modern pits, quite different from the old Black Country pattern."

Furthermore, he clearly acknowledges this 'timeframe-contradiction', in trying to define the geographical borders of the Black Country: -

"So, what else controls the confines of the Black Country? Geologically the area coincides with the presence of coal, though Baggeridge, Hampstead and Sandwell pits are often considered outside its boundary, the original field being now worked out".

So, it can certainly be argued that the Black Country Society definition, specifically the part which geographically defines the area through the 'existence of the thick-coal seam, irrespective of its depth', is a part of that definition which for many loses considerable credibility.

Even if you choose to accept the stance that the borders of the Black Country can change with time and change, the borders of the 'original Black Country' cannot be changed. It is imperative to differentiate between the two.

F) Wolverhampton's incorrect ommission from the Black Country adopting the Black Country Society's thick-coal seam definition.

There was undoubtedly a considerable amount of coal-mining in Wolverhampton before and during the Industrial Revolution, far more than many local historians have ever acknowledged. The Black Country Society barely ever acknowledged Wolverhampton's mining legacy, in fact not really until late-2017.

Yet large-scale commercial mining commenced in the town in the early-1800s, highlighted by Samuel Griffiths in describing Chillington Colliery in east Wolverhampton, in his book on the iron trade written in 1872, where he said: -

""*They leased 110 acres of land within a mile of Wolverhampton, and here they found some of the richest mines of coal and iron in Staffordshire".*

Critically for this argument, there is also concrete evidence that the thick coal seam existed at some Wolverhampton Collieries.

A rare, early record highlighted that in the 1600s the seam at Moorfields Colliery, at Parkfields was noted to be around 14-yards thick. This colliery lay slightly closer to Bilston, but within Wolverhampton's Stow Heath manor, one of two manors that at that time made-up Wolverhampton, the other being Deanery.

There is also plenty of evidence of the existence of the thick coal seam around Monmore Green, Rough Hills, and East Park in Wolverhampton. An advert from an edition of the Wolverhampton Chronicle on 23 November 1842, highlighted that colliery owner Edward Lowe: -

"………informs residents of Wolverhampton that his 'Hill Park Colliery' on Bilston Road, Wolverhampton is raising thick coal, heathen coal, and bottom coal".

Harrold's Colliery at Rough Hills, near the 'Wolverhampton Furnaces' was offered for sale within the same newspaper, stating that: -

"the brooch coal and the thick coal was being mined".

The nearby Wolverhampton Colliery also advertised its thick coal for sale.

On 24 March 1845, the Birmingham Aris's Gazette highlighted that it was common knowledge that the thick seam lay within Wolverhampton's borders, stating: -

"It is a notorious fact that the Oxford and Wolverhampton line, from its first entry into the mineral district near Stourbridge, til it reaches the vicinity of the Chillington Iron Works near Wolverhampton, passes over ground the entirety of which has been under-worked in the thick coal."

Furthermore, local geologist Mr H Beckett wrote a report in 'The Wolverhampton Chronicle and Staffordshire Advertiser' on 3 February 1858, in which he confirmed the existence of the thick coal seam at both the Chillington Colliery and the Wolverhampton Colliery: -

"A small amount of the thick coal was worked in the Chillington Colliery, and the Wolverhampton Company also worked it on the north side of the Lanesfield fault".

He also spoke of the 'Great Bentley Fault', which he stated commenced at Fighting Cocks in Wolverhampton, the location where the thick seam ceased. Fighting Cocks was a district in Blakenhall, Wolverhampton, just south of the town centre.

Joseph Beete Jukes in his 2nd edition 'The South Staffordshire Coalfield' (1859) also confirms the presence of the thick coal seam at Wolverhampton's larger collieries of Stow Heath, Chillington, Rough Hills, Parkfields, and the Ettingshall Collieries.

He stated: -

"The entire coalfield can be divided in two - the principal line of division is that which runs from Parkfields through Sedgley, Dudley and Rowley".

But in relation to the existence of the thick coal in Wolverhampton he importantly also confirms that: -

"The thick seam outcrop has a detached piece thrown in towards the Wolverhampton furnaces. A small east and west fault with a down-throw to the north, throws in another little detached piece towards Monmore Green".

This would have been close to Cable Street, less than a mile from the town centre of Wolverhampton.

Finally, on 15 August 1860, the 'Wolverhampton Chronicle and Staffordshire Advertiser' published a report of the annual provincial meeting of the 'Institution of Mechanical Engineers', where Mr William Mathews of Corbyn's Hall Iron Works in Dudley gave a speech 'On the Ten-yard coal of South Staffordshire', in which he described the boundaries of the thick coal seam: -

"The limit of the thick coal in the northern portion of the area might be roughly defined by a line drawn from Monmore Green, to a little to the north of the town of Bilston, to Darlaston, where it proceeds in a south-westerly direction to West Bromwich where it is there terminated by a fault."

Monmore Green, as we all know, is a district of south-eastern Wolverhampton, less than a mile from the town centre.

So, we have plenty of conclusive evidence that some of the thick coal seam was mined in Wolverhampton, albeit not in the same quantity as in some neighbouring Black Country towns. Most of Wolverhampton's collieries mined the thin coal seam and precious iron-ore.

Nevertheless, this proves beyond doubt, that even if one chooses to adopt the Black Country Society 'thick coal seam' definition, some of Wolverhampton, even excluding Bilston, qualifies as being in the Black Country. Again, this is a fact very-rarely acknowledged by the Black Country Society.

G) The boastful figures within five-miles of Dudley

The Black Country Society website proudly boasts that 'within five-miles of Dudley there were 441 pits, 181 blast furnaces, 118 iron works, 79 rolling mills, and 1,500 puddling furnaces'.

Yet many of those included within this 'boastful Black Country figure' were in Wolverhampton, which is exactly five miles from Dudley. The town it often finds difficult to credit or acknowledge as being part of the Black Country.

From that impressive 1860s figure, of the 441 pits some 225 were in Wolverhampton (75 in Wolverhampton, 150 in Bilston), of the 181 blast furnaces 52 were in Wolverhampton (28 in Wolverhampton, 24 in Bilston), of the 118 major iron-works 47 were in Wolverhampton (23 in Wolverhampton, 24 in Bilston), of the 79 rolling mills at least 60 were in Wolverhampton (40 in Wolverhampton, 20 in Bilston), and of the 1,500 puddling furnaces 528 were in Wolverhampton (290 in Wolverhampton, 238 in Bilston).

A significant proportion of each figure.

Surely it should deduct from those impressive figures, any of those in Wolverhampton, or clearly acknowledge its Black Country contribution?

H) Industry - did the thick coal seam really determine the location of developing Industry? Or was this primarily determined by other factors such as the location of the iron-stone tract and thin seam of the coal-field, or by the location of the canal system?

We have already touched on this issue, but for the credibility of the Black Country Society definition, this issue is critical, because in effect they define the Black Country in precise geographical terms through the existence of the thick seam section of the coal-field, as they proposed that this dictated where the iron industry developed thereafter. There was a presumption that the thick coal seam and the iron industry were inextricably reliant on each other, perhaps due to the famous work of Dud Dudley whose thick seams were used in the smelting process in earlier times. The thick seam west of Dudley was better-suited for smelting, whilst across much of the South Staffordshire coal-field, it was too crystalline in nature and only suited for domestic-household use.

So, it is essential to examine exactly where the heaviest concentrations of the iron industry actually did develop, and to examine why those iron works developed exactly where they did, to see if the credibility of the Black Country Society definition stands to scrutiny.

This section ended up being lengthier than intended, but the evidence proposed retains a simple message – that factors 'other than the location of the thick coal seam' determined the location of the great iron industry, that so-shaped the region during the Industrial Revolution.

In examining this issue, two 'sub-points' are now examined to highlight that other factors were critical to industrial growth: -

i)   The location of industry in relation to different parts of the coal-field.
ii) The location of industry in relation to the canal system.

i) The location of industry in relation to the different parts of the coal-field

Crucially for this question, we again highlight Joseph Beete Jukes geological research, and his observation that the location of the iron industry in the Black Country, was determined by that 'central portion of the coal-field' which specifically contained iron-stone, or iron-ore.

So, taking that position, it is evident that the Black Country Society definition can already be brought under considerable question, as the best quality iron-stone usually lay adjacent to thinner seams of coal, and was often of poorer or less quality and quantity adjacent to the thick seam. Jukes emphasised this critical point in the Wolverhampton Chronicle in 1858: -

"The seat of the great iron manufacture of South Staffordshire is not co-extensive with the whole coalfield, nor is it ever likely to become so, since it is the middle part only of the coalfield which has ever been productive of ironstone."

Jukes drew a 'Black Country boundary' built around this identifiable 'iron-stone' core section, from Wolverhampton to Bloxwich and Walsall, from Wolverhampton to Stourbridge, Stourbridge to Halesowen, and Halesowen to Walsall on the eastern side, an area approximately ten miles by five miles.

In support of Jukes theory, it is a little-acknowledged but an already highlighted fact, that most of the thick coal of the Black Country was not always naturally suited to use in the blast-furnaces, and hence the iron industry was not so reliant on it. On the 23 December 1857, the 'Wolverhampton Chronicle and Staffordshire Advertiser' published a discussion regards a proposed reduction in wages of the South Staffordshire colliers, with the Chairman of the Iron Trade Mr Philip Williams stating: -

"The thick coal men are not associated with the iron works. The thick coal comes into the market, while the thin coal is consumed in the blast furnaces".

So, it is a bit of a myth that the unique thick coal was critical to the growth of the mighty Black Country iron industry. The major iron works were often more reliant on iron-ore and the thin coal seam.

ii) The Location of the Industry in relation to the canal system.

Small iron-producing companies were able to evolve and expand, simply because of the creation of a canal system. It has even been argued that the construction of the canal system not only created the market economy, it created the birth of the Industrial Revolution. Most iron works were built in the early-1800s, shortly after the canal system opened.

In 1768, an 'act of Parliament' was passed for the 'Birmingham Canal Company' to build a line of canal northwards from Birmingham, to link to the 'Staffordshire and Worcestershire Canal' just north of Wolverhampton.

The main BCN Birmingham Canal Navigations system was completed by May 1772, so that all sorts of goods, including coal and iron could be transported around the region. Potentially, collieries and the iron industry could benefit from its creation. The construction path of the canal between Birmingham and Wolverhampton, that linked Birmingham with the north, utilised James Brindley's 'contour method', where it primarily followed the natural lie-of-the-land, to keep the number of necessary locks and tunnels to a minimum. In linking Birmingham to Wolverhampton, it ran through the Black Country.

With the coal and iron-ore field close at hand, and additionally connected to the canal by a series of narrow-gauge railways called 'canal tram-roads', the major iron-works generally located immediately adjacent to the newly-constructed canal system, as it was evidently critical to them as they relied heavily on water to power and cool their equipment, as well as to receive coal and transport iron products. So, it made sense to locate there on two key grounds.

The map below (Figure 6) produced by Paul Quigley for the University of York, and titled 'Black Country Historic Landscape Characterisation' (2009-10), shows that the primary location of the Black Country's major iron works, highlighted by dark dots, were situated in a line immediately adjacent to the main BCN Birmingham-Wolverhampton canal, shown by the light-blue line, leading south-eastward from the centre of Wolverhampton, through Bilston, Coseley, Tipton, Wednesbury, to the north-west of West Bromwich.

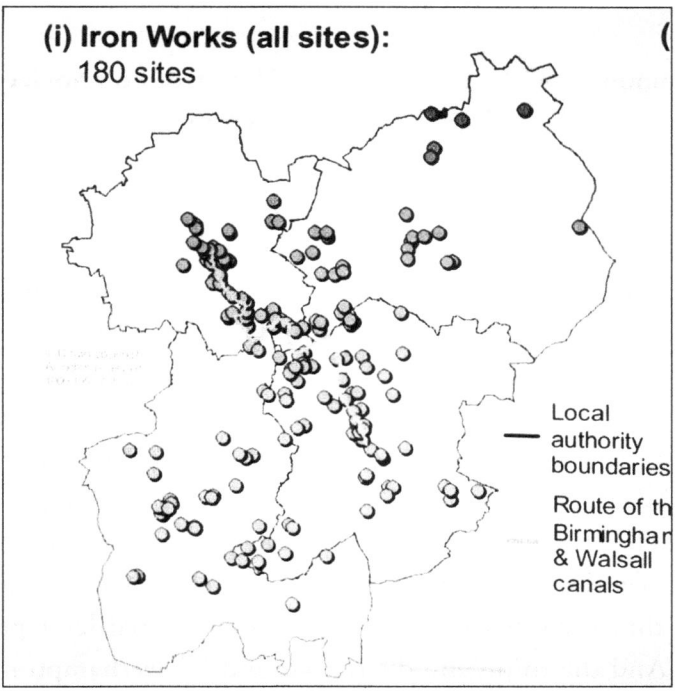

Figure 6 – Black Country Historic Landscape Characterisation 2009-10 by Paul Quigley for the University of York, showing location of main iron works in Black Country

However, by the 1830-40s, the over-burdened canal system was no longer cost-effective, as it took two weeks to transport iron goods to the coast for export. Yet the Black Country struggled on for another four decades, with the help of the newly-constructed railways that usually ran immediately alongside the canal system, and due to its land-locked location, the Black Country iron industry increasingly struggled to compete financially with coastal iron-works.

Nevertheless, this evidence shows that that the location of the rapidly-developing Black Country iron industry throughout the Industrial Revolution was chiefly determined by the location of the canal, and not primarily by the location of the thick coal seam.

Summary of the eight inherent Black Country Society definition contradictions

a) The 'original Black Country' only lay in South Staffordshire, which naturally excludes Dudley but includes Wolverhampton.

b) There was no open belt of countryside separating the commercial town centre of Wolverhampton from the mineral-producing plateau.

c) There was no clear distinction or difference in occupations of residents of the larger so-called commercial town of Wolverhampton and the central mineral-producing towns.

d) The Black Country was clearly never defined by just one aspect of geology – the thick coal seam. Quite clearly the iron-ore and thin seams were just as important for industrial development. And the thin seam district around Wolverhampton was evidently the most damaged and blackest tract of land.

e) The 'original Black Country' and its boundary arguably cannot be shifted or expanded over time and with subsequent economic change.

f) Even if you still adopt the thick coal seam definition of the Black Country, it is evidently wrong to exclude Wolverhampton as some of its districts possessed the thick seam.

g) To emphasise the scale of the Black Country iron industry, the Black Country Society includes statistics from Wolverhampton, but arguably it should deduct Wolverhampton's impressive figures from their overall figures if it does not wish to acknowledge or include the town and its legacy within Black Country history.

h) The iron-ore tract of the coalfield with adjacent thin seams of coal, and the newly-constructed canal system were arguably more important factors than the location of the thick coal seam in determining where the great iron industry located and developed.

5) CONCLUDING THOUGHTS - WHICH DEFINITION OF THE BLACK COUNTRY IS RIGHT?

Having looked in considerable detail at the chronological development of the region, and having examined the growth of both the coal and iron industries in terms of production and manpower, having looked at the precise geographical location of Black Country industry during the Industrial Revolution, and finally having also examined the thought-processes and views of historians and writers that relate to the four different definitions of the Black Country, it is possible to draw valid and sensible conclusions.

First of all, it is evident that mining of coal 'in isolation' did not define the Black Country, and the process of coal-mining did not in isolation, create the environment that led to the area being named 'The Black Country'. There had not been the merest sniff of the term 'Black Country' being used to describe the region, prior to the establishment of the iron industry in the region around

1820-40, with the thick coal having been mined in the area for the previous 500 years, albeit in lesser though ever-increasing quantity.

And so, there is simply no evidence that the area was ever named the 'Black Country' because of the coal-mining alone, nor because of the effect on the environment of coal-mining alone.

Secondly, although mining of both coal and iron-ore undoubtedly came first, the subsequent and hugely-increased level of extraction of these minerals was inextricably linked to two factors. Primarily, it was linked to the unyielding demand for production of pig-iron and associated finished cast and wrought-iron products. Secondly, it was linked to the demand for domestic household fuel.

Whilst the process of iron production could not have happened on such a scale without the coal, it was truly the desire and demand to create iron that led to this great industrial area evolving in the way it did. Arguably, iron defined the Black Country more-so than coal.

And it was the processes of smelting iron-ore and creating iron products, albeit fuelled by coal, and the smoky atmosphere this created, that visually struck such an impression on people. The black clouds of smoke 'belching-out' from the furnaces and 'forest of chimneys' hung permanently above the towns and blocked out the sun, killing any vegetation and leaving a layer of soot on anything and anyone. It was quite evidently this dramatic, impacting, industrial process, when first occurring on a large, consuming scale, that coincided with the area being first so-called the 'Black Country'.

Evidence produced has also shown that the Black Country was the top producer of iron in the Country, yet only the third highest producer of coal, and in terms of man-power, more workers were employed in the iron-producing industry than in the mining industry, at the height of the Industrial Revolution.

The great iron industry, as highlighted by Jukes, established itself chiefly near to the iron-ore tract of the coal-field and by the thin-coal seam, and critically, close to the canal system.

But, in arriving at any sensible definition of the Black Country, I would ask, why choose one industry or the other?

Surely a sensible approach is to accept that both coal and iron industries fundamentally defined the Black Country. One industry could not exist without the other. The availability of minerals, coal, including the thick and the thin seam, the iron-stone, clay, and limestone, 'enabled its existence', the demand for iron 'created its existence'. So, both coal and iron 'defined' it.

At times, it feels like a somewhat muddled concept to grasp, but it is also a simple analogy. Clearly, both coal and iron were critical industries for the region's industrial development, you could literally take your pick regards which of the two you felt was most important in 'defining the Black Country'. And that is exactly what the Black Country Society have done in choosing to define the area through the thick seam of coal alone. It is a flawed, one-sided, and misrepresentative summary of the Black Country's industrial heritage.

And consequently, their definition is simply too idealistic, too restrictive, and arguably plainly wrong. Concurrently their restricted geographical borders of the Black Country are also wrong.

This sweeping and impacting conclusion casting doubt on the Black Country Society definition is evidently and sometimes-inadvertantly supported by the thoughts of virtually every writer who wrote about the Black Country during the 1800s, including Reverend William Gresley, Samuel Sidney, Joseph Beete Jukes, Walter White, Samuel Griffiths, Elihu Burritt, and The Earl of Dartmouth, each whom described the Black Country in different, wider geographical terms than the Black Country Society, with an emphasis on both coal mining and iron production, and viewing both as inseparable and inter-twined processes or activities, that equally shaped the lives of thousands of Black Countrymen and women.

KEY CONCLUDING BULLET POINTS - Correctly defining the Black Country

- There is no concrete evidence that the term 'Black Country' was ever used to solely describe the area where the coal seam outcropped. The coal, including the thick seam, was mined and picked on a smaller scale near, or at the surface, for up to five-hundred years before the term 'Black Country' was first used around 1820-40.

- There is very little evidence that the Black Country was named as such, due to coal-mining in isolation. Nor is there any apparent evidence that suggests that it was so-named because of the 'effect of coal-mining' alone. Even if one still chooses to adopt this theory, it seems likely, and somewhat ironic, that the heavily-damaged Wolverhampton thin coal mining-district was the tract of land that led to it being called 'the Black Country'.

- It is also important to acknowledge that the thin coal seam and iron-stone in the ground were equally important for the economic development of the great iron industry, whereas a good proportion of the thick coal seam was only suitable for domestic-household use or for drawing-off gases from furnaces. Mainly west of Dudley was its content suitable for smelting purposes.

- The name or term 'Black Country' was first used around 1820-40 to describe a part of South Staffordshire alone, which excludes the town centre of Dudley which lay in a small Worcestershire enclave. The term 'Black Country' became widely-known nationally, around 1850, and was by then clearly used to define a wider area including South

Staffordshire and part of Worcestershire, including Dudley. Nevertheless, the 'orginal Black Country' only comprised the South Staffordshire part.

- There is little evidence that the areas where the thick coal seam was mined, were necessarily the same areas where the heaviest iron-production occurred, nor where the 'Black Country was perceived to be at its blackest'. There is no direct correlation. In fact, the thin seam tract around Wolverhampton was the part of the Black Country where the greatest concentrations of iron works with their smoking furnaces and chimneys lay.

- The location of the canal, constructed in the 1770s, was a key determining factor for the location of iron works, and it was this that enabled a market economy and consequently the great industrial Black Country to evolve.

- Technological advances in mining within the late-1800s and early-1900s played no part in defining the 'original Black Country' and its original boundary. These technically-advanced mining practices thereafter enabled amounts of coal to be extracted on a large scale from the deeper, concealed part of the coal-field at peripheral green-field sites. These advanced mining practices did not scar the environment nor define the original Black Country of the previous 100 years. These operations constitute at best, a continuation of mining around the edge, or even just outside the Black Country, at the collieries at Baggeridge, Walsall Wood, Sandwell Park, Jubilee, Hamstead, Holly Bank, and Hilton. The Black Country Society view that the Black Country should be geographically defined by the area where the 30-foot, thick coal seam existed, irrespective of its depth, therefore appears contradictory and fundamentally flawed, as it spans two different periods of time that involve slightly different geographical areas of the region.

- Using an historic, evidence-driven assessment with equal emphasis on both coal and iron to define the 'original Black Country', the boundary would thus expand slightly further out than the geographical borders defined by the Black Country Society. This slightly different 'original Black Country' correlates with that geographical definition held by a clear majority of historians and writers from the highly relevant period of the 1800s, as will be further clarified in the following chapter.

- Dr Fletcher, on behalf of the Black Country Society, was wrong to propose that there was a belt of open countryside separating Wolverhampton town-centre from the mineral-producing areas, and they were wrong to omit Wolverhampton from the list of towns in the Black Country where coal, including some of the thick seam, though mainly the thin seam and iron-ore were mined.

- The Black Country Society in 'redefining the Black Country' in the late-1960s, have arguably re-written 19th-Century history based on a somewhat idealistic 20th-Century interpretation, and hence they have misrepresented it. Inadvertantly, it might be concluded that they have stolen Wolverhampton's Black Country legacy and status. A sweeping and controversial statement, but one that stands to scrutiny.

- It is arguable that those within the Black Country Society used their definition as a way to emphasise what they perceived as Dudley's pre-eminence and stature in Black Country history, whilst diminishing and depreciating Wolverhampton's Black Country legacy, and this clear misrepresentation has self-perpetuated, or been allowed to persist ever since.

- It may be considered today, that the residents of certain districts around Dudley where the thick coal seam was mined, typically characterise the Black Country, but the area did not earn its name because of this.

- Many local people are adamant that they know where the Black Country lies, and why it was so-named. They have grown up with concrete-mindsets without in many cases, fully-understanding the history, growth, and emergence of the Black Country. Whilst this view sounds deeply condescending and patronising, it is evident that many simply believe the status quo view expressed by the Black Country Society, that being that it was defined solely by the thick coal seam. But it is necessary to thoroughly study the history of the Black Country, to properly understand its origins and growth, as there are fundamentally complex considerations which have been discussed and analysed.

In conclusion, having used all available evidence, the 'fourth Black Country definition' proposed at the start of the chapter, is therefore deemed to be the correct one. This quite clearly resembles the view that existed throughout the 1800s Industrial Revolution, and therefore it is this definition with an equal emphasis on both coal and iron, that should be accepted today. Therefore, to conclude this complex chapter, the definition proposed to quite clearly be the correct one, is shown again overleaf.

The CORRECT DEFINITION OF THE ORIGINAL BLACK COUNTRY

"The original Black Country was defined by those areas of South Staffordshire where the 'shallow seams' of thick or thin coal and iron-ore were mined, which gave the general landscape a pitted appearance, and it was defined at least equally by the adjoining districts where the great iron and brass-manufacturing industries developed with their resultant piles of furnace-slag, spoil, scrap metal, and cinder ash, and with their numerous furnaces and chimneys constantly spewing out dense clouds of smoke that blackened the general atmosphere and everything underneath it".

CHAPTER THREE

Wolverhampton – 'in', 'out', or 'of the Black Country'? Correctly Defining the Original, Geographical Borders of the Black Country and Its Original Capital

CHAPTER BREAKDOWN

1) **Introducing Wolverhampton within The Black Country.**
2) **Wolverhampton a Black Country Town? The views of writers, historians, and geologists** - Including: - A) Writers descriptions of Wolverhampton before the term Black Country evolved. B) Writers descriptions of Wolverhampton in a 'Black Country' context during the Industrial Revolution. C) Post-Industrial Revolution descriptions of Wolverhampton. D) The views of 20th-Century local historians - is Wolverhampton a Black Country town?
3) **Is, or was there really a true 'core-area' of the Black Country?**
4) **Innovation and creation in the Black Country.**

5) **Wolverhampton or Dudley considered to be The Capital, Metropolis, or Queen of the Black Country?**
6) **Conclusion - Wolverhampton a Black Country town?**

Figure 7 – Photograph of central Wolverhampton in the 1970s by unknown photographer

Whilst the previous chapter concentrated on analysing how to correctly define the Black Country, concluding that both iron and coal industries equally created its growth and therefore defined it, this chapter naturally follows on from that, concentrating on the views of writers and local people regarding the perceived Black Country geographical boundary, especially during the Industrial Revolution, particularly with Wolverhampton in mind.

Where did people back then, view the original Black Country to be?

The photograph above (Figure 7) shows a canal scene in central Wolverhampton in the 1970s, showing the canal running through the area around Horseley Fields and Monmore Green. It sets the scene nicely, highlighting the industrial legacy of the previous two-hundred years, particularly that of the huge iron industry that once existed.

The views that are highlighted regards Wolverhampton, or 'Ironopolis' as it was labelled by the Manchester press in 1866, I think you will agree, are convincing and compelling.

1) INTRODUCING WOLVERHAMPTON WITHIN THE BLACK COUNTRY

The arguments of the previous chapter have I hope, highlighted fairly-convincingly that the fourth definition of the Black Country should clearly be adopted, with an emphasis on both coal and iron, which in turn determines that the Black Country was thought to have been a little larger geographically than that district defined through the Black Country Society thick coal seam definition.

These days however, since the 1960s, it seems that many people have adopted the stance that Wolverhampton is not and was not in the Black Country at all. Wrongly in my opinion. And clearly so, as will be evidenced in this chapter.

Back in the 1800s, a polar-opposite attitude existed, as it was seen very much as being part and parcel of the heavily-industrialised region that in that era became known as the Black Country, and it was perceived as its 'Capital' or 'Metropolis', much more so than Dudley.

Much of Wolverhampton's landscape, albeit unphotographed back then, was very much blighted by coal-mines and iron-works, and its environment was as smoky as any other district, possibly the worst of all. Its present-day expansive western and northern suburbs were pastoral green fields at the time, but the Ordnance Survey map of eastern and southern Wolverhampton from around 1900 below (Figure 8), 'over-marked' in 'circled-stripes' where a colliery existed, and simply 'circled' where a major iron works existed, clearly highlights the degree and concentration of industry at the end of the Industrial Revolution. The town centre is at the top left, and it shows the area of east and south Wolverhampton, but only as far south as Parkfield and Ettingshall Collieries, which were mid-way between Wolverhampton and Bilston.

It is unclear where Dr Fletcher's open tract of countryside lay, that 'apparently' separated the commercial centre of Wolverhampton from the mineral producing area.

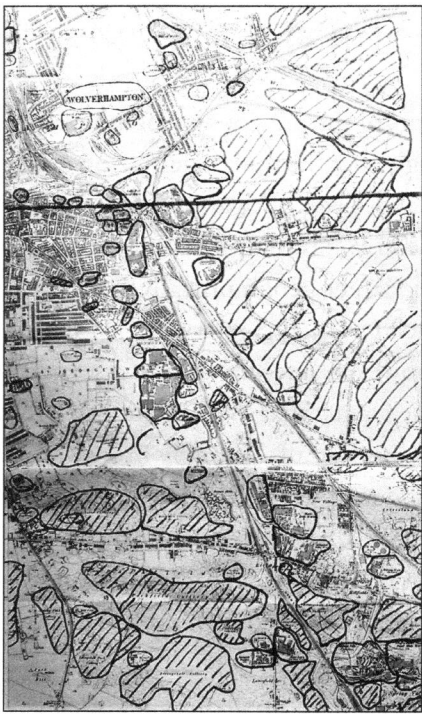

Figure 8 – Map of Wolverhampton from around 1900 over-marked with collieries and major iron works.

In this chapter, a huge weight of evidence will show that Wolverhampton was quite clearly originally considered to be a Black Country town, and as stated, perceived as the 'Capital' or 'Metropolis of the Black Country' throughout the Industrial Revolution, at least from the inception of the term.

The visit of Queen Victoria in 1866 was a key event in the history of the town, but it perhaps marked a time when Wolverhampton gained much-needed self-esteem and civic pride, and a sense of worth and self-identity. As its natural resources of coal and iron-ore expired, and spoil-banks were gradually levelled, it was in the late-1930s that a few elite and prominent Wolverhampton people perhaps first began to question their status of being within the Black Country, at that point alternatively proposing it was 'Of the Black Country, but not in it', due to its position on the edge of the district.

Within this chapter, the views of every writer or historian who commented on Wolverhampton, especially in a Black Country context, are highlighted chronologically. And there are many, so it does make for quite a lengthy read, but that only supports Wolverhampton's Black Country status.

There may be a few more out there, but the evidence has certainly not been gathered in a selective way. The issue of Wolverhampton's position within the Black Country was approached with an open mind, initially I was unsure what views existed, perhaps it was indeed just a market town during the Industrial Revolution, away from the dirt, grime, and hardship? But the evidence on the contrary is quite compelling. Some of the remarks about the towns environment make grim, but interesting reading.

2) WOLVERHAMPTON A BLACK COUNTRY TOWN? THE VIEWS OF WRITERS, HISTORIANS, AND GEOLOGISTS

There are many contributions from various writers and travellers throughout the Industrial Revolution period in relation to Wolverhampton and the Black Country. It is certainly interesting to highlight different people's descriptions of Wolverhampton during the 1800s, as they reveal whether it was considered to lie within the original Black Country, or at least before that term emerged whether it was fitting of an area shortly to be named as such.

Before concluding this chapter, the notion of a 'core Black Country area' will also be examined, and then finally the issue of the region's 'Capital' – Wolverhampton or Dudley throughout the Industrial Revolution?

A) Writers descriptions of Wolverhampton before the term 'Black Country' evolved

Right at the start of the Industrial Revolution, Wolverhampton's metal trade was of international repute. As previously highlighted, Swedish commissioner **R.R. Angerstein** during his visit to the UK in 1754, stated: -

"Wolverhampton is one of three towns in England famous for its fabrication of iron and steel-ware."

He noted some gin-pits and iron works, and he noted that nailers shops and black-smiths lined the entire road from Wolverhampton to Wednesbury. He also stated in his diaries that: -

"Upon arrival in Wolverhampton, I found a lot of people buying and selling. Scores of smiths came to offer their wares for sale - nails, tools, locks, hinges, buckles, flat-irons, and other similar goods in iron and steel."

In 1792, **Lord Torrington** rather condescendingly described Wolverhampton in simple but derisory terms, highlighting a bleak landscape even at that early time, as: -

"A large, black swelling, with commerce".

A year later, in 1793, West Bromwich mine-owner and geologist **James Keir**, in his work 'Mineralogy of the South-West part of Staffordshire' stated that: -

"Mining focussed around Wolverhampton, Wednesbury, Bilston, Dudley, Oldbury, Albion, and Smethwick".

As highlighted, in that document he 'never-once' referred to the area as 'the Black Country' despite owning a colliery at Tividale.

Only subsequently has the title of his work been re-worded to incorporate the words 'Geology of the Black Country'. Nevertheless, Keir clearly considered Wolverhampton to be part of an identifiable, industrial, coal-mining region.

Other writers, some of world-wide renown, have described Wolverhampton's industrial environment of the 1800s in striking terms, possessing landscape features that people would readily accept as being reflective of the Black Country without naming it as such, because the term 'Black Country' was not well-known or had not even evolved at that time.

Frank Mason in 'The Book of Wolverhampton' (1979), stated that in 1828 an unnamed writer even 'congratulated Wolverhampton' for: -

"Standing in-the-midst of exhaustless mines of coal and ironstone".

The same writer concluded that: -

"For the manufacture of every other article of brass, iron, and steel, its claim to supremacy is justly acknowledged".

The well-journeyed traveller and writer **William Cobbett**, in Volume Two of his 1830 book 'Rural Rides', referred to the region in the following alternative terms: -

"In the Iron Country, which Wolverhampton seems to be some sort of central point."

This is strong independent evidence that Wolverhampton was perhaps already then perceived to be 'the major commercial and industrial town of the district', even before the term 'Black Country' evolved, though in 1831 a census report rather condescendingly described the males of the town's 58,000 population as: -

"A ragged bunch of drunken men of the lowest order".

In the 1834 'History, Gazetteer and Directory of Staffordshire' by **William White**, he described Wolverhampton in the following manner: -

"Though not remarkable for the beauty of its streets and buildings, and though seated in the heart of the great midland mining district, surrounded by coal and iron works, the town is very salubrious and picturesque".

But he also pointed out that: -

"Being situated upon the summit, as Plot pointed out, "it is so liable to the winds that what noxious fumes come from the mines, are quickly dispersed".

Two writers, as we will now see, made-reference to 'Vulcan's Forge', in describing Wolverhampton's landscape. Vulcan of course, was the mythical 'God of Fire   including volcanoes', and 'God of metal-working and the forge'.

In 1835, German traveller and writer **Friedrich von Raumer** was evidently stunned by the dramatic landscape that he saw, when he recorded the following in his travel diaries: -

"About Wolverhampton, trees, grass and any trace of verdure disappear. As far as the eyes can reach, all is black with coal mines and iron works, and from this gloomy desert rise countless, slender, 'pyramidical' chimneys whose flames illumine the earth while their smoke darkens the heavens. The whole is exceedingly striking, probably unique in its kind, but the interest of movement would quickly vanish if I were obliged to prolong my stay in this Vulcan's forge".

And he went on to remark: -

"......if the world had remained as black and gloomy as a chimney at Wolverhampton".

These are telling descriptions of the town's landscape. Remarks about Wolverhampton, not Dudley, nor West Bromwich, though they may of course equally apply. But certainly, they are remarks characteristic of a true Black Country town.

Of worldwide renown and fame, **Charles Darwin** wrote the following in his famous book of 1835, 'Voyaging' (A Biography Volume One), when he described the volcanic landscape of a Pacific island: -

"The beach was black lava, buckled and crippled like an ocean of stony waves, giving way to a low horizon of black cones".

In relation to the scene, Darwin wrote the following to describe what he and his companion witnessed: -

"It reminded them of the smoky, industrialised Midlands – the iron furnaces of Wolverhampton. Dismal heaps of broken lava, piles of cinders, large circular pits, fumaroles, stacks and chimneys made it a port of call suitable for Vulcan".

This quote has subsequently sometimes been subtly-corrupted by local historians to 'furnaces near Wolverhampton', as opposed to 'furnaces of Wolverhampton'. Hence it has sometimes wrongly been concluded that he was referring to Bilston, but in fact the huge concentration of iron works around central and east Wolverhampton contained many furnaces and hundreds of smoking chimneys, and the adjacent thin seam mines of the town created a black, pitted appearance, and it is this district on its central and eastern portion that he was seemingly referring to. Spring Vale furnaces (to become known as Spring Vale or Bilston Steelworks in the 20th-Century) were no more productive at that time, in terms of iron tonnage per annum, than any of those at Chillington, Victoria, Swan Garden, Shrubbery, Osier Bed, Parkfield, or Mars Iron works, all in central and east Wolverhampton.

Perhaps this subsequent, 'grammatical-adaption' of Darwin's quotation is further evidence of a cynical determination by some people to distance Wolverhampton's industrial heritage from that of the Black Country.

Whilst on the subject of famous writers, **Charles Dickens** described Wolverhampton from his 'Old Curiosity Shop' in 1838: -

"It had tall chimneys crowding on each other, and presenting that endless repeating of the same, dull, ugly form, pouring out their plague of smoke which obscured the light, and made foul the melancholy air".

In writing to his wife, he stated: -

"We were compelled to come to Shrewsbury by way of Birmingham and Wolverhampton..........through miles of cinder paths and blazing furnaces and roaring steam engines, and such a mass of dirt, gloom and misery as I have never- before witnessed ".

Dickens was often struck by the hardship and poverty of London's East End, but also by the Black Country region, even if it was not referred to as such in his writing. He highlights this in a scene within the same novel 'The Old Curiosity Shop', where Nell and her grandfather stay overnight at a foundry in the area. Dickens does not highlight geographical place-names in the novel, but in studying the book the Japanese writer and Dickens expert Fumie Tamie stated that this foundry was in Wolverhampton, though others consider it to be in Birmingham. In the novel Dickens said: -

"In this gloomy place, moving like demons among flame and smoke...……….a-number-of men laboured like giants…………others drew forth, with clashing noise upon the ground, great sheets of glowing steel, emitting an insupportable heat, and a dull deep light that which reddens eyes of savage beasts."

The man who offered them shelter at the foundry is described by Dickens as: -

"A black figure, who is miserably clad and begrimed with smoke. The night in this dreadful spot – night, when the smoke was changed to fire, when every chimney spurted up its flame, when the people looked wilder and more savage".

To be truthful, it might have been in any foundry in the region.

But these striking descriptions of Wolverhampton's landscape by Charles Darwin, Charles Dickens, William White, and Friedrich von Raumer are fitting of a true Black Country town even if the term 'Black Country' had not yet emerged.

B) Writers descriptions of Wolverhampton, in a 'Black Country' context during the Industrial Revolution

Once the 'Black Country term' evolved some time before 1840, authors and writers routinely described the area, and the scenes they witnessed, with Wolverhampton often prominent in their thoughts as a key Black Country town.

In relation to the first recorded use of the term 'Black Country', and as already highlighted earlier in the work, a significant discovery was made in June 2016 - a written reference to 'The Black Country' that pre-dates all other known references.

This was discovered in newspaper archives, within an edition of the 'Staffordshire Advertiser' on 27 November 1841, where Lichfield town clerk **Mr C Simpson Esquire** gave a toast at a meeting of leading Liberal reformers at Lichfield Guildhall on 24 November 1841, in-reference to 'the valuable working-classes of the Country', whom he claimed formed 'the staple of the Empire'. He said: -

"Who could go into what was called the 'black Country' in Staffordshire...............Wolverhampton, Bilston, Tipton".

This new evidence is simple and unremarkable, but it clearly refers to Wolverhampton as being a key Black Country town. A local man with local knowledge.

Clearly, this pre-dates the previous, earliest-known written reference to the Black Country, made by **William Gresley** (Reverend of Lichfield) in his now-famous 1846 book 'Colton Green, a tale of the Black Country', in which he referred to the region in the following way: -

"That district of South Staffordshire commonly known as the Black Country, is a dismal region of mines and forges."

He also stated: -

"The Black Country, for so the region is appropriately called, is a district of about twenty miles in length, and five miles in breadth, reaching from North to South".

Great emphasis is often placed by local historians on Gresley's first statement that the Black Country was already 'commonly known as such', but it is somewhat ironic that to my knowledge, none of those same historians highlight what he said about its proportions. Of great relevance is the fact that his 'twenty-mile long, commonly known Black Country' would quite clearly and inevitably have included Wolverhampton at one end. Furthermore, they also oversee the fact that he too, like the Lichfield Town Clerk, described the Black Country as being 'that part of Staffordshire' only, and not Worcestershire including Dudley.

Nevertheless, this forms abundantly clear evidence that the Black Country, at the time it first became known as such, was quite clearly not considered to be as restricted in size as the smaller geographical area that the Black Country Society 1960s 'thick-coal seam' definition would deem it to be.

On 3 January 1850, the 'Morning Chronicle' published a report called 'Labour and the Poor – Manufacturing Districts', in which it highlighted the unique effect of shallow thin seam mining on the landscape earlier described by Charles Darwin: -

"The appearance of the country around Wolverhampton, Willenhall, and Bilston, where the thin seams principally lie, is strange in the extreme. For miles and miles, the eye ranges over wide-spreading masses of black rubbish, and hills on hills of shale, and masking, as it were, the whole face of nature".

The 1851 'Gazetteer of Staffordshire', emphatically and categorically labelled the town in the following way: -

"Wolverhampton, the Metropolis of the Black Country".

That same year, **Samuel Sidney** in 'Rides on Railways' (1851) specifically named Wolverhampton as a Black Country town, when he wrote: -

"In this Black Country, West Bromwich, Wednesbury, Dudley, Darlaston, Bilston, Wolverhampton and several minor villages, a perpetual twilight reigns during the day, and during the night fires on all sides light up the landscape with a fiery glow".

He went on to say: -

"Flaming by night in conjunction with hundreds of fiery furnaces and natural gases blazing, do produce on a night's journey from Dudley to Wolverhampton not the effect of one of Etna, but of a broad inferno from which even Dante might have gathered some burning notions".

Such was the 'hellish scene' Sidney witnessed.

Subsequently however, in reference to Sidney's work, some recent articles such as that in the 'Black Country Bugle' publication, omitted Wolverhampton from that quote that listed six key towns. One can only conclude that this is possibly further evidence of an anti-Wolverhampton agenda when it comes to Black Country history. Or evidence of a selective memory at best?

The dense, industrial smog that lingered grimly over Wolverhampton was often much discussed by politicians, but in 1855 the iron-master **John Neve** reminded those who were highlighting concern, that Wolverhampton owed its existence and prosperity to heavy industry and manufacture, when he said rather succinctly: -

"If there was any town in the kingdom which had a right to smoke, it was Wolverhampton".

And the town was referred to in rather demeaning terms when the House of Lords convened to discuss the 'Wolverhampton New Water Supply Bill' in July 1855. Its supposed-promoter **Mr Alexander** said the following to the panel headed by the Lord of Lucan: -

"It is a bill for the supply of the town of Wolverhampton with water. Wolverhampton, my Lords, is as well known, is the centre of the great iron and coal district of South Staffordshire, and in point of situation, it is about as undesirable a place in which to reside as any place on earth, for it is surrounded by tall chimneys, which vomit forth a vast quantity of smoke".

Indeed, the town was often simply referred to as: -

"smoky Wolverhampton".

And it was no surprise that it was exceedingly smoky and dirty. As posted in the previous chapter, the famous geologist **Joseph Beete Jukes** made a very poignant statement in a Wolverhampton Chronicle article on 8 December 1858: -

"The Black Country was based on the location of the seat of the great iron manufacture."

And critically for him, the iron industry was to be found within an identifiable core section of the region. He said: -

"This was not co-extensive with the whole of the coalfield, nor is it ever likely to become so, since it is the middle part only of the coalfield, which has ever been productive of iron-stone."

He clarified where the Black Country lay: -

"…….the area with Dudley at its heart, from Wolverhampton to Walsall via Bloxwich, and Wolverhampton to Stourbridge, and from Stourbridge to Halesowen, then connecting with Wolverhampton on the west side, then across to Walsall again, constituted the main iron-producing area, which was referred to as the Black Country".

For the highly-respected Jukes, despite being a geologist, the Black Country was defined by iron, and Wolverhampton was a key part of it. He was another local man whose view should carry much weight and significance.

In reference to the famous 'Black Country smog' created by the furnaces and countless rows of chimneys belonging to the many iron works and brick works, the author **Walter White** made a particularly telling remark about Wolverhampton in his 1860 book 'All Round the Wrekin', where he observed The Black Country from the elevated position at Dudley Castle, stating: -

"We mount to the castle, and to the top of the keep. A strange prospect it is. Smoke prevails, rolling and drifting, blackest over the clusters of furnaces. Only on the west and south-west is there cleanliness. There lies Netherton, a place of heavy work. Wolverhampton is visible to the north-east and thereabouts the smoke is densest".

Even if his directional sense is a little awry - the town lies to the north, White clearly recognised Wolverhampton's distinctive landscape from a distance, and he found its industrial smog impressionable, stating: -

"If you look at Wolverhampton from a distance, you see a great deal of dusky roofs, of sluggish smoke, and tall chimneys, so numerous that to describe them as a forest is hardly a figure of speech. As to reconcile

the townsfolk to their fate by something more depressing, one of the stupid Russian guns has been mounted in the market-place".

The gun was a gift to the town, a tribute to its iron works that produced so much armoury for the Crimean War in the 1850s. White's statement provides compelling evidence that Wolverhampton was considered to be a true Black Country town in the blackest part of the Black Country, at the time the Black Country was at its most industrious - during the height of the Industrial Revolution. The numerous tall chimneys he alludes to were famously sketched when Queen Victoria visited the town fifteen years later and shown at the very start of the work as an introduction.

Netherton, a Dudley suburb, on the other hand, the town most-free of industrial pollution based on White's observations, is these days considered a 'true, core Black Country town' by most people. A poignant consideration.

White also describes Wolverhampton's suburb or neighbour Bilston as: -

"Rolling in over-whelming clouds, dark and fearsome. Havoc has fixed its head-quarters here without a doubt".

Dudley, he interestingly described as: -

"The chemical corner of the Black Country".

Whilst he described Wednesbury as being: -

"built on a hillside, and with this abrupt height the Black Country here terminates".

What does that say for Walsall and part of West Bromwich, which lie beyond Wednesbury?

Interestingly, he also fleetingly described Longton, Stoke-on-Trent as a 'second black country'. Though this term was clearly used merely to draw comparison to 'The' Black Country. He was not suggesting that Longton was really referred to as such.

White also specifically identified Wolverhampton as a town belonging to the Black Country when he stated: -

"Few besides students of the Registrar General's census returns associate a population of 50,000 with Wolverhampton, 23,000 with Bilston, 36,000 with West Bromwich, 37,000 with Dudley, and swarms in other places – a grand total of 350,000. Not without reason did the Black Country figure in the extended franchise schedule of Mr Disraeli's Reform Bill".

In 1861, one source highlighted that Wolverhampton township's adult male population was 34,000, of whom 10,000 worked in iron-manufacturing industries, and 5,000 were miners. That is nearly half the adult-male population. Figures indicative of a true Black Country town surely?

Another report from the **'Birmingham Daily Gazette'** on the 8 August 1862, highlighted the occupations of Wolverhampton's residents, from the official census. Over 25% of men aged over twenty were involved in some form of metal manufacture - 10.8% were locksmith's, 9.1% were employed in iron manufacture, and 5.7% were nailers or involved in brass manufacture. 16% were miners, and 9.4% surprisingly still worked the land. In summary, these figures also highlight that 41% of men aged over twenty were involved in metal manufacture or mining.

An excerpt from the **'Wolverhampton Chronicle'** from 17 September 1862, described a field day undertaken by the 'Dudley and Midland Geological and Scientific Society', commencing in Wolverhampton, examining the fault at the Parkfield coal-mine, and eventually moving onward to the elevated position at Sedgley Beacon, where the following description of the view was recorded: -

"The party obtained a splendid view of the Black Country and the surrounding district. The coalfields and Wolverhampton seemed to be smoking at their feet, but to the left and behind them the country had been allowed to remain as nature had made and adorned it, save where the land was cultivated, and the hand of man had added to its beauty with golden corn fields and deeper tinted ground crops. One could hardly refrain contrasting the view from one side of the

hill with that obtained from the other side, for the country here seemed like half made or half destroyed, and the country there was like a world perfected".

The '**Commercial Directory Shippers Guide**' of 1862 clearly considered that Wolverhampton was a Black Country town, as its companies were advertised under a clear section titled: -

"Black Country Section".

And an edition of the 'Wolverhampton Chronicle' from February 1864, carried an advert for '**Jones Mercantile Directory of the Iron District of South Staffordshire and East Worcestershire**', which it stated: -

"*......was generally known as 'The Black Country', and consisting of Wolverhampton, Bilston, Brierley Hill (with Brockmoor and Quarry Bank), Darlaston, Dudley, Kingswinford, Moxley, Oldbury, Rowley Regis (with Cradley), Sedgley, Smethwick and Soho, Stourbridge, Tipton, Walsall and Bloxwich, Wednesbury, Wednesfield, West Bromwich, Willenhall".*

Indeed, there are numerous references in newspapers from the 1800s that demonstrate that Wolverhampton was considered as being 'part and parcel' within the Black Country.

On 4th June 1866, the '**Birmingham Daily Post**' issued the first of a series of detailed reports on the individual towns of the Black Country, from its 'special reporter', in what it titled: -

"The Sanitary Condition of the Black Country" - *"No.1 - Wolverhampton".*

In this report, it referred to Wolverhampton in the following way: -

"*Wolverhampton, the metropolis of the Black Country, stands upon the extremist edge of the iron and coal district of South Staffordshire - looking out from the one side upon smoke and glare, upon sooty chimneys and haggard mine gear, looking out from the other upon fields and trees, and hedgerows, upon meadows enameled with daisies and buttercups, and farmlands dotted with homesteads and cattle- pleasant villas in the foreground, misty hills in the dim distance".*

That same year, on 23 October 1866, the '**Birmingham Daily Gazette**' reporter also highlighted the polar-opposite environments of the town in rather poetic terms, when he reported the town being the unlikely venue for the 'Poultry, Root, and Grain show' of 1865: -

"Who that has ever entered the town by rail – choose what railway you like – can do aught but rail at the country he has passed through and say: 'This land is black and blasted here, fair nature cannot bloom, her bosom's torn with gaping wounds, and blurred, scarred, and blotted o'er, her gleaming is all in gloom. Talk of its fields, and the mind refers to coal-fields, speak of hills, and one cannot but think of Rough-hills made up of cinder mounds. Cottages there are none, but strange dwellings that seem to have grown out of the ruin of the ground and run like blighted-cauliflowers manured with brick-ends, and in place of rosey-cheeked peasantry you have long, gaunt, lean 'sons of toil' who are ever-fighting 'mother-earth' and coming from the conflict with black eyes all over their faces. But there are two sides to anything that has sides at all, and there are two sides to Wolverhampton. Though better known as the 'Metropolis of the Black Country of Staffordshire', Wolverhampton is nontheless the "Metropolis of its country-green.""

Again, this polar-opposite, contrasting environment of its eastern and western districts was notable to writers, but nevertheless, it was placed firmly within the Black Country.

But 1866 was an important year for Wolverhampton for a very different reason.

Queen Victoria famously visited the town, this being her first public appearance after a long period of mourning following the death of her husband Albert in 1861, and she described it as: -

"a large but dirty town".

It is well-documented that the Queen had previously asked for the blinds of her train window to be pulled down as the train travelled through the Black Country on its way to Scotland, as she was so offended by the dirt and grime of eastern Wolverhampton.

Upon her visit in 1866, a great triumphal-arch was erected as a tribute near the railway station, comprising huge lumps of coal, one which weighed four tons, and containing iron bars, picks and shovels. A true reflection of the town's Black Country economy at that time. The famous photograph of this arch is seen below (Figure 9), courtesy of Wolverhampton City Archives.

Figure 9 – 1866 photograph of triumphal arch comprising coal and picks, to mark Queen Victoria's visit to Wolverhampton

Interestingly, the comic publication '**Punch**' reacted with 'abusive-astonishment' that The Queen had to 'endure' such a tribute, by writing a poem belittling Wolverhampton, titled 'The Queen in the Black Country', which made-reference to: -

"the pale and toil-stunted children who leave their nailing for the show".

The poem went: -

"Gracious Queen Victoria, Wolverhampton greets you
Pranks her unlovely face in smiles, with homage as she meets you
Underneath her arch of coal loyally entreats you
Wreaths, nails, locks, and bolts, and near the iron trophy seats you
Grimy labour washes and puts on its Sunday clothes
For holiday unwanted, forges cool and smithies close
The stream of subterranean work, idly, above ground flows
In honour of the Queen, whose very name sounds strange and odd
To many here that know no more of a Queen than of a God
Slaving from dawn to darkness at nail-hammer and nail-rod
Their backs bowed to the anvil, and their souls chained to the clod
The Queen comes honouring those who honour him she loved
*   and lost*

Albert, good, wise, and thoughtful who in-spite-of chill court frost
Kept the green spring of head and heart alive, not counting cost
Of time, or toil, or scorn that scoffed, or doubt his work that crost
Tis well his statue should stand high, in this Black Country core
Looking across these cindery wastes, seamed, scathed, and ashy-hoar
Where the eviscerated earth knows' seasons change no more
Where the only seed is gold, the only harvest coal and ore."

The poem went on still further, but it is noteworthy that 'Punch' referred to Wolverhampton, as highlighted above, as 'in this Black Country core'.

Many residents of Wolverhampton were deeply offended by the words of 'Mr Punch', resolutely defending 'our Black Country' in letters sent to local and national press. But notably and tellingly, amongst these letters of protest, not a single person debated that Wolverhampton was wrongly deemed to be in the Black Country, as would likely happen today.

'Punch' defended their stance, responding in a general letter to the 'Wolverhampton Chronicle', in which it rather damningly highlighted a recent 'Report on Trades in the Wolverhampton district', which said: -

"The large working population of this district are peculiarly isolated from the rest of society. All the large employers live far away from the work people they employ. A few ministers of religion are almost the only representatives of the upper-class residents in The Black Country. No-one, unless compelled by duty or necessity, resides in a district from which nature has been so roughly excluded. Huge, ugly heaps of refuse, spoil from the pits, or cinder from the iron furnaces, cover the whole surface of the country, to the very doors of the very houses in which its denizens live, whilst smoke, issuing night and day from the hundreds of furnaces, shuts out the sun and stifles what little vegetation the few patches of soil left unoccupied by buildings of rubbish might afford".

Queen Victoria's own official diaries were released much later in 1986, and are easily accessible on-line, and they perhaps partly explain why she accepted Wolverhampton's invitation, whilst declining those of other major cities and towns. Some fourteen years earlier in 1852, her diaries clearly expressed sincere sadness at the plight of the people of Wolverhampton's 'Iron Country'. After visiting Wales and Shrewsbury, her train had stopped at Wolverhampton, on her way back to London, and she wrote: -

"Shortly after 3pm we stopped at Wolverhampton where we entered the 'Iron Country', one of the most dreadful parts of the Country one can imagine, which I had seen many years ago, but was new to Albert. It is like another world. In-the- midst of so much wealth, there seems to be nothing but ruin. As far as the eyes can reach, one sees nothing but chimneys, flaming furnaces, and many deserted but not pulled down, with wretched cottages around them and heaps of refuse and dross of the metal which has been worked. They have the effect of gigantic mole-hills. Add to this a thick and

black atmosphere, and a few miserable trees, on which no leaves can live, and you have but a faint impression for the life, under these circumstances which a third of a million of my poor subjects are forced to live. It makes me sad! What a contrast to the life, and invigourating, healthful hills, with its robust inhabitants, which we left two days ago".

And of her widely-acclaimed 1866 visit to the town, she remarked on the journey along Peel Street and around the edges of Wolverhampton's famous Caribee Island slum: -

"We drove back through quite another and the poorest part of town which took half an hour.........there was not a house that had not got its little decoration, and though we passed through some of the most wretched-looking slums, where the people were all in tatters and many very Irish-looking, they were most loyal and demonstrative. There was not one unkind look, or dissatisfied expression, everyone without exception, being kind and friendly".

At the end of an emotional and long day where she was welcomed and cheered by many thousands in Wolverhampton, the Queen wrote her diary of the day, evidently moved by the affection shown by the people of Wolverhampton. She remarked: -

"We reached Windsor safely a little before seven, less tired than I should have expected...............gratified at the love shown to me by my people, a happy day, full of emotion".

Furthermore, upon command from The Queen, her Private Secretary Lieutenant-General **The 'Honourable' Mr C. Grey** wrote the following letter to the 'Mayor of Wolverhampton': -

"Her Majesty is anxious that you should hear, less formally, and as it were, more directly from herself, how much she was gratified by the heartiness and cordiality of the reception she met with from every individual of the vast assemblage that yesterday filled your streets, and how deeply, how very deeply she was touched by the proof which the days' proceedings afforded of the respect and affection entertained at Wolverhampton for the memory of her beloved husband".

CHAPTER THREE

Various national and regional newspapers, including the London press, highlighted The Queen's visit to Wolverhampton, and for some reporters, it was clearly their first visit to the region.

The '**Illustrated London News**' report of The Queen's visit featured a famous picture in its edition of 8th December 1866 called: -

"*The Black Country round Wolverhampton*". (Figure 10)

Figure 10 – 1866 drawing of central Wolverhampton and its easten coalfield, by editor of Illustrated London News

This impressionistic landscape, also depicted at the start of the work, and drawn apparently by the newspaper's artistic editor, once found itself being displayed in Paris's George Pompidou Centre.

The thoughts of the London press at the time of the Queen's 1866 visit confirm that the painting depicted Wolverhampton, as the report in the newspaper accompanying the famous picture stated: -

"By night, as seen in our illustration, viewed from the neighbourhood of Wolverhampton, presents a very remarkable spectacle. The lurid smoke and flame of the countless furnaces and forges, with the fire of the many heaps of burning refuse thrown up at the mouth of the pits, fill the sky with a fierce glare, which throws out in a gigantic shadow the shapes of buildings, tall chimneys and machines, or of passing

workmen, carts and horses, railway-trains, and barges on the canal, rendering the scene one of the strangest and most fantastic that can be witnessed anywhere".

The report placed great emphasis on Wolverhampton's industrial power and reputation as a hard-working town. It described Wolverhampton and its environments in the following terms: -

"Wolverhampton admittedly had a smoke-begrimed aspect, but it was a handsome town having a fair church and pleasant suburbs".

This famous sketch depicted Wolverhampton's famous 'forest of 240 chimneys', according to local iron-trade expert **Samuel Griffiths**, when two years later, on 3 September 1868, he stated: -

"Before leaving this portion of the district we may say that the whole of the 240 chimneys depicted in the 'Illustrated News', on the occasion of the Queen's visit to Wolverhampton, appear in their normal state of emittance, excepting in the few cases where old stacks are being replaced by larger ones".

He clearly differentiated between this Wolverhampton sector containing the 240 chimneys, and those of neighbouring towns, as he then proceeded to say: -

"Passing along the line we see the Bilston furnaces."

Many in Wolverhampton were unhappy with what they considered to be an exaggerated image of their town being portrayed across the nation. At a Council meeting reported in the Wolverhampton Chronicle and Staffordshire Advertiser on 18 December 1866, **Councillor Mander** stated: -

"It was a well-known fact that immediately adjoining the south, north, and west sides was some of the most beautiful and picturesque country in England, and therefore it was untruthful to call the representation of chimney stacks which appeared in the 'Illustrated News' "A scene around Wolverhampton". Unfortunately for Wolverhampton, the railway entrance to the town on both lines was on the east side, which was its most smoky part and strangers took their impressions of the place from the appearance of the different iron works immediately adjoining".

He challenged the artist to show him the viewpoint where there were so many chimneys, but stated: -

"But whilst they were aware that Wolverhampton on the east side was singularly unpleasant, yet at the same time they did not want to be painted blacker than they were".

It seems likely that he 'crowded' all of Wolverhampton's chimneys together in a tight line, and it has been suggested that he drew the picture from Chillington Colliery or Old Heath Colliery, looking towards east central Wolverhampton, where there were indeed many tall chimney stacks.

Many national newspapers reported Queen's Victoria's visit to Wolverhampton.

'**The Times**' for instance, reported the visit by stating: -

"Nothing could exceed the enthusiasm and devotion displayed by the whole population, town and country, assembled in the streets. The colliers, the puddlers, and the forgemen from the iron districts, the workers in metal, jappan, papier-mache, the hollow ware, which have of recent years been added as staple trades of Wolverhampton, raised a mighty shout when the royal carriages appeared in sight, renewing it again and again with a heartiness that could not be mistaken. Those who thought that the population of the Black Country might prove unruly in such a crowd, were agreeably disappointed".

'**The Daily News**' expressed admiration of the town and its working people, by commenting: -

"Those who only know Wolverhampton in its normal workday livery of smoke and soot would hardly have recognised the change which the will of a people in earnest and the skill of practiced decorators had effected in one short week".

More locally, '**Aris's Birmingham Gazette**' provided a detailed report of the day, and it celebrated what it called 'The Queen's weather' on what was an unusually bright sunny November day, though the reporter gave a reason for this: -

"..........even through the dense haze that hangs ever like a grimy pall over the Black Country, the sun was seen beaming with a jolly red face, like an immense danger lamp hanging between earth and sky. The atmosphere was unusually clear, for nearly all the works were stopped. The tall gaunt chimneys did not send forth their volleys of inky smoke to darken all the air, the fires were for the most part extinguished or banked down, and the opaque bands of white waste steam came from the little funnels of the boilers, like atmospheric streamers waving in honour of the Queen's visit."

'**The Standard**' meanwhile offered an alternative explanation as to why Wolverhampton succeeded at the expense of Liverpool and Manchester: -

"The 'Capital of The Black Country', more-lucky, asked for the presence of the Queen when no very lengthy journey was necessary, and when no domestic or social duties intervened".

The Liverpool press, however, were none too complimentary, as highlighted by **John Butland Smith** in his University of Leicester thesis 'The Governance of Wolverhampton 1848-1888'. He highlighted that the 'snubbed Liverpool press', who had hoped that she would visit their great, sea-port city, belittled her 1866 choice by referring to Wolverhampton as: -

"That dirty, little coal-box".

The Manchester press seemed to praise the town's efforts, albeit through gritted-teeth, as on 1 December 1866 the '**Manchester Courier and Lancashire General Advertiser**' reported: -

"What the industrious and hard-working inhabitants of 'Ironopolis' had done to merit the special honour which has been denied to the populations of the two, great manufacturing and maritime enterprises in the north, we are at a loss to imagine, but no-one who penetrated to the heart of the 'Black Country' yesterday, for the first time, could venture for one moment to gainsay the assertion that Wolverhampton is truly loyal to the backbone".

It even went on to afford quite generous praise: -

"The transformation of a grimy and inelegant iron-working town, full of smoke and dirty streets, into a scene of beauty, animation, gaiety, and splendour was a 'fait accompli' which we should have supposed could only have been achieved by our more volatile and fanciful neighbours across the channel."

Either way, **Queen Victoria's** visit was clearly one that benefitted her, and perhaps more importantly, it benefitted Wolverhampton. Both gleaned great satisfaction, which was reflected in obviously different ways.

Some twenty years later however, in 1886, she was still saddened by what she saw as she travelled through the region on the Royal Train, stating: -

"Wolverhampton and the Black Country looked dismal and horrid".

A year after The Queen's visit, on 2 November 1867, the well-known medical publication '**The Lancet**' released a report condemning social conditions in Wolverhampton's Workhouse, which according to the author: -

"reflected the character of the surrounding district".

The Wolverhampton Workhouse was situated near the town centre, at the junction of Commercial Road and Bilston Road, in the heart of the industrial and impoverished Horseley Fields and Monmore Green areas in eastern Wolverhampton. 'Going into the house' was considered-to-be 'worse than going to jail', described as 'a terror to the poorest of the poor' by the Wolverhampton Board of Guardians, upon revealing plans for a new workhouse, which was then proposed to be built in 'the green borderland of the Black Country' at New Cross, Wednesfield.

The rate of pauperism was twice as high in Wolverhampton than even in Birmingham, and it took the inspectors five hours to inspect Wolverhampton Workhouse's 120 wards with over 800 residents. To highlight the sheer scale of people using the Wolverhampton Workhouse, just under 10,000 people, mainly men, had used it during 1846, and similar numbers throughout subsequent decades.

In one ward the Lancet investigators noted 'fifty men huddled around a coal fire, sat in stony silence', and they remarked: -

"*We have never seen criminal prisoners in such dirty clothes, or with such filthy persons. Their life is practically one of perpetual confinement, with the sole prospect of being released by death*".

But it was the introductory remarks at the start of their report which were of most relevance with the Black Country issue in mind: -

"*If cleanliness be as nearly related to godliness as is generally supposed, it is to be hoped that the Church Congress in Wolverhampton will not have been held in vain, for assuredly the introduction of the former virtue is greatly needed in this dirty town. The roads are black with coal, and soot begrimes the houses and the people. The Smoke Prevention Act, if it exists, is never put in force, and hundreds of chimneys vomit forth volumes of dense black clouds, which darken the atmosphere around*".

These are very telling remarks regards the environment of central and east Wolverhampton, at that point in time.

American diplomat **Elihu Burritt** is arguably the writer most-frequently quoted in relation to Black Country history, perceived as being responsible for spreading the region's fame worldwide, through his famous book 'The Black Country and its green borderland' (1868). But he held the contentious view that: -

"*Birmingham was the Capital of the Black Country.*"

He stated that the 'greater Black Country' encompassed an area within a 'twenty-mile radius sweep of Birmingham Town Hall', which for him was the manufacturing centre. He devoted a good portion of his book to describe this city, but importantly he also described the towns of his 'Black Country proper' in separate chapters, and regarding Wolverhampton's peripheral location in the 'Black Country proper', he said: -

"*Wolverhampton is the border town of the district. On its' western outskirts the scene changes with surprising and sudden contrast. In a few minutes, you are in 'green borderland'* ".

As highlighted in the previous chapter, Burritt visited Dudley Castle to view the different towns of his 'Black Country proper' at night, and he compared the furnaces of the iron industry at work to a 'battle-scene' before him. His wonderful description of the iron industry's furnaces at work in his 'Black Country proper' commenced with the following line: -

"Wolverhampton on the extreme left stood by her black mortars which shot their red volleys into the night."

He was very impressed by the industrial prowess of the town, and in-reference to one of Wolverhampton's leading, land-owning families, the 'Leveson's, he remarked: -

"At the time, they (The Leveson's) flourished here, they made the wool trade the great business of Wolverhampton. Then the district around had not begun to be a black country. Then, white sheep, with fleeces unstained by smoke, fed over a green and undulating surface, now buried fathoms deep in the debris of mines, furnace, and forge".

Burritt highlighted Wolverhampton's key industrial role in the Black Country, especially in iron production with its innovative and diverse industries, including the manufacture of locks (mainly lever locks - a speciality of Wolverhampton locksmiths) with over 100 manufacturers in the town employing up to 2,000 people, with similar numbers employed in the tin-plate and japanned-ware industry. He noted 15 iron foundries that employed 1,000 men, 20 brass foundries that employed 1,200 men, 10 iron-plate works that employed 300 men, 3 cut-nail manufactories that employed 450 boys and men, and 15 steel-toy manufacturers that employed 250 men, concluding: -

"Wolverhampton, if not the central, is the leading town of one of the most industrial counties in England".

Quite an accolade from this most respected source, but again, a rarely highlighted one, which further provides evidence of the widely-held view that Wolverhampton was perceived as the 'Metropolis of the Black Country' during the Industrial Revolution.

This notion of Burritt's, regarding the existence of a 'Black Country proper' was further discussed by prominent local dignitories, in an article within the 'Staffordshire Sentinel and Commercial and General Advertiser', on 14 August 1869.

This report, titled 'Spiritual Destitution in the Black Country', is therefore of critical relevance as it portrays the 'common local view' of that important period. Reverand **J.H. Isles** (Wolverhampton) and the **Earl of Dartmouth** (West Bromwich) discussed exactly which areas should be classed as the 'Black Country proper', as their research covered a slightly wider geographical area, but they clarified where the 'core Black Country' area lay: -

"In making the enquiry, the Committee have taken as their field the four rural deaneries of Wolverhampton, Himley, Walsall, and Handsworth, but they omit as not fairly included in the 'Black Country' the parishes on the west side of Wolverhampton, and the parishes of Handsworth, St Peter's and St John's Harborne, Smethwick Old Church, Himley, and Great Barr".

But they clarified that 14 parishes in central and eastern Wolverhampton were considered to lie in the 'Black Country proper', whilst 5 parishes on the western side did not. Interestingly though, there was yet again no reference made to the thick coal seam as being a defining factor, just reference to the general 'South Staffordshire coal-field', that the Earl of Dartmouth preferred it to be called, as opposed to the Black Country as he thought the latter painted the area as being 'black in every respect'.

In August 1871, the reporter of the '**Ipswich Journal**' expressed considerable dismay about simply finding himself present in Wolverhampton during a visit from the 'Royal Agricultural Society'. He was clearly shocked by what for him were unfamiliar scenes of street-life, which he described in the following unflattering terms: -

"Wolverhampton is one of the blackest, grimiest, and dingiest of the Black Country towns. Agriculture in the immediate vicinity, there is none. The town has some good streets diverging from the market place

or square. At the centre of town these streets are well built, but they soon degenerate into mean-looking and even squalid lines of cottages, extending for miles into the heaps of slag which surround the town on every side. To speak of Wolverhampton in mild terms, we might say it is not a clean town. It really deserves to have far worse things said of it. 'Where there's muck there's money', it is said, and we sincerely hope that is the case for the lower classes in this town".*

He hadn't finished there, he then moved on to describe the town's youngsters: -

"The children of the back slums of Wolverhampton are the grimiest of the dirty. In one long street - and we did not see a single child, they ran about in swarms - whose face was not clean enough for a passing stranger to say whether-or-not its possession had a fresh or sallow complexion. In the same street, boots or shoes worn by children were the exception".

But all was not bad, he did report that the children appeared well fed and that the streets appeared relatively orderly for a Saturday night. And to be fair, he obviously did not visit its beautiful western 'green borderland'.

If readers wondered whether such writers, many of whom were outsiders, may have misconstrued where the Black Country's borders were thought to have been, due to a lack of local knowledge, then just like the Earl of Dartmouth and Reverand Isles, Bilston-born **Samuel Griffiths** can allay any such concerns. Born to West Bromwich parents, he reveals a great deal about the Black Country in his book 'Griffiths Guide to the Iron Trade of Great Britain' (1872).

First of all, a little about the life of Samuel Griffiths.

According to local historian Bev Parker, Bilston-born Griffiths led a charmed life, starting off as a supplier of oil and grease in Bilston, then standing as a local councillor, before being made insolvent with a £163,000 debt owed to 'The Wolverhampton and Staffordshire Bank' which ceased trading for three weeks. Dressed in poor man's clothes, he convinced people that his desperate situation was sincere, before somehow managing to recover, and later acquiring an iron works in West Bromwich. But he was somewhat-maligned and deemed a failure in most of his business enterprises, and he also failed when he stood as a Member of Parliament in 1861.

But iron was a field of work that Griffiths felt totally at home with. He claimed to have patented a process to create more malleable, unsulphurised iron at his Staffordshire Iron Works in West Bromwich, in 1862. He also produced regular reports regards the local iron trade, which were published in regional as well as national newspapers over many years, to the point that Wolverhampton became known as 'The Centre of the Iron Trade'.

Griffiths was an intelligent and well-intended man whose ideas often ran away with him, according to Parker. She highlighted that 'he always managed to pay the local tradesmen and shop-keepers in full, and he was open-handed and generous to the poor'. In fact, he was very highly regarded amongst local miners and iron-workers, and they often turned to him for advice at times of strife and strikes. For instance, on 19 October 1864, the 'Wolverhampton Chronicle and Staffordshire Advertiser' encapsulated this train of thought, where they reported his involvement in a local trade dispute: -

"Last they went to Mr Samuel Griffiths, whose connection with, and practical experience of the staple trade of the district is well known, and who, too, is a native of Bilston, and has ever been a favoure with the working-classes of this portion of South Staffordshire, to ask his advice of how they were to act."

So, whilst Griffiths's work may be discredited by some, there is no evidence that he was dishonest when he wrote about the iron trade, although as Bev Parker highlighted, he sometimes 'sailed close to the wind'. Although small bits of information in his book on the UK's iron trade are said to be incorrect or exaggerated, it is still seen as one of the most comprehensive accounts of the industry at that time, and it must have taken him several years to finalise after visiting iron works the length and breadth of the Country, which he describes in intricate detail, along with the districts in which they lay. His telling accounts of Bilston, Wolverhampton, Dudley, Willenhall, Brierley Hill, and Oldbury are especially descriptive. There is no reason to disbelieve or discredit those elements of his work. And that is an important point.

And tellingly this writer, primed to the hilt with local knowledge, stated: -

"Wolverhampton was considered to be 'The Capital of the Black Country' ".

Griffiths also described the eastern Wolverhampton landscape in vivid and engrossing detail: -

"Being now within two miles of Wolverhampton, which is considered to be the 'Capital of the Black Country', we must refer to it. Situated on the very top of old mines, the land all around for miles is devastated and thrown into heaps. Attempts have been made to level the ground and recultivate the surface, but nature, after the torture which she has undergone, refuses to give her increase; the trees all withered away, the sun appears to frown on the efforts of man, and refuses to force his genial, sparkling rays through the murky atmosphere which enshrouds this devoted spot. The road and the country all round has been disemboweled in all directions. Nothing can be seen all round for miles, as far as the eye can reach, but blast furnaces and tall chimneys, vomiting forth volumes of dense smoke which form a dark canopy, resembling in some measure a moderate London fog; fortunately, the latter is quickly dispelled by the suns rays. Here however, he seems to have lost his power, obstruction of the smoke renders a thickened state of the atmosphere a normal condition of the country".

Compelling evidence regards eastern Wolverhampton, and its industrial 'Black Country' landscape and environment.

And in reference to local iron-master Isaac Jenks becoming Mayor of Wolverhampton, Griffiths made a further significant accolade to the town, stating: -

"He is the third iron-master who has been mayor of the 'Capital of the Iron Trade in the Black Country' ".

Griffiths clearly placed the town at the head of the Black Country iron industry.

But like others, Griffiths recognised that Wolverhampton had two distinctive sides, though noting that its prosperous western suburbs were at that time separate and detached from it. He described Wolverhampton in the following terms: -

"One side of Wolverhampton develops to view the Black Country in earnest, the other presents a beautiful landscape, with the charming country village of Tettenhall, two miles distant from the town".

Critically though, he too clarified exactly where the Black Country's borders were considered to lie: -

"The Black Country commences at Wolverhampton, extends a distance of sixteen miles to Stourbridge, eight miles to West Bromwich, penetrating the northern districts through Willenhall to Bentley, The Birchills, Walsall and Darlaston, Wednesbury, Smethwick and Dudley Port, West Bromwich and Hill Top, Brockmoor, Wordsley and Stourbridge. As the atmosphere becomes purer as we get to the higher ground of Brierley Hill, nevertheless here also, as far as the eye can reach, on all sides, tall chimneys vomit forth clouds of smoke."

It is somewhat suprising how the Black Country Society appear to have ignored and disregarded the very relevant thoughts of Samuel Griffiths, and those views of Joseph Beete Jukes too, or the Earl of Dartmouth, which are surely amongst the most significant and telling of any from the Industrial Revolution period.

But Griffiths is not alone with his thoughts regarding Wolverhampton's Black Country status.

John Bartholomew's 1887 'Gazetteer of the British Isles' described Wolverhampton in the following emphatic terms, again highlighting the perception that it was known as the 'Metropolis' of the region: -

"It is now the largest manufacturing town in the county and is known as the 'Metropolis of the Black Country'. Situated in the heart of the great midland mining district, with extensive beds of coal and

ironstone in its vicinity, it possesses enormous iron foundries where articles of every description of iron-ware are produced."

Local newspapers were in little doubt that Wolverhampton was the principal Black Country town.

In the '**Birmingham Daily Post**' edition on 13 May 1893, the reporter resolutely defended Wolverhampton from the abuse which it often attracted, describing it as: -

"The metropolis of the mining district of South Staffordshire".

But he went on to say: -

"Now there is no denying the fact of furnaces and long chimneys, with their volumes of smoke as the consequence. The real charm is not in the town itself. It is in the country roundabout. On one side, it is the Black Country, sure enough - the murky atmosphere speaking of industrial activities and grimy hands siding in the trade and manufacture of the nation. On the other we have a perfectly rural and unspoilt country."

Reverend **Henry Hampton** highlighted in straightforward terms how the residents of the industrial side of Wolverhampton were perceived to be, when in 1895 he said of his All Saints, central Wolverhampton parish: -

"It is not decent for a woman with any sense of propriety to walk down Steelhouse Lane".

He also highlighted that 'the area was known to be full of dog-fighters, pigeon-flyers and other rough characters', and of the church built here the Reverend stated: -

"This is essentially a poor man's church to provide for the miners and grimy iron-workers of Steelhouse Lane, Monmore Green, and part of Rough Hills".

J.G. Phelps 'Illustrated Towns of England - Business Review of Wolverhampton 1897', described Wolverhampton as a town, in the following manner: -

"In point of size and manufacturing importance, Wolverhampton easily holds premier position among the chief towns of Staffordshire."

However, as with Griffiths, Burritt, and others, whilst highlighting its heavily-industrialised side, Phelps also described the split appearance of Wolverhampton: -

"Being an essentially manufacturing town, possessing localities of somewhat grimy character particularly as seen in travelling through on the railways, many people want of closer acquaintance with the place imagine it to be a typical Black Country town of altogether unprepossessing appearance and character, but such is by no means the case, Wolverhampton has really beautiful suburbs and its high streets are clean and attractive. It may be said to lie on the fringe of the Black Country, partaking somewhat of the character of this renowned neighbourhood on one side, but embracing charming country in extensive residential districts on the other".

Local writer **William Highfield Jones** (W.H. Jones) in his 1903 book 'The Municipal Life of Wolverhampton' highlighted the town's central or pivotal role in the regions industries, stating: -

"Wolverhampton, being in the centre of Staffordshire, was the Capital of the coal and iron trade. The town was surrounded by large numbers of smelting furnaces and collieries".

A 1904 article in the Wolverhampton Journal by **James P. Jones** titled 'Tettenhall – The bright, green borderland', was clearly making-reference to Burritt's earlier description. He said: -

"Few busy towns of the size and importance of the 'Metropolis of the Black Country', can boast of such a wealth of charming rural villages in close-proximity as does Wolverhampton. Strangers who are carried through the town by the various railways have the impression that the town and district are equally black. Those more fortunate, who stay, are delighted with the picturesque country they discover. The transition from town to country is sudden, the discovery so unexpected. The scenic beauties of the village are undeniable, it is a haven of rest after the heat and burden of the day, and its freshness and charm are enjoyed and shared alike by the toiler and dweller in the slums of Wolverhampton and the civic magnates who have it their home".

Nevertheless, Tettenhall's actual physical detachment from Wolverhampton, as highlighted by Samuel Griffiths, was all too evident back then, portrayed by an 1800s description of Wolverhampton, as seen 'from' Tettenhall, which stated: -

"Further south is the town of Wolverhampton with its great forest of tall chimneys belching forth their soot-laden clouds and obscuring the horizon".

Local evidence that Wolverhampton itself was being described in this way, as seen from a western geographical perspective.

The editor of the '**London Daily News**' also made-reference to Wolverhampton's contrasting aspects on 30 April 1908: -

"On its western side, Wolverhampton is an agreeable town which spreads through pleasant suburbs to a charmingly rural countryside. On its east side are all nearly all the factories and workshops, and the route to the various industrial villages in this far-reaching division is blackened and bleak. One need not be a tee-totaller to become depressed by the remarkable multiplicity of public-houses in the terribly-mean streets."

Nevertheless, these descriptions by Burritt, Griffiths, Parker, Phelps, and Jones indeed typify the dilemma Wolverhampton creates for some people. The industrial central section and eastern side being atypical of that 'gritty Black Country character', and the smaller, western side and its adjoining but then separate, picturesque villages, which were less populated at the time than today, being as far-removed from dirt and hardship as one could possibly imagine.

And when it was proposed to include the parishes of Tettenhall, Penn, and Bushbury in the Poor Law Union of Wolverhampton in 1870, there was strong opposition from the residents and inhabitants of those areas, as encapsulated in one letter to the local newpaper where they considered themselves to be: -

"too purely agricultural to be counted as bona-fide suburbs of Wolverhampton".

In modern times, when detractors argue that Wolverhampton does not represent the Black Country, they often depict scenes from its 'leafy suburb' of Tettenhall but choose to ignore the fact that during the Industrial Revolution, the village of Tettenhall, as highlighted, was detached from Wolverhampton, nor was it at all representative of the town.

This divided east-west situation was one that the smaller, so-called 'core Black Country towns' did not really experience due to their central position within the district. But there will always be this complexity and conundrum regards Wolverhampton, and its polar-opposite sides and environments.

John Butland Smith in his fairly-recent thesis 'The Governance of Wolverhampton 1848-1888' poignantly highlighted this situation, when he stated that: -

"Wolverhampton in the 1870s was a polarised society divided between the lower classes, and the middle-class who were the principal controllers of governance, and who saw themselves as separate, respectable and more refined."

Wolverhampton's deeply-divided society was also highlighted by **Henry Pelling**, in his book 'Social Geography of British Elections 1885-1910' (1967), when he said: -

"The political gulf between east and west Wolverhampton in 1885 required little explanation. Wolverhampton East was 'more uniformly working-class' than other Black Country seats and therefore more anti-Conservative".

To summarise, these numerous descriptions of Wolverhampton and its landscape and environment from throughout the Industrial Revolution period, clearly cement Wolverhampton's Black Country legacy.

C) Post-Industrial Revolution descriptions of Wolverhampton

After the Industrial Revolution, writers continued to describe Wolverhampton as a Black Country town, and a leading one at that.

On 5 July 1913, a writer from Stroud named **Charles Allen**, wrote of his time living in the Black Country in the Gloucester Journal, stating: -

"If ever there was a place rightly-named, this was. Anyone who stood on the hills outside Wednesbury and Wolverhampton and looked down on those places after dark and saw nothing but a mass of flame and black smoke, would rightly describe it as "hell with the lid off". "

Local newspaper the **Tamworth Herald** reported the King and Queen's pending visit to the region on 24 January 1914 by stating: -

"In continuance of the King's inspection of the principal industrial centres of the United Kingdom, it is now considered to be the turn of the Black Country, of which Wolverhampton is the industrial, though not the geographical, centre."

This is further evidence of local knowledge confirming Wolverhampton's prominent position within the Black Country, even if it was becoming an industrial shell, with a rapidly declining metal industry in the early-1900s.

Not unlike Charles Dickens, in the first half of the 1900s, Halesowen-born-and-bred writer **Francis Brett Young** used 'variant names' to describe the towns of his local area – he called Birmingham 'North Bromwich', Dudley 'Dunston', Wednesbury 'Wednesford', and Wolverhampton 'Wolverbury'.

Young described Dudley as: -

"the self-proclaimed Capital of the Black Country".

This highlighted a potential shift in thinking after the end of the Industrial Revolution.

He described the towns of the Black Country in three of his books named 'A Portrait of Clare' (1927), 'This Little World' (1934), and 'Mr Lucton's Freedom' (1940).

Like other writers, he viewed the Black Country from the elevated position of Dudley Castle, and in 'Mr Lucton's Freedom' (1940) he geographically identified what he considered to be the core area of the Black Country: -

"To the north, The Black Country smouldered beneath its perpetual smoke pall; there lay Wednesford (Wednesbury), Dulston (Dudley), and Wolverbury (Wolverhampton), clasped in the grimy tentacles of North Bromwich (Birmingham)".

In 'This Little World' (1934), he said: -

"The town of Dulston (Dudley), a conglomeration of mean dwellings, foundries and workshops stood at the very heart of the blighted zone, in-the-midst-of slagged and cindery wilderness".

And in 'A Portrait of Clare' (1927), he said: -

"To the north is Wolverbury (Wolverhampton), where towering smoke stacks shook out funereal pennons', and the shriek of tortured iron issued from rolling mills".

So, Wolverhampton, in the eyes of this 1900s Halesowen-writer, was clearly considered a Black Country town, which is surely especially telling and revealing not only because of his local upbringing, but because it demonstrates a 'confirmation' and indeed 'a continuity-of-acceptance' that Wolverhampton still was, at that point in time, and had been for the previous one-hundred years, perceived as a key Black Country town.

But there was undoubtedly a shift in thinking as the 1900s progressed, as Wolverhampton's economy evolved and became more highly-skilled, based largely on engineering, with its landscape gradually becoming less-bleak and less-riddled with worn-out mine-workings and furnace slag-heaps, and less smoking chimneys servicing the great iron-works that were mainly closed down.

On 4 February 1938, the '**Birmingham Daily Gazette**' reported the annual exhibition of the 'Wolverhampton Art Circle', and interestingly at that point it stated: -

"The Black Country is still the best description of the Black Country, despite improvements that have been made by the reclamation of waste-land and the building of housing estates".

But critically it went on to say: -

"Although the official view – which has been modified in recent years – is that Wolverhampton is 'of' rather than 'in' the Black Country."

So, it certainly appears that with some certainty, we can identify the late-1930s, some decades after the Industrial Revolution ended, as being the time-period when a new strand of thinking emerged regards Wolverhampton and its position within the Black Country. A view possibly endorsed by some of its own politicians, especially those representing its expanding middle-class western suburbs into which newer residents from other areas moved into.

The late-1930s therefore, was the point in time when Wolverhampton's position within the Black Country was first queried. This is a critical piece of evidence.

Nevertheless, the environmental physical damage created by the effects of that heavy industrial period of the 1800s, continued to shock writers who visited the region. The famous author **J.B Priestley** in his book 'English Journal' (1934) highlighted this blitzed effect of the landscape.

He first went to Dudley, which he described as: -

"a fantastic place".

Like Burritt, White, and Young before him, he went to the elevated position of Dudley Castle to look across at the Black Country. And like White and others, he suggested that the 'blackest section' was not around Dudley nor Cradley, but for him too, in the opposite direction. This was clearly where Priestley considered the Black Country to be. He said: -

"The view from there is colossal. On the Dudley side, you look down across roofs and steeply mounting streets and pointing factory chimneys. The view from the other side, roughly I suppose, to the north-east, was even more impressive. There was the Black Country unrolled before you like a smouldering carpet. You looked in to an immense hollow of smoke and blurred buildings and factory chimneys, there seemed to be no end to it."

Priestley clearly emphasised where his 'blackest' areas were: -

"There was a cynical abundance of these patches of wasteland which are as shocking as raw sores or open wounds............drunken troops have passed this way, there are signs of atrocities everywhere, the earth has been left gaping and bleeding. The places I saw had names, but these names were merely alliterations: Wolverhampton, Wednesbury, Wednesfield, Willenhall, Walsall. You could call them all wilderness and have done with it."

Later in his book Priestley poses the question whether 'the people' were better off or worse off in England'? He answered this by suggesting that the Industrial Revolution had changed a once pleasant green country, in the following way: -

"It had blackened fields, poisoned rivers, ravaged the earth, and sown filth and ugliness with a lavish hand. You cannot become rich by selling the world your coal and iron and cotton goods and chemicals without some dirt and disorder. What you see looks like a debauchery of cynical greed. As I thought of some of the places I had seen......... Wolverhampton, St Helens, Bolton, Gateshead, Jarrow, and Shotton - who gave them leave to turn this island into their ash-pit? It is as if the country had devoted a hundred years of its life to keeping gigantic sooty pigs. And the people who were choked by the reek of the sties didn't get the bacon".

Priestley was from a humble, working-class northern background, but the iron works and industrial environment of Wolverhampton, Jarrow, and Shotton clearly left a 'marked' impression on him. He was particularly struck by the scenes of desolation he found in Wolverhampton, Gornal, and West Bromwich within what he considered to be 'his Black Country'.

Even the famous English author **John Betjemen**, made-reference to the town, in his book 'Coming Home: An anthology of his prose 1920-1977', where he was reminiscing of his life back in England, whilst away on his travels during the period 1940-1945. He stated: -

"Not until you have been away from it for more than a year, do you realise how friendly, how beautiful is the meanest English town..........

even a town like Wolverhampton looks splendid through Memory's telescope."

As recently as 1970, 'blog writers' visited Wolverhampton to revel in its industrial wastelands and urban decay, the legacy of the ravages of the Industrial Revolution nearly one-hundred years previously.

A **Stephen Dowie** recorded his thoughts of Horseley Fields in the following way: -

"I had just waked half a mile from Wolverhampton station and dropped down onto the towpath of the canal. This was the scene that greeted me. What a wonderland! At every turn of the canal some monstrous vista of colossal buildings was disclosed to my eyes. In places, the water of the canal steamed, in others it was so polluted that if you stirred it with a stick you created rings and patches of opalescent hue. 'Beautiful' is not quite the word to use of such places, yet I loved them with a holy zeal."

Another 'blogger' **Stephen Boisvert**, from outside the area, stated: -

"My trip out to RAF Cosford Museum took me through Wolverhampton on the train and I thought it looked quite fantastic in that way that run-down industrialisation does. Giant pipe collections which have no obvious purpose other than connecting this derelict building to that derelict building. Old red brick warehouses with cracked yellowed windows. Weeds and trees pushing their way through asphalt, concrete and brick".

In 1977, author **Charles M Young** reported on the Sex Pistols secret 'gig' in Wolverhampton at the Club Lafeyette under the guise of the 'Spots' – 'Sex Pistols on Tour', and he was none too complimentary about the condition of the town when he remarked: -

"Wolverhampton turns out to be an industrial sump hole, resembling Cleveland if Cleveland had been built two-hundred years earlier".

He was presumably comparing the town to the famous American steel-producing city of Cleveland.

Personally, I can recall departing Wolverhampton Railway station on the train in a northerly or southerly direction even as recently as the late-1980s and being taken aback by the dirt and grime etched upon the faces and hands of foundry workers milling around in yards directly below the railway line. The scene constituted some sort of industrial throwback to times gone-by. And looking at the faces of other passengers, many were equally aghast at the scene they witnessed on the other side of their train window, especially if it was new to them. Wolverhampton 'High Level' station and its adjacent sections of railway have always provided an elevated panorama and an insight into Wolverhampton's industrial might and legacy, and the filth and grime that came with it, collected during the previous two-hundred years. Only the council skyscrapers of Heath Town that seem to nearly reach the clouds, created a stark chronological contrast, and acted as a backdrop to remind the observer that they are not in fact viewing some absorbing recreation of the Industrial Revolution.

But make no mistake, they could have placed the Black Country Museum here at half the cost, adjacent to the town centre of Wolverhampton, and there would have been no need to change anything! Even today, some of that dereliction is still being cleared or is left rotting away.

To summarise, these fairly-compelling descriptions and quotations clearly highlight that Wolverhampton was undoubtedly perceived as one of the principal, heavily-industrialised, coal and iron-reliant 'Black Country towns' throughout, and indeed for some time after the Industrial Revolution.

However, most of Wolverhampton's huge iron works and coal and iron-ore mines had closed or expired by the late-1880s and certainly by the early-1900s. And as many of the chimney stacks and furnaces were knocked down, and the spoil banks levelled, Wolverhampton gradually began to take on a different appearance, perhaps ahead of neighbouring, smaller Black Country towns.

Jon Lawrence highlighted Wolverhampton's partial, economic shift away from primary heavy industry in his work 'Speaking for the People - Party, Language and Popular Politics in England 1867-1914', where he stated: -

"In 1906, Wolverhampton's economy suffered acutely from the migration of its great iron industries to coastal sites. Wolverhampton Tories found their most vocal working-class supporters not among the impoverished iron-workers and tool-makers of the east end, but amongst skilled workers in more prosperous trades such as engineering and brass-ware".

Of course, the whole region and indeed the entire Country's economy changed and evolved over time, but this 'new progressive Wolverhampton' was the one that many local Black Country historians and commentators grew up with, especially as the 1900s progressed. A 'different beast' to the 'Black Country Wolverhampton' of the Industrial Revolution. And this economic change was a critical one, as it is quite likely that it was this change that shaped opinion in the late-1900s, when some within the Black Country Society considered Wolverhampton not to be a Black Country town.

The weight of evidence highlighted so far in this chapter, in conjunction with the views of local historians that now follow, does therefore raise the question of whether the Black Country Society were entirely subjective with their 1960s 're-assessment' of the 'definition of the Black Country', and of where its borders lay.

And it is the views of local historians that we finally examine.

D) The views of 20th-Century 'local historians' – is Wolverhampton a Black Country town?

Fascination with the history of the Black Country reached almost mythical proportions as the 1900s progressed and as its bleak environment was being gradually transformed, and as highlighted, this was the period when a number of writers and local historians published their work. These individuals lived in and experienced the Black Country during the mid-to-late-1900s, and it is of some irony, and rather revealing in my opinion, that only since Dr Malcolm Fletcher's 1960s controversial definition, have some of these writers 're-defined' the Black Country in specific and restrictive 'either / or', coal / iron' terms.

So, let's examine the views of these 1900s local historians.

Clearly it is difficult to summarise their overall thoughts in just a few selected, isolated lines or quotes, therefore it might be argued that it is necessary to read their work, in each case, in its entirety.

So, I stress, as a disclaimer, 'that the following conclusions are simply my own interpretations', having read the books of the historians that are now discussed. They do not therefore necessarily therefore reflect their own overall thoughts. Nevertheless, any highlighted quotes or lines are still critical defining ones, so they are unquestionable, in case it is suggested that they do not represent the required degree of accuracy and impartiality.

In 1945, **Professor S.H. Beaver** distinguished between the conurbation as a whole, and the 'Black Country proper', which he equated to the 'shallow or exposed coal-field'. He stated that 'such an area excluded the centres of Wolverhampton, Walsall, and West Bromwich'. Though of course he therefore included mining areas of those towns.

In 1946, **H Rees** defined the borders of the Black Country as a smaller area based on earlier 18th-Century forges and foundries located on the South Staffordshire Coal-field. This in his view excluded Wolverhampton, though it is unclear exactly why. He was adamant the Black Country should be defined by the iron works, and that the number of forges and foundries would be where the Black Country was at its blackest, close to the coal-field. In his view, 'black' refers not to underground blackness in the form of coal, but to serious pollution, or the smog created by the processes of smelting and forging.

Perversely then, Rees concluded that Wolverhampton was not in the Black Country, but perhaps he simply and incorrectly concluded that anything east and south of Wolverhampton town centre counted as Bilston.

Birmingham-born writer **Walter Allen**, in his book 'Black Country' (1946) stated that 'it was difficult to define the Black Country' but stated: -

"It is true that coal and iron had been mined there for centuries, but it was steam power that gave the district its distinctive character, made it a phenomenon, and caused the populations of towns like Wolverhampton, Walsall, West Bromwich, Kingswinford, Rowley Regis and Tipton to increase by seven or eight times in three generations".

He also made the following telling statement: -

"The suburbs of Wolverhampton are pleasant, and the country, not the Black Country, is close at hand. But in the centre of Wolverhampton the taste of the air is definitely that of soot".

Walter Allen clearly concluded that Wolverhampton itself was a Black Country town, or the bulk of it.

Bloxwich-born author **Phil Drabble** highlighted the conundrum in defining the borders within his beautifully-written 1952 book simply titled 'Black Country' in which he captured the somewhat confused mixture of opinion of local-residents: -

"The Black Country, in fact, is the whole area bounded by a line from Bloxwich to Wolverhampton to Stourbridge to Smethwick to West Bromwich and back to Bloxwich again. The whole area that is, except the towns bounded on one side by country, like Wolverhampton and Walsall and Stourbridge".

He goes on to say however: -

"No one knows just where the boundaries lie".

Though I would suggest that he clearly considered Wolverhampton to be a Black Country town, as he made the following statement: -

"I always associate this thriving, throbbing, flaming Black Country with Wolverhampton church. For one thing, the very character of the place has always been so full of vivid, searing contrast. Bullbaiters and cock-fighters have marched cheek-by-jowl with Bible-bashing hellfire Methodists. Rough, hard-swearing illiteracy has been combined with some of the shrewdest, sharpest business in the land. As far as eye could see were gibbety pit-winding gears and smoking spoil-banks, clanging rolling-mills and teeming, verminous tenements. Yet St Peter's harmonised with this whole melancholy picture as naturally as a swan on a city lake. There it stands as it has always stood, its warm, red sandstone mellow and friendly, its massive tower dominating the countryside, symbolic of the triumph of good over evil. As the centuries rolled on and the rash spread, the proud old church remained immune, 'sallowed' a little, perhaps, by the smoky breath of the land around".

Drabble also confirmed that he perceived Wolverhampton to be a Black Country town, where he stated: -

"From Sedgley Beacon, from this farm at the Delves, from Barr Beacon, or any high ground in the area, you can see all the east and north-east side of the Black Country. You can see Wednesbury's twin churches. You can see Bilston, the very heart, and Wolverhampton and Walsall on the edge. But you can't see what happens to the west."

So, I think it is fair to suggest that Drabble concluded that in his view Wolverhampton was in the Black Country, at least in part.

The well-known authority on the Black Country iron industry **W.K.V. Gale**, or **Keith Gale** (1966), a West Bromwich-born historian, reminds us that the 'Black Country has an industrial history all of its own, based on iron'. He accepts that the borders of the Black Country are arbitrary and often up for dispute, but for him the Black Country was defined by the iron industry. He stated: -

"We are concerned with the district enclosed by a line drawn in a westerly direction from the Birmingham-Halesowen road at Quinton, round Halesowen, Stourbridge, Wolverhampton, Bloxwich, and

Walsall, and returning to the Birmingham-Walsall road at Hamstead. This district was, in its day, the greatest iron producing area in the British Isles".

So, he too concluded that Wolverhampton was within the Black Country.

George Barnsby, born in London but a resident of Wolverhampton, in his 1971 article 'The Standard of Living in the Black Country during the 19th-century' stated: -

"The Black Country is an area about one-hundred miles square, including the towns of Dudley, Walsall, West Bromwich, and Wolverhampton, together with Stourbridge and Halesowen".

So, he also concluded that Wolverhampton was in the Black Country.

That same year, 1971, **Roy Millward and Adrian Robinson** wrote a short book named 'Black Country', where they stated: -

"The Black Country belongs to the coalfield of South Staffordshire and North Worcestershire".

But in their introduction, they also geographically describe where the main section of the region lay: -

"The greater part of the Black Country lies to the north and east of the central backbone of hills".

However, they went on to describe certain towns where the thick coal seam was mined, notably Wednesbury, Dudley, Halesowen, Cradley and Cradley Heath, Quarry Bank, and Brierley Hill, which they clearly considered to be classic Black Country towns. But they neglected to describe other towns at all, such as Tipton, Sedgley, Coseley, Darlaston, Willenhall, Bilston, West Bromwich, and Wolverhampton. Nevertheless, they do not really attempt to define specific borders of the Black Country, and so no conclusions can be really drawn from their work.

Edward Chitham (1972) uses both coal and iron to define his Black Country borders. He named Dudley the 'Capital of the Black Country' and said: -

"Defining the area of the Black Country has always been difficult. At one time, it was generally regarded as starting at the next village or town to the one you lived in yourself. Nowadays, though, people have begun to be proud to be associated with an area where so much inventive and productive labour has taken place."

Although he acknowledged the existence of iron-stone, fireclay, limestone, and other minerals as being the reason the area was riddled with mines and quarries, Chitham highlighted coal as being the main factor in Black Country life, defining the Black Country in the following, somewhat ambiguous way: -

"Perhaps if we take coal as a main factor in Black Country life we can arrive at a working definition of the area. The coalfield as stretching from Walsall and Bloxwich, down through Bilston, Darlaston and Wednesbury to Dudley at its centre. On the east and west lie West Bromwich and Sedgley respectively. On the south, the coalfield stretches through Brierley Hill to Amblecote, the Lye and Cradley, and around in an arc from Halesowen, through Old Hill and Rowley, Oldbury and Tipton. Add to these towns places where coal was marketed and used, together with the parishes where the overspill population now lives, and you have some ideas of the boundaries".

So, he too concludes that Wolverhampton is within the Black Country, even though he somewhat surprisingly omits it from his list of 'coal-field towns'. It is likely he was highlighting the towns where the thick coal was prominent, but 'his Black Country' also included those nearby towns where coal was marketed and used. That clearly includes Wolverhampton even if he wrongly omitted it, because the coal was used in its huge foundries.

D.M. Palliser, in 'The Staffordshire Landscape' (1976) implied that the Black Country 'core area' comprised of 'smaller colliery settlements' in the villages such as Bilston and Tipton, but overall it also included the 'messy urban landscapes' of Walsall, Wednesbury, Wolverhampton, and Dudley.' So, he included Wolverhampton within his Black Country, at least in part.

Harold Parsons, a Dudley-man and ex-editor of the 'Black Countryman' until the 1990s, worked at a major iron works in Wolverhampton during his younger life. He was also author of the book 'The Black Country' (1986), in which he exhibited the wariness typical of late 20th-Century local writers, where he stated: -

"Wolverhampton is a town in which it is necessary to tread warily when linking it with the Black Country. For this reason, I shall ignore residential (western) areas such as Tettenhall and Pendeford, which by no stretch of the imagination can be included. As to the rest...... there are historic pointers to warrant inclusion".

Despite this initial expression of doubt, he then argued and concluded that Wolverhampton was a Black Country town due to its original coat of arms as it incorporated a brazier, and that this was indicative of the Black Country. He also highlighted that Wolverhampton suffered from the collier's strike action in 1831 and 1842, and emphasised Wolverhampton's close Black Country links by highlighting that when Queen Victoria visited the town in 1866 to unveil the famous 'Queen's Square' statue of Albert - commonly referred to locally as 'The Man on the Horse' - a great triumphal archway of coal and iron bars, containing picks and shovels, was erected near the railway station by its dignitaries, full of civic pride.

He also clarified in detailed geographical terms where the Black Country lay, stating: -

"Let us place Wolverhampton at twelve o'clock and work round the perimeter, that is not to say that the whole of Wolverhampton is within the region, only its eastern and southern aspects. Wednesfield now part of Wolverhampton, Willenhall, and Walsall, down to West Bromwich at 3 o'clock. Smethwick, Oldbury, then Halesowen, ...to Stourbridge at 6 o'clock, round to Brierley Hill, Sedgley and Kingswinford at 9 o'clock, then back via Himley to Wolverhampton".

So, Parsons clearly considered that Wolverhampton was in the Black Country, at least in part.

He referred to the eastern side of Wolverhampton as: - *"Bilstonised Wolverhampton"*.

Why not 'east Wolverhamptonised-Bilston', as an alternative? Infact, neither phrase is really appropriate, as both evolved independently in their own way before and after they joined-up, though undoubtedly being close, adjoining neighbours who felt a close bond and unison, and who shared a great deal in common.

Parsons geographical definition of the Black Country fairly-closely aligns with that conclusion determined through this work and clarified at the end of the previous chapter.

George Barnsby can again be referred to, as he inadvertently highlighted Wolverhampton's little-acknowledged status in Black Country coal-mining, where he listed the 'male employment figures' of all Black Country parishes in 1841, in his 1990 book 'Social Conditions in The Black Country'. Already highlighted in Chapter Two, he revealed that Wolverhampton parish had more miners than any other Black Country parish except its near neighbour and suburb Bilston.

These figures were obtained from parish records so would have been reasonably accurate. The number of miners was to increase two-fold over the next twenty years, and the number of iron-workers would multiply around ten times, but nevertheless, these figures demonstrate that Wolverhampton has a significant and proportionally comparable mining legacy to other Black Country towns.

So, it was at this point in time, the 1840s, that being when the term 'Black Country' was first recorded, that after Bilston, Wolverhampton had more miners than any other Black Country town, even Dudley or West Bromwich. A very significant point when Wolverhampton's mining legacy is next 'rubbished' or dismissed.

And Barnsby also highlighted that there was further evidence pointing to Wolverhampton's mining legacy. The principle way that Coal-masters maintained discipline in coal-mines, was through the

'Master and Servant Acts', which were used to penalise breaches of contract and default of duty. He stated that: -

"Between 1858 and 1867 there were 10,000 prosecutions in Staffordshire under these Acts. Many of these would be mass prosecutions involving up to 50 men. Wolverhampton had a higher incidence of these prosecutions than any other borough in the Country".

Overall, it is clear, that Barnsby considered Wolverhampton to be a key part of the Black Country. And those mining statistics substantiate that view.

In 1998 **Dave Ogden**, a well-known local historian, tried to define its boundaries based on the 'thick-coal seam', which aligns with the Black Country Society view, though he acknowledged that the definitions were 'subject to heated debate'. His definition more closely reflects the post-1960s view, he said: -

"The undisputed Queen of the Black Country is Dudley which is virtually at its centre, but starting from the southern edge and going round clockwise, it includes the top end of Halesowen, Lutley, Pedmore, Oldswinford, Stourbridge, Amblecote, Wordsley, Kingswinford, it then cuts across skirting Himley up to the Gornals and Ruiton, Sedgley, Coseley, part of Wolverhampton, across to Wood End and Willenhall, Wednesfield and New Invention, the bottom end of Bloxwich through to Harden and Coalpool, and Rushall (at a push!). Part of Walsall coming back through Bentley down to Wednesbury, across to Hill Top, Great bridge/Tipton. Part of west Bromwich, part of Oldbury, Langley, part of Smethwick (as far as Brindley's canal). Part of Cape Hill across to Bearwood (as far as The Bear Hotel), up to Hill Top (another one) down to White Heath, and through Black Heath running back again through Cradley to the top end of Halesowen."

In the above statement, he tried to define the edges or borders of the Black Country, though, as highlighted earlier, he goes on to say that: -

"The real heart of the area is from Cradley Heath to the Gornals, Woodside, Netherton, Quarry Bank, Pensnett, Rowley etc."

So, he too concluded that part of Wolverhampton was in the Black Country, though at this late point in time he clearly considered Dudley to be the 'undisputed Queen of the Black Country'.

The current owner and editor of the **'Black Country Muse'** website, highlighted that he was fairly-frequently asked by some, 'why he persisted with the notion that Wolverhampton is in the Black Country', replied: -

"Because it is".

He then highlighted its mining and iron industry history and legacy to explain why.

Furthermore, his website included an article that described Monmore Green, an area of east Wolverhampton: -

"Monmore Green was once a hive of industry. It contained four coal mines - Cockshutts Colliery, Monmore Green Colliery, Rough Hills Colliery and New Rough Hills Colliery. There were two Iron Works including the Wolverhampton furnaces - later the Victoria Iron Works, a chemical works, and two brick works. A very busy and smoky part of Wolverhampton. Cockshutts Colliery, as well as bringing up coal also brought up ironstone. These were all horse driven gin pits, at Monmore a pit wench fell to her death whilst fitting on the net used to lower and haul up the horses, she was just twenty-one and the shaft was over one-hundred feet deep".

So, he too concluded that Wolverhampton, certainly in part, is within the Black Country.

As an aside, the 'Black Country Muse' website is quite superb and wonderfully laid out, and worthy of regular visits as it is routinely updated with fascinating historic information. However, on-line forum discussion is controlled to some considerable degree, which always devalues its significance in my eyes. If you look at the various sub-forums, you will quite likely note a virtual absence of Wolverhampton-related sub-headings. Sadly, the site-owner seemed to take some offence at my post suggesting Wolverhampton should have its own mining sub-section, as other towns did, and he may well have taken further offence when I suggested that Wolverhampton was perceived as the 'Capital of the Black Country' for long periods during the Industrial Revolution. He also somewhat bizarrely described my own post as 'a mild rant', before closing the sub-topic and banning me from posting. Which was a shame, because I was just trying to make a point, albeit strongly, and in fairness he is an advocate for Wolverhampton being an integral part of the Black Country.

Nevertheless, one still gets the feeling that 'Wolverhampton' is a bit of a dirty word there, and a sensitive topic not to be aired too frequently on his website in case it offended the loyal followers of his website. For instance, there is no reference to any coal-mining deaths in Wolverhampton, despite three pages of incidents across the Black Country. And the town's industrial districts such as Monmore Green, are often referenced in a way that would never occur with Hill Top, West Bromwich, or Woodside, Dudley. For example, it would report a mine as being at 'Monmore Green, near Wolverhampton', as opposed to 'Monmore Green, Wolverhampton'. I have seen such subtle tactics adopted by many Black Country historians, who just seem to find it fundamentally difficult to accept that Wolverhampton could possibly have had coal-mines and associated industrial grime within its boundaries. But again, it is a quite fantastic site, despite my somewhat-cynical observations.

Local historian **Alec Brew** inadvertently contributed to this dispute in his 1999 book, 'Ettingshall and Monmore Green' which he described: -

"As a region of Wolverhampton typical of the Black Country".

He added: -

"There is a perennial argument about whether-or-not Wolverhampton is actually part of the Black Country. Anybody that wandered through the Rough Hills area, from Monmore Green to Ettingshall, around the turn of the century would have been in no doubt. They would have been confronted by the sight of worn

out workings of Rough Hills Colliery and Cockshutts Colliery, set against a line of chimneys belching out smoke and flames and iron production, steel and products made from them. The Ettingshall area was surrounded by the soot-blackened landscape of abandoned mine workings, slag heaps, and brick works. It is said that Queen Victoria visited Wolverhampton, she was so appalled by the view as her train passed through Ettingshall that she drew the curtains. Ettingshall and Monmore Green, like the rest of the Black Country, where local people are justifiably proud of coming from the Black Country".

In summary, it is evident that although the vast-majority of 20th-Century local historians accepted that defining the Black Country was open to debate, their conclusions generally aligned with earlier writers, authors, and visitors, who considered Wolverhampton – at least in part – to be a key Black Country town.

Finally, **Esther Asprey's** (Doctor of Philosophy) 2007 research at Leeds University into Black Country linguistics, highlighted the divergent views of present-day residents, clearly influenced by the Black Country Society's 1967 re-definition.

She revealed how residents from different areas had entirely opposing views regards the Black Country's boundaries, and that there was considerable annoyance among locals she interviewed that other areas tried to high-jack the name, with every area except Dudley, Netherton, Old Hill and Cradley coming under fire. Western Wolverhampton was certainly problematic for many but others generalised and did not see any part of the town in the Black Country. The same discussion and difference of opinion applied to Walsall, Smethwick, Stourbridge, and West Bromwich.

In her work, Asprey also highlighted that local historians and experts with great knowledge of the region's industry had specifically looked at the borders of the Black Country. Most of these views were at odds with the views of the newly-formed Black Country Society's 'panel of experts' who convened in the late-1960s.

3) IS, OR WAS THERE REALLY A TRUE 'CORE-AREA' OF THE BLACK COUNTRY?

It is worth examining the routinely-aired view of the late-1900s and today that there is, or at least was 'the real Black Country', or a 'true core area' seemingly centred round Dudley and its adjoining towns, especially Cradley Heath, Quarry Bank, and Gornal.

To be honest, I have always been somewhat bemused when someone claims to originate from the 'real Black Country'. Do they really think that their ancestors worked in different types of coal-mines or iron foundries than people elsewhere in the region? Arguably, a sort of inverse sobbery exists.

These days, such a perception seems to very much be based on strength of accent, especially the Dudley / Gornal / Quarry Bank / Cradley accent. Concurrently, it is true that such districts of the Black Country have perhaps more-strongly retained their original character, less affected by cosmopolitan influences and immigration than other parts of the Black Country. The larger towns such as Wolverhampton and Walsall have arguably changed and dare I say it, modernised more than some of the smaller Black Country towns, over the past century. Changed for the worse, some would argue.

Surprisingly however, the picture of Dudley below (Figure 11) in the mid-19th Century, the peak of the Industrial Revolution, surprisingly suggests an environment reminiscent of Burritt's 'green borderland' around the centre of Dudley and its hillside castle. Dudley town itself, like Wolverhampton town, was also sat on high ground, with streets of great historic antiquity.

Some 20th-Century local historians, especially those originating from that area, routinely highlight the notion of this 'true Black Country core area' around Dudley. And it is a notion that has persisted for the last fifty years at least.

Figure 11 – Mid-1800s drawing of Dudley Castle and surrounds by unknown artist.

Much is often made these days, of the fact that Wolverhampton was still partly a market town, but Dudley too held agricultural shows, such as the Worcestershire Agricultural show of 1874, when up to 50,000 visitors attended. It certainly wasn't all black in Dudley. The town was described as 'fantastic' by one famous writer, and its castle and grounds were elevated, green, and airy. Gornal was noted to produce the best roses in the Black Country, and Sedgley held its annual flower show. No lingering black smog there as there was a few miles away over eastern Wolverhampton.

Nevertheless, John Ogden for instance, in 1998, stated: -

"The real heart of the area is from Cradley Heath to the Gornals, Woodside, Netherton, Quarry Bank, Pensnett, Rowley etc."

Why is this? There is no direct correlation between the areas where the famous thick-coal seam was mined, and the areas considered the most affected by the clouds of sooty, black smoke from the chimneys and furnaces of the great iron industry.

If one adopts the Black Country Society definition, where the Black Country was indeed 'solely' defined only by the presence of the thick coal seam, it is plausible that some sort of core area exists. But even then, it would not be solely restricted to the area west of Dudley around Cradley, Brierley Hill, Rowley Regis, Netherton, and Lye Waste as is often suggested, where chain and nail-making were also prominent. Those areas were not noted to have been as affected by the famous Black Country smog because this district lay on higher, rolling hills.

Arguably, the 'shallow-bowl area' comprising the mineral plateau, running eastward and south-eastward, from central Wolverhampton, through to Willenhall, Bilston, Darlaston, Tipton, Wednesbury, to the northern part of West Bromwich was where the Black Country was 'at its blackest' due to the greatest concentration of chimneys and furnaces, the piles of furnace slag, combined with the numerous shallow pits. This core area of collieries and iron-works lay just outside the commercial centres of Wolverhampton, Walsall, West Bromwich, but it also lay just outside, or at least below Dudley too.

But interestingly, as highlighted in the previous chapter and again here, the thin coal seam tract in the triangle of land between Wolverhampton, Bilston, and Willenhall was perhaps the most damaged in the entire Black Country. Was this the 'core area' during the Industrial Revolution? Many writers from that time-period appear to suggest as much.

And can those mid-to-late-1900s historians who write about a 'core Black Country', show that there were clear differences for instance, between east Wolverhampton and Dudley or West Bromwich during the Industrial Revolution, at the time when the Black Country truly existed? That for me is the critical question. I am not sure that there was.

Certainly those 'nailing-areas' around Cradley were deeply-impoverished, and its inhabitants hard-working to the extreme, with entire families notably having to work from Friday morning through to Saturday evening. The 'nailers' undoubtedly developed a unique character, traits that might conceivably still be present within their ancestors, but they weren't the only workers to suffer extreme hardship, and they didn't necessarily represent or typify the Black Country more than some other groups of trades-people.

Perhaps as the 1800s progressed, communities around Lye and Cradley continued to resemble a collection of industrial villages with smaller cottage-industry type workshops, rather than a transforming into a continuous, industrial, urban mass with large factories running continuously, for example from the centre of Wolverhampton to Bilston. But that characteristic image of the typical Black Countryman as a self-employed nail-maker grafting from a workshop at the back of his home, gradually evolved to a worker reliant on factory-based employment as more advanced methods of creating metal products inevitably evolved, including nail production.

What else might identify where the 'core-area' of the Black Country lay?

The social conditions of the masses were equally harsh in all these areas. Cholera and other air and water-borne diseases struck where the housing was worst during three key outbreaks in 1832, 1848-49, and 1854. Bilston and Wolverhampton suffered more than any other Black Country district due to the insanitary slum conditions of its residents. The average life expectancy of Wolverhampton residents was just 19 years and 1 month during that decade, the third lowest, or worst in the Country, and the annual death rates on its eastern side during the height of the Industrial Revolution were generally always the worst in the Black Country area, varying between 33-41 in every 1,000.

It has become popular to portray and characterise real hardship as a fact of life once present only in the smaller, so-called core-area towns. Perhaps the type of housing poverty was different in the larger towns of Wolverhampton, Dudley, Walsall, and even Bilston, where densely-packed, alleyway slums without sanitation existed, whereas as ramshackle miner's huts and tumbledown houses often existed in the smaller villages. But east Wolverhampton had both types of slums – dense alley-way slums and courts at Caribee Island and Horseley Fields, as well as many squalid, miner's cottages and huts that lay close to its collieries, at Rough Hills for instance.

Perhaps looking at the economies of the towns will reveal differences and help reveal a 'core district'.

Wolverhampton's economy, like much of the rest of the Black Country, was certainly over-reliant on coal and iron production during the entire-1800s. Richard Trainor in his 1993 book 'Black Country Elites – The Exercise of Authority in an Industrialised Area 1830-1900' highlighted socio-economic similarities between Wolverhampton and Dudley, and he also drew comparison with West Bromwich. In discussing the period of 'the Great Depression' around 1870 he stated: -

"Dudley partly duplicated the residential, social and trading facilities of Wolverhampton".

He highlighted that: -

"Between nine and eleven per cent of the adult population of Dudley and Wolverhampton paid income or assessed taxes in 1859-60."

He also highlighted that in 1852, less than one in five properties in West Bromwich, Bilston, and Dudley met the £10 valuation threshold, whilst one in four met this value in Wolverhampton, due to its slightly larger middle-class belt on its western side. Conversely, over half the properties in 'leafy Handsworth' parish met this value.

Trainor also highlighted the differences of the role of Poor Law Unions in Wolverhampton, Dudley, and West Bromwich, which supported their impoverished workers and their destitute, during the industrial Revolution. He stated: -

"Overall, potential claims on the guardians were probably greater in Bilston than in Dudley and certainly higher than in West Bromwich. For, aside from their corresponding levels of general prosperity and proportions of highly paid workers, West Bromwich had relatively few of the miners and nailers who, in Bilston and Dudley respectively, put

most pressure on the Poor Law. Yet these contrasts among the towns, like those among their respective Unions, were merely variations within an area-wide pattern of high levels of destitution which became severe. In the late-1870s for example, cases of starvation were reported even in West Bromwich. The three unions substantially though unevenly increased their spending per head of population. The scale and persistence of the increases are too great to be explained solely by rising distress during the local Great Depression. The upward movements affected each of the Unions, though Wolverhampton ended the period spending far more than more prosperous and more ratepayer-conscious West Bromwich, with parsimonious but needy Dudley in-between."

All good evidence that at the height of the Industrial Revolution, Wolverhampton and Bilston experienced perhaps the greatest social pressures of the entire Black Country.

Perhaps the core-area was defined by the lifestyle of its residents.

Famous Black Country pass-times such as cock-fighting, and bull-baiting using Staffordshire Bulldogs took place notably in Wolverhampton, and even at Tettenhall, as much as they did in Wednesbury, Gornal, or Cradley. There is even a district of south-east Wolverhampton named Fighting Cocks, by Cockshutts Colliery, less than a mile out of Wolverhampton centre.

The author William White inferred that 'bull-baiting' originated in Wolverhampton, in his book 'History, Gazetteer, and Directory of Staffordshire' in 1834, when he stated: -

"The Tettenhall Wake, held on the first Sunday and Monday after Old Michaelmas day, has, with its brutal sport of bull-baiting, extended itself to Wolverhampton. This cruel sport, which has been abolished in almost every other county, still prevails at many of the villages of Staffordshire, especially in the mining district, but we trust it will not long be tolerated in this populous town, where the custom is said to have originated some years ago in a mob of the Wolverhampton artisans, who stole the Tettenhall bull for the purpose of baiting him here".

Another little-known pastime, thankfully fairly-rare in Black Country public houses was 'rat-fighting', of which a few instances were even reported in the press across the nation. On one occasion in November 1892 a man bit off the head of a live rat in a Wolverhampton public house at Monmore Green, all for a wager of '20 quarts of ale', only to die several days later with a severe infection of his intestines. On another occasion, in May 1894, various newspapers including 'The Leeds Times' reported another instance of this unsavoury sport in the town: -

"*A disgusting exhibition of Black Country sport has just come to light at Wolverhampton. At a public house, a man was matched against a rat tied to a wooden peg in the middle of the table by a long line, which allowed it a complete circuit of the board. The man attacked with his teeth, with hands fastened behind him. After a savage engagement, the rat was killed, but not until it had inflicted severe injuries.*"

Prize-fighting, more aptly described as 'bouts of street-fighting', was a crude form of boxing with money-stakes inevitably the driving force. It was a common interest of working-men in the Black Country before football became established. Over 4,000 spectators travelled from Wolverhampton and Dudley in March 1845 to watch respective home-town boxers Tranter and Jenkins 'slog it out' at at a greenfield site at Sutton Coldfield, and in December 1918 two Wolverhampton boxers named Abe Hicken and Jack Weston battered each other for a staggering ninety-nine rounds over two hours at 'tranquile Water Orton', before a winner was fairly declared, with both covered in blood.

In fact, such fights were common-place in the Black Country. It was a tough, rough place to grow up, where 'grey pays and bacon' was a staple diet throughout the district.

Overall, it is hard to find substantive evidence that there was thought to have been a true core-area 'limited to the area around Dudley and Cradley' at the time the Black Country truly evolved and existed, throughout the Industrial Revolution of the 1800s.

After the Industrial Revolution, during the early-to-mid-1900s, Wolverhampton saw considerable change. And these natural changes coincided with the period when many late-1900s Black Country historians would have grown up, and when painters such as Edwin Butler Bayliss started to produce 'landscapes' of its industrial wastelands. Wolverhampton saw new industries evolve based upon engineering and transport.

Many of these new industries, especially those based on engineering, attracted a more highly-skilled workforce, and so a large new, upper working-class emerged on the western side of Wolverhampton as the 1900s progressed. Nevertheless, iron foundries and steel works still existed in the Wolverhampton area until the 1980s, notably of course at Bilston Steel Works.

But overall, perhaps the Wolverhampton of the mid-1900s, with these innovative, new transport and engineering industries, did not seem 'quite-so-Black Country' in nature to some historians, at that later point in time when they grew up, whilst towns like Cradley and Quarry Bank perhaps retained the primary, metal-bashing industries, and some coal-mining, more prominently.

It seems likely therefore, that any noticeable differences between towns, may primarily rest upon a perception that was based upon growing up in the mid-1900s, but there is little evidence that key differences existed between the towns during that entire-1800s Industrial Revolution period, when the Black Country earned its name, or that there was perceived to be a 'core-area' based around the thick coal seam around Dudley.

4) INNOVATION AND CREATION IN THE BLACK COUNTRY

It is worth highlighting at this juncture, that Black Country life wasn't all about endless toil and hardship. It was about creativity and invention too.

Although the natural resources in the ground - coal, iron-stone, clay, and limestone, created the potential for the area to a mighty industrial entity, it still required human intervention for that potential to be realised. And it wasn't all down to the thousands who toiled endlessly in the great iron works, in the mines, in the thousands of small manufactories, or from workshops in their home.

Abraham Darby and Dud Dudley of course, were largely responsible for significant advances in the process of smelting iron.

But Wolverhampton played a part too.

There is now strong evidence that the first Newcomen steam-powered engine was successfully used to drain a coal mine at Horseley Fields, Wolverhampton in 1711, though this is still subject to dispute.

But there is no doubting the innovative metallurgy undertaken at Bradley, Bilston around 1767 by John 'iron-mad' Wilkinson, who devised cast-iron and cylinder-boring equipment, as well as developing more effective blast furnaces using the more-efficient steam-engines of James Watt.

A 'General and Commercial Directory' for the Black Country area, produced in Wolverhampton in 1794, was perceived by some as being critical for first creating the trading conditions necessary to generate a market-economy. As far back as 1770, Wolverhampton and Birmingham had their own rather basic trade directory.

There were other examples of innovation in Wolverhampton, that are worthy of mention.

The galvanising process using a hot zinc-dip, was sometimes recognised as being first perfected by Mr Edward Davies at his Crown Works in central Wolverhampton in the 1830s.

Horatio Gibbs Powell discovered a process of applying enamel to iron-ware whilst in employment at the Shakespeare Foundry, that enabled the firm owned by Messrs T. and C. Clark to really prosper over many years.

Safety-fencing was first introduced around the pit-mouth at a Wolverhampton coal-mine, and the system's inventor wanted to see its design replicated across the Black Country, to reduce the number of tragic pit-deaths, tragically sometimes involving wandering or playing children. In this he was fairly-successful.

A safety device was also first introduced at a Wolverhampton coal-mine, which could prevent the skip that lowered and raised the miners from over-running, which often resulted in men falling out of the skip and back down the shaft.

The skill of its artisans was renowned, and the town's japanning and enamelling industry was prominent in the UK, as was its steel-toy industry. Some of the finest gun-lock producers in the U.K originated in Wolverhampton, and its locks of course, were renowned worldwide, especially the Chubb brand.

In 1880, 80% of steel exported to the USA originated from Issac Jenks Horseley Fields Minerva and Beaver Works, such was the high quality of the steel produced. It was even preferred to Sheffield steel at that point in time.

Thomas Parker opened an electrical engineering plant in Wolverhampton where he used electrical accumulators and dynamos to power the first electric light schemes in the Country, such as at Liverpool and Oxford. But perhaps his most famous invention is that of 'Coalite', the smokeless form of coal, in 1904, and that was then widely used in towns and cities across the Country. It arguably transformed the general atmosphere of some towns and cities.

Clearly, the Industrial Revolution in the Black Country was not only about graft, dirt and grime, it was about invention and craft too, and Wolverhampton's industrial legacy possessed all of these qualities, in abundance.

5) WOLVERHAMPTON OR DUDLEY CONSIDERED TO BE THE CAPITAL, METROPOLIS, OR QUEEN OF THE BLACK COUNTRY?

Today, Dudley is recognised by some, even many, as the unofficial and self-proclaimed, but nevertheless: -

"*Undisputed Capital of the Black Country*".

This view is now routinely accepted in many quarters, and I am sure that any other view would simply be 'scoffed at'. That stance is supported by many in the Black Country Society, and by some late-1900s writers and local historians such as Edward Chitham and Dave Ogden. After all, Abraham Darby was born there, and Dud Dudley before him.

But it does appear that during and indeed throughout the Industrial Revolution of the 1800s, when the district truly first earned its 'Black Country' title from around 1820-1840, Wolverhampton was consistently and fairly-widely perceived as 'The Capital, or Metropolis of The Black Country'.

Impartial writer John Smith, within his 2005 research, confirmed Wolverhampton's perceived status during this period when he stated: -

"*By the 1860s, Wolverhampton was described confidently as the 'Capital of the Black Country'*".

And a great amount of any evidence suggests that he was right, which follows shortly.

Wolverhampton undoubtedly became the main administrative centre, with coal and iron-masters holding their 'Quarter Day' to settle accounts and carry out trade at the Lion Hotel in Wolverhampton, through a sustained period of the 1800s, superseding the Dudley meeting that more-or-less faded into obscurity. Eventually, such meetings would be centred on the Birmingham Exchange as well as Wolverhampton.

Newspaper Archive Evidence

Critically, there is a considerable amount of evidence to support Wolverhampton's pre-eminent status as 'Capital', from newspaper archives which only in recent years have become easily accessible on-line.

The Britishnewspaperarchive.co.uk website, for a small monthly cost, enables precise 'phrase-searches' from either specific or all newspaper publications, which is very useful for research like this. Is there any better way of ascertaining the views of the nation than through such examination? And those views are very revealing.

For instance, a search of the phrase 'Capital of the Black Country' between the parameters of 1750-1950 in all newspaper publications in the U.K., revealed that Wolverhampton was referred to as such 77 times, as well as being referred to just once as 'The Great Capital of our Staffordshire Black Country', whilst Dudley, Walsall, and West Bromwich were each referred to as 'Capital' just twice each.

The only serious contender to Wolverhampton to the title of 'Capital' was Birmingham, which was referred to as such 30 times. So much for Elihu Burrtt's 'Greater Black Country' description having no influence! Those references in support of Birmingham were made mainly by newspapers based in distant and peripheral parts of the Country, whilst those who gave Wolverhampton this status included publications from across the Country, but also a number of local newspapers including those from Birmingham and Tamworth, for instance, who critically for this discussion, would have had that regional knowledge. As highlighted, the same 'search' only twice awarded Dudley that title of 'Capital of the Black Country', in newspapers in 1871 and 1882.

Similarly, figures for the term 'Metropolis of the Black Country' using a similar newspaper phrase-search, were also very heavily slanted towards Wolverhampton, during this crucial time-period.

CHAPTER THREE

These 'search-results' are highly significant, as they directly contradict modern-day thinking. There are many examples of newspaper references that support Wolverhampton's Black Country 'Capital' or 'Metropolis' status.

On 30 August 1854, The Right Honourable Arthur Wrottesley urged Wolverhampton to open a Mining School for the impoverished children of the region's colliers, as a few other mining districts had already championed. In the 'Wolverhampton Chronicle and Staffordshire Advertiser' he wrote: -

"Wolverhampton was the metropolis of the mining district of South Staffordshire."

On 4 June 1866, the 'Birmingham Daily Post' commenced a series of reports on 'The Sanitary Condition of the Black Country', commencing with a damning verdict on Wolverhampton, which it referred to as: -

"The Metropolis of the Black Country".

More of that issue in Chapter Seven.

On 5 November 1866, the 'Birmingham Daily Gazette' published 'Sketches of the Black Country in olden times - number VL - the first mayor of Wolverhampton'. This report was a tribute to Tipton-born, Wolverhampton iron-founder George Thorneycroft. But critically the report, in looking at the history of Wolverhampton, stated: -

"At the time Mr Thorneycroft became an adopted son of Wolverhampton - now the proud 'metropolis of the Black Country' - the entire population did not number more than 18,000 and the streets were dingy and awkwardly constructed".

Following Queen Victoria's famous visit to Wolverhampton that same year, 1866, 'The Standard' newspaper referred to Wolverhampton as: -

"The Capital of the Black Country".

Wolverhampton was also referred to as such, in other newspaper reports, for example in the 'Wolverhampton Chronicle' on 5 December

1866, the 'Oxford Journal' on 5 October 1867, the 'Staffordshire Advertiser' on 19 March 1870, the 'Birmingham Daily Gazette' on 21 October 1870, the 'Dublin Daily Express' on 16 August 1875, the 'Staffordshire Advertiser' on 15 July 1933, and the 'Lichfield Mercury' on 18 December 1936. There are a significant number of others.

The 'Birmingham Daily Gazette' presented an article on 13 December 1869, where it referred to Wolverhampton as: -

"*The Metropolis of the Black Country*".

And as already highlighted, some forty-four years later, in 1913, local-newspaper the 'Tamworth Herald' reported the King and Queen's pending visit to the region, stating: -

"*It is now considered to be the turn of the Black Country, of which Wolverhampton is the industrial, though not the geographical, centre*".

The County issue - Staffordshire and Worcestershire

Within his book in 1868, Elihu Burritt described Wolverhampton as: -

"*The border town of the district*".

But this was within what he described as being within his: -

"*Black Country proper*".

Critically however, he also added: -

"*Wolverhampton, if not the central, is the leading town of one of the most industrial counties in England*".

And that 'county issue', in a nutshell, may highlight why there was little competition to Wolverhampton's status, and it might explain why Dudley could not vie for 'Capital' or 'Metropolis' status at the time. The so-called Black Country was spread over two counties during the entire Industrial Revolution period, unlike today where the whole district is contained within the 'unifying' 1974 'West Midlands' county-creation. County-status was extremely important to people back then.

The Black Country coal-field was split into two distinct regions, mainly lying in the great 'South Staffordshire Coal-field', but also in the distinctly separate 'North-east Worcestershire Coal-field'. Wolverhampton and most of the region's towns, along with their huge iron works, historically sat in Staffordshire, whilst parts of Dudley lay in Worcestershire.

Wolverhampton was certainly perceived as the 'Capital of South Staffordshire', or 'The Capital of South Staffordshire Black Country', perhaps Dudley perceived itself as the 'Capital of the Worcestershire' section of the Black Country? But again, I can find very little literature laying claim to such status.

The bottom line was that Dudley, lying in a separate county, could not be considered the Capital of a region that primarily lay in an adjoining one.

The view of writers during the 1800s and early-1900s – Wolverhampton or Dudley?

As has already been highlighted, in 1872, at the peak of the Industrial Revolution, Bilston-born Black Country iron-master **Samuel Griffiths** stated that: -

"Wolverhampton was considered to be The Capital of The Black Country".

He also gave it the accolade of being: -

"The Capital of the Iron Trade in the Black Country".

This was a man who was primed to the hilt with local knowledge. Did he have a Wolverhampton-bias? Brought up in Bilston and born to West Bromwich parents, you would think not, though he did settle in the town. Either way, why would he make these proclamations, if it was not considered to be the case at that time? His statement only supports the stance of others, highlighted in numerous newspaper articles.

In 1887 Scottish cartographer and geographer **John Bartholomew** described Wolverhampton within his 'Gazetteer of the British Isles' as: -

"*The Metropolis of The Black Country*".

Ten years, in 1897, writer **J.G. Phelps** stated: -

"*Wolverhampton easily holds premier position among the chief towns of Staffordshire*".

In 1903, local writer **William Highfield Jones** described Wolverhampton as: -

"*The Capital of the Coal and Iron Trade in Staffordshire*".

A year later in 1904 another local writer **James P. Jones** also referred to Wolverhampton as: -

"*The Metropolis of the Black Country*".

These views from the mid-1800s through to the early-1900s are important as they highlight a somewhat-continued train of thought through that time-period, during the height of the Industrial Revolution, and indeed for a period afterwards.

The view of writers as the 1900s progressed

As the 1900s progressed, evidence emerges of a challenge to Wolverhampton's widely-perceived status as 'Capital', which arguably reflects the period its industrial economy started to evolve with new engineering industries, moving gradually away from a sole reliance on the 'dirty' coal and metal-bashing industries. Whilst its spoil-banks and pit-mounds gradually disappeared from its eastern environment, other parts of the Black Country, such as the Dudley and West Bromwich districts, found new deeper, coal within the concealed seam.

And, as has been shown, it was in the late-1930s that it was first suggested by prominent local people that Wolverhampton was 'Of the Black Country' but not 'in it'. Concurrently, pehaps its 'Capital' status started to be questioned at that time.

Although Halesowen-born writer **Francis Brett Young** described both Wolverhampton and Dudley as key Black Country towns within his novels written between 1920-1940, he referred to his local town in the following interesting manner: -

"Dudley was the self-proclaimed Capital of The Black Country".

Why did he state that it was 'self-proclaimed'? Was it because this reflected a new strand of thinking? Or was it because at that time, Wolverhampton was still considered to be so, and Dudley's claim was considered a new challenge? Either way, the 1930s mark the time when Dudley was first seriously proposed as such.

Yet even in 1936, local press articles highlight that Wolverhampton was still perceived to hold that title. On 18 March 1936, the '**Lichfield Mercury**' reported a new garden housing estate planned for the town: -

"It is interesting to hear of another scheme for establishing a large model village on the out-fringes of Wolverhampton, the Capital of the Black Country."

In the 1950s, there was some talk amongst local politicians of creating an official 'metropolis of the Black Country', one that could challenge Birmingham and vie for more Government funding to improve its general environment still further. But it seems that idea never really progressed further than mere discussion.

Subsequently, as we already know, in the latter half of the 20th-Century, a number of local historians, most of whom it has to be said originate from the Dudley area, such as **Edward Chitham** and **Dave Ogden**, unequivocally consider that: -

"Dudley is the undisputed Capital of The Black Country".

And this position has been supported strongly by many within the Dudley-based Black Country Society since the late-1960s when it was formed, to the point that this status is rarely challenged these days.

But you cannot re-write history, and in summary, during and throughout the key period of the Industrial Revolution of the 1800s, Wolverhampton was widely perceived to be 'The Capital or

Metropolis of the Black Country'. History confirms that. Although that stance is scorned today, it is very relevant to the overall discussion.

Alternatively, Wolverhampton could today perhaps start to promote its status as 'The Capital of the Iron Country', as the region was also widely known during the Industrial Revolution.

5) CONCLUSION - WOLVERHAMPTON A BLACK COUNTRY TOWN?

The previous chapter proved fairly-categorically, that the 'original Black Country' should be defined by both iron and coal, rather than solely by the somewhat-restrictive presence of the thick coal seam as proposed by the Black Country Society since the late-1960s to the present day.

The evidence contained within this chapter also shows fairly-categorically, that historically the Black Country was perceived to include a larger geographical area than that suggested through the definition of the Black Country Society. It is evident that in effect, the Black Country Society have re-written the history of the 19th-Century using a contemporaneous 20th-Century interpretation, and by doing this it is arguable that they have inadvertantly misrepresented it.

Whether you assess the Black Country through its coal or its iron, or both for that matter, Wolverhampton was clearly considered to be a Black Country town. And, not only that, Wolverhampton was also clearly considered to be 'The Metropolis of the Black Country', or 'The Capital of the Black Country' throughout the Industrial Revolution. Wolverhampton's 'Capital' status only seems to have become an area of debate or discussion from the late-1930s, when its economy was in a transitional phase. It may at that point, after the Industrial Revolution, have been a title that some Wolverhampton politicians were happy to shed.

Nevertheless, its 'Capital' status throughout that time-defining industrial period were provided by numerous relevant 19th-Century sources, including 'straight from the mouth' of Bilston-born writer Samuel Griffiths. Not some ill-informed outsider. A point worth remembering.

Many Wolverhampton residents have every right to consider themselves proud Black Country folk. No one can tell them otherwise.

CHAPTER FOUR

Wolverhampton's Borders Over Time

CHAPTER BREAKDOWN

1) **Wolverhampton's Historical Boundaries** Including: - A) Grant of Land from The King. B) Role of the Manors. C) The Parish system. D) Poor Law Unions, Local Boards, and Urban Sanitary Districts. E) Civil Parishes and Urban District Councils (UDC's). F) Municipal Boroughs, County Boroughs, and Parliamentary Boroughs.
2) **Conclusion** - What constitutes Wolverhampton?

Figure 12 – Early-1900s photograph of east Wolverhampton's furnaces and chimneys, from unknown photographer at St Peter's Church.

For those that still wish to exclude Wolverhampton from the Black Country, it helps to look in more detail at what 'constituted Wolverhampton' over time, in this somewhat shorter chapter.

Some people still take the stance that only the Bilston part of Wolverhampton was within the Black Country, a stance that is quite clearly incorrect, as has been demonstrated, and further to that they seemingly highlight that Bilston has an entirely different history, detached and totally separate from Wolverhampton. This chapter will hopefully put that theory to bed, to some degree at least.

The grainy photograph above, from the early-1900s (Figure 12), shows the view from St Peter's Church in the heart of Wolverhampton, looking through the smoky atmosphere that often hung over it, in to the 'forest of chimneys' belonging to Wolverhampton's 'east-end' iron-works.

Though it must be acknowledged that Bilston, Willenhall, Wednesfield, and numerous other Black Country towns do indeed have strong independent identities, those-named towns have always been strongly connected to Wolverhampton, and they have undoubtedly shared a joint-community interest with it, for many hundreds of years.

Much of this information has been obtained from the article by K Farley 'A History of Wolverhampton 985-1985', as well as from highly-informative websites such as

distinctlyblackcountry.org

historywebsite.co.uk

newmanlocalhistory.org

Wolverhamptonhistory.org

Wikipedia and others.

Guy Williams at Wolverhampton City Archives has also been very helpful.

Without the wealth of information that these sites and people provide, such detail would have been difficult to obtain. This is true throughout the work, not just this chapter.

1) WOLVERHAMPTON'S HISTORICAL BOUNDARIES

Boundary or border changes of any town or city are inevitably complex over long periods of time, but within this chapter, key changes that have affected Wolverhampton's boundaries are summarised.

As you will see, Wolverhampton has not simply 'swallowed-up' the likes of Bilston in recent years. Though of course the individual sense of identity of these towns should never be over-looked. But in this case, the two towns were always closely connected, as this 1835 description highlights: -

"Bilston, a market town in the parish of Wolverhampton. Bilston is intimately connected with Wolverhampton. Their proximity and their increasing wealth and population render it probable that the buildings of the two towns will soon be united".

A) Grant of Land from The King

Looking as far back in history as we can, it is plainly clear that those villages then surrounding Wolverhampton initially grew up as separate entities, with a couple of miles of pasture between them and Wolverhampton. But even then, people relied upon, and travelled to their larger neighbour for trade and religious practices. People in Bilston, Willenhall, and Wednesfield looked to Wolverhampton, with owners of the land in between, living in both. So, there was historically some community of interest between them.

The Foundation of Wolverhampton

The year 985AD saw the foundation of Wolverhampton and clarification of its borders, when a 'Grant of Land' was given by King Aethelred to the monastery at 'Heantune' (or Hampton) and specifically to Lady Wulfruna, this became Wulfrun's Hampton then Wolverhampton. This included Bilston, Sedgley, and Tettenhall.

The Doomsday Book of 994AD further confirmed that Ettingshall, Bilston, and Bradley as being land that comprised part of Wolverhampton.

Further proof that Ettingshall, that immense industrial district 'smack inbetween' Wolverhampton and Bilston including the area where Spring Vale, or Bilston Steel works was located, originally belonged to Wolverhampton, exists through a 1261 transaction where the Baron of Dudley gave so many 'pounds of wax to the church at Wolverhampton for land at Ettingshall, Brierley (Bradley), and Sedgley Park'.

And it is little known that the name 'Spring Vale', where the mighty steel-works were to evolve centuries later, was named after a washing-well apparently imbued with healing powers, where Lady Wulfruna used to bathe and wash. Well and truly within her Wolverhampton land.

So, there is no doubt that Bilston, Willenhall, Wednesfield, and even part of Sedgley parish, belonged to, or were often classed as Wolverhampton from very early days. Tettenhall was also a separate village but linked to Wolverhampton through Trysull parish which was rural and agricultural. So overall, Wolverhampton was a mixture of urban and rural environments.

Much early coal-mining took place between the villages, as it was uncertain who precisely owned the land. Indeed, this is why mining took place so prominently for example, at Ettingshall, halfway between the towns and parishes of Wolverhampton, Bilston, and Sedgley.

B) Role of Manors

After 1066 the Dean of Wolverhampton split Wolverhampton into two manors, 'Deanery' and 'Stow Heath'. Stow Heath Manor spread eastward and south-eastward from the centre of Wolverhampton and included eastern Wolverhampton, Bilston, and Willenhall. Stow Heath Manor supposedly at some point came to be run from the 'Greyhound and Punch Bowl' public house in Bilston. This manor system remained in place for a number of centuries, but over time their role gradually diminished because their key role was to manage agricultural land. All the Black Country towns, once just hamlets or villages, as with Wolverhampton, were originally agricultural.

C) The Parish System

Running alongside and eventually replacing the manors, the role of the local Parish became increasingly more important due to ecclesiastical and burial issues, and as land became less reliant on manor ownership. Nevertheless, the boundaries of both manor and parish for a while co-existed and would often be very similar. Hence the residents of smaller towns such as Bilston and Willenhall relied upon Wolverhampton, until they obtained funding to build their own church. Even then, small parishes would still often be reliant on the main neighbouring parish, by forming 'chapelrys' to their larger neighbouring church. The relationship between Bilston and Willenhall, to Wolverhampton for example developed in this way. Bilston, Wednesfield, Willenhall, Essington, Hilton were historically part of the Parish of St Peters, Wolverhampton, as each formed a chapelry to Wolverhampton Parish.

St Peters Church, Wolverhampton started records of burials and marriages for Wolverhampton, Bilston, Willenhall, and Wednesfield in 1538. This forms strong evidence that there was a reliance on, and a strong community link with Wolverhampton for many centuries.

St Leonard's, Bilston, which started to keep Bilston records from 1684, became its own ecclesiastical parish in 1723, and it had its own Parish from 1866.

Sedgley was once an important parish stretching as far north as Parkfields, and as far south as Dudley town, but Dudley's and Wolverhampton's increasing influence meant that eventually Sedgley's importance reduced.

So, boundaries and borders chopped and changed a little over time.

The 1851 'Gazetteer of Staffordshire' described Wolverhampton Parish, stating that: -

"Wolverhampton was the 'head of a populous parish' including Bilston, Willenhall, Wednesfield, Hilton, Featherstone".

It also described Wolverhampton as being head of a Parliamentary Borough, Poor Law Union, and County Court system.

D) Poor Law Unions, Local Boards, and Urban Sanitary Districts

These bodies predominantly determined local affairs, and increasingly became very important for residents, especially during the Industrial Revolution.

'Local Administrative Boards' were set up across the Country in the 1750s to oversee local affairs, as was the case in Bilston and Willenhall. Bilston Town Hall was built in 1788, and as divisions and alleged corruption within the administrative 'parish system' increased in the early-1800s, parishes progressively lost their administrative powers to these other ad-hoc boards, such as the loss of control of Poor Relief through the 'Poor Law Amendment Act' 1834.

Of course, the Industrial Revolution affected many towns and cities from the late-1700s onwards, and increasingly-so during the 1800s, a period when the population boomed, this being when we know the Black Country became so-named, and when it evolved as a physical, industrial entity.

In 1777, Parliament passed an 'Improvement Act' for Wolverhampton which appointed a 'Local Board' comprising 125 Commissioners to run the town, together with the stewards of Deanery and Stow Heath Manors, and they did indeed succeed to some degree to improve conditions as the town was belatedly provided with some lighting, a limited water supply, and slight increased cleanliness. But the great population boom during the Industrial Revolution brought with it uncontrolled overcrowding and slum housing, and many other social problems.

Hence, the role of 'Poor Law Unions' increased during the 1800s as industry developed and associated poverty increased.

'Wolverhampton Poor Law Union' or 'Wolverhampton Union of Parishes' was formed officially in 1837, and it represented its 4 constituent parishes of Wolverhampton, Wednesfield, Willenhall, and Bilston for nearly 100 years until 1930.

Similarly, the 'Wolverhampton, Bilston, and District Trades Union' actively represented the workers of the area from 1865 onward, to modern-day times.

Incidentally, in 1870, when it was proposed to include the agricultural parishes of Tettenhall, Penn, and Bushbury in the Poor Law Union of Wolverhampton, it drew vigorous opposition from those localities, as they considered themselves 'too purely agricultural to be considered bona-fide suburbs of Wolverhampton'.

Overall, this evidence highlights that throughout the key phase of the Industrial Revolution, Wolverhampton was even then, as it is today, perceived to be an all-encompassing area including Bilston, Willenhall, and Wednesfield.

In response to cholera outbreaks and other widespread illnesses in society, smaller 'Urban Sanitary Districts' were created across the U.K. via the 'Public Health Act' of 1872. These were small districts within existing Municipal or Parliamentary Boroughs, such as Willenhall Urban Sanitary District or Short Heath Urban Sanitary District. They were prominent across the country by

1875, still running alongside the diminishing Parishes whose role and responsibility progressively reduced.

E) Civil Parishes and Urban District Councils (UDC's)

These, in effect constituted what we now know as Local Councils, or were the nearest structure to them, in their modern sense.

In the 1890s, it was noted that Wolverhampton had official clerks, as well as a 'Wolverhampton Board of Guardians', comprising a Chairman, Vice-Chairman, 18 members for Wolverhampton, 5 for Bilston, 3 for Willenhall, 2 for Wednesfield, and 1 each for Heath Town and Short Heath. Further strong evidence that a 'greater Wolverhampton' existed at that time.

There was overlap regarding civil or local administrative responsibilities, perhaps as there is still today. But Bilston and Willenhall for example, were still part of 'Wolverhampton Parish', and then part of the granted status of 'Wolverhampton Borough'.

UDC's were first created by the 1894 'Local Government Act', after the Industrial Revolution. This turned Urban Sanitary Districts into 'Urban District Councils', some initially from 1894, and some later from 1933, and these existed until 1966. This 'Local Government Act' created 1,013 Urban District Councils for smaller towns or districts across the country and representing a single parish, each with a population no bigger than 30,000, so that specific local problems could be addressed within existing Municipal Boroughs.

The creation of 'UDC's, particularly from 1933, marked the first time that smaller towns gained 'full independent status', so it is worthwhile highlighting that many of the older population still alive today might take to the preconception that Wolverhampton 'swallowed up Bilston' for instance, with the abolishment of UDC's in 1966.

'Bilston UDC' was created in 1894, and was given full, independent, borough status in 1933. In 1966 all UDC's, including Bilston's full borough status were abolished, and Bilston returned to Wolverhampton despite a lot of local opposition.

Willenhall only became independent from Wolverhampton in 1910, after many years of dispute with St Peters church in Wolverhampton regards burial fees.

Tettenhall, which was also a 'UDC', was also incorporated into Wolverhampton in 1966 amidst much local opposition. 'Leafy Tettenhall' often perceived itself as being disconnected from, or better than Wolverhampton, and there was a clear belt of green fields between it and Wolverhampton, until the 1900s at least, unlike Bilston or Willenhall.

Sedgley these days, is understandably keen to highlight that some Parkfield and Ettingshall collieries lay within that parish in the early-1800s, despite both originally and subsequently belonging to Wolverhampton, as they were the main mining areas near Sedgley village. Interestingly, Sedgley could equally lay claim to much of Dudley's coal-mining legacy, as Sedgley parish previously spread as far as Dudley Castle. The three Ettingshall Collieries and the Parkfield Colliery, even during the 1800s Industrial Revolution, gave their addresses as being either Wolverhampton or Bilston, as these towns were their nearest principal towns. Sedgley was then part of Wolverhampton Borough anyway, at least from 1823 (Parliamentary), and 1848 (Borough). Similarly, coal mines in Dudley gave their addresses as Dudley rather than Sedgley despite lying in Sedgley parish, further highlighting Sedgley's diminishing status locally. Along with Bradley and Coseley, the districts of Parkfields and Ettingshall broke away from Sedgley Parish in 1897.

Parkfields and Ettingshall's historic link or belonging to Wolverhampton is rightly seldom disputed, though as highlighted above, they sat within the parish of Sedgley for a period. Both have clearly developed as distinct Wolverhampton districts.

F) Municipal Boroughs, County Boroughs, and Parliamentary Boroughs

More and more people in towns were demanding more say in local affairs. For Local Government responsibilities, larger towns like Wolverhampton were made 'Municipal Boroughs' under the 'Municipal Reform Act' 1835, and these had a slightly higher status than local boards, and they could elect a mayor as well as executing local government duties.

Wolverhampton nominated 2 Members of Parliament, and encouraged by this system, it sent a 'petition of the householders of Wolverhampton' to the Queen, who in 1848 then granted Wolverhampton a charter officially making it a borough with a Mayor, 36 Councillors, and 12 Aldermen.

The newly created borough included Bilston and Willenhall.

On the 2 May 1849, the 'Wolverhampton Chronicle and Staffordshire Advertiser' reported the meeting of the 'Willenhall Copyhold Enfranchisement Society', that perhaps reflected the mood of its residents, with the Vice-President Mr James Tildesley stating: -

"Willenhall formed part of the parish of Wolverhampton, they were neighbours, indeed one body, as they were fellow parishioners, and intimately connected in trade".

He then raised a toast: -

"To the Mayor and Corporation of Wolverhampton".

'Wolverhampton Municipal Borough' existed from 1849-1889 and then 'Wolverhampton County Borough' existed from 1889-1974, and 'Wolverhampton Borough' from 1974 onwards. These structures included Bilston, Wednesfield, and latterly, only a reduced area of Willenhall.

In terms of parliamentary Representation, the 'Parliamentary Borough (or Parish) of Wolverhampton', was created in 1823 and this existed until 1918, incorporating its neighbouring towns of Bilston, Willenhall, and Wednesfield.

John Bartholomew's 1887 'Gazetteer of the British Isles' described Wolverhampton as a Parliamentary Borough containing Bilston, Wednesfield and Willenhall, and a Municipal Borough and township containing Bilston, Wednesfield, Willenhall, and part of Sedgley. In 1891 the Parliamentary Borough of Wolverhampton included Bilston, Willenhall, Wednesfield and Sedgley (including Gornal), and had a population of 164,000, so there was a close connection at that time, at the end of the Industrial Revolution. In 1918, it was split into Wolverhampton East, West, North West, North East, and South West, but South East became Bilston which had its own parliamentary seat from 1918, though it again later became known as Wolverhampton south-east, to present day.

This history shows that there has virtually always been a strong historic link between Wednesfield, Bilston, Willenhall, and that Wolverhampton had not simply 'swallowed-up' its smaller neighbours from 1966. A deeper relationship had existed for many years.

2) CONCLUSION - WHAT CONSTITUTES WOLVERHAMPTON?

It is abundantly clear that each Black Country town had, and certainly has strong individual identity, and ultimately it is the choice of each individual living within them at any point in time, and no-one else, to decide whether they consider or feel that they want to be part of Wolverhampton or not, irrespective of ever-changing borders. But, legislatively, there is a strong evidence of a 'greater Wolverhampton' incorporating its smaller neighbouring districts over many centuries.

These debates occur across the nation as once small independent villages and communities amalgamate into a larger neighbouring town or city, whether it be Manchester, Liverpool, Leeds, or Glasgow. It is the natural way that large towns and cities evolve and develop.

But it is clear too, importantly for this discussion, that through the past one-thousand years, Bilston, Willenhall, and Wednesfield, although existing as proud, individual villages and now towns, have historically always had a very close link to Wolverhampton, and up to 1900 and again after 1966, have always been part of Wolverhampton.

There are consistencies throughout history in relation to Wolverhampton's borders, and whilst it should be acknowledged that for periods some people fought for independence, the following points can be concluded: -

'Bilsateena' (Bilston) and other towns such as 'Seeges League' (Sedgley) including key mining areas like Ettingshall, were areas of land granted to Lady Wulfruna (Wulfruna-hampton) by the King through a "Grant of Land" back in 985AD.

East Wolverhampton, Willenhall, and Bilston were linked as part of 'Stow Heath Manor' pre-industrial revolution, for a several hundred years. Wolverhampton at that time was split into Stow Heath and Deanery manors.

Bilston, Willenhall, Wednesfield, Featherstone, and Hilton were all historically part of St Peter's Parish, Wolverhampton, and remained so for centuries.

Bilston formed its own ecclesiastical parish in 1723 though was still linked through a chapelry to St Peter's, Wolverhampton, and it formed its own parish at the end of the Industrial Revolution in 1866.

The towns of Bilston, Willenhall, Wednesfield, and Wolverhampton were all linked from 1836 to 1930 through The Wolverhampton Poor Law Union, and the associated Wolverhampton Work Houses. There was also a Wolverhampton Board of Guardians in place in the 1890's, which covered Wolverhampton, Bilston, Wednesfield, and Willenhall.

Although Local Administrative Boards of 1750, Local Sanitary Boards 1875, and Urban District Councils in 1894 and 1933 provided local politics and some level of control to individual towns, they were still part of Wolverhampton Parish, or from 1848 part of Wolverhampton Municipal Borough and Wolverhampton Parliamentary Borough. Sedgley was part of Wolverhampton Parliamentary Borough from 1823 through to 1918.

From 1966 to present day, Bilston, Wednesfield, Tettenhall, and part of Willenhall, have been returned to Wolverhampton Borough, and constitute parts of the 'City of Wolverhampton' from 2001 when it gained full City status.

For over a thousand years, there has been some form of 'greater Wolverhampton', managing local affairs in Wolverhampton, Wednesfield, Willenhall, and Bilston.

And finally, it is poignant to highlight that when King Aethelred granted lands to Lady Wulfruna in 985AD, that led to the creation of Wolverhampton, it included Bilston, Willenhall, Sedgley, and Tettenhall, with the charter specifying: -

"what torments in hell awaited anyone who tried to violate it".
You should never argue with a King!

CHAPTER FIVE

A Closer Look at Coal-mining in Wolverhampton and the Wider Black Country Area

CHAPTER BREAKDOWN

1) **The Black Country Coal-field**
2) **The Wolverhampton Coal-field** - Including: - A) Wolverhampton's thick coal. B) The value of Wolverhampton's iron-ore and thin coal seam. C) Newcomen's first successful steam engine. D) The truck system and its tommy shops.
3) **Wolverhampton Collieries** - Including: - A) Known Collieries Pre-Industrial Revolution. B) Collieries of the main Industrial Revolution period 1800-1880. C) Later operations of the 'Concealed' coal seam.
4) **Coal-Mining Statistics** - Including: - A) Analysis of Coal-mining Casualties in The Black Country in the 1800s. B) Black Country Working Collieries 1880. C) Coal-miner statistics 1841 and 1896.
5) **Brief history of Coal-mining in West Bromwich** (for comparison).
6) **Conclusion** - Wolverhampton's role in Coal-mining in the Black Country

Figure 13 – Early 1900s photograph of miner's family at Rough Hills, Wolverhampton.

If you accepted the views of many Black Country historians over the past fifty years or so, you would have fallen for the myth that Wolverhampton did not have a coal-mining legacy at all, well Bilston aside. A myth seemingly happily perpetuated over the decades by many of those within the Black Country Society.

In the 2005 book 'Towns, Regions, and Industries – Urban and Industrial change in the Midlands', John Smith wrote chapter eight which he titled 'Industrial and Social Change – Wolverhampton Transformed 1700–1840'. In this work, he emphasised Wolverhampton economy's reliance on coal when he stated: -

"Until the coal seam became exhausted, or at least prohibitively difficult to work, after 1860, it was the foundation of most of the wealth for Wolverhampton".

This statement highlights the pivotal history that coal played in the growth and prosperity of Wolverhampton during the Industrial Revolution. No less than thirteen major coal merchants situated themselves along Wolverhampton's canal routes, fed by the numerous collieries in the town.

I must again draw attention to websites such as
Wolverhamptonhistory.org
newmanlocalhistory.org
blackcountryhistory.org
historywebsite.co.uk
distinctlyblackcountry.org
lostwolverhampton.co.uk
and Wolverhampton City Archives, whose photograph opposite shows families picking coal from the shallow coal-field at Rough Hills, Wolverhampton in the early-1900s (Figure 13).

The 'Wolverhampton Chronicle and Advertiser' placed an advert for the Moseley Hole and Neach-hill's Collieries on 18 October 1834, and in this it highlighted the significance of the Wolverhampton Coal-field: -

"Wolverhampton, as a mining district, stands unrivelled, the local advantages unexcelled, and the widely-extending manufactories in the vicinity, secure a demand which experience demonstrates requires new mines to be opened in rapid succession. Mining in the neighbourhood of Wolverhampton is moreover so well understood that it partakes little of the precarious character which attaches to mining property in many parts of the Kingdom".

Quite clearly, Wolverhampton had a substantial mining legacy all of its own.

1) THE BLACK COUNTRY COAL-FIELD

The rather primitive nature of the Black Country coal-field in the 1800s was quite crudely described in the book 'The Victorian Working Class' edited by P.E Razell and R.W Wainwright, which comprised a selection of letters to the Morning Chronicle: -

"The change from the collieries of Northumberland and Durham to those of Staffordshire seems like going back at least a century in the art

of mine engineering. On the banks of the Tyne and the Wear, science the most profound, and practical skill the most trained and enlightened, are brought to bear upon the excavation of coal. In the Staffordshire coal district, on the contrary, everything seems to be done by the roughest rule of thumb. The pits, as regard depth, are mere scratches, compared with those of the north, and except in the case of a few of the thick seam mines, they are ventilated solely by the agency of the vast number of shafts with which the whole coalfield is honey-combed. The workings in such excavations are, of course, very limited. The labourers could not breathe at any considerable distance from one of the shafts, and the consequence of the whole system is, that the coal is worked in the slowest, most dangerous, and least economical fashion. There are scores of coal-pits scattered through the Wolverhampton district, worked without any steam engine at all, simply by the aid of a rude gin and a blind old horse".

The Black Country Coal-field was split into two distinct geographical sections, the 'great South Staffordshire Coal-field' covering east Wolverhampton, Wednesfield, Bilston, Willenhall, Darlaston, Wednesbury, Tipton, and northern West Bromwich, as well as parts of Dudley, and then the 'East Worcestershire Coal-field' that included other districts close to Dudley. These included areas of thick and thin coal, iron-stone, limestone, and clay. Despite its basic practices, the famous 1800s geologist Joseph Beete Jukes highlighted the unique importance of the Black Country coal and iron-ore field in layman's terms: -

"In no other coalfield of the United Kingdom is a thickness of 30-feet of coal to be found together, while in South Staffordshire twelve or thirteen beds of coal rest one upon the other. In the same way, I believe the quantity of ironstone to be found in some parts of this district within a vertical space of 100-150 yards is greater than is known anywhere else".

Coal was first mined in the Black Country purely for domestic purposes, from as early as 1300 when it was easily picked from the surface. Detailed mining records from these early times do not exist, though we know that there are records of mining in the Wolverhampton area from as early as 1315, including 'open-cutting' in Wolverhampton. Over the centuries more and more coal was mined, and pits became slightly deeper. By the late-1700s, local mines were often in the form of rather-rudimentary, horse-driven gin-pits, or bell-pits, or they used the 'pillar-and-stall' method, where small boys crawled down narrow tunnels and propped up the roof using a wooden support. 'Long-wall' methods were then introduced, which were a little safer.

In simple terms, coal in the Black Country was close to the surface, and more easily retrieved than anywhere else in the land. And for that reason, mines were quickly worked and abandoned. By the mid-1700s mines were as deep as 50 yards, or 150 feet in the Black Country. Nationally, for contrast, the average depth of coal-mines in the UK in 1700 was said to be about 300 feet, in 1750 around 600 feet, and then in 1820 around 950 feet. And it was this 'shallow-depth' feature of Black Country mining that affected the landscape so profoundly and uniquely and became characteristic of the 'original Black Country'. The heavily-scarred, or heavily-pitted appearance that these mining methods and practices created across great swathes of land was eye-catching, and nowhere was this effect more noticeable during the 1800s Industrial Revolution period than in the Wolverhampton thin coal seam district. Many of the mines were small, employing just 25-30 men. In Wolverhampton there were many such operations, but there were also much larger collieries such as those ran by the Chillington Iron Company or the Parkfield Iron Company, who employed far higher numbers as their expansive tracts of land contained around 100 shafts. The Parkfield Company for instance operated many shafts as well as 5 blast furnaces to create pig-iron, employing 1,500 men. It is likely that around half of these were colliers. Similar numbers of men were employed by the Chillington Company. In contrast, the Wolverhampton Colliery was a mid-sized operation with around 130 colliers.

But as the Industrial Revolution progressed during the 1800s, the value of coal was affected not simply by the cost of its deeper excavation, but increasingly by haulage, drainage, and ventilation costs too. Mines would often become flooded, though great attempts were made to pump water out using steam engines. Eventually many mines were abandoned, as they were no longer economically viable to operate, and by the late-1800s and early-1900s, it has been said that the Black Country Coal-field resembled a 'giant, water-logged rabbit-warren'. The exhaustion of the coal-field in the Black Country led to the 'great depression' around 1870-1880, and of course this directly affected the 'entirely coal and iron-stone reliant' local iron industry too, even though technological advances in mining practices at the end of the century meant that coal from the much deeper, concealed field was extracted in great quantity around the periphery of the Black Country area, particularly at Cannock Chase, which continued until it expired in the 1970s.

Understanding the original Black Country Coal-field is not easy, it was not as many perceive simply a continuous thick bed spread over large areas. The coal-bed varied in thickness due to the existence of geological faults such as the 'Great Bentley fault', which created a series of alternating beds of coal, iron-stone, fireclay, and sandstone, all of them varying in thickness and extent, and pushed up to the surface or pushed deeper down, so a diagram of it might be said to resemble a gigantic sea-wave. There were also different names for different types of coal. But unlike other areas of the Country, here, coal seams came together in certain districts, resting one upon the other, until they formed a unique thick coal seam, thirty-foot, or ten-yards in thickness. This famous thick coal was notably present around Wednesbury, Tipton, Halesowen, Brierley Hill, Kingswinford, and Bilston, but just south of Wolverhampton town centre, a separation formed by a bed of shale and often containing valuable bands of iron-stone, occurred in the middle of the seam, and a white coal sometimes formed the upper bed of the thick coal.

Contrary to modern-day perception, the average thickness of the Black Country thick coal seam was in fact just over eight-and-a-half yards, rather than ten-yards as is often suggested. This little-known fact was confirmed in a report within the 'Wolverhampton Chronicle and Staffordshire Advertiser' on 10 August 1864, when a meeting at the committee room of the 'Mechanics Institute', Dudley discussed 'the yield of coal in South Staffordshire'. Mr Johnson opened the debate, producing a plan of thirty-five square miles of thick seam collieries, and after contacting thirty mine-owners in the region, he concluded the following regards the thickness of 'gettable coal': -

"The replies to these enquiries have brought me 82 measurements, the average of which is 8 yards, one foot, 6 inches. This, it should be remembered, is from a perfectly independent and disinterested source, and the thickness which I have my self taken in 40 different collieries confirms to 2 inches above 8 and a half yards".

It is seldom highlighted that much of the thick coal seam was sent for sale in the domestic household market as it was more crystalline in texture and not suitable for use at the furnaces, but mainly in the district west of Dudley the thick seam was 'more-earthy' and hence better-suited for smelting purposes. On Dud Dudley's land. And contrary to popular opinion, the thin coal seam prominent around Wolverhampton was prefectly suited for use in the blast furnaces and iron-works.

The amount of each type of coal mined varied at different points in time, as it was intrinsically linked to demand. The thin seam coal-miners, for instance, had to take a pay cut because local iron-ore resources expired during the late-1870s 'Great Depression', and with it the ability to competitively make iron products. At the same time, the thick seam workers did not have to take a pay cut because the demand for coal for use in domestic households remained as strong as ever.

The iron-stone, or iron-ore tract of the Black Country Coal-field was critical for industrial development. Generally, the better-quality beds of iron-ore, called the 'new mine iron-stone', 'gubbin and ball ironstone', the 'blue-flats iron-stone', or the 'Rough Hills white iron-stone', lay adjacent to thinner seams of coal where it was prominent in the Wolverhampton Coal-field, and this iron-stone was notably of great financial value. These under-appreciated thin beds of coal with their adjacent iron-ore beds notably extended for a few miles in a northerly direction from Bilston, at Chillington, Monmore Green, Rough Hills, Cockshutts, Parkfield, Ettingshall, and Stow Heath collieries for instance. Though small amounts of the thick seam were also mined there.

Various attempts to explain the make-up of the different sectors of the Black Country Coal-field have been made by different experts, and it is interesting to view these explanations as there are a few possible contradictions contained within them. The following descriptions, between 1750-1871 by Swedish commissioner R.R. Angerstein, Thomas Tancred, William Matthews, Samuel Bailey, and Henry Johnson are now summarised.

Reinhold Rucker Angerstein

Better known simply as R.R. Angerstein, the Swedish commissioner described in simple terms, some of the differences in the area's early-Industrial Revolution coal-mines, in his diaries later translated and published in 2001, in 'Illustrated Travel Diary - Industry in England 1753-1755'. He visited a few Wolverhampton, Bilston, and Wednesbury coal-mines in April 1754, noting some obvious differences.

Of those Wolverhampton coal-mines he visited, he said: -

"The coal mines of Wolverhampton do not have such thick seams as those at Wednesbury four miles away, but they are still rich, and supply an abundance of coal, giving the industries in the town and neighbourhood great satisfaction and a price advantageous over other manufactories."

Of the mines in nearby Bilston, he said: -

"A coal mine in the vicinity that I visited was working the seams which dipped very little. Two quite thick seams were being mined and a fire engine had been installed to keep the water out. The coal mined here has a rather high content of charcoal. The interspersed layers of charcoal make the work of the miners infinitely easier because the coal splits very readily into pieces along the layers, which saves much effort".

Of the mines in Wednesbury, he said: -

"The mines here are the most famous in the world for its tremendous thick seams of coal that measure 30, 33, 36, and 39 feet in height. A result of this abundance of coal is that the mines nowhere else are worked so carelessly, as the miners can see quite plainly that the coal cannot come to an end in their lifetime."

Thomas Tancred

In his 1843 'Midland Mining Commission' report, Tancred stated that there were two distinctly different sorts of mines in the South Staffordshire Coal-field: -

"Those of thick coal chiefly in the district south of Sedgley and Rowley hills, and mines of thin coal and ironstone in the northern part of the coal-field towards Wolverhampton, Bilston, and Darlaston".

Interestingly he also made the following distinction: -

"It is necessary to keep in mind the two distinct classes of labourers in each sort of mine respectively, the wages of the thick coal colliers are always higher than those in the thin coal and ironstone mines".

This probably reflected the increased risk of danger in the thick seam mines. Although the rate of accidents in thick and thin seam mines were similar, the death rates were higher in the thick seam operations. But working in the iron-stone and thin seam mines was tough and demanding, in cold, damp conditions.

William Matthews

On 11 August 1860, Aris's Birmingham Gazette reported the meeting of the 'Institute of Mechanical Engineers', where Matthews, of Corbyn's Hall Iron Works, Dudley stressed the different characteristics of the region's thick coal seam. He said: -

"*There was a marked distinction in the mineralogical character of the thick coal in the two portions of the district. In the Wednesbury district the coal was of a more crystalline character, breaking up into large fragments, burning with a strong heat, and leaving but a comparatively small residue of ash. It was therefore better adapted for domestic use and gas making. In the region west of Dudley, although the qualities ascribed to the Wednesbury coal attached, in some degree, to a portion of the thick coal, yet, generally-speaking, it had a more-earthy texture. It was therefore better adapted for iron-smelting and had been held in high estimation for that purpose from the days of Dud Dudley, downwards*".

Samuel Bailey

Samuel Bailey, in the book 'Birmingham and Midland Hardware District' (1866) by S. Timmins, explained the complex make-up of the original, shallow coal-field in the South Staffordshire section of the Black Country, by dividing it into five distinct geographical divisions, four of which affect Wolverhampton. He placed an approximate economic value on the land within each division, though Murchison, as will be highlighted shortly, placed the highest financial value on the Wolverhampton iron-stone tract.

Division One runs southward from a line drawn at its northern boundary from West Bromwich to Tipton to Deepfields (Coseley), nearly reaching Sedgley. This division only affects the extreme southern tip of what we consider to constitute Wolverhampton today. The prominent coal mined is as follows: -

* Brooch coal - for domestic purposes, as it burnt swiftly. Widely available.

* Thick coal - comprised of ten or more excellent beds (1,2,3,4 and 9 being the best beds) - used mainly for smelting iron-ore, hence in high demand. 'The Brazils' bed of thick coal excellent for use in reverberatory furnaces (puddling).

* Heathen coal - the coal seam just below the surface - good for raw smelting, of a very fine quality. Also, good for making gas.

* New Mine coal - much inferior in quality but used in mills and forges as it is well adapted for that purpose.

* Iron-stone measures limited but include 'gubbin' and 'white iron-stone'.

Value of land (1865 estimate) per acre up to £28,000.

* Wolverhampton Collieries lying within this division include only the Deepfields Colliery at Woodcross. Some of Bilston and certainly Bradley lay over this field.

Division Two - the southern boundary of this division is effectively the same as the northern boundary of Division One, whilst its northern boundary is formed by drawing a line from the 'old West Bromwich church near Wednesbury, through Wednesbury, Darlaston, Bilston, into the western fault north of Bilston until just a little south of Wolverhampton town centre'. The prominent coal of this division is: -

* Thick coal - same as in Division One.

* Heathen coal - same as in Division One.

* New Mine coal & Fireclay together form a bed 3-4 yards thick, which is purer than in Division One, much preferred for certain smelting and special uses in iron-work.

* Bottom coal - the cheapest coal but eleven-foot in thickness and used for less important purposes in mills and forges. Not of great quality.

* Gubbin Ironstone, Balls Ironstone, White Ironstone, Blue Flats Ironstone - this division is rich in ironstone.

There is no brooch coal in this division.

Value of land (1865 estimate) per acre between £3,000 and £20,000. Though fast expiring.

* Wolverhampton Collieries lying within this division would include the Parkfields Colliery, Rough Hills Colliery, New Rough Hills Colliery, Harrold's Colliery, The Wolverhampton Colliery, Hincks's Colliery, Blakenall Colliery, Cockshutts Colliery, Monmore Green Colliery, Hill Park Colliery, Fighting Cocks Colliery, Blakenall Colliery, Dudley Road Colliery, Stow Heath Colliery, Chillington Colliery, and the 3 Ettingshall collieries. So, the thick seam reached as far as the Monmore Green or Cockshutts Collieries, close to central Wolverhampton.

Division Three runs from Rushall through Bloxwich, into Wednesfield Heath (Heath Town). The prominent coal mined here is as follows: -

* Heathen Coal - same as Division One above

* New Mine coal - same as above

* Yard coal - similar as New Mine coal, but of superior quality here, used for domestic purposes and for smelting and for making gas.

* 4-foot coal - a fireclay seam

* Bottom coal - same as above, uniformly 11-foot in thickness, used widely in mills and forges.

* Rich in Ironstone including Brown Ironstone, Gubbin Ironstone, Blue Flats Ironstone, Poor Robins Ironstone, New mine Ironstone, Silver thread Ironstone, and Diamond Ironstone.

NO cost per acre of land given but said to be the cheapest, other than its iron-stone measures.

* Wolverhampton Collieries lying within this division would include New Cross, Wednesfield Heath, Horseley Fields, Willenhall Road, Barnfield, Deans, Old Heath, Bowman's Harbour, Moseley Hole, Natty Stack, Portobello, Castlebridge, and Neachells collieries, and probably the later Ashmore Park Colliery.

Division Four runs from Goscote to Essington to Cannock. The main coal mined is as follows: -

Cannel coal - for domestic purposes.

Bottom coal - 8-foot coal - a superior coal.

4-foot coal - fireclay of great quality.

The coal and ironstone here is said to be of the same quality as that within the ten-yard thick seam.

NO cost per acre of land is given but this division is extensive and valuable.

* Wolverhampton collieries here are those right on the north-eastern periphery, such as 'Hilton Main' at Featherstone, and possibly Ashmore Park Colliery.

Division Five is in effect the 'later' Cannock Chase coalfield.

This description does not of course describe the Worcestershire section of the Black Country coal-field, but it is helpful to the lay person nevertheless.

Henry Johnson

An 1871 summary of the Black Country Coal-field by Mr Henry Johnson called 'The geological features of the South Staffordshire coal-field', divided it into four fundamentally, different geographical sectors.

a) South Central - where the thick coal, fine and very thick, is free from partings, with under-measures thin and poor in quality.

b) North Central - where the thick coal was wanting altogether, but where the under-measures of both coal and iron-stone being of fine quality, and being nearly double the thickness, as compared to areas where the thick coal exists.

c) Extreme North - where the thick coal is absent as one bed, and the iron-stone is absent too, but where there are seams of coal of fine quality and great thickness.

d) Extreme South - where the thick coal is split up into numerous and separate beds, of almost worthless character, and lacking ironstone, but with two beds of pure fireclay, counter-balancing the loss of the thick coal of fine quality.

Clearly, the complex nature of the Coal-field cannot be summarised in just a few lines, but it is difficult to understand the ever-changing character of coal mined as you move around different areas of the Black Country.

2) THE WOLVERHAMPTON COAL-FIELD

Although we have established that Bilston, Willenhall, Wednesfield, Essington and had a strong historic Wolverhampton connection, during the Industrial Revolution and indeed today, this section now specifically examines the coal industry within the Wolverhampton alone, for the sake of argument. Mining was first recorded in the Wolverhampton area around 1325, and from the early-1500s around Monmore Green, Rough Hills, and Blakenhall. Much of the coal that outcropped was mined in early history, including some of the thick seam which was present very close to the surface in Wolverhampton. The 'Staffordshire Advertiser' highlighted this in a report on the 'South Staffordshire coal-field' on 2 June 1838, which stated: -

"It may be mentioned, as a remarkeable fact, that coal is stated to have been obtained near Wolverhampton, by 'open cutting', probably the only instance of the kind which has ever occurred in the kingdom".

The City Council produced a map of 'known coal-mines' (Figure 14), as part of a risk assessment, in 2016. The town centre is seen towards the top-left, encircled by the ring-road. Bilston is in the bottom-right. The entire eastern and south-eastern side of Wolverhampton is littered with hundreds of coal-shafts, indicated on the map by dots. Intense concentrations of mines are marked at

Blakenhall, Monmore Green, Parkfield, Rough Hills, Heath Town, Old Heath, Lanesfield, and around Bilston of course. Remains of mines have recently been found closer to the centre of the town centre.

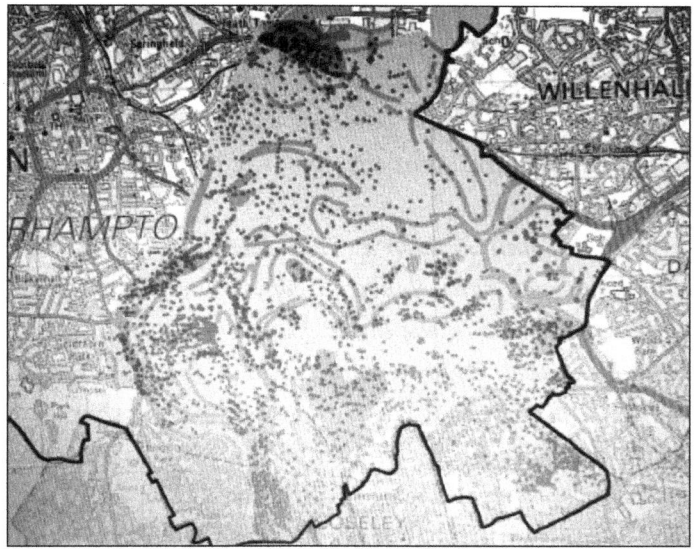

Figure 14 – Wolverhampton City Council 2016 map
showing known mine-shafts

Mining in Wolverhampton on a commercial basis commenced in the late-1700s and especially the early-1800s, prominently through shallow bell-pits, or gin-pits, and they continued in operation throughout the Industrial Revolution until they were exhausted at different points in the latter half of the 1800s. The early practices often used 'primitive soughs' to help drain the mines. Suhail Rana has recently unearthed a map, pin-pointing commercial Wolverhampton mine borings in 1770, so clearly at that point coal-mining was already fairly, well-established.

In 2007, Stourbridge-based researcher P.W. King, in his work 'Black Country Mining Before the Industrial Revolution', highlighted that coal-mining had occurred in the Wolverhampton area some centuries earlier, where he stated: -

"In 1564, the lords of the manor of Wednesbury tried to stop John Leveson of Wolverhampton from mining in competition with them. Leveson had pointed out that two to three years before, the matter had been referred to arbitration, and the arbitrators had determined that Leveson was entitled to enjoy mines in his own ground."

He also pointed out that there was mining in Ettingshall in 1620, but also highlighted some of the difficulties that arose regards ownership and rights to mine the land within the Black Country: -

"Some of the manors, such as Stow Heath in Wolverhampton, were large, but most of it belonged to copy-holders, leaving its lords with few direct rights in the land. There the lords unsuccessfully tried to exercise their right to mine in about 1760".

But in 1811 an 'Act of Parliament' was passed that critically for commerce, enabled the Dean of Wolverhampton and his successors 'to grant leases and licenses for opening and working mines within the lands belonging to the Manor of Wolverhampton, for any term not exceeding fifty years'. So, from this point in time, the scale of commercial mining in the town rapidly increased, in fact it literally exploded. Coal and iron-ore mines could often be found immediately adjacent to each other all-across the Wolverhampton coal-field, and the same miners often worked at both, at different times and on different days.

Women were also employed at the mines, mainly assisting in unloading the iron-stone and coal, chiefly in the Wolverhampton area according to Thomas Tancred. They were known as 'pit-bank wenches'.

Within Black Country history, the importance of what was once called 'The great Wolverhampton coal-field' is significantly under-appreciated. As highlighted, the importance of its iron-ore (or iron-stone) and thin coal seam, that was often relied upon by the iron works of Dudley as well as its home-town works, are very much under-valued.

It is evident that the 'greatest concentration of coal-mines' sat in a great tract of land between the centres of Wolverhampton, Willenhall, Bilston, and Sedgley, yet it is often suggested or inferred that the town had no mining legacy at all, which is evidently sheer ignorance.

But the 'Great Bentley fault', a geological fault running from the north-east to south-west across part of Wolverhampton meant that comparatively smaller amounts of the thick coal seam were mined in Wolverhampton. In fact, several geological faults affected the area. Local geologist Mr H. Beckett wrote a report in 'The Wolverhampton Chronicle and Staffordshire Advertiser' on 3 February 1858, where he described the western boundary of the coal seam, which cut across in a north-easterly direction, virtually to the centre of Wolverhampton, closer to the town centre than many Black Country historians acknowledge: -

"A similar upheaving has raised the whole level of the coalfield and caused the most extraordinary rents in the various beds. One great line of dislocation forming the western boundary has been traced to a point near Hagley, passing between Stourbridge and The Lye, and skirting Wordsley, Kingswinford, and taking part of Himley Park. It then strikes a little west of the Sedgley limestone hills and of the Fighting Cocks, passes east of Bilston Street bridge, and near the junction of Walsall Street and Horsley Fields of Wolverhampton, from thence it has been stripped as far as the railway tunnel at Wednesfield Heath (Heath Town). It has again been proved eastward of Essington brickyard, and extends northwards towards Rugeley".

Although much of Wolverhampton's coal-mining involved shallow operations, there were some deeper operations too. Geologist Sir Roderick Impey Murchison remarked that a Wolverhampton colliery owner named as a Mr Barker, referring to the co-owner of Chillington Colliery, commented that operations at his mine bored down to a depth of 150 yards, or 450 feet.

In the late-1800s and early-1900s, just after the Industrial Revolution period, large quantities of coal were mined from the much deeper, concealed seam around the periphery of Wolverhampton at Ashmore Park, Wednesfield, and at Holly Bank, Essington, and finally at Hilton Colliery near Featherstone where it even tunnelled underneath Bushbury. Furthermore, Baggeridge Colliery near Dudley also mined under a small section of Wolverhampton.

But these later mining operations clearly did not define the 'original Black Country', nor did similar operations elsewhere in the region such as Sandwell Park, Baggeridge, or Hamstead Heath.

A) Wolverhampton's thick coal

As already alluded to, the thick coal was brought up at some Wolverhampton mines, much of it in earlier centuries before records were kept.

As highlighted, a geological fault called the 'Great Bentley fault' ran north-eastward from Sedgley to Fighting Cocks, and then onto just south of the centre of Wolverhampton at Horseley Fields, and this meant that the thick seam generally tapered away at ground level at these points and was the first coal to be picked, probably in earlier centuries. Any thick coal was seldom more than forty yards deep in Wolverhampton's collieries.

In the 1916 W.W. King produced flexographic maps of Dudley and Wolverhampton pin-pointing the exact districts, highlighted in black, where the thick coal seam outcropped. These were superimposed on to later maps of Wolverhampton. East Park for example which is clearly seen, did not exist at the time. It was built over the expired Chillington Colliery. In his map opposite (Figure 15), Wolverhampton town-centre is in the top left corner, and Bilston is off the bottom right-hand corner of the picture. East Park is top-right.

CHAPTER FIVE

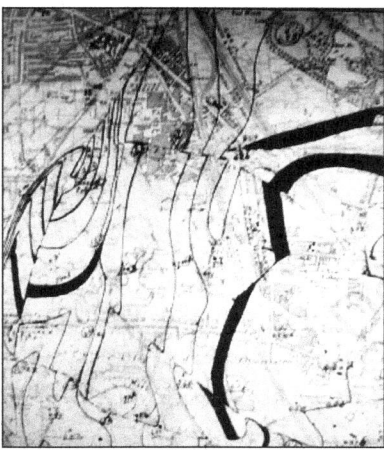

Figure 15 – W.W. King's 1916 flexographic map showing the outcrop of the thick coal seam in eastern Wolverhampton.

The geologist Sir Roderick Impey Murchison in the publication 'Silurian system based on Geological researches' (1839) highlights that the thick seam in Wolverhampton was exhausted during early times, where he stated: -

"The manner in which the coal is cut off at the edges of the field near Wolverhampton, is worthy of notice. The bed there, called the thick coal, and the underlying iron stone measures, instead of dipping under the red sandstone, rise gently as they approach it, and taper away and deteriorate in quality. To the north of the field, chiefly between Wolverhampton and Walsall, the thick coal outcrops, alternating with beds of iron stone rising to the surface. Sometimes shafts are sunk through shale and clunk with bands of sandstone to 100-yard depth, before coal is found, but in many cases like Wednesbury, all overlying coal seams are removed and hence the ten-yard seam rises to the surface. Hence our early ancestors worked it from open quarries. When it was exhausted, shafts were sunk, and the thick coal was found at a depth of 100-200 yards."

The comments of Joseph Beete Jukes in his 2nd edition 'The South Staffordshire Coalfield' (1859) are also poignant. He confirms the presence of the thick-coal seam at Stow Heath, Chillington, Rough Hills, and at Ettingshall Collieries within the Wolverhampton Coal-field. He goes on to explain the 'Bentley fault', highlighting that: -

"*The entire coalfield can be divided in two - the principal line of division is that which runs from Parkfields through Sedgley, Dudley and Rowley*".

He explained that the make-up of the thick coal near Wolverhampton took on 'a different-strata', stating: -

"*Between Wolverhampton and Bilston, the 'white coal' is always looked on as the top of the thick coal. Here however, we get still another change in the central part of the thick coal, as a considerable mass of shale, sometimes containing ironstone. There is exhibited in these facts that tendency in the thick coal to split up towards the north.*"

Furthermore, he describes how the thick coal out-cropped near the surface in the Wolverhampton field: -

"*The thick coal, when it does take the ground between Wolverhampton and Bilston, declines so gently into it as never to be more than forty yards deep. Between Wolverhampton and Walsall, the coal measures crop gradually so that first the thick coal, then the heathen, then the new mine coal, rise to the surface of the ground and end towards the north. The thick coal, between Wolverhampton and Bilston, has lost the two upper beds, which have gone off as the 'flying reed', and cropped out south of the Lanesfield fault*".

In terms of the precise geographical location of the thick seam outcrop, he states: -

"*The crop of the thick coal runs along Ettingshall Lane nearly up to Monmore Green. A little south of Catchem's Corner, it is broken through by the branches of the Great Lanesfield fault. Here, between Ettingshall Park farm and Monmore Green, there is a very broken and disturbed district of coal measures. It appears that a rude anti-clinal curve runs north from Hurst Hill to Ettingshall Park farm, the Parkfield furnaces, and Rough Hills Colliery............a fault running north and south by the Wolverhampton Furnaces has a downcast to the west of about 150 feet and brings in a good-sized patch of the thick coal in that direction. South of this, on the west side of the Parkfield Colliery, the coal-measures are completely smashed up by the faults. The thick seam outcrop has a detached piece thrown in towards the Wolverhampton furnaces. The outcrop runs along the west side of Ettingshall Lane for some distance, and then turns across it and across the Wolverhampton and Bilston round towards Batchcroft and Priestfield. A small east and west fault with a down-throw to the north, throws in another little detached piece towards Monmore Green".*

This thick coal was less than a mile from the town centre of Wolverhampton, and to further confirm this, newspaper archives from the 1800s prove beyond doubt that certain collieries in the town produced the thick coal seam. Such adverts are shown in the list of Wolverhampton mines that follows in due course,

B) The value of Wolverhampton's Iron-ore and thin coal seam

The iron-ore, often referred to as the 'New Mine iron-stone', was especially rich in the Wolverhampton coal-field. Iron-ore of course, is the raw material used to make pig-iron, and it has been argued recently in one international economical report that: -

"*iron-ore is more integral to the global economy than any other commodity except oil*".

Iron-ore was found in many shallow coal-mines across eastern Wolverhampton. In 1754 Swedish Commissioner R.R. Angerstein visited the region, and he described the region's iron-ore mines, and exactly what he saw in the ground: -

"*Clay adjoining the coal seam is called the 'clunch' and is black and impregnated with smoke and has no vegetable matter in it. As soon as the clay takes on bluish colour it is impregnated with iron, and, also contains quantities of vegetable matter. The iron-ore is bluish and* is under the thin coal. The seam is 12 inches to 18 inches thick and consists of a blue clay-like kind of rock, that is heavy and rich in iron. The ore is sold per blume, which is a pile 5-foot long, 6-foot 6-inches wide, and 1-foot 6-inches high".

He also confirmed that iron-ore was mined further into the southern area of the South Staffordshire coal-field where the thick seam had been exhausted, stating: -

"Between Bilston and Wednesbury on what he called the large plain, where the thick seam has been exhausted many years ago, there were several small shafts sunk down to the thin coal seam, which here is only 2-3 feet thick, in order to remove the iron-ore lying above it".

As highlighted earlier on in the work, an important writer of that period W. Fordyce, in his book 'A History of Coal, Coke, Coalfields, and Iron Manufacture in Northern England' (1860) emphasised the significance of the iron-ore field of Wolverhampton: -

"From the low cost at which the ore is generally raised, the number and variety of measures of coal and ironstone, and the superior quality of the iron produced, the Wolverhampton division of the South Staffordshire coal-field is considered as one of the most important in proportion to its area, of any of our iron-making districts."

Quite an accolade for a district that the Black Country Society usually deems to lie outside its borders.

The iron-ore or iron-stone in the Wolverhampton coal-field was of the highest quality, and hence of the highest value too. The famous geologist Murchison emphasised the much under-appreciated value of iron-ore in the Wolverhampton coal-field, where he stated: -

"The general reader may be informed, that land in the productive iron-stone tract of Wolverhampton, where the lower coal only exists, is much more valuable than in the southern district, where both the thick coal and lower coals are present. The latter is much less rich in iron-ore than in the northern Wolverhampton field. It is seldom, indeed, that the mere existence of coal of any thickness and of the *very finest quality, will of itself repay the speculators, and hence it is usual to transport the iron-ore from the Wolverhampton field to the pit of the thick coal, south of Dudley, and there to smelt it. In Dudley, under the ten-yard seam, three courses of workable iron-ore have been ascertained, whilst in the Wolverhampton coal-field six valuable bands are wrought".*

These comments from Murchison and Fordyce certainly highlight the immense value of Wolverhampton's iron-ore to the development of the Black Country.

But working in the iron-ore mines was generally considered more unpleasant and prejudicial to health than in the thick coal-mines. The miners in the iron-stone pits were constantly wet and cold, leaving workers with painful arthritic conditions even at a young age, along with chronic asthma. They also had to work longer hours for less pay than the thick seam miners. The 'Morning Chronicle' report on 3 January 1850, described the work at the iron-ore mines of the district: -

"The ironstone seams are generally thinner than the coal-belts, the work is more severe than at the thick seam, and a great number of boys are employed to load the refuse into small iron skips".

It is evident that the significance of iron-ore mining, and its value to the wider Black Country, has been overlooked and under-appreciated, yet it was critical for the industrial progress of the area. The British Army was involved in 41 years of war between 1750-1845 and it acquired two-thirds of its armoury from iron made in the Black Country. Victoria Iron Works at Monmore Green, Wolverhampton was a great producer of iron for armoury, as were several iron-works at Horseley Fields, barely half-a-mile away such as Chillington, Swan Garden, and Shrubbery Iron Works.

In Wolverhampton and the Black Country, iron-ore started to expire around 1850-1860, after which time it had to be imported from elsewhere to supplement the ever-diminishing local supply, signaling the gradual and slow decline of the Black Country iron industry.

But its significance should never be under-valued or under-appreciated. The legacy of the Black Country was quite clearly, not simply due to the existence of the thick coal seam.

C) Newcomen's first successful steam engine

There is a very important historical development that Wolverhampton can perhaps quite proudly claim to have hosted.

The steam engine can with some justification be viewed as the most important single invention of the Industrial Revolution, and Wolverhampton can potentially lay claim to the significant accolade of having the first steam engine that ever successfully operated, to pump water out of a coal-mine. This was the creation of Devonshire-born Thomas Newcomen.

His rather primitive, stationery, early machines could still pump forty-two gallons of water out of water-logged coal-mines at each motion, which could be achieved ten times per minute. This single invention was critical as it meant that deeper pits had a longer life-span, as they could pump out water much more efficiently. The number of steam-engines increased rapidly over time and with technological improvement. In effect, they transformed the coal-mining industry within a few decades, largely replacing the horse-driven gins for drainage purposes.

By 1730, it was estimated that Thomas Newcomen had built up to 50 engines, located across the coal-fields of the U.K. His engines were in effect heat engines, but they did not actually use the power of steam to move a piston. The steam was used to create a vacuum, and it was the air pressure above the piston and the vacuum below that moved the piston. In fact, a more appropriate description for it is that it was an 'atmospheric engine'.

His mode of condensation by cooling the outside of the cylinder at every stroke proved to be inefficient, according to

W.W. Smythe in his 1880 book 'Coal and Coal-mining'. It was only when he introduced an internal jet of cold water that success became achieved.

As the 1800s progressed, up to 2,000 of what were called steam-engines were operating across the Country. Most of these were indeed used to pump water out of coal-mines, but others were used with blast furnaces. At least 800 of these were Newcomen's engines, whilst around 500 of the more-advanced James Watts engines were built, which were twice as efficient as their predecessor, largely replacing them in the 1830s and 1840s.

The Black Country Living Museum exhibits an example of a steam-powered 'Newcomen engine', describing the 'worlds first ever successful steam engine', as being used at Coneygre Pit, Tipton, close to Dudley Castle, in 1712.

That presumption was based on the statement of a Swedish engineer Martin Trieweld, a close companion of Newcomen, and who stated in 1734: -

"Mr Newcomen erected the first fire engine in England in the year 1712, which erection took place at Dudley Castle in Staffordshire".

A photograph of this engine exists from 1719, so its existence is uncontestable.

Veteren Black Country engineer John Allen also produced a paper in the early-1990s in support of the Dudley location.

But there has also been long-standing evidence supportive of the existence in 1711 of an ultimately unphotographed Newcomen engine at the 'half-mile stone on the road to Walsall from Wolverhampton'. Letters written in French by Newcomen engineer John O'Kelly in 1721 to a business associate, and by J.T. Desaguliers (FRS) in his work 'Course of Experimental Philosophy' in 1744, both support the earlier existence of the Wolverhampton engine.

Both men stated that: -

"the first successful Newcomen engine was used to draw water for a Mr Back of Wolverhampton".

But there were still missing pieces to the jigsaw.

Then in 1948, W.O. Henderson in a Newcomen Society paper, identified Mr Back as Mr William Bache, but could not link him directly to the Wolverhampton engine. But Henderson did propose the location of the engine based on what were 'at the time', unverifiable quotes from the lost diaries of the locally well-respected Doctor Wilkes from Willenhall.

So, in 1948 it was felt that there was insufficient evidence to prove Wolverhampton's claim.

But the relevant Doctor Wilkes diary has now come to light, confirming that the 'engine was built near another Wolverhampton engine belonging to a Mr Sparrow off the Willenhall Road'. The diary even confirmed the exact location: -

"Newcomen fixed the first engine that ever raised any quantity of water at Wolverhampton, on the left-hand side of the road leading from Walsall to the town, over against the half-mile stone".

But it was then wrongly claimed by some that there were no coal-mines half-a-mile from Wolverhampton town centre, and that the location must refer to the 'one-and-a-half mile-stone' further towards Willenhall. More of that shortly.

Suhail Rana, Chairman of 'Wolverhampton Civic and Historical Society', undertook further investigations and produced a paper in 2009 titled 'New Evidence supporting Wolverhampton as the location of the first working Newcomen engine', which carries significance credence as it was published by the 'Newcomen Society' in their International journal.

His research arguably unearthed the final pieces of the jigsaw in support of the Wolverhampton engine, through the critical discovery of old Wolverhampton mining maps from 1770, which show both the old engine pit of Mr Sparrow mentioned by Dr Wilkes near to the end of Cross Street, just off Willenhall Road and behind Moore

Street - a 22-yard deep engine pit. This was situated on land known to have belonged to William Bache in 1712. This would, as was originally proposed, have indeed been against the 'half-mile stone' at lower Horseley Fields, just off the Willenhall Road and just east of Wolverhampton town centre.

He also discovered an account book that confirmed the existence of another engine for William Bache at Bilston in 1714, so his previously unclarified links to the Newcomen engine were now firmly established. He also discovered a deed from 1732, and a diary entry from 1736, which support the Wolverhampton case.

It is strongly suggested therefore, that this further evidence supports the location of Newcomen's first successful steam engine to have been in Wolverhampton.

Despite this significant new evidence being presented, it has been seemingly ignored by the Black Country Society and the Black Country Museum who continue to hold the view that the first engine was used at Tipton, near Dudley Castle a year later in 1712.

The local newspaper Express and Star highlighted and summarised the key findings of the paper released by Suhail Rana in 2009, in response generating the somewhat childish and patronising remarks of Black Country engineer John Allen: -

"It is very easy for a presenter to address an audience who largely have no knowledge of the subject and then impress them with their conclusions, particularly if they relate to Wolverhampton, which would please a Wolverhampton audience".

He then went on to say: -

"There is no record of any so-called engine in Wolverhampton".

These remarks seem to be rather defensive and ill-considered comments, and to be frank it seems somewhat bizarre how the record of the Wolverhampton engine continues to be disregarded and dismissed.

What other evidence is there?

Certain respected publications from the early-1800s support the Wolverhampton claim.

In 'A Topographical history of Staffordshire' by William Pitt in 1817, he confirmed the Wolverhampton location, stating: -

"The first steam engine that ever-raised water in considerable rate quantity was erected near this town, a short distance from the half-mile stone on the Walsall road."

And then in 1834, the author William White stated in his book 'History, Gazetteer, and Directory of Staffordshire' that:

"The first steam engine that raised any considerable quantity of water was set up for the purpose of draining a mine on the Walsall road, about half a mile from Wolverhampton".

W.W. Smythe in his 1880 book 'Coal and Coal-mining' stated: -

"Newcomen appears to have been assisted by the suggestions of Dr Hooke, and to have first tried his 'fire-engine' on the large-scale at a colliery near Wolverhampton".

So, the claims for both locations prevail, despite what is becoming an increasingly strong, but perhaps not quite yet a sufficiently proven case for Wolverhampton's engine pre-dating the Dudley one. Is it even conceivable that the Wolverhampton engine was moved to Dudley? This seems possible.

Either way the debate rages on. Perhaps there are simply too many permutations for the Newcomen Society to officially accept the Wolverhampton case just yet, but they remain open-minded and I suspect we will hear more of this in the future, with the Wolverhampton claim surely now more or less assured.

But the case still-remains an open one.

D) The Truck system and its tommy shops

This system of payment to colliers, where the great proportion of wage was paid through the provision of goods such as necessities, was prominent in the Wolverhampton area especially, and it was often criticised and much-despised.

The employers of the workmen provided their own so-called 'tommy-shops' where goods 'had' to be acquired from, as part of the conditions of employment.

The problem was, these tommy-shops often charged more for goods than other local shops, so became deeply unpopular. But the system was a good way for colliery owners to control their workmen, and to make further profit.

Thomas Tancred highlighted the practice in his 1843 'Midland Mining Commission Report', and the impact of the practice on the poor workers: -

"As regards those employed by the owners of mines and iron-works, the truck system is at present confined to Wolverhampton, Bilston, Darlaston, and Wednesbury, and north of there. In that part of the district where the thick coal lies, the owners have as yet abstained from the evil practice, whilst in the thin seam district, or where the thick coal is for the most part exhausted, the pressure of bad times has compelled the mine-owners to maintain their ground in the competition with their more fortunate neighbours by this unlawful expedient."

Tancred also pointed out that a butty in the Dudley thick coal district was asked the following question about the impact of the truck system on the miners: -

"Is there much difference between the two sides of the country?"

He responded: -

"They do not work so laborious on this side, they have to work harder on the other side".

The thin seam miners in the Wolverhampton area evidently earnt less than their Dudley area thick seam counterparts, and were paid largely through the truck system, meaning they had to work harder to maintain a very basic standard of living.

Another butty interviewed by Tancred named the worst abusers of the truck system as all lying in the Wolverhampton and Bilston coal-field, at Ward's Priestfield Colliery, Sparrow's Osier Bed Colliery, Jones's Chillington Colliery, and Underhill's Parkfield Colliery.

The miners of Wolverhampton and Bilston clearly endured tough working conditions, for worse levels of pay.

3) WOLVERHAMPTON COLLIERIES

As highlighted, huge swathes of eastern Wolverhampton are littered with old coal shafts, including a newly discovered and previously unchartered mine at Horseley Fields, just a couple of hundred metres from the city centre. Discovered in November 2014, it significantly delayed the relaying of the 'Midland Metro' track. These mines, immediately adjacent to the town centre, were the first to expire.

The main concentrations of coal mines and shafts lay either in east Wolverhampton, or south-east and south Wolverhampton.

In all there were around 80 collieries, which varied greatly in size.

Within these, around 160 mine shafts could be found around Heath Town, Old Heath, and Deansfield at the collieries of Old Heath, Deans, Barnfield, New Cross, Wednesfield Heath, and Bowman's Harbour. In 1908, it was estimated that there were 600 miners in the Heath Town area alone, this being a point-in-time when Wolverhampton's coal-field had largely expired. These operations mined iron-ore, fireclay, and the thin-seam.

Moving southward, another 140 mine shafts were situated in another area of east Wolverhampton, immediately south of Willenhall Road at the vast Chillington and Stow Heath Collieries, and at Moseley Hole, each located around East Park. These mines were also rich in iron-ore and fireclay, but they also mined some of the thick coal seam.

The third major concentration of mine shafts lay south and south-east of Wolverhampton town centre, with 130 shafts at the collieries of Horseley Fields, Cockshutts, Monmore Green, Fighting Cocks, Dudley Road, Blakenall, Harrolds, Hill Park,

Wolverhampton, and Rough Hills. Additionally, there were another 170 shafts at the expansive Parkfield Colliery, and over 150 shafts at the three Ettingshall Collieries which sometimes classed themselves as lying in Wolverhampton, or sometimes in Bilston. These mines were also rich in iron-ore, but they also mined good quantities of coal including patches of the thick coal seam.

Up to 70 mine shafts could be found on the periphery of Wolverhampton around Ashmore Park, Neachell, and Castlebridge at Wednesfield, and around 50 mine shafts around Portobello towards Willenhall. Again, thinner seams of coal and iron-ore were mined in quantity.

Finally, there were several substantial mines around the north-east periphery of Wolverhampton, such as at Essington, Hilton-Main, and Holly Bank, though these were mined later-on.

In total, around 900 shafts were sunk for coal and iron ore in Wolverhampton, excluding Bilston which probably had even more. The names of these collieries sometimes changed over the centuries depending on who owned them. Most of the substantial operations in Wolverhampton were first mined commercially in the mid-to-late-1700s, and most had expired by 1870 when the shallow coal seam was virtuallly exhausted.

Technological advances meant that a few large-scale, deeper operations of the concealed seam then emerged around the periphery of the core Black Country mining district. Such new concerns were at Ashmore Park, Wednesfield, at Holly Bank at Essington, and Hilton at Featherstone, and outside the Wolverhampton area also at Baggeridge near Sedgley, at Sandwell Park, Jubilee, and Hamstead near West Bromwich, and at Walsall Wood.

The following list of collieries, around 80 in total, includes both the major ones as well as lesser known ones in Wolverhampton, but excluding those 'clearly' listed as being at Bilston. The Ettingshall, Priestfield, and Millfields collieries are situated on the border of the Wolverhampton and Bilston Coal-fields, but only around a mile-and-a-half from Wolverhampton town centre and situated on land we know originally belonged to Wolverhampton, and crucially, which classed themselves as Wolverhampton coal-mines rather than Bilston ones at the time they existed.

Many of these collieries were owned by rich businessmen or landowners, such as George Jones, The Sparrow family, George and William Bishton, or by the Southan Brothers for example, but they also changed hands frequently.

A) Known Collieries Pre-Industrial Revolution - before 1800

1) **Moorfields Colliery** – this mine was situated at the south-eastern end of what was to become the Parkfield Colliery, though at the time in Sedgley parish but in the Manor of Stow Heath, Wolverhampton. It was first mined as early as 1490. Later owned by a Mr Persehouse, in 1600 it was noted that the thick seam was fourteen yards, or forty-two feet thick, and amongst the best in the entire district.

2) **Willenhall Road Colliery** - a mine was noted to have existed in the early-1700s at this location, as the first fixed Newcomen steam engine that pumped water out of mines is now considered by many to have been located near the half-mile stone along Willenhall Road at Lower Horseley Fields. But it is unclear what name the mine used, though a colliery of this name existed here and was owned by William Bache.

3) **Waterloo Colliery** – this was a small colliery further along and just south of the Willenhall Road, but west of Stowheath Lane, East Park. In 1725 the coal seam on Stowheath Lane was noted to be around one-hundred and twenty yards in length and at seven and a half yards wide. This colliery was active until the mid-1800s.

4) **Priests Meadow Colliery** - this mine was noted to be situated around Monmore Green, perhaps opening in the late-1700s, but little else is known.
5) **Bull Pleck Coal Pits** – these series of pits were located at Portobello between Wolverhampton and Willenhall, though the latter town probably lays claim to ownership of this pit. At the time, Willenhall had very close ties to Wolverhampton, certainly the Portobello part, which still lies within its boundaries.
6) **Neachell Colliery** - this Wednesfield Colliery was noted to be established in the early-1700s. In 1735, the owner Thomas Thomkys of Wolverhampton had to compensate the owners of the adjacent land when their mining operations flooded and damaged it.
7) **Essington Wood Colliery** - this was a substantial colliery first mined in the 1790s. This village now lies just outside Wolverhampton, but it used a Wolverhampton address, and was also considered part of Wolverhampton at that time.

B) Known collieries of the main Industrial Revolution period 1800 - 1880

8) **Parkfield Colliery** – owned initially by George and William Bishton until 1836, and then by John Underhill and the Parkfield Iron Company, it was thought to have been first-mined commercially in the early-1800s, though there is evidence of mining in the area from the 1600s. The remains of an ancient forest were famously discovered by geologists here. This substantial and productive colliery was situated just off the main Parkfield Road and accessed off Martin Street, directly opposite Cockshutts and Rough Hills Collieries, and close to the three Ettingshall Collieries, the Catchem's Corner Colliery, and Lanesfield Colliery. It covered a significant area, some 250

acres in total, and the prime section covering 105 acres was walled-in by the owners as the land was so highly valued. It is likely that some of the thick coal seam was mined here, as well as thinner seams, but notably fireclay that contained extremely valuable iron-ore. The fireclay seam was noted to be 19-feet thick, with 11 bands of the highly-sought after iron-ore, said to be the best in the entire Black Country. It is estimated that around 175 shafts were sunk at this expansive colliery, though the seam in its western aspects was 'smashed up' by the fault. Like much of the Black Country coal-field, Parkfield Colliery became flooded in the 1850s, though via ambitious plans it was successfully drained by two pumping engines in 1857, when despite cynicism, a huge amount of water was pumped into the nearby canal every day, until the mines were successfully free of water. One of these, the 'Bandy Gay Engine' belonged to the Parkfield Iron Company. The Company employed 1,500 miners and iron-workers at its height.

9) **New Parkfield Colliery** - this colliery covered 57 acres, and probably lay close to the Parkfield Iron Company's existing estate. The shaft here was sunk to 160 yards, considerably deeper than most of the shallow pits in the area. High-quality iron-stone, and probably some of the thick seam would have been mined here.

10) **Chillington Colliery** – this major operation owned by the John Barker, James Foster, and George Jones of the Chillington Iron Company, was situated where Wolverhampton's 'East Park' now stands, covering an area of 110 acres. It was first mined commercially in the early-1800s. Along with the adjoining Stow Heath Colliery, around one-hundred shafts were sunk, mainly for 'gubbin' and iron-stone, especially the valuable 'blue-flats iron-stone', fireclay coal, new-mine coal, and the bottom coal. The thick coal seam was mined here in its southern section. Even in the 1870s, up to 200,000 tonnes

of coal and iron-stone were being mined at Chillington each year, such was the wealth and quantity of mineral matter in the ground here. Approximately 1,500 miners and iron-workers were employed by the company. It was owned by Messrs J. and J. Southan in the early-1890s when it was still being worked for what was left. Samuel Griffiths described Chillington Colliery in the following impressive manner when coal measures were first discovered: -

"They leased 110 acres of land within a mile of Wolverhampton, and here they found some of the richest mines of coal and iron in Staffordshire".

11) **Stow Heath Colliery** – this was another substantial colliery, first mined in the early-1800s, covering around 98 acres. It was owned by brothers William Hanbury Sparrow and John Sly Sparrow. A nephew John William Sparrow later joined the Company. The colliery was set immediately adjacent to Chillington Colliery, covering part of the current 'East Park', west of Stowheath Lane and south of Willenhall Road. Some of the thick seam was mined here, along with fireclay containing valuable iron-ore, as well as the new mine coal and the bottom coal. By 1855, when the colliery was rated, 86 acres were deemed as spoilt and worked out, with just 12 acres of unworked land remaining, and containing two gin-pits, four pillar-pits, and nine whimsey-pits at that point.

12) **Osier Bed Colliery** - this colliery was also owned by the Sparrow family, under the name of W. and J.S. Sparrow. It was situated south of Willenhall Road, off Moseley Road and close to Moseley Hole and several other pits. William's eldest son, William Mander Sparrow later became involved in managing the Company. Their iron works of the same name were situated closer to the centre of Wolverhampton, roughly around one-mile along the Willenhall Road. Coal and iron-ore was heavily mined here.

13) **Horseley Fields Colliery** - this early-1800s colliery was situated very close to the centre of Wolverhampton, by Walsall Street. In the 1820s, it was owned by Messrs Jones and Barker, according to 'Pigot and Co's National Commercial Directory' of 1828. They were also heavily involved with the nearby Chillington Colliery. It seems likely that a mine discovered under the 'metro-line' in 2014, might well have belonged to this colliery, as coal-mines existed around Walsall Street and Bilston Street in Horseley Fields, where many miners resided. The thin seam and iron-ore was mined here.

14) **Willenhall Road Colliery** - this colliery was situated close to Horseley Fields and owned by George Jones in 1840, and later by J. Edge and Co. Iron-stone and coal were mined here, and the shafts were noted to be at a depth of at least 150-200 yards.

15) **Old Heath Colliery** – this colliery was sandwiched between Willenhall Road and Heath Town. Owned by Henry Caswell, it was a fairly-substantial operation with many shafts sunk for coal and iron-ore. The residents of Wolverhampton Workhouse were heavily involved in levelling its many spoil-banks. It was situated over quite a large area around what is now Old Heath Road and Colliery Road, but it became flooded in 1880, and offered for sale, along with all the plant including seven steam engines, by the then-owner Benjamin Caswell. As there were no takers it was eventually abandoned.

16) **Moseley Hole Colliery** – this was a colliery that lay between Portobello and East Park, with several pits situated off Moseley Road, but south of Willenhall Road and east of Stowheath Lane, and totalling 39 acres. It was later taken over by the Chillington Company. Iron-ore and coal were mined here.

17) **Cleveland Colliery** - this was a small operation between Moseley Hole and Portobello where iron-stone was mined. It was owned by Messrs Bradley, Barrows, and Hall. A tragic

accident occurred here in 1842, when seven died, including five teenagers and young boys, when an explosion occurred as they were being lowered.

18) **Portobello Colliery** - this medium-sized colliery owned by H. Ward, was situated immediately adjacent to the village of the same name, close to Willenhall. Several pits were sunk here, and the entire Portobello community was involved in coal-mining.

19) **Wednesfield Heath Colliery** - this colliery was also owned by Henry Caswell and situated close to Park Village and Heath Town. Fireclay and thinner seams of coal were mined here. This was probably the most northerly mine in the Wolverhampton field.

20) **Bowman's Harbour Colliery** – this major operation was located by Heath Town and owned by Mr H.B. Whitehouse. Over one-hundred shafts were sunk during its early history, though it was mainly for three seams of shallow fireclay that contained iron-ore, as well as for coal but not of the thick seam, though deeper shafts were also sunk. The 'blue flats iron-stone' and 'gubbin and ball iron-stone' were highly prized here.

21) **New Cross Colliery** – this colliery was also owned by Mr H.B. Whitehouse and situated just north of Deans Road, close to Heath Town. It had at least fifteen shafts sunk down to 300 feet, mainly for coal and fireclay containing rich seams of iron-ore. A number of deaths occurred here, including seven who were killed during a horrific accident in 1860 at the 'Blue Fly pit'. Three of these victims were twelve-to-thirteen-year-old boys.

22) **Deans Colliery** – this fairly-substantial colliery was adjacent to a few other collieries in the Eastfield area of east Wolverhampton, alongside the Birmingham canal and comprising 30 acres. The 'mealy coal' was mined here in quantity.

23) **New Deans Colliery** - this 1860s colliery was presumably close to the original Deans Colliery. It was owned and run by a W.F. Fryer. Iron-ore, fireclay and coal would have been mined here.

24) **Barnfield Colliery** – this colliery covering 18 acres, and owned by Edward Poole, was also situated at Eastfield around what was then known as Wednesfield Heath, on the immediate northern-western side of Deans Road. Coal and iron-stone were mined here, and it was noted to have been fairly-productive.

25) **Cockshutts Colliery** – this substantial operation covering 44 acres of land was owned by Messrs Aston and Shaw. It was first mined in the early-1800s and was situated off Dudley Road, at Cockshutts Lane, Blakenall. At this point in time, the 'h' in the name 'Blakenhall' was omitted. It was spread over a considerable area that now encompasses Phoenix Park. The pits here were mined mainly for fireclay and iron-ore, 'new mine' and 'bottom coal', as well as a patch of the thick coal seam. Around 130 shafts were sunk here and at the adjacent Monmore Green and Rough Hills Collieries. By 1871 it was no longer in operation, as its resources had expired.

26) **Monmore Green Colliery** – this substantial colliery was first owned by John Fereday and first mined in the 1820s. It later passed into the ownership of Messrs Corbett and Hartsthorne. It was situated at the junction of Cable Street and Caledonia Road between Monmore Green and All Saints. It is thought that a small amount of the thick seam was mined here, as well as thinner seams of coal and iron-ore. The shafts were mined to a depth of about 80 yards, but it was exhausted by 1870.

27) **Monmore Green New Colliery** - it seems likely that this colliery was situated close to the 'old' Monmore Green Colliery, though very little is known about it. It was thought to have been owned by John Fereday.

28) **Hinck's Colliery** - also known as Hinckes Colliery, this was a small colliery situated at Monmore Green, just off the junction of Bilston Road and Ettingshall Road owned by Messrs James Cadman, Benjamin Francis, and James Dodd. The thick seam would have been mined here as well as iron-ore.

29) **Hill Park Colliery** - this Monmore Green colliery seems to have passed through the fingers of any Wolverhampton historians, as there is no other reference to it anywhere I can find. It was first mined in 1842, situated on the Bilston Road at Monmore Green. An advert from the Wolverhampton Chronicle highlights that the thick coal as well as the heathen and bottom coal were mined and sold here by colliery-owner Edward Lowe. This advert is exhibited below (Figure 16).

Figure 16 – 1842 advert from Wolverhampton Chronicle for coal at Hill Park Colliery, Monmore Green.

30) **Rough Hills Colliery** – this extensive colliery covering 61 acres was first mined around 1800. It was situated adjacent to Cockshutts Colliery, situated off Rough Hills Road, and owned by Messrs Aston and Shaw, and later by Messrs James Cadman, Benjamin Francis, and James Dodd. It was offered for sale in 1824 as an entire colliery though partly worked, comprising 39 acres known as 'The New Mines', and the remainder known as Hen Birch Lower and Upper, and St Leonards Hill. Fireclay, iron-ore, and coal, including some

of the thick seam, were mined here. A number of shafts were sunk, but five men were killed here in 1834 when the chain lowering them into the pit, suddenly broke. Over 100 miners were still employed here in 1860.

31) **New Rough Hills Colliery** - a second series of pits first mined around 1840, adjacent to the original colliery at Rough Hills, covering at least 12 acres and with 12 shafts. Coal, iron-stone, and fireclay were mined here.

32) **The Harrolds Colliery** - this was a productive colliery situated close to the 'Wolverhampton Furnaces' by Dixon Street at Monmore Green. An advert from 20 January 1855 below, in an edition of the Staffordshire Advertiser, highlights that the thick coal was mined here, as well as the brooch coal, 'little gubbin', 'Rough Hills white iron-stone', and bottom coal. The colliery, along with a brick works, was advertised for sale or available on a 21-year lease, with 12 acres yet to be mined at that point. Part of this colliery was as close as half-a-mile from the town centre, as it states in the advertisement below (Figure 17).

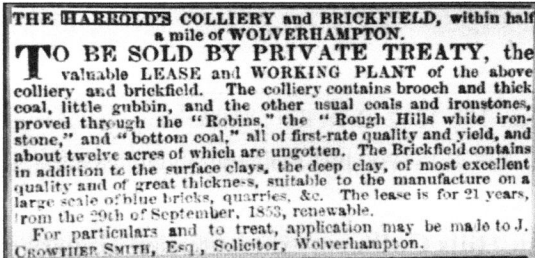

Figure 17. 1855 advert from Staffordshire Advertiser, for The Harrold's Colliery, Wolverhampton

33) **The Wolverhampton Colliery** - previously known as Timmins Colliery, was situated at Green Lane, off Dudley Road, Blakenall. This colliery was first mined around 1815, and after Mr Timmins sold the colliery it was owned by Messrs Aston and Shaw, becoming particularly productive for

iron-stone around 1825, with a considerable amount being transferred to Corngreaves Iron Works near Dudley. Plenty of coal, including the thick seam, was also brought up here. Around 1830 it was taken over by Messrs Small, Shears and Taylor, but then sold to Messrs Whitehouse and Poole in 1850. At least 130 miners were still employed here in 1860, when its resources were close to expiry. Their advert from the Wolverhampton Chronicle below, confirms that the thick coal was mined there (Figure 18).

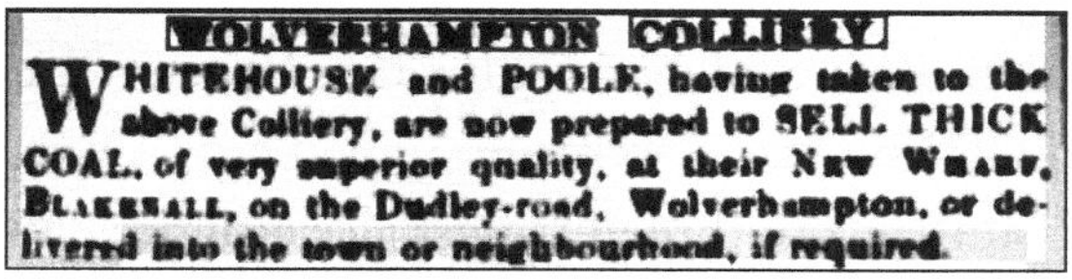
WOLVERHAMPTON COLLIERY.
WHITEHOUSE and POOLE, having taken to the above Colliery, are now prepared to SELL THICK COAL, of very superior quality, at their New Wharf, Blakenall, on the Dudley-road, Wolverhampton, or delivered into the town or neighbourhood, if required.

Figure 18 – Mid-1800s advert from Wolverhampton Chronicle, for coal at the Wolverhampton Colliery

34) **Blakenall Colliery** - this little-known colliery was situated one-mile from Wolverhampton railway station, near Cockshutts Colliery. Owned by John Southan, it was mined extensively until it was exhausted by 1857. The 'h' in the 'Blakenhall' name was then unused. Coal and iron-stone were mined here.

35) **Dudley Road Colliery** - a small mine that operated during the 1870s. This must have been close to several others in a compact geographical area around Blakenall at that point in time.

36) **Pettit's Colliery** - this mine was a busy operation in Monmore Green, which expired by 1846, when a lot of equipment including 700 yards of pit-chain and two steam engines were offered for sale.

37) **Fighting Cocks Meadow Colliery** - this was a small concern only covering 5 acres, which contained the thick coal and iron-stone, offered for sale in 1832.

38) **Highfields Colliery** - this colliery located off the Bilston Road in Monmore Green is yet another little-known mine that produced thick coal. It was owned by Messrs Shale and Fowler and was active until the late-1860s. Not to be confused with the same named concern in Bilston.

39) **Ettingshall Colliery** – this fairly small but productive colliery owned by Mr James Cadman was situated immediately south of the Parkfield Colliery, consisting 16 acres of land. In 1836 this included an acre of the thick coal seam and 13 acres of 'heathen coal' that then remained. The bottom coal, fireclay, and iron-ore including the 'blue-flats ironstone', and 'gubbin and balls iron-stone' were also mined here. Over 150 shafts were sunk at the three Ettingshall collieries covering over 75 acres of land, which were sometimes described as being at Bilston and sometimes at Wolverhampton. This colliery tended to use a Wolverhampton address.

40) **Ettingshall Park Colliery** – this was the second major colliery at Ettingshall, situated just south-west of Parkfield Colliery, where iron-stone and some of the thick seam were mined. This colliery covered around 33 acres of land.

41) **Ettingshall Lodge Colliery** – this colliery was situated just east of the other two Ettingshall collieries and was another major colliery where the thick coal seam was mined as well as the mealy and bottom coal, and iron-ore including the 'blue-flats' and 'gubbin and balls iron-stone'. It covered around 30 acres of prime mining land and was owned by a Mr Harper and Co. By 1896, just 90 men were working the 3 Ettingshall collieries, for what little coal was left.

42) **Lanesfield Colliery** – this was a smaller colliery covering 15 acres, sandwiched between the Ettingshall collieries, just south of Catchem's Corner, where the thick coal seam was mined.

43) **Sedgley Park Colliery** – this colliery was situated just west of what is now the Birmingham New Road, a few hundred yards

south of the junction with Parkfield Road, leading out to Sedgley from Blakenhall. The thick coal seam was mined here.

44) **Rookery Colliery** - this was a small colliery of just four acres at Ettingshall where the new mine coal, fireclay, and iron-stone were mined. It had just three shafts.

45) **Catchem's Corner Colliery** - this was another colliery situated around Rough Hills and Ettingshall, which covered 17 acres of land. Iron-stone and the thick coal seam were mined here.

46) **Deepfields Colliery** - situated at Woodcross, on the extreme southern tip of Wolverhampton and north-east of Sedgley, this mine arguably belonged to the Sedgley or even the Bilston Coalfield at the time. The thick seam was mined here as well as fireclay.

47) **Priestfield Colliery** - this colliery was situated west of Stowheath Lane and north of Wellington Road at Stow Heath, on the border of Wolverhampton and Bilston. The thick coal seam was mined at this substantial mine.

48) **New Priestfield Colliery** - this was a second mine situated near the above operation.

49) **Millfields Colliery** - this major colliery was situated between Wolverhampton and Bilston, closer to the latter, and covered around 78 acres of land. The thick coal seam was mined here as well as different types of iron-stone.

50) **Heath Colliery** – this early-1800s colliery was located at Eastfield, at the junction of Willenhall Road and Deans Road. Fireclay, new mine coal, and bottom coal were mined here.

51) **Heathfield Colliery** - a colliery based at Heath Town, this would mainly have been mined for thinner seams of coal as well as fireclay and iron-ore.

52) **Natty Stack Colliery** – little is known about this small colliery, though it was situated in Wednesfield by the border with Essington. It was not thought to have been particularly productive.

53) **Neachell Colliery** - sometimes also referred to as Neach-hill Colliery, this was one of the earliest and busiest pits in the Wednesfield area where coal, fireclay, and iron-stone were mined. A number of shafts were sunk here as it expanded in the 1800s.
54) **Neachells Hall Colliery** – this was a small colliery in central Wednesfield where several shafts were sunk, though it was not particularly productive, and it closed fairly- quickly.
55) **Castle Bridge Colliery** – this Wednesfield colliery was situated close to where the Castlebridge Gardens local authority flats are now situated. It too was not thought to have been a particularly productive pit although several shafts were sunk.
56) **Park Hall Colliery** - this colliery was said to lie just south of Wolverhampton, possibly around Monmore Green, but little is known about it.
57) **Gibbet Meadows Colliery** - this colliery was situated off Stowheath Lane, by the 'gibbets' at the junction of Bilston Road, close to Monmore Green. Iron-stone and the thick coal seam would have been mined here.
58) **The Hen Birch Colliery** - little is known about this small colliery in the Rough Hills area, but it only covered 5 acres of land.
59) **The Laue's Field Colliery** - this was yet another fairly-small colliery containing 15 acres of land, also within the Rough Hills area.
60) **Masonfield Colliery** - this colliery was situated near Moseley Hole. Owned by a Mr Mass, this operation was mined during the 1850s.
61) **Moseley New Colliery** - this colliery was owned by a Thomas Millership, in the 1840s, and was thought to have been close to the Masonfield Colliery.
62) **Perry Hall Colliery** - this was a small colliery north-east of central Wednesfield owned by Messrs N. Blakemore and R. Harper, that ceased trading in 1882.

63) **Ward's Bridge Colliery** – this was a small colliery just north-east of Wednesfield centre.
64) **Merrills Hole Colliery** - this was a small mine situated south-east of central Wednesfield, later owned by the Chillington Iron Company.
65) **Trentham Colliery** - this was a small colliery north-east of central Wednesfield, approaching Willenhall.
66) **Buggins Lane Colliery** - this was a small mine situated in Wednesfield owned by P. Williams and Co.
67) **Lock House Colliery** - this was another small mine situated adjacent to the canal between Heath Town and Wednesfield, owned by Messrs Aston and Shaw.
68) **The Meadows Colliery** - this colliery was located near Wednesfield Heath and owned by Joseph Hill. It was mainly mined for fireclay.
69) **The Hampton Colliery** - this was an early-1800s mine owned by Messrs Smallshears and Taylor, at Temple Street, according to 'Pigot and Co's National Commercial Directory' of 1828. It seems unlikely that Temple Street was the location of the mine, but they may have had offices there.
70) **Priest Leasowe Colliery** - this was another Wolverhampton colliery, though little is known about its exact location, though it was possibly situated by Stowheath Lane.
71) **The Penn Mine** - this was a small pit on the south-western side of Wolverhampton situated by Penn church, and close to the Rose and Crown public house on the Penn Road, where fireclay was mined.
72) **Vicarage Colliery** - little is known about the location of this colliery, possibly near Wednesfield.
73) **Wards Meadow Colliery** - this colliery was situated in Wolverhampton, but little is known about it, though it was not a large operation. It may have been situated around the Wednesfield area.

74) **Jenny's Piece Colliery** – a small colliery containing 6 acres of land where coal and iron-stone were mined. This was situated at March End, Wednesfield.

75) **Thacker's Crofts Colliery** – another small Wednesfield colliery, also containing no more than 6 acres of land, where coal and iron-stone were mined.

76) **Frost's Field Colliery** – a small colliery thought to be located between Monmore Green and Stow Heath, owned by M. Frost and Co.

77) **Morris's Piece and Minshaws Garden Colliery** – despite the unusual name, this colliery containing two adjacent parcels of land at Monmore Green, covered more than 10 acres, and was offered for sale by the owner Mr John Pountney in 1820.

78) **The Bridge Colliery** – another small colliery owned by Mr L. Lloyd.

79) **The Compton Colliery** – a small stone quarry on the west side of town.

C) Later Operations of the 'Concealed' coal seam post-Industrial Revolution

80) **Ashmore Park Colliery** – this large pit was a later and deeper, substantial mine on the edge of Wolverhampton, that started operations in the 1870s. Over 350 miners worked here at its peak. Coal and iron-ore were mined here. Many miners employed here had previously worked at New Cross Colliery. It was a successful and productive operation which mined productive measures of different bands of coal including top and bottom robin's coal, charles coal, brooch coal, benches coal, wryley eight-foot bottom coal, little coal, old park coal, heathen coal, stinking coal,

yard coal, bass coal, cinder coal, shallow coal, deep coal, and mealy grey coal. It started to struggle financially as the price of coal dropped, and it finally closed in 1911.

81) **Holly Bank Colliery** – this large colliery was first mined in 1891. It was a major operation situated just outside the official Wolverhampton boundary at Essington, at Bursnips Road behind the Mitre Inn, and it bordered Ashmore Park Colliery. Around 460 miners were employed here at its peak. But operations were closed in 1927, after 'Hilton Main' opened. They usually used a Wolverhampton address, and as we know, Essington did originally belong to Wolverhampton.

82) **Hilton Colliery, Featherstone** – 'Hilton Main' was also a substantial operation just outside Wolverhampton that first opened in 1924 and continued until 1968. At its peak 350,000 tonnes of coal were mined per annum. Some shafts were mined into and under nearby Bushbury, Wolverhampton. Similar bands of coal were mined as at Ashmore Park Colliery, less than a mile away. They usually used a Wolverhampton address.

Finally, it is worth again recalling the fact that an old pit was recently found just a couple of hundred metres from the town centre of Wolverhampton, which highlights that a lot is still unknown about the scale of Wolverhampton coal-mining in earlier centuries.

It is difficult to gauge the scale of some of these mining operations, partly because detail of their activity at specific points in time are hard to find, and therefore it is unclear whether available information regards any specific pit relates to a time of prominence or near exhaustion of coal measures.

As we know, by the late-1800s, at the end of the Industrial Revolution, much of the shallow coal had been exhausted and so the 'Great Depression' set in. Between 1860-1928, 73 mines were exhausted in Wolverhampton and Wednesfield, and 132 in Bilston. Famous Wolverhampton names that closed were Chillington, Harrold's, Old Heath, Cockshutts, Bowman's Harbour, and Natty Stack.

Even after the closure of these mines, the legacy of intense and uncontrolled mining in east Wolverhampton left its mark. East Park, known as 'East-End Park' when it was first created and opened in 1896, was described by the mayor as: -

"A most excellent resort for the toiling thousands of the smoke-begrimed district situated in the eastern or industrial portion of Wolverhampton".

This lovely park originally had pools and a boating lake, but these drained away into the old mine shafts beneath. East Park still stands today, without the pools. Once, however this was an area of coal pits and banks of cinder ash and blast-furnace spoil.

To summarise, Wolverhampton clearly has its own mining legacy within Black Country history, and I think this is the first attempt to list all the coal-mines of Wolverhampton.

4) COAL-MINING STATISTICS

The final section of this chapter is mainly statistical, but these statistics are very important as they truly demonstrate the scale of mining in Wolverhampton compared with other Black Country areas.

The reader may wish to skip this section, if it does not appeal. But the records of tragic incidents highlighted shortly, make sad but fascinating reading.

As the reader will see, until the post-Industrial Revolution period Wolverhampton played a more significant part in the history of Black Country coal-mining than is generally ever now acknowledged.

A) Analysis of Coal-mining Casualties in The Black Country in the 1800s

An article from the 'Wolverhampton Chronicle' from 20 December 1843 highlighted a table of mortality-levels at coal-mines in each Black Country parish over a five-year period from July 1837 - December 1842, courtesy of the 'Mining Journal'.

Dudley	186
Sedgley	153
Bilston	152
Wolverhampton	142
West Bromwich	134
Tipton	117
Oldbury	79
Rowley Regis	75
Wednesbury	47
Willenhall	25

Virtually all of the Sedgley deaths occurred at Ettingshall Collieries, which at the time lay in Sedgley parish but were very much part of Wolverhampton historically and of course today, as well as being part of the Manor of Stow Heath, Wolverhampton.

A snapshot of casualties in The Black Country 1838

The Coal Mining History website also has an article from 1838, during the middle of the Industrial revolution, where the Registrar General gave an analysis of death for that year, in relation to industrial-related death.

In the South Staffordshire Coal-field he recorded as 'Deaths by Accidents around Shafts of Coal Pits' as Bilston 8, Sedgley 6,

Tipton 3, Dudley 2, Wolverhampton 2, Darlaston 2, and 1 each at West Bromwich, Oldbury and Rowley Regis.

'Deaths by falling of Coal, clad or rubbish into coal pits' included 9 in West Bromwich, 8 in Wolverhampton, 7 each in Dudley, Sedgley and Rowley Regis, 4 each in Tipton, Oldbury, Sedgley and Wednesbury, and 3 at Bilston. The youngest killed was a nine-year old boy worker at a Wolverhampton pit.

Wolverhampton mines did not experience what might be called devastating incidents with large numbers lost because the mines in relative terms, were shallow operations. Nevertheless, it was certainly a dangerous occupation, as the following newspaper archive reports highlight. A quite-staggering 400-600 miners died in accidents at Wolverhampton coal-mines during the 1800s, 80% of which involved individual deaths. An appalling waste of life. Many of these miners were killed in the Monmore Green and Rough Hills Collieries, which both had unenviable safety records. The rate of accidents at thin seam and ironstone mines was about the same as at thick seam mines, but the risk of fatality at the latter was higher, though working the thin seam and ironstone was notably a tougher occupation that paid less well.

Incidents at Wolverhampton Coal-mines

A search of 'Wolverhampton Chronicle and Staffordshire Advertiser' archives, reveals some fairly-typical but dreadful accidents in Wolverhampton mines.

In August 1813, a number of men were buried after a shaft collapsed at an unnamed mine in Wolverhampton. But after seven awful days for the buried men, on 27 August 1813 voices were heard, and miraculously, thanks to the efforts of hundreds of people who gathered to escalate the rate of the operation, nine miners including a boy were saved, with only a man named as John Keeling presumed killed and buried by the initial mine collapse.

In September 1816, Noah Lees and Thomas Win were killed in a stone pit at Compton.

In May 1814, a young 'pit-bank wench' named as Margaret Davis was killed at Cockshutts Colliery when her clothing got caught on the ladder pulley and she was pulled into the shaft, where she plunged 70 yards to her death.

In June 1820, three young men were killed at Monmore Green Colliery. Thomas Punford, John Walker, and Christopher Dodd were hit by falling rock as they ascended the pit.

In November 1821, a miner named William Ball was killed at the Wolverhampton Colliery when the skip he was descending in, suddenly started to come back up again. At the mouth of the pit he jumped from the skip to prevent being drawn over the pulley and held on to the side of the pit frame, but one foot became caught in one of the chains and having to let go of his grip he was lifted in the air briefly, before falling eighty yards to his death.

In April 1824, a 'pit-bank wench' named as Maria Speak fell down the shaft at Cockshutts Colliery, whilst working on the bank.

In March 1825, Eleanor Speke, Jeremiah Kidson, and Richard Edwards were killed at Monmore Green Colliery when they were instantly catapulted into the 56-yard deep pit when trying to pull the waggon, but the pulley which they were attempting to wind suddenly malfunctioned.

The Wolverhampton Colliery was to prove a curse for three young children who fell down its unguarded shafts that decade.

In April 1824, 9-year old WIlliam Sumner fell to his death down a sixty-yards shaft. Tragically, the little lad had simply gone to take his father some dinner when he slipped into an all-too-typically, unguarded shaft.

In May 1827, a 9-year old boy named James Sutton died after falling backwards into a shaft near to which he was playing at the same colliery, The Wolverhampton Colliery.

And in July 1827, an 8-year old girl named Elizabeth Harsthorne was walking home from work when she fell down a shaft at the Wolverhampton Colliery, dying instantly.

In September 1827, the paper reported the death of 12-year old Thomas Eaton, who was killed whilst at work in a pit at Chillington Colliery, when a large amount of iron-stone and rock fell upon him. Two others were also seriously injured.

In another snapshot of time, August 1829, the paper reported three deaths that month.

At Rough Hills Colliery, a group of men had ascended the pit, and just as they got to the top and just before the wagon was drawn over the mouth of the shaft, a man jumped out, but the wind blew him back into the shaft, which was 70-80 yards deep.

Secondly, a Samuel Lawley was struck on the temple by a piece of coal, after a section gave way at Wolverhampton Colliery.

Thirdly, 12-year old William Lawley was killed at Chillington Colliery when he fell out of a skip which was ascending out of a shaft, after the chain gave a sudden jerk.

In July 1830, the chain lowering the skip containing eight men and a boy down the shaft of a pit eighty yards deep at Chillington Colliery suddenly snapped, and they fell to the bottom of the shaft, where the heavy chain fell upon them. One man broke his spine, and all received very serious injuries. It was unclear if they ultimately survived their injuries.

In August 1832, 13-year old Richard Baker was killed by a fall of coal at Catchem's Corner Colliery.

In May 1834, five men were killed at Rough Hills Colliery when one of the chains got caught on the pulley as they were ascending the pit in the skip, resulting in instantaneous death for four of the men who suffered numerous fractures as they fell back down the pit which was fifty yards in depth. The other man was brought up alive but died soon afterwards. The dead were named as William Adams, Thomas Green, William Davis, Thomas Hartshorne, and

David Jones who all lived in central Wolverhampton. The horse at the bottom of the pit was uninjured. The accident left fifteen children orphaned. The men had frequently complained of the worn out, problematic chain used to take them down. Examination of the chain after the incident revealed that two links were noted to have completely gone on it, with another severely cracked, and sixty-eight rivet links put in where it had broken previously. A verdict of accidental death was returned nevertheless, highlighting what little value was placed on health and safety and on the lives of the ordinary working man.

In November 1836, a collier named Thomas Jones was killed when half-a-ton of coal suddenly gave way and fell upon him whilst he was working at Chillington Colliery.

In November 1838, a 12-year old boy named William Mattocks died when he fell down an unnamed iron-pit after pushing a skip towards the pit-mouth. He and the skip tumbled down, and he was killed instantly.

In August 1839, a 12-year old girl named Jane Rowley accidentally fell down a pit at Chillington Colliery, when she was working at the pit-mouth. She died instantly.

In October 1839, four men were killed at the Wolverhampton Colliery when a large overhanging piece of coal weighing around ten tonnes suddenly gave way, instantly killing Samuel Haynes, John Aston, William Jones, and Joseph Evans who were working at the mine.

In August 1841, three miners were killed at the Willenhall Road Colliery when they were descending to the bottom of the pit in a water barrel. At a depth of 145 yards it suddenly slipped from the chains and descended into the sump, where the chain fell on top of them. A William Richards drowned, and Thomas Jones and John Mason were killed instantly by the three-ton chain, which ripped the top of Mason's skull clean off. A fourth man miraculously survived.

In June 1842, a dreadful accident occurred at Cleveland Colliery, Willenhall Road. Thirteen men and boys descended the shaft in a skip, and at a depth of 50 yards they came across foul air. As several had lighted candles, an almighty explosion occurred. Seven of the group fell to their death from the skip to the bottom of the shaft, whilst the other six held tightly and were hoisted back up the shaft but were badly burnt. The dead were named as 27 year-old William Smith, 46 year-old James Love and his 14 year-old son, 15 year-old Walter Marshall, 16 year-old Edward Dawson, 17 year-old William Dunn, and 11 year-old William Jones. Of those brought back up in the skip, three were aged just 11, and one aged 14. At least two of these were said very unlikely to survive. There was immense distress as relatives gathered around the pit mouth. The Moseley Hole and Portobello mining communities were severely affected by this dreadful incident, and the victims were badly-burnt and mutilated.

In July 1842, 17-year old 'pit-bank wench' Ela Glover was killed at Cockshutts Colliery, when she was leading a horse pulling two fully-loaded tubs of coal, but a tub became detached and struck a timber support. The shaft roof suddenly gave way, and Ela and the horse plunged to their death.

In February 1847, two men, William Powell and William Marsden were killed by falling bricks as they descended the shaft at Wednesfield Heath Colliery.

In November 1848, a 23-year old collier named Simeon Colbourne, was killed when a large quantity of clod fell upon him at Chillington Colliery, and he expired within quarter of an hour.

Two days later, Emmanuel Taylor was hit by falling coal at Rough Hills Colliery. He stumbled back to his Steelhouse Lane home, where he died an hour and a half later.

In December 1853, a 14-year old boy named Peter Harper fell from a skip at the Wolverhampton Colliery, and died a day later at his home, after badly banging his head.

In June 1857, 21-year old 'pit-bank wench' Mary Swift, fell one-hundred feet to her death whilst fitting the net used to lower and haul up the horses, when her clothing got caught in the tub and she was dragged into the shaft at Monmore Green Colliery.

In June 1858, three men were killed and several injured when a huge overhanging section of coal collapsed and buried them alive at the Masonfield Colliery, Moseley Hole. They had been warned just ten minutes before the collapse to vacate the area, but stubbornly continued to work.

In November 1858, 21-year-old Enoch Brown and 12-year old John Bate were approaching one of the pits at New Cross Colliery when a pocket of gas exploded, killing John instantly and Enoch a few days later.

In January 1860, four men and three boys were killed at the 'Blue Fly Pit', or 'number 15 pit' at Wednesfield Heath Colliery, Heath Town. Everything was fine for the first ninety feet of their descent, but then a chain snapped, and they fell the remaining two-hundred feet at great speed. The snapped wire decapitated some of the victims, and a fire also broke out. It took four hours to recover the tangled bodies at the bottom of the pit. The deceased men were named as John Cheese, Emmanuel Giles, Henry Davis, and Thomas Kelly, along with 13-year old's George Jones and Samuel Stych, and 12-year old John Jones. It was noted that the engine used to lower and raise the men from the shaft was without the legally-required 'safety-brake'.

That same month, January 1860, 18-year old Phoebe Davis threw herself down a pit just forty yards from her home, at Monmore Green, after an argument. She fell to the bottom of the shaft, that was 80 yards deep, dying instantly.

That same year, 1860, 14-year old 'pit-bank wench' Bridget McHale was killed when she was thrown down the pit after her clothing became entangled in the winding gear at Wednesfield Heath Colliery, Heath Town.

In October 1862, a dreadful accident happened at Priestfield Colliery. Five men were descending to the bottom of the eighty-yard deep mine, and were about half way down, when a skip fell down the shaft and fell on top of them with such violence that four were killed instantly. Miraculously the fifth man was uninjured. The dead men were unnamed.

In 1863, 18-year old 'pit-bank wench' Elizabeth Blaney died at Stow Heath Colliery when she fell down the pit after the guard rails were pulled away.

In 1864, 16-year old Charles Guy was leading his horse down in the pit at Bowman's Harbour Colliery, Heath Town, when a large lump of coal fell and killed him.

In 1867, 3 'shaft sinkers' were repairing a shaft at the Ettingshall Colliery when one of the supports to the scaffold suddenly gave way. One of the sinkers managed to hold on, but William Edwards and Matthew Hinglam, both from Blakenall, Wolverhampton were 'dashed to the bottom, and their bodies proving difficult to retrieve'.

In 1875, 38-year old Thomas Brant, a shaft sinker, was killed when the shaft collapsed upon him at New Cross Colliery.

That same year, 1875, another unnamed shaft-sinker died when jumping prematurely out of the ascending cage after finishing his shift at New Cross Colliery. He fell back into the shaft, dying instantly.

On 8 October 1878, a boy named only as Porter was pushing the skip into the shaft at the Dudley Road Colliery, when he was pulled down into the shaft with it, which resulted in the boy dying of terrible head injuries.

In 1884, 31-year old Samuel Harper blew himself to pieces at Ashmore Park Colliery after trying to ram home a charge of powder using an iron bar and lighting a candle to see better.

A year later, in 1885, 23-year old John Davis was killed and almost decapitated when he got stuck between the loaded tub and a roadway wall at Ashmore Park Colliery.

In April 1892, the paper reported an incident at Chillington Colliery, where three men were working close together, when one of them went to his powder-box for a cartridge of compressed powder. He placed his candle on a dry-stone wall, but as soon as he opened his box, the lighted candle rolled into it and exploded the powder. He dived out of the way, but the man working near him received the full force and died of horrific injuries a few days later.

In 1894, a 24-year old named Richard Jeavons was killed by a gas explosion when leading horses to their underground tunnel at Ashmore Park Colliery. The horse was uninjured.

These were just a selection of the accidents that highlight the perilous nature of mining in the 1800s particularly, when health and safety was pretty much non-existent. The number of children who perished whilst working at Wolverhampton mines is staggering.

Many incidents clearly happened at the pit-mouth because they were often crudely fenced or roped-off, but Wolverhampton colliery owners devised important safety improvements.

In 1856, Mr Griffiths of Chillington Iron Works designed a 'safety-brake' to colliery engines, that could stop at a stroke a 30-horse power engine, and bring it to a standstill, hence helping to prevent those dreadful accidents where the cage or skip, often with people in it, was drawn over the pulley. The adaption cost £10 per engine. The device was introduced by George Thorneycroft to all of his fourteen colliery engines that same year.

The Osier Bed Company's mining manager, Mr W. Blakemore of Heath Town, devised a significant safety improvement that was introduced across the Black Country, at its pit at Stow Heath Colliery on Willenhall Road on the edge of Wolverhampton in 1864. The complex design involved metal rods and pulleys that were attached to both the fence surrounding the pit entrance, and to the wagon that ran into it. It is hard to envisage exactly how it worked, and although the design was patented, his generous nature dictated that he wanted it to be freely copied and widely adopted at as many pits as possible.

The design was described in detail in the 'Wellington Journal' on 4 June 1864. It was adopted by some of the large mine owners in the Black Country, such as by the Chillington Company, The Osier Bed Company, and at Dud Dudley's mines, but not so widely by many of the smaller colliery owners of the region.

All in all, by 1873, around 50 of the 200 Black Country colliery proprietors in South Staffordshire had adopted this fencing protection scheme.

B) Black Country Working Collieries - 1880

In the 1850 there were said to be around 26,000 miners in the entire Staffordshire Coal-field, and there was reported to be around 75 pits in Wolverhampton, and over 140 in Bilston.

In 1865, 24,000 workers were still employed in coal mines and 2,500 in iron-stone mines in the Black Country. The iron-ore of the region had virtually expired at this point.

But by 1880, the 'Great Depression' had set in, and the Black Country Coal-field of the Industrial Revolution was rapidly expiring, and only around half of the original figure remained. A total of 413 collieries were registered in the Black Country in 1880.

The following list uses the 'address town' the collieries themselves gave at that point in time: -.

Bilston	71
Brierley Hill / Rowley Regis / Cradley	37
Dudley / Gornal	35
West Bromwich	35
Tipton	34
Wolverhampton	31

Wednesbury	20
Walsall	17
Oldbury	17
Darlaston	12
Willenhall	10
Sedgley	3
Stourbridge	6
Halesowen	2

The 31 collieries giving Wolverhampton as an address are as follows: -

Ashmore Park, Chillington x 3, Deans, Deans Old x 4, Ettingshall Lodge x 10 (4 more at Ettingshall classed as being Bilston), Essington Wood, New Cross, Neachell Hall, Old Heath, Parkfield x 3, Perry Hall, Portobello, Stow Heath, Vicarage, Wolverhampton. Many pits, including Monmore Green, Cockshutts, Bowman's Harbour, & Rough Hills were already closed at this point.

Nevertheless, using these figures, in terms of the four Black Country borough's today, or alternatively what was classed as Wolverhampton during the Industrial Revolution, Wolverhampton had more coal mines than any of its neighbours - 102 collieries in Wolverhampton, 100 in Dudley, 89 in Sandwell, and 46 in Walsall.

Perhaps an important fact to remember when Wolverhampton is next referred to as 'just a market town'.

Furthermore, the map produced by the website 'Distinctly Black Country' of 'Collieries at Work in 1861', shows the distribution of collieries across the Black Country area. This persuasive map clearly shows that east Wolverhampton was littered with various coal mines and was a key mining area, along with Bilston.

The map is shown on the following page (Figure 19).

'IRONOPOLIS'

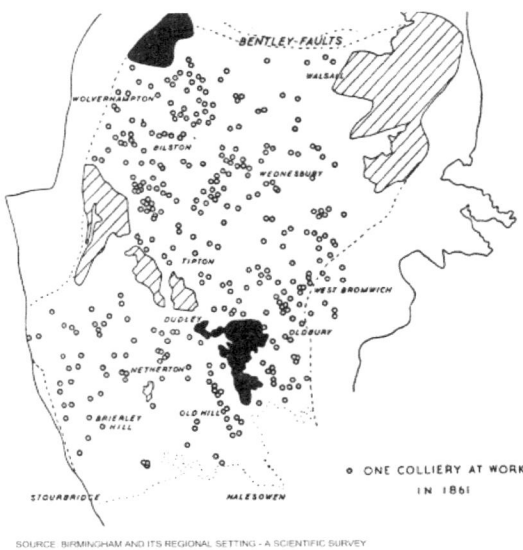

Figure 19 – Collieries at Work in 1861 by 'Distinctly Black Country'.

C) Coal-Miner Statistics from 1841 and 1896

As already highlighted, in 1841 local historian George Barnsby in his 1990 book 'Social Conditions in The Black Country' scrutinised and revealed official census records of Black Country towns. It is appropriate to again remind the reader at this juncture, of these revealing figures, highlighted in descending numbers. They accurately demonstrate the amount of mining activity in each town, as without transport, miners resided very close to the pits where they were employed: -

'Bilston had a male population of 10,540, of whom 2,474 were miners (23% of male population).

Wolverhampton had a male population of 18,789, of whom 1,886 were miners (10% of male population).

Sedgley had a male population of 12,586, of whom 1,818 were miners (14% of male population). Most of these pits lay in Ettingshall, originally and now part of Wolverhampton.

Dudley had a male population of 15,689, of whom 1,606 were miners (11% of male population).

West Bromwich had a male population of 13,480, of whom 1,340 were miners (10% of male population).

Kingswinford had a male population of 11,466, of whom 1,333 were miners (11% of male population).

Tipton had a male population of 9,773, of whom 1,151 were miners (12% of male population).

Walsall had an adult male population of 10,967 of whom 718 were miners' (7% of male population)'.

So contrary to many people's perception, Wolverhampton had more miners at this point of the Industrial Revolution than anywhere else except its adjoining suburb town of Bilston. Parishes or townships were roughly of equal size population-wise, but even proportionately, these figures show us that Bilston was arguably the greatest mining town in the Black Country, where over 23% of males worked in mines, followed by 14% of Sedgley males, and 12% of Tipton males. Wolverhampton, Dudley, West Bromwich, and Kingswinford each had around 10-11% of males who worked in mines, with Walsall in last place with just under 7%.

Just ten years later, according to the 1851 census, 16% of men of working age in Wolverhampton were miners or quarrymen, reflecting the general increase during that decade.

These figures arguably constitute a fairly-accurate reflection of where the greatest concentrations of mines were situated. It seems that the greatest mining area of the Black Country at that time was the triangular area of land linking Wolverhampton, Bilston, and Sedgley.

By 1896, at the end of the Industrial Revolution, most of the shallow mines that characterised the Black Country were exhausted, with just small areas being still left to mine.

This was particularly the case in the northern part of the Black Country, in Wolverhampton, where iron-ore and the thin seam were mined. This is reflected in figures from that year that show large numbers of miners being employed at the new, deeper, concealed coal-mines around the periphery of the Black Country.

Sandwell Park had 483 underground workers and 162 surface workers at this point. On the Wolverhampton outskirts, Holly Bank Colliery, Essington had 462 underground workers, and 100 surface workers, Ashmore Park Colliery had 279 underground workers, and 63 surface workers, and Hilton Colliery had 127 underground workers, and 36 surface workers.

For contrast, older, virtually 'worked-out mines' in Wolverhampton such as Chillington Colliery had just 12 underground workers and 3 surface workers at that point, Ettingshall Park had just 17 underground workers and 14 surface workers, Parkfield Colliery had just 21 underground workers and 11 surface workers.

It was a similar story accross the Wolverhampton coal-field at New Cross, Barnfield, Deans, Neachells, Old Heath, Moseley Hole, and Rough Hills Collieries, as the shallow seam expired.

5) BRIEF HISTORY OF COAL-MINING IN WEST BROMWICH (for Comparison)

For contrast, West Bromwich, on the opposite end of the Black Country and like Wolverhampton also right at the edge, and similarly affected by a geological fault, had a similar number of collieries, in fact considerably less if one includes the Bilston Collieries as being part of Wolverhampton.

West Bromwich's early mining operations were inevitably where the coal outcropped, in the 1700s set in the north and west of the parish such as at Balls Hill in 1707 and Golds Green 1760s, and Swan Village in 1808. The old centre of West Bromwich was situated around this area. Neighbouring Wednesbury first had mines in 1315, and by the mid-1700s it had coal-pits all around.

Coal-mining really expanded in West Bromwich in the 1800s. By 1829 there were 18 collieries in West Bromwich, then 40 by 1835. At its height during the Industrial Revolution, in the 1850s there were 60 collieries in West Bromwich, but quite a few of these were small scale in conjunction with iron works, as is the exact case with Wolverhampton. Nearly all of these pits were in the northern part of West Bromwich, close to Wednesbury. By 1868 only 40 of 65 pits were still active, and just 14 by 1896. The 'Great Depression' was said by some to be between 1874-1890. Thereafter the concealed section started to be mined around the periphery of the West Bromwich area in the very late-1800s, just after the Industrial Revolution.

As alluded to, like Wolverhampton, West Bromwich was affected by a geological fault, in its case the 'eastern boundary fault' that had a down-throw of 354 feet. But due to technological advances, in 1870 a pit was sunk at a depth of over 1250 feet at Sandwell Park colliery in the parish of Smethwick, and this operation sank a mine on the West Bromwich side of the border at Jubilee Pit, Warstone Field in 1897. These rich, much deeper reserves were successfully mined until the 1970s. The Sandwell Park Colliery was situated right on the edge of West Bromwich, in a similar peripheral location to Ashmore Park Colliery or Holly Bank Colliery on Wolverhampton's edges, and both operations occurred after the main stage of the Industrial Revolution, or arguably after it altogether. Nevertheless, with these technological advances in mining practices, huge amounts of coal were mined from the concealed coal-field, though they certainly did not define the Black Country.

But prior to this small geographical area being mined at Sandwell Park Colliery, allotments and green fields were situated all around south-west West Bromwich throughout the Industrial Revolution, very much llike the western side of Wolverhampton. This part of the town had no history of mining, and it certainly had no 'battle-scarred' landscape like other Black Country areas, paricularly eastern Wolverhampton and Bilston where the thin seam was prominent. In the northern part of the 'new' West Bromwich town centre, there were newer deeper pits at Heath Colliery, which had been first-mined in 1833. This operation included Lewisham and Victoria Pits.

In summary, the-majority-of coal mining and iron industries in West Bromwich were to be found at the northern end of West Bromwich, close to Wednesbury during the 1800s Industrial Revolution. This was not dissimilar to the area between Wolverhampton and Bilston. Yet despite these similarities, West Bromwich's place in Black Country history is secure and fully acknowledged by the Black Country Society, whereas Wolverhampton's is often wrongly derided or dismissed.

6) CONCLUSION -
Wolverhampton's role in Coal-mining in the Black Country

To conclude, it is evident that considerably more mining took place in Wolverhampton excluding Bilston, than seems to be generally appreciated or acknowledged, though much of this was for the uncelebrated thinner seams of coal, and especially for its invaluable seams of iron-ore.

East Wolverhampton's coal-field expired at the end of the 1870s, whereas new measures in the concealed seam were discovered around the periphery of the Black Country, including areas around the border of Wolverhampton. But in general, the coal-field in Wolverhampton was amongst the first to expire in the Black Country. But even at Wednesbury, once in the heart of the thick seam, the last mine closed in 1915, and the spoil-banks began to be levelled. Its famous thick seam had expired well before that.

Ironically, some people still ignorantly suggest Wolverhampton has virtually no mining legacy at all, yet the town had the highest incidence in the whole Country of 'Coal-master' prosecutions between 1858-1867 utilising the much-despised 'Master and Servants Act'. This was the most industrious and productive period of the Industrial Revolution.

The importance of its thinner seams of coal for use in the blast-furnaces and iron works, and especially of its iron-ore for the development of the Black Country seems to be very much under-appreciated. The high-quality iron-ore from the Wolverhampton Coal-field was often transported to the Dudley Coal-field where it was utilised. Without the iron-ore that was mined the great Black Country iron industry would not have developed as it did. The thick coal by itself, was sometimes not of great financial value, but of course it was always in high demand especially for domestic household use.

Furthermore, contrary to popular belief, some thick coal was mined at a number of Wolverhampton Collieries, even if it was not mined in the same quantity as in some neighbouring areas. So, even when the 'thick coal seam' definition is adopted, the Black Country Society have wrongly concluded that Wolverhampton should be excluded.

As a concluding and defining point for this chapter, it is again worth recalling and remembering that official census records reveal that during the decade the Black Country was first named as such in the 1840s, the parish of Wolverhampton had the second highest number of miners in the Black Country, lying only behind Bilston. Many of these worked longer hours and were paid less than those miners in the southern part of the Black Country where the thick seam was more prominent. Large numbers of young men, children and 'pit-bank wenches' were routinely employed at Wolverhampton mines, and has been seen, many paid the ultimate price.

CHAPTER SIX

Iron Production in Wolverhampton and the Wider Black Country Area

CHAPTER BREAKDOWN

1) **The history of the Process of Iron Production**
2) **Wolverhampton's Iron and Brass Industry** Including: - A) A general Introduction. B) An Imaginary Journey through Horseley Fields in east Wolverhampton during the height of the Industrial Revolution. C) The Iron Works of Wolverhampton – a summary of operations. D) Dangerous places of work.
3) **Black Country and National Iron Industry Statistics Including:** - A) Blast Furnaces (producing primary pig iron). B) Puddling Furnaces (in Rolling Mills and Forges) (producing finished wrought-iron). C) Iron Works of the Black Country.
4) **Conclusion** - Wolverhampton's Iron Industry

Wolverhampton, during the key part of the Industrial Revolution of the mid-to-late-1800s was known throughout the kingdom as the 'centre of the iron trade'.

CHAPTER SIX

Figure 20 – Rollers at Mars Iron Works, Ettingshall, Wolverhampton

Ellen Thorneycroft Fowler, a local novelist, said of Wolverhampton in her 1899 novel 'A Double Thread': -

"The staple commodity of the citizens of this place is iron, which they manufacture and buy and sell. Iron gets into their blood and makes strong men of them".

Such was the perceived significance of iron to the town.

'Rollers' from the Mars Iron Works, one of the town's major operations, are seen in the superb, atmospheric photograph above (Figure 20). Wolverhampton had huge Rolling Mills.

In this chapter, we look at the history and development of iron-production, and inevitably we then concentrate of the iron trade in Wolverhampton and the wider Black Country. The final section of this chapter specifically provides 'Black Country town-by-town' statistical detail, in-reference to the iron industry. They show that Wolverhampton, including Bilston, was arguably the prominent iron-producing area of the entire Black Country during the 1800s, despite Dud Dudley's revolutionary, earlier work.

Today, the iron and brass industry, and belatedly the subsequent steel industry that were once so dominant during the 1800s and even to some degree in the 1900s, have all-but-gone, but the legacy left behind in the form of its numerous factory buildings has been present for many subsequent decades.

If anyone feels that Wolverhampton's role in coal production is often under-represented as far as Black Country history is concerned, then that is certainly true of its iron industry, which was vast. It was pivotal to the Black Country, in simple terms.

1) THE HISTORY OF THE PROCESS OF IRON PRODUCTION

Over many centuries the methods of extracting pig iron from iron-ore, and 'working' it so that it could produce cast-iron and then wrought-iron products evolved and improved continuously in relation to the quality of the iron and in relation to production-levels too. The systems and methods inevitably became more complex as the 1700s and 1800s of the Industrial Revolution progressed.

In the 1500s the iron-ore (or iron-stone) was simply placed into the few blast-furnaces with the charcoal, where it was 'smelted' and then poured into ingots to create cast-iron products. But it comprised a somewhat granulated texture, and when cast-iron cooled it was often brittle when placed under duress. It was recognised that the more pig-iron was reheated, cooled, and re-worked (or 'puddled'), the more malleable and stronger it became because impurities had been 'driven-out'. To achieve this, a second process took place in the forge. In the refinery section of the forge, the pig-iron was reheated and refined by hammering out the impurities, and then in the chafery part of the forge it was again heated and shaped into bars by hammers, or into various iron products.

Early blast-furnaces, as well as the forge, relied heavily on water-power, as the bellows that produced the cold-air blast were powered by a water-wheel. Early, small blast-furnaces and forges employed at most a dozen men, with many in the Black Country area making rudimentary nails for instance, and these small operations were often still situated alongside farming. The nailers required strips of thinner iron, so to fulfill this demand, so-called slitting-mills were built.

But the amount of deforestation taking place to produce the necessary charcoal to fuel these furnaces was increasingly becoming a major concern, with huge swathes of the nation's trees disappearing rapidly, so the process of using coke, which was widely available locally, continued to be tested. But the fundamental problem was that when coal was used as a fuel, the smelted iron-ore that became pig-iron, absorbed sulphur from the coal, and this made it brittle and difficult to work in a forge. At this point, it produced relatively-poor quality iron.

It was in 1620 when Black Country Lord Edward Dudley first claimed his son Dud Dudley made a technological invention within iron production and obtained a patent from the King. Dud invented a blast-furnace which separated the iron-ore from the fuel using burning, coke, at Pensnett Chase. He claimed to have invented this process in 1618. It is thought his trials were fairly successful, as his new quality iron was sent to the King to be tested for its malleability and strength, in connection with the production of muskets and other armaments, and it was deemed to be 'good, merchantable iron'. He was only able to produce three tonnes per week however, so Dudley then also built a large, more-powerful, stone furnace with extra width, at Hasco Bridge, between Himley and Sedgley in 1626. But he was plagued with problems, including damage to his furnace and ongoing friction and opposition from local charcoal-utilising iron-masters, and to compound it all, by a terrible flood.

Dud Dudley then became heavily involved in domestic military affairs that plagued the Country, on the side of the King, but some years later when things had calmed down he continued experimenting, highlighting his achievements in his famous book

'Metallum Martis' published in 1665. Yet he continued to find enemies locally in the owners of charcoal-fuelled furnaces, who suggested that he somewhat exaggerated his success. In 1686, it was argued by the reputed historian Robert Plot that the furnaces at that earlier time could not have heated the raw coal to a sufficiently hot temperature to smelt iron properly, whereas the charcoal-fuelled furnaces could do. Dudley was neither fully-endorsed nor entirely discredited it seems.

That process of using coke to smelt iron-ore would finally be perfected by the widely-acclaimed Black Country-born metallurgist Abraham Darby around 1709, and hence the district of Shropshire where he operated his blast-furnace, can truly lay claim to be the pioneer of the iron trade and even the 'birthplace of industry'. He indeed managed to use coke rather than charcoal to make forgeable iron-castings in his single blast-furnace at Coalbrookdale, and it has been argued that this single technological development kick-started the Industrial Revolution. But he was a touch fortunate as the coal mined and used there happened to be more-or-less sulphur-free. Either way, the next generation of Darby's family further utilised the process by around 1740, and thereafter pig-iron was sent in increasing quantity to the forges and slitting-mills.

But they only mastered the process of utilising liquid iron-ore for castings through the use of moulds, and contrary to popular opinion, the best bar-iron was actually still produced by charcoal-fuelled furnaces until the early-1800s.

Further developments in the iron industry continued to be devised. Cumbrian-born John 'iron-mad' Wilkinson developed a blowing-device for his blast- furnace, greatly increasing its efficiency, at his Bradley Iron works at Bilston on the edge of Wolverhampton in 1767. Through his rolling-mills, he was the first to make iron truly smooth and malleable, and furthermore he invented a precision boring-machine to produce cast-iron cylinders such as those used in the steam-engines of James Watt, whom he was close friends with. In effect, he was the inventor of the 'machine-tool'. He also invented cupola-furnaces, where pig-iron was reheated before castings were made. These inventions really took the iron industry into a new hemisphere. Specifically, his invention of using steam-engines to provide blast for the furnaces and to power forge-hammers, and later the great rolling-mills, removed the need for iron works to be situated immediately by sources of water, so this was a fundamental change, and hence existing iron works started to evolve in the 1800s, with some containing blast-furnaces, puddling-furnaces, rolling and slitting-mills, whilst smaller operations prospered by specialising in just one aspect of iron production.

Iron-production processes and improvements were complex, and different types of furnaces evolved over time, one often little different than its predecessor, and each performing a specific role within the process.

Blast-furnaces that produced the pig-iron simply became bigger and more efficient, powered by the blast from steam-engines, so they were able to meet the huge and increasing Government orders for arnaments or railways. Hot-blast ones became more productive, but in the Black Country primary pig-iron was smelted from the ore mainly in cold-blast-furnaces, for a specific reason. The coke in the Staffordshire field and the Dudley field, according to a report from 'The Engineer', published in the 'Birmingham Daily Gazette' on 23 March 1868, was said to limit the ability to use large, powerful blast-furnaces, for a specific reason: -

"It was not able to bear more than half the burden carried by either South Wales or north country coke, so the prospect of large furnaces was not possible in the district. Hence, the oven system of coking, except with a large admixture of other coal or bitumen, was out of the question. So highly-heated or hot-blast was purposely avoided by most of the major pig-iron suppliers of the Black Country, so as to maintain the quality of their pig-iron."

The report looked closely at the 'once-Dud Dudley-owned' Round Oak Furnaces, stating: -

"They were typically for the Black Country, quite small, averaging a height of just 48 feet, and a width of just 10 feet at the mouth. As usual, the blast was supplied by a Cornish engine with a 72-inch blowing cylinder and was always employed in cold-blast in at least one furnace, and never heated beyond 200-250 degrees in any of them. The small coal in this district will not coke well and is instead coked in open fires heaped round a small, square-brick chimney with a damper on top. Without admixture of pitch or coking coal, bad results are obtained in ovens from the Dudley coal, even in a round state, and the slack is unusable."

Nevertheless, the Wemlock limestone and shale from the area just west of Dudley in isolation, was excellent for use in blast-furnaces. And the abundant thick coal, when pitched and topped up with Welsh coal, could be widely used in the blast-furnaces.

So, the Black Country iron industry evolved with busy but medium-sized works, in contrast to the new 'super-plants' of South Wales or the North-east.

Iron production during the late-1700s and 1800s Industrial Revolution could be split into two fundamental areas – the production of 'primary pig-iron' through the blast-furnace, which could then be used for cast-iron products, and the production of 'wrought-iron' products through the puddling-furnaces, rolling-mills, and foundries. It was the need to produce stronger and better products in the form of wrought-iron, that drove continued improvements in furnace-technology.

The 'pot-and-stamp' method was an early practice widely used in the 1700s, where the ore was simply washed, and 'stamped-on' before being heated in a 'pot-furnace' where it was stirred continuously.

Different types of heating and re-heating furnaces were used to reheat the ingots of pig-iron from the blast-furnaces into a workable state, so the blacksmith could work on the iron in the foundry.

In 1784 Henry Cort patented a process where the molten liquid was stirred in a 'reverberatory-furnace', which was really the first type of puddling-furnace, where fuel and ore were separated. This was a critical invention, removing the need for charcoal-fuelled furnaces. But his patented process for successfully puddling iron only worked on 'white cast-iron', not the more common 'grey cast-iron' that was found in the Black Country, so further developments were necessary.

An innovative and game-changing process called 'boiling' or 'wet-puddling', where iron-rust contents were repeatedly stirred into the molten-iron, evolved in the Black Country. Then, the 'rabbling-bar' which had a hook, would be repeatedly twisted by the shingler (or puddler) until enough molten iron was gathered, and when he assessed that it was of exactly the right heat and of a perfect 'pasty consistency', it was rolled into a ball or a 'bloom', before being removed from the puddling-furnace and placed into the rollers. Long, red-hot, snake-like coils of iron came out of the roller, with the rollers working as a team. Using special tongs, the rollers placed them back into the roller until they were of a satisfactory shape in the form of long sheets, strips, or even squares. The whole process required immense skill, technique, and of course great strength. 'Puddling' in the great rolling mills was extremely physically demanding, and puddlers were often prematurely worn-out.

As techniques developed, the molten iron was put into a 'shingle', or a forge-train that squeezed it into oblong blocks called 'bar-iron', or alternatively into large sheets or plates, which could then be used for ship-building, bridges, and boilers. From around 1850, giant steam-hammers and drop-forges were introduced, able to cope with the output of thirty puddling-furnaces, and railways and girders were produced in huge quantity in specially-designed mills. Work was still extremely demanding, but these advanced processes undoubtedly reduced the sole dependency on individual human strength.

In those large works with both blast and puddling-furnaces, combustible gas from the blast-furnaces mixed with heated-air produced an intense heat in the puddling-furnace, enough for the iron to be refined satisfactorily, so larger works had better production levels.

Different types of furnaces evolved - 'air-furnaces' produced nuts and bolts, 'annealing-furnaces' produced pipes and tubes, and 'mill-furnaces' produced nails. 'Ball-furnaces' also performed specific roles. Foundry-cupolas, or Cupola-furnaces, a kind of miniature reheating blast-furnace, increasingly replaced some 'reverberatory-furnaces' by the 1850s.

Clearly, the production of iron goods through the use of different furnaces was a complicated process, well beyond the author's understanding. But the fact that iron could be re-heated repeatedly was ideal for the different iron works, especially those not possessing or situated by blast furnaces, as it could be transported in pig-iron ingot form or bar-iron blocks to the foundry, where the shinglers and later the steam-hammers got to work, or onward to the huge rolling-mills which produced sheet-iron in vast quantity, or perhaps to the slitting-mills which cut the sheets into thin strips for the purpose of producing nails. Wrought-iron became widely used on key structures such as bridges, and famous structures such as the Eifel Tower as it could take more tension and pressure and was hence more durable. Cast-iron was more suitable for some products even though it was more brittle. Iron sheets were often corrugated, for the roofing industry.

Finally, any iron products could be protected from rust through the galvanising process, where it was dipped in a boiling hot-zinc liquid. Alternatively, tin-plate was applied to some products. It also became popular to finish some products decoratively, through japanning or enamelling processes. 'Japanning' was a specialised process of finishing, especially to tin products, by applying a decorative heavy black lacquer. This process evolved in South Wales and spread to the Black Country, where the practice became established in Wolverhampton and Bilston. Products could be finished in a green, red, or blue lacquer. A great variety of enamels were also applied to products.

The Bessemer process of creating steel from iron-ore introduced in 1856, was followed by further technological improvements in steel manufacture between then and 1880. This led to a reduction in the dominance of the iron industry, though steel production only outstripped iron production nationally for the first time in 1918, and even then, cast-iron production continued. Steel was created from pig-iron using oxygen to remove impurities. Carbon, manganese, and an alloy-of-iron is added, creating a huge reaction, where the carbon converts the iron into steel. High carbon steels had the advantage that they proved to be extremely strong and durable, and for that reason alone steel production replaced iron production as the 20th-Century progressed.

These complex processes inevitably evolved, modified, and advanced over time, and as local iron-ore resources started to expire, it was increasingly imported to South Staffordshire from as close as Northamptonshire and as far away as from North America and Russia.

Wolverhampton's iron industry was vast and varied, and specialised in every stage of iron production from its extraction from the ground, at one extreme, to the cosmetic finishing and sale of items in shop-windows at the other.

2) WOLVERHAMPTON'S IRON AND BRASS INDUSTRY

Figure 21 – Graiseley area of Wolverhampton in the early-1900s

A) A General Introduction

Wolverhampton's position in the nation's iron trade is evidenced by the fact that most respected local newspapers throughout the Country would seek updates from their 'Wolverhampton Correspondent' regards the state of the iron trade and market. People throughout the nation were routinely updated through these 'State-of-Trade' reports, that often referred to overall sales of pig-iron, bar-iron, and sheet-iron in the Wolverhampton area, and they were notified of the 'degree of distress' when trade slumps occurred, such as early as December 1811 when an un-named but major Wolverhampton iron-master went into liquidation, leaving 1,500 out of work, and perhaps more significantly in 1857, when many furnaces were blown-out and 10,000 people in Wolverhampton were said to be out-of-work, destitute, and reliant on Poor Law handouts, and then yet again in 1877 when many works closed during the 'Great Depression'. Western central Wolverhampton is seen in the photograph above (Figure 21), from an unknown source.

Furthermore, the Black Country 'Iron-masters Quarter-Day' was for some time held at the Lion Hotel in Wolverhampton, after the Dudley Quarter-Day faded more-or-less into obscurity. Iron merchants and colliery owners from across the Country would attend these meetings where contracts and deals were signed, and where accounts were settled, and sales were made, and where general trade was carried on. Inbetween Quarter-Days, trade continued, with buyers often trying to purchase at a lower rate and manufacturers holding out for those of Quarter-Day. Depending on demand, lulls in the market often occurred and profoundly affected production rates.

The largest stock of iron outside London was always kept at the great warehouse of G. and W. Underhill at Castle Street in central Wolverhampton, according to Samuel Griffiths. This was reputed to be the oldest iron-merchant in the Black Country.

Wolverhampton's economy was certainly at one point, largely reliant on the iron trade, with 15,000 people in the town actively working in the metal-trade during the height of the Industrial Revolution, which is more than the combined workforce of Bilston Steelworks (2,500), Round Oak Steel Works (3,000), and The Orb Steel Works in Newport (3,000) at their respective height in the relatively recent times of the 1970s, before recession hit. In the wider Black Country some 46,000 workers were employed in some form of metal manufacture around 1860-70, after which time it gradually started to lose its dominant position in the trade to other geographical areas of the UK, especially from 1880 onwards.

In fact, as far back as 1700, Wolverhampton companies were producing small brass articles in addition to steel-toys and iron products, and there were numerous households producing nails and buckles. The Swedish Government even sent commissioner R.R. Angerstein to Great Britain to examine the iron and steel industry in 1754, noting Wolverhampton's pre-eminence at that point, when he stated: -

"Wolverhampton is one of three towns in England famous for the fabrication of iron and steel-ware."

Angerstein also recognised the critical value of the work of women and children in Wolverhampton's early iron industry, as they carried out what he described as 'time-consuming, finicky-work that required more time than skill'. He said: -

"The main reason the manufacturers in Wolverhampton can undersell the iron and steel products of other manufacturing towns is the great help they get from women and children. As far as filing and forging is concerned, this is done by the master."

Boys in Wolverhampton started work at an earlier age than many of their counterparts elsewhere in the Country. They were generally in some form of employment from the age of seven or eight. Furthermore, as Angerstein observed, girls in the town were heavily involved in both the production of washers, and in the cut-nail trade where they were employed as 'feeders'. They were also heavily involved in the production of steel-toys, so much so that the Birmingham Daily Post proposed in a report of Wolverhampton Industry on 5 February 1866, that the 'old-adage' applied: -

"English children break, what the German children make" be changed to *"The German children can't break, what the girls of Wolverhampton make"*.

The commercial directory for Wolverhampton in 1770 highlighted that the town had at least 30 steel-toy makers.

Wolverhampton's children were also employed in iron works, in foundries, in nailing factories, in galvanising and japanning works, as well as in the coal and iron-ore mines of the town. Their invaluable but for many, costly contribution is worth remembering and recognising when recalling the legacy of the region's industrial revolution.

With the opening of the Birmingham Navigations Canal at that time, the scale of industry vastly increased in the Wolverhampton area, with the first blast-furnaces at Spring Vale in 1780. By 1790,

'Wolverhampton Parish' had 15 of the 21 coke-fueled blast furnaces in the wider Black Country, highlighting a dominant role in the iron trade as the Industrial Revolution was in its early stages, and by 1798 2,000 tonnes of coal were being used each week in Wolverhampton's iron works. For contrast, only 5,000 tonnes of coal were being used across the entire district of Walsall, Wednesbury, Bilston, Tipton, Dudley, Oldbury and West Bromwich. It is self-evident where the concentration of smoke might well have been, as-a-result-of its use in iron-producing processes. To further emphasise the town's dominance, in 1842 six of the nine Black Country iron-works containing blast-furnaces producing 200 tonnes of iron per week lay in the Wolverhampton area, with five of those occupying the top five positions.

The owners of the great iron-works of Wolverhampton - George Thorneycroft, Isaac Jenks, John Lysaght, William and Moses Bayliss, William Hanbury Sparrow and John Sly Sparrow, and William's son William Mander Sparrow, George Jones, George Adams, John Underhill, Edwin Thomas Wright, and of course Sir Alfred Hickman, along with famous Companies such as Chillington and Chubbs, all became household names in the Wolverhampton area. George Thorneycroft and Sir Alfred Hickman of course, both went on to become prominent political figures in the town, and the latter heavily involved with the development of Wolverhampton Wanderers.

These great works produced iron in huge quantity at the industrial revolution peak between 1860-1880, with John Lysaght's Swan Garden and Osier Bed Iron Works producing a combined total of 40,000 tonnes of iron per annum, G.B. Thorneycroft's Shrubbery Iron Works producing 36,000 tonnes per annum, Chillington Iron Works producing 35,000 tonnes per annum, both Parkfield Iron Works and Alfred Hickman's Spring Vale Iron Works (later to become Bilston Steel Works) producing 30,000 tonnes per annum, and Stow Heath Furnaces producing 25,000 tonnes per annum.

The author John Smith wrote chapter eight of the 2005 book 'Towns, Regions and Industries – Urban and Industrial Change in the Midlands 1700–1840', which was titled 'Industrial and Social Change – Wolverhampton Transformed 1700–1840', in which he encapsulated and summarised the importance of Wolverhampton's iron trade at the height of the Industrial Revolution, stating: -

"At maximum capacity in 1871, the Wolverhampton area was capable of producing 20,000 tons of iron per week, nearly one-third of national production".

It is unclear what Smith classifies exactly as the 'Wolverhampton area', but nevertheless it is a very telling and significant point, which somewhat supports the poignant and very relevant earlier-made comment of the writer and traveler William Cobbett in Volume Two of his 1830 book 'Rural Rides', where he alternatively labelled the area in the following terms: -

"In the Iron Country, which Wolverhampton seems to be some sort of central point."

In eastern Wolverhampton, mainly around the Horseley Fields and Monmore Green areas and spreading into the Ettingshall area, there were at least 40 blast-furnaces and around 300 puddling-furnaces, and what was often described as 'a forest of 240 towering, smoking chimneys'. Indeed, the central and eastern Wolverhampton area during the industrial revolution throughout the 1800s, was arguably the main iron-producing area of the Black Country, along with the continuous industrial district between the centres of Wolverhampton and Bilston, running onward to Tipton and Wednesbury.

A Staffordshire-gazetteer described the Horseley Fields area in the following 'impressive' terms: -

"This half-square mile was the most industrious and commercial quarter of the whole of South Staffordshire".

Those who employed large numbers in the peak, mid-to-late-1800s through to the early-1900s included G.B Thorneycroft's Shrubbery Iron Works with 2,000 hands, the Bushbury Engineering

Works with 2,000 hands, Bayliss, Jones and Bayliss's Victoria Iron Works and Monmore Rolling Mills with 2,000 hands, the Chillington Iron Company with 1,500 hands, the Parkfield Iron Company with 1,500 hands, John Lysaght's Swan Garden and Osier Bed Iron Works also with 1,500 hands, Chubbs Lock and Safe Works with 1,200 hands, George Adam's Mars Iron Works with 750 hands, Terence and Charles Clark's Shakespeare Foundry with 600 hands, Isaac Jenks Minerva and Beaver Iron Works with at least 500 hands, and the Sparrow family's Stow Heath Iron Works with up to 500 hands. Hundreds of smaller works operated with as few as 50, but often up to a few hundred hands.

Famous writers such as Elihu Burritt noted around sixty substantial iron, steel, and brass foundries in Wolverhampton in the mid-1800s, and several writers allude to this iron-town, powerhouse status. Samuel Griffiths confirmed its significant position in his 1872 book on the nation's iron trade, when he referred to Wolverhampton as: -

"The Capital of the Iron Trade in the Black Country".

And Scottish-writer John Bartholomew described Wolverhampton in the following 'impressive' terms in his 1887 'Gazetteer of the British Isles': -

"Wolverhampton, known as the 'Metropolis of the Black Country', possesses enormous iron foundries, where articles of every description of ironware are produced".

In a wider context, the Black Country iron industry was vast, and according to H.C. Derby in his 1973 book 'A New Historical Geography of England after 1600', the region was the top producer of iron in England in 1851, of all those areas where coal and iron was produced. Iron for many, understandably defined the Black Country.

Francois Crouzet, in his 1982 book 'The Victorian Economy' highlighted the dominance of two geographical areas regards the production of primary pig iron at the peak of the Industrial Revolution, these being South Wales and the Black Country. In

1830, South Wales produced 278,000 tonnes of pig-iron per annum, the Black Country 212,000 tonnes. In 1839, South Wales produced 454,000 tonnes per annum, the Black Country produced 346,000 tonnes per annum. Then finally, in 1852, South Wales produced 666,000 tonnes of pig-iron, the Black Country 725,000 tonnes. Gradually, after that final date, the iron industry in the Black Country slowly lost its influence and dominance as its natural resources started to run out. In 1854, the Black Country was producing 31.7% of pig-iron in the whole Country, but just 9% by 1880.

Each Black Country town found its own niches within the iron industry, and they evolved and developed over the decades. Wolverhampton's major iron works produced 'primary pig-iron' through the blast-furnaces, and along with Bilston it was also well known for its huge rolling-mills that produced squares, rounds, strips, plates, sheet-iron, nails, armoury, and railways in huge quantity, and the town was also known for the production of railway nuts and bolts, locks, fenders, bridges and girders, chains for shipping and mining, wrought-iron safes, iron fencing, welded-iron tubes, blister-steel springs, corrugated roofing, galvanised products, brass products, tin-plate, and japanned-ware. And later-on, in the 1900s, heavy engineering and of course vehicle and motor-bike manufacture found a significant niche within the town's economy. Wolverhampton's suburb of Wednesfield belatedly became famous for its production of animal-traps, and there were around 100 such works in the Wednesfield area, many of them small operations. Walsall and Wednesbury gained a reputation for their gun-barrels and welded tubes, Darlaston for its railway nuts and bolts, Cradley for its chains and nails, Dudley and Tipton for its cables, iron fencing, and anchor-making, West Bromwich for its metal springs and numerous finished products, and Willenhall of course for its locks.

The Wolverhampton area was famous too for its gun-makers, of which an incredible 431 were registered in the 1800s. Nearly all of these were cottage-industries, mainly operating in family names.

CHAPTER SIX

The Brazier family of Wolverhampton were probably the most-respected gun-lock producer in the Country. 144 of these were substantial enough to have forge operations. Others specialised in gun-sight making, gun-barrel making, boring, finishing, polishing, assembling, filing, or repairing, whilst some produced guns as well as other products.

To highlight Wolverhampton's dominant role in general iron production, the map produced by Chief Landscape archeologist Paul Quigley, from his 2009-10 University of York work titled 'Black Country Historic Landscape Characterisation' is again shown, highlighting the location of the '180 main iron works of the Black Country' during the mid-to-late-1800s (Figure 22). On the map Wolverhampton is top left, Walsall top right, Dudley bottom left, and Sandwell bottom right.

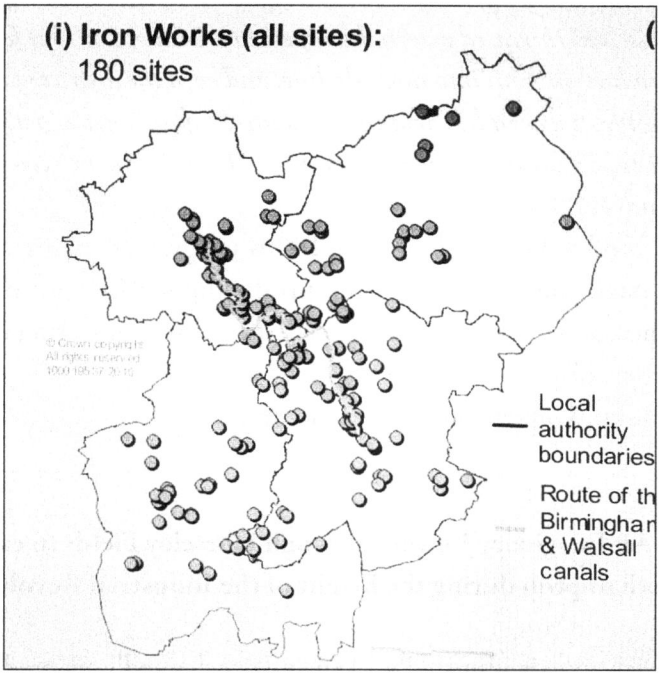

Figure 22 – Paul Quigley's map showing location of
main iron works in Black Country

Whilst the Black Country evolved and thrived because of the demand for finished-iron products, by 1880, after several economic slumps, the 'Great Depression' was to effect and change the economy of the district forever. Wolverhampton, along with other Black Country towns, lost many of its blast-furnaces and iron works in the late-1800s and early-1900s. Richard Trainor, in his 1993 book 'Black Country Elites – The Exercise of Authority in an Industrialised Area 1830-1900' summarised the various economic slumps towards the end of the Industrial Revolution: -

"Even in the 1840s and 1850s there were signs of increasing instability in the region's basic trades, notably during the 1857 financial panic which plunged 23 substantial firms in Wolverhampton alone into bankruptcy. Although the Franco-Prussian War produced a brief local boom, between 1860-1890 the economic performance of the Black Country suffered from declining natural resources, inefficient methods, and increased external competition. Mineral output fell, pig iron production went into rapid decline, and even the district's famous wrought iron was in less demand as South Staffordshire experienced serious trade slumps in the early and late-1860s, mid-to-late-1870s, and mid-1880s".

As the 1800s ended and the 1900s progressed, many of the older established primary metal-producing works went out-of-existence, and newer, more advanced, specialist engineering works took their place.

'Smoky Wolverhampton' was no more.

B) An Imaginary Journey through Horseley Fields in east Wolverhampton during the height of the Industrial Revolution

This notion is admittedly taken and unashamedly adapted from an article on the Wolverhampton History Website, produced by Bev Parker. Apologies Bev.

The iron works of Horseley Fields were closely packed. The following description of the two-and-a-half-mile journey from Portobello on the Willenhall Road to the town centre of Wolverhampton, journeying through its eastern aspects when it was at its industrial peak around 1850-1860, attempts to describe in vivid detail, the scene that people travelling into the town on this route would have witnessed: -

"Leaving Willenhall, around three miles from Wolverhampton, one would first pass the Bull Pleck Coal Pits and a few rows of small, ramshackle terraced houses at Portobello, and a little further on the Cleveland Colliery which was an iron-stone pit. Then to the left, stood the Moseley Hole Furnaces with its adjacent colliery, with the Osier Bed blast-furnaces nearby. A number of spoil-banks belonging to smaller collieries, were visible to the right as you entered eastern Wolverhampton's prime coal-mining district, and for the next mile the adjacent and adjoining collieries of Deans, Barnfield, Bowman's Harbour, and then Old Heath would appear one after the other on the right-hand side of the Willenhall Road, stretching across a wide area towards Heath Town and then towards central Wolverhampton, whilst the profitable and adjoining Stow Heath and Chillington Collieries with their many spoil-banks, were situated on the left-hand side of the road. One-hundred pits were sunk for coal and iron-ore at these large, adjacent collieries. Stow Heath Iron Work's four blast-furnaces would be visible in operation distantly, to the left.

The forest of chimneys and furnaces belonging to Wolverhampton's vast central iron works would be seen straight ahead as one approached its eastern industrial quarter at 'Lower Horseley Fields', now less than a mile from its grand, central, commercial streets, and on a slight incline. The whole iron-quarter reverberated and shook to a wall-of-sound emanating from its huge iron works, as furnaces and steam-hammers operated in the foundries, forges, and rolling-mills, and an acrid, chemical, burning smell filled the air. The consuming atmosphere would have left a distinct impression upon the visitor, with flashing, combusting 'blasts-of-fire' catapulted into the sky from the blast-furnaces and puddling-furnaces, whilst lingering, sooty, clouds of smoke from the forest of chimneys hung grimly and menacingly across the whole area, reminiscent of an imaginary Doomsday smog, or perhaps of a hundred steam-trains leaving a train-station at the same time. When approaching the area at night, the view might have resembled some giant bonfire-night party, with fire lighting up the sky and the noisiest of noisy fireworks reverberating in human ears.

Just off Hickman Avenue, to the left of the Willenhall Road, and behind several rows of terraced houses, was the impressive Chillington Iron Works, with 4 blast-furnaces, 56 puddling-furnaces, 6 rolling-mills and forges, and many tall chimneys. It was said that the flames would be interspersed with dark clouds each time a furnace was charged, and an intense orange glow would be seen when a furnace was dropped at the end of the day. In 1839, it was producing 16,600 tonnes of iron per annum, making it the most productive iron works in the whole Black Country at that point, and at its peak it produced 35,000 tonnes of iron per annum.

The furnaces and chimneys of the vast Victoria Iron Works of Bayliss, Jones, and Bayliss, along with those of the Monmore Rolling Mills, and other smaller works of Monmore Green may have been visible in the distance behind it.

As the journey progressed, on the right-hand side of the Willenhall Road, between Colliery Road and Griffon Street, were the New Griffon Iron Works with its forges and lime kilns, and next to it the Cleveland Iron Works with its 9 puddling-furnaces. It specialised in horse-shoe production. The British Oil Works was set further back and was a smoky operation and may just about have been visible in the distance on the right, over the spoil banks of Old Heath Colliery.

Moving a little further towards the town centre along the Willenhall Road, on the right-hand side, and just off Swan Street, was the mighty Swan Garden Iron Works which had 30 puddling-furnaces and 7 rolling-mills, whilst the next street on the right quickly led to the setback and equally impressive Osier Bed Iron Works, also known as the Horseley Fields Iron Works, which had 26 puddling-furnaces, 6 mills and forges, and many smoking chimneys. This works was owned initially by the Sparrow family, but later by Isaac Jenks, who also purchased Swan Garden and employed 1,500 workers to operate the adjoining operations in the 1870s, producing 35,000 tons of iron per annum.

Moving a little further along the main Willenhall Road, but before the railway bridge and to the right, stood Isaac Jenks Beaver Iron and Steel Works with its 14 puddling-furnaces and 5 tall chimneys, with John Neve's Union Iron Works that produced cut-nails, tucked in just behind it. Both were busy operations.

Directly opposite, to the left of the Willenhall Road, sat the Thorneycroft family's sprawling, mighty Shrubbery Iron Works with its towering, smoking chimneys. The works was split by Lower Walsall Street into two sites. By 1873, it had 74 puddling-furnaces plus heating and annealing furnaces, 3 large steam-hammers, and several large rolling-mills with forges, producing 36,000 tonnes of iron per annum. This was one of the town's leading works, employing 2,000 workers at its peak, and it created a wall of sound close to the road, as forges dropped, and furnaces discharged. A circle of puddling-furnaces and tall chimneys could be seen close to the road by passers-by, and dark, smoke-begrimed figures darted busily around the furnaces, like bees feeding the Queen.

The journey then passed under the railway bridge, up into 'Upper Horseley Fields'. The final section was equally industrious as that that had preceded it. Wulfruna Coal was, and still is located immediately to the left of the main road, adjacent to a busy canal wharf where coal and iron-stone would be continuously unloaded from a procession of barges from the nearby mines, and adjoining it was the impressive Minerva Iron Works, with its 21 puddling-furnaces and 4 mills and forges. The road would shake and vibrate as the forges operated, and deep thuds could be heard for some distance around, whilst its 15 large chimneys belched out continual black clouds of smoke. Owned *by Isaac Jenks, Minerva was said to have produced 80% of all UK steel exported to USA in 1870, such was the high quality and reputation of its steel products.*

Next to Minerva were several smaller but equally industrious works - the Bridge Iron and Engine Works, Atlas Iron Works, and Crosbie Coatings, whilst set behind them, located on Lower Walsall Street were the Crown Nail Works, one of the most successful nail-shops in the region, and the Brunswick Iron Works, as well as a Varnishing Works, and a Gas Works that was later to become established as BOC – the British Oxygen Company.

Directly opposite Minerva, across the Willenhall Road, stood the Griffon Iron Works, producing edge-tools and which had numerous smoking chimneys of various sizes. Immediately next to the Griffon Iron Works sat the Clark family's impressive Shakespeare Foundry, that employed 600 workers at its industrial height, and which specialised in finished hollow-ware. It was the largest foundry in the region. Just behind it, was the equally-productive Crane Foundry, as well as a large Chemical Works and a Gas Works. Nearby, the Union Mill and Albion Mill Warehouses lined the canal, with its old flour mill, and the old Wolverhampton Workhouse stood alongside the busy Wulfruna Canal Wharf. Its residents were often tasked with breaking stones and levelling out the spoil-banks of the nearby coal-mines, such as at Old Heath Colliery.

Back on the main Willenhall Road, and situated in buildings on either side of it, were the Albion Iron Works, the St James Iron Works, and the St James Brass Foundry. Chubbs Locks was also based in this area from 1836. Although there were numerous small iron works and foundries all around, these works were the last substantially-sized operations one would see, with rows of small, incredibly cramped houses scattered all around, along dimly-lit and often out-of-view court-yards and streets, before the impressive town centre streets welcomed the traveller to the considerably cleaner and healthier commercial heart of Wolverhampton. Out of darkness cometh light!

And there the journey ends".

C) The Iron Works of Wolverhampton –
a summary of operations

The following iron-works, varying in size from substantial to small, totalling around an incredible two-hundred and sixty operations, were all active at some point either during the period of the late-1700s, but mainly at some stage through the 1800s Industrial Revolution, or in some cases during the early-1900s. Many of them worked not just with iron and belatedly steel, but often with tin-plate, zinc, or brass. A great range of iron products were made in the works, all within two miles of the town centre.

Wolverhampton's thriving iron industry certainly declined greatly in the late-1800s, probably more markedly than in neighbouring towns, and the town became overall less prominent in the Black Country iron-producing sector. Though Alfred Hickman's Spring Vale Iron Works continued to thrive, and Bilston Steel Works (as it became known as) evolved to become the Black Country's biggest metal producing operation in the mid-to-late 1900s. It was said that 50,000 people lined the streets of Wolverhampton for the funeral when Alfred Hickman passed away, such a prominent role had he played in the lives of many of the town's residents. The metal industry economy suffered peaks and severe dips, but at its industrial peak, iron, brass, tin-plate, and galvanising works of varying sizes were scattered all around the eastern and southern side of Wolverhampton.

Bilston itself was also host to a huge number of iron works, such as Stonefield Iron Works, Bovereux Iron Works, Barbor's Field Iron Works, Albert Iron Works, Bankfield Iron Works, and Bradley Iron Works. For arguments sake, such works are omitted from the following section unless they were geographically located roughly midway between the two towns, such as at Ettingshall or Priestfield, and then 'only' when they gave their address as 'Wolverhampton'. Works at Wednesfield are included in the list.

Finally, immense credit must be given to the Wolverhampton History Website, particularly Bev Parker who has researched the history of the iron trade in the town in great detail, and from which a good proportion of the following information is gleaned, but most is from my own research.

The following 'directory of works' is separated firstly into those of the main Industrial Revolution period between 1760-1900, and then secondly from the 1900's onwards, though there is a little inevitable overlap of both periods involving some companies. Most research is based on the Industrial Revolution period, so those firms listed after 1900 are only larger, well-known works.

Iron-based works during Industrial Revolution of 1760-1900

1) **Chillington Iron Works (The Chillington Iron Company)** situated mid-way between Horseley Fields and Monmore Green, was founded around 1780 when it had one blast furnace, but it became a substantial operation in 1822 when it was jointly owned by John Barker, James Foster, and George Jones in creating 'The Chillington Iron Company'. It was the first major iron works in Wolverhampton, and by 1829 Chillington Iron Works had 4 cold-blast-furnaces situated just east of Cross Street at Lower Horseley Fields, as well as 6 rolling-mills and forges. Its giant steam-hammers worked at ten blows a minute, day and night. By 1839 it was producing 16,600 tons of iron per annum through its blast-furnaces and 56 puddling-furnaces, making it the most productive of any iron works in the entire Black Country. At its peak, it employed up to 1,500 workers, a combination of iron-workers and miners, and it received huge orders for the manufacture of railways, such as from the 'Great Western Railway' who signed an order in 1846 for 17,500 tonnes of railways to be delivered

over three years. As well as producing pig-iron through its blast-furnaces, Mr Barker ensured that Chillington was one of, if not 'the first works' in the Black Country to create steel using the 'Bessemer' process, with an experiment on 19 September 1856, where he successfully heated and rolled a bar out to a thin sheet at one end of the rolling-mill, before being rolled again and annealed, after which it was tested by a tobacco-box maker in the town, who stated - 'a better piece of iron I have never worked'. This followed Bessemer's famous speech a month earlier at Cheltenham on 11 August 1856, where he released his famous paper called 'The manufacture of iron and steel without fuel'. This innovation was typical of the Chillington Company who were always at the cutting edge of metalurgic technology. In the 1860s, Chillington's blast-furnaces were demolished and replaced with 5 more powerful ones capable of hot-blast, and the company's overall output increased to over 35,000 tonnes of iron per annum. At this point the works also had 3 forge-trains, and 7 mills, including 3 mills for rolling sheet-iron, 2 mills for rolling nail-rods and merchant iron, and 2 mills for rolling hoop-iron. Chillington was fortunate to own 110 acres of land immediately adjacent to the iron works, containing some of the richest seams of coal and iron-ore in Staffordshire, where over 100 shafts were sunk. It also purchased 6 locomotives to transport coal and iron-ore to the works and onward to the canal system, as well as connecting Chillington to its other furnaces and collieries at nearby Moseley Hole, Bunker's Hill, Rosehill, Merrill's Hole, and Bull Pleck. In all, by 1872, 'The Chillington Iron Company' owned a vast 750 acres of land across the eastern Wolverhampton district, and operated a total of 6 blast-furnaces, 108 puddling-furnaces, 17 mills and forges, several steam-hammers and squeezers, around 50 steam-engines, and 65 canal-barges at its eastern

Wolverhampton works. Following the 'Great Depression', the company opened an 'Edge-Tool and Horse-shoe Works' in 1876, becoming the largest producer of horseshoes in the world, and in 1881 the company decided to build a plant to build cheap steel, as a that time only nearby Minerva Iron and Steel Works, and the Patent Shaft and Axletree Company at Wednesbury produced steel in the region. Nevertheless, the blast-furnaces were blown out for a final time in 1884, when its natural mineral sources had all but expired, and the Chillington Iron Company's shareholders voted to liquidate the loss-making company in January 1885. A small group of workers are photographed below (Figure 23).

Figure 23 – Iron workers at Chillington Works, early 1900s.

2) **Shrubbery Iron Works** at Horseley Fields was founded in 1824 by Edward Thorneycroft, who was later joined by his more illustrious brother George Thorneycroft, who undertook a prominent role in its development. In 1843, they patented a machine that was capable of rolling, squeezing, or compressing puddled balls of iron, and in 1848 it was producing huge sheets of iron weighing 1680lbs, or around a tonne. When the much-loved and revered George Thorneycroft died in 1851, more than 1,000 workers there contributed to a bronzed,

cast-iron monument. Thereafter, the company continued under the ownership of G.B. Thorneycroft and Co for many years, though run mainly by Edward Bagnall Thorneycroft. This vast operation was situated off Willenhall Road in large buildings either side of Lower Walsall Street, and in the 1850s it contained 44 puddling-furnaces and several rolling-mills and forges. It continued to expand, producing an impressive 36,000 tons of iron per annum by 1873. It produced high-quality wrought-iron, including huge quantities of railway-axles and railways for which it became renowned, as well as shells and armour-plating for use in the Crimean War. It took over bullet-iron production from the Old Bradley Works owned by the late John Wilkinson, and in conjunction with one of the other great Horseley Fields iron works close by, Swan Garden Iron Works, it produced the largest iron rolling-plates, rounds, and squares in Staffordshire. The northern half was where most of the iron was produced, as that was where most of the furnaces and many chimneys were situated within the foundry. With the 'Great Depression', when local natural resources expired, the cost of producing iron became uneconomical, and the Thorneycroft Company very reluctantly closed the works in 1877, throwing over 1,000 iron-workers out of work. All in all, 2,000 hands had been employed in their iron works and collieries, but this signalled the end of the Thorneycroft family's long involvement in Wolverhampton's iron industry. They sold off all the existing plant machinery, advertised in the South Wales Daily News on 21 January 1882. The stock for sale was split into what were called 'Shrubbery's northern and southern sections'. At that point, the 'northern section' consisted of 60 puddling, scrap-pile, and mill-furnaces, 2 large steam-hammers, 4 metal helves, 14 forge and mill-trains, 3 powerful roll-lathes, refinery with blast-engine, cast and wrought iron cranes, 8 powerful condensing beam-engines, and 26 'furnace and firing' boilers. The southern so-called 'Stour-Valley' section (adjacent to the Stour-Valley railway terminus that served the works) consisted of 14 puddling and ball-furnaces, as well as heating and annealing-furnaces, five-ton steam-hammer, metal helve, 2 forge-trains, boiler-plate trains, girder-mill trains, merchant-bar trains, 2 condensing beam-engines, and 10 'furnace and firing' boilers. Many buildings and a lot of stock were also included in the sale. So overall, the 'mighty' Shrubbery Iron Works, was closing-down with its 6 huge, rolling-mills containing more than 80 furnaces, including 74 puddling-type furnaces as well as heating and annealing-furnaces, 3 large steam-hammers, 5 metal helves, around 20 twenty forge-trains, 3 roll-lathes, refinery with powerful blast-engine, 10 condensing beam-engines, and 36 'furnace and firing' boilers. An incredible amount of stock. Thereafter, in the early-1880s, the furnaces and chimneys were demolished in the northern half. It was later used by vehicle manufacturer A.J.S. and then by battery-producer 'Ever-Ready'. In the 1880s, the southern half of the works was taken over by the 'Wolverhampton Corrugated Iron Company', formed by brothers John and Joseph Jones, who relocated their operation from nearby Graiseley. They vacated the site by 1905, moving to Ellesmere Port, but the works carried on as an iron-producing works until 1912. The British Oxygen Company (B.O.C.) then purchased the southern section of the works and are still located there today.

3) **Victoria Iron Works (Monmore Green Chain Works, and later The Victoria Iron Company, then Bayliss, Jones, and Bayliss)** at Monmore Green was founded in 1826 by William Bayliss. It evolved and developed from a busy but small foundry and rolling mill into a huge operation specialising in the production of a huge range of finished metal products. His brother Moses Bayliss soon joined the operation, and from 1854 the works was known as the 'Monmore Green Chain Works', when it

specialised in making huge chains for shipping and naturally also for for mining operations and industry. With Moses knowledge from his previous operation, it commenced making heavy-duty nuts and bolts for railways in huge quantity, as well as railways themselves. It also produced a huge amount of armoury. Edwin Jones joined the company in 1859, and he ran its London office very successfully, under the name of Bayliss, Jones, and Bayliss. Spread over a large area it had a number of drop-forges and a large foundry with massey-hammers, and a number of furnaces specifically designed for producing nuts and bolts, as well as many heating and cupola-furnaces. There were also large pattern and finishing shops. The adjoining 'Wolverhampton Furnaces', with 3 blast-furnaces, may have worked in conjunction with the works as they were virtually attached, though separately owned. In 1893, the firm purchased the adjoining Monmore Green Rolling Mills, which at this point had 11 puddling-furnaces, a powerful blast-furnace, and 3 huge rolling-mills. And that same year it received an order from the Indian Government for a 120 miles of iron fencing to run adjacent to its new railway lines. A new stack and mill were built at the works in at the turn of the century, and it continued to produce railways, and railway springs and nuts in quantity, along with huge anchors and cables. At its peak in the late-1800s and early-1900s, 2,000 workers were employed here. The advertisement below is for the 'Chain Works' (Figure 24), with a photograph of this huge works below that (Figure 25), courtesy of Britainfromabove.org.

Figure 24– Advertisement for Monmore Green Chain Works in the 1850s.

'IRONOPOLIS'

Figure 25 – Photograph of Victoria Iron Works, Wolverhampton, early-1900s

4) **Monmoor Green Rolling Mills (Monmore Rolling Mills)** was founded in 1826 by Mr Edwin Thomas Wright and Mr David North, but from the 1850s the works were managed by the revered George Adams, owner of Mars Iron Works. The works was situated directly across Cable Street from the Victoria Iron Works. This was also a substantially-sized works containing three large rolling-mills, forges, including a large steam-hammer, and 11 puddling-furnaces. It became particularly famous for its 'Monmore boiler-plates'. It closed in 1892, but a year later it was acquired by Bayliss, Jones, and Bayliss, and merged with the adjoining Victoria Works at which point it also possessed a powerful blast-furnace. The works continued to prosper well into the 1900s. The huge rolling-mills can be seen to the left of the canal, in the image below (Figure 26), courtesy of Britainfromabove.org, with the Imperial Tube Works to the right of the canal, and the Mitre Iron Works situated where the canal joins the Bilston Road towards the cooling tower. The town centre of Wolverhampton is just beyond the cooling-tower. The photograph below, from the mid-1900s, highlights just how industrial the town was

at this point, with the tightly-packed residential streets of All Saints seen in the top left-hand corner, the fringes of the town centre to the top right behind the cooling tower, and other smaller iron works and scrap-yards adjoining the Bilston Road.

Figure 26 – Monmore Green Rolling Mills, early-1900s

5) **The Parkfield Furnaces and Iron Works (Parkfield Iron Company)** with its 5 hot- blast-furnaces was a large operation founded in the 1820s by John Underhill and 'The Parkfield Iron Company', and he was soon joined by John Bishton. In 1852, it was taken over by Mr Edward Bagnall Dimmach, and managed with the help of his son-in-law Henry Marten Esquire. Situated a mile from both Wolverhampton and Bilston, it produced around 10,000 tonnes of pig-iron per annum in 1839, making it one of the top dozen producers of pig-iron in the Black Country, and by 1865 it was producing 30,000 tonnes of pig-iron through its furnaces, forges, and rolling-mills, making

it one of the most productive in the area. It was a key producer of boiler, bridge, and boat-plates, and angle, guide, bar, strip, and hoop-iron. It was estimated that at its peak, it employed 1,500 workers, though that included its iron-workers and its own miners too. It was surrounded by collieries including Parkfield Colliery, Cockshutts Colliery, Rough Hills Colliery, the 3 Ettingshall collieries of Ettingshall Park, Ettingshall Lodge, and Ettingshall, as well as Moorfields Colliery, and Lanesfield Colliery. It had its own two locomotives to bring coal from the nearby pits and being the largest group of furnaces in South Staffordshire, it reputedly drew many visitors to observe operations and to see gases drawn off. It was purchased by a group of London and Sheffield businessmen in 1881 with the purpose of converting the pig-iron into steel, but it closed in 1887 and the works was demolished not long afterwards. Today, there is no visible reminder whatsoever, that this famous works once stood proudly in the town.

6) **The Stow Heath Furnaces and Iron Works** was founded around 1788. It was one of the towns first major iron works, situated on the edge of the eastern part of the town, just west of Stowheath Lane and below Thornton Road at the northern edge of East Park, which of course was only constructed later-on. Owned in the early-1800s by the prominent Wolverhampton and Bilston iron-master brothers William Hanbury Sparrow and John Sly Sparrow, it operated with 4, or possibly later with 5 blast-furnaces, 26 puddling-furnaces, and 3 rolling-mills at its industrial peak. In 1839, it was producing 12,750 tonnes of iron per annum, making it the 6th most productive iron-producing operation in the Black Country at that point in time, and Wolverhampton's second most productive operation. Sadly, there appear to be no photographs of this works in the archives, and there are no visible signs left today of its existence, but it must have employed several hundred workers

and covered a substantial area, lying adjacent to the profitable and rich mining land of Stow Heath Colliery and Chillington Colliery which over-lapped.

7) **Swan Garden Iron Works** at Horseley Fields was founded in the early-1800s, but it exchanged hands several times. In 1843 Ironmaster Thomas Murray Gladstone patented his process there using a machine for cutting or shearing iron and other metals. The works, which covered an area of 13,000 square yards, contained a forge and 30 puddling-furnaces, as well as dedicated rolling-mills producing sheet-iron squares and rounds, boiler-plates, rail-iron (railways), and tin-plate. Swan Garden became famous for production of iron-plate, and later galvanised sheet-steel, at its rolling-mills. It was registered as being owned by Mr E.T. White in 1851, but in 1858 George Thorneycroft and Company, who also owned the nearby Shrubbery Iron Works, purchased Swan Garden. However, it closed in 1877 during the 'Great Depression', but was re-opened in 1878 by John Lysaght, and by 1883 it operated with several rolling-mills, employing 700 workers and producing 25,000 tonnes of iron per annum, much of it iron-sheet that was exported to Australia. Lysaght also purchased the nearby Osier Bed Iron Works and between them they had 24 sheet-mills in operation by 1896, but that year he decided to move production from both works to his giant, new 'Orbs Works' at Newport in South Wales, due to a lack of space to expand in Wolverhampton, and due to the cost-advantage of a coastal operation. This move was complete by 1902. He moved equipment from 13 rolling-mills at his two Wolverhampton plants to Newport, which eventually had over 30 rolling-mills. A few hundred of his 1,500 workers at Swan Garden and Osier Bed moved to Wales, but there was no offer of work there for the 'puddlers'. He sold Swan Garden to a Mr A.H. Marks in 1911 and some of

the empty rolling-mills were converted to a foundry under an agreement with Lysaght to supply chilled cast-iron rolls to his new Orbs Works. The works stood empty for a number of years, before being purchased by Qualcast in 1953. Two men are seen standing by a steam-hammer in the photograph below (Figure 27), courtesy of Wolverhampton City Archives

Figure 27 – Workers at a steam-hammer, Swan Garden Iron Works, Wolverhampton early-1900s

8) **Osier Bed Iron Works (Horseley Fields Iron and Tin-plate Works, or the Osier Bed Company)** has a distinguished history, having been founded in the early-1800s and built adjacent to Old Heath Colliery. It was established as a major works in 1843 by William Hanbury Sparrow and his brother John Sly Sparrow, though John died young. William's son William Mander Sparrow later joined the Company. The works was initially involved in the production of finished iron-ware and tin-plate, employing around 300 workers. They had 3 blast-furnaces producing pig-iron at this point, but it appears that these were situated away from the main works, a mile along the Willenhall Road at Stowmans Lane, which later became Stowheath Lane. The Sparrow's, through 'The Osier Bed Company', also owned the nearby Stow Heath Furnaces, which also produced pig-iron through its blast-furnaces there. An advert from the Staffordshire Advertiser on 24 July 1847 highlighted that Osier Bed Iron Works was offered for sale at that point. The equipment included a forge with hammer and rolls used in the production of tin-iron, a sheet-mill and 2 pairs of planishing-rolls, 2 tin-mills with a five-and-a-half-ton steam-hammer, 9 puddling-furnaces and one ball-furnace, 6 tin-plate-furnaces, 2 annealing-furnaces, 2 scaling-furnaces, 1 heating-furnace, and 1 annealing-sheet-iron-furnace. There was also a sheet-mill with 2 sheet-iron-furnaces, 1 heating-furnace, and 1 annealing-furnace - totaling 26 puddling-type furnaces. There was a large iron foundry on site and included in the sale were 4 steam-engines, 5 iron coal-boats, tin-houses, washroom, stables, and a dozen houses for essential workmen. The works was capable-of-producing 15,000 tonnes of iron per annum, but the site evolved over the next few decades, and at its peak in 1873, Osier Bed had 4 blast-furnaces, 26 puddling-furnaces, and 6 rolling-mills and forges. But it

ran at an operating loss, resulting in Mr W.H. Sparrow and his partners deciding to close the works in 1878, throwing 700 men out of work during 'The Great Depression'. Two years later in 1880, Irishman John Lysaght bought the works, initially employing just 400 hands, but he then built an additional 6 rolling-mills here and at Swan Garden, which he also acquired. Together, the two works were-capable-of producing 40,000 tonnes of iron per annum. 800 workers were employed here and 700 at Swan Garden - a total of 1,500 hands. Lysaght died in 1895 and workers funded a memorial statue that still stands in East Park. In 1901 the company transferred production to Orb Iron Works, Newport when some workers transferred to Wales. Parts of the works were demolished in 1906, but in 1912 a new owner re-opened the works with 16 new puddling-furnaces and several rolling-mills, to produce bar-iron.

9) **Minerva Iron and Steel Works** at Horseley Fields was founded by Isaac Jenks in 1849, and in its early days the works produced just 60 tonnes of iron per week. It operated with 13 puddling-furnaces, but by 1867 it had expanded considerably, possessing a forge, 21 puddling-furnaces, and 4 rolling-mills, as well as four-storey warehouses. 80% of the UK's steel exported to the United States was made here around 1870, as the 'Minerva-steel' brand was considered at that point to be of the finest quality and even preferred by the Americans to Sheffield steel. At its height Minerva employed up to 500 workers, and it produced all sorts of iron and steel goods, with its 'spring-steel', mainly railway springs and rolled-taper-break-lever bars being a speciality. The works also produced cast and blister steel, merchant bars and sheets, and wire rods. Although the works were expanded in 1902, trade continued to slump, and it closed in 1914, when its furnaces and chimneys were demolished.

10) **The Mars Iron Works** was situated at Ettingshall, midway between the centres of Wolverhampton and Bilston, and was founded in 1866 by George Adams. Through its 3 blast-furnaces, 12 puddling-furnaces, and 3 rolling-mills, it produced primary pig-iron and high quality galvanised bar-iron and iron sheets, as well as iron plates, rounds, squares, and strips, amongst other goods, and employed 750 hands. It managed to continue through the 'great depression', and by 1896 it was operating with 6 sheet-mills. It eventually closed in 1925, with 500 thrown out of work. An advert for the works is shown below (Figure 28). A photograph of rollers at the works, is shown at the start of the chapter (Figure 20).

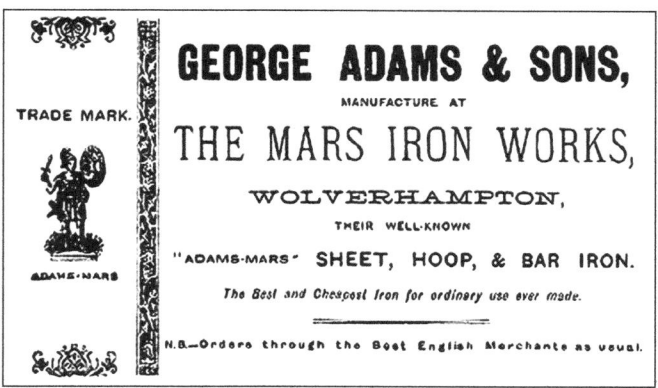

Figure 28 – Advert for Mars Iron Works, Wolverhampton

11) **The Spring Vale Furnaces and Iron Works (later Alfred Hickman, then Stewarts and Lloyds)** was founded in 1768, situated in the Ettingshall area between Wolverhampton and Bilston but usually classed as being in Bilston, which it was nearer to. However, it often gave its address as 'Wolverhampton', especially in national directories, and sometimes as 'Sedgley' for instance when owners James and John Broad were declared as bankrupt in 1833. Spring Vale Furnaces originally comprised of 3 brick-built blast-

furnaces, and owned by Jones and Murcott it rapidly expanded, possessing an impressive 68 puddling, ball, or mill-furnaces by 1862, but in 1865 John Jones went into bankruptcy owing £260,000 of debt, though the works were carried on under the name of Murcott, Wright and Co, until Alfred Hickman purchased the site in 1866 and amalgamated it with the adjoining works, that were to become known as the Staffordshire Steel and Ingot Works. The two works were based on the same site comprising some 200 acres of land, but until then owned by two different owners. Hickman amalgamated the two works and built 6 new blast-furnaces that produced just shy of 30,000 tonnes of iron per annum in 1880, still slightly less tonnage than some of the central Wolverhampton works. With the discovery and development of the 'Bessemer' process for the manufacture of steel, Spring Vale (Bilston) Steelworks evolved and developed greatly, producing steel from around 1883. Under Hickman, as the 1900s progressed, the works clearly became the prominent metal works in the Wolverhampton area.

12) **The Staffordshire Steel and Ingot Iron Works (later Alfred Hickman)** was founded in the mid-1800s and formed the second half of the site purchased in 1882 by Alfred Hickman, and then amalgamated with the adjoining Spring Vale Furnaces. The whole site, which became known simply as Alfred Hickman, and later Bilston Steel Works, became the major works in the Wolverhampton area in the 1900s. It produced galvanised steel sheets and other goods using the Bessemer process from around 1883.

13) **The Shakespeare Foundry** at Horseley Fields was founded by Terence and Charles Clark in 1795, and it employed 600 workers by 1881. It was renowned for being the largest hollow-ware foundry in the district. They pioneered and patented production of enamelled cast iron-ware that eliminated lead

and any other potentially hazardous materials, and it was also a general iron-founder that specialised in the manufacture of tinned, cast-hollow-ware, including what was claimed to be the first enamel-coated iron or brass bath. Casting processes using moulds to produce finished items was the speciality of this operation, and the works had re-heating furnaces and foundry cupolas to continuously produce molten liquid-iron, for use in its moulds. The atmospheric photograph below (Figure 29), from Wolverhampton City Archives shows workers posing briefly, including a young boy stirring boiling liquid iron.

Figure 29 – Workers at Shakespeare Foundry, Wolverhampton, early-1900s

14) **The Griffon Iron Works (The Griffon Edge-Tool Works) (later Edmund Vaughan Stampings, Falcon Iron Works)** was founded by William Edwards in the 1840s. This works was also situated along Willenhall Road in Horseley Fields, and with its numerous chimneys, including three towering ones, it generated a smoky sight. It had re-heating furnaces and foundry-cupolas to create molten iron to pour into its

many moulds. The site was taken over by 'Edmund Vaughan Stampings', and later became known as the Falcon Iron Works. Like Shakespeare Iron Works, which sat immediately next to it, it too specialised in finished iron-ware. Garden and edge-tools were one of its most famous products including all sorts of hammers to use in quarries and mines, railway tools, horse-shoes, enamel products, and many drop-forge products and stampings. Up to 400 hands were employed. Edmund Vaughan Stampings later took over the site, when it was named the Falcon Works, producing drop-forgings for motor cycles predominantly.

15) **The New Griffon Iron Works (later Vulcan Manufacturing Company)** was purchased by William Edwards and Sons in the 1870s, and situated at Lower Horseley Fields, off what is now Colliery Road. With its forges and lime-kilns, it specialised for long periods in the production of hollow-ware, edge-tools, horse-shoes, railways, and mining products. It also specialised in the production of wrought-iron wheel-barrows. It was a fairly, large operation with forging-shops possessing heavy steam-hammers weighing four tons, as well as grinding and polishing-shops. It was noted to have had 180 employees, a number that almost certainly grew over time.

16) **The Victoria Iron Works** was another operation owned by William Edwards and Sons. This operation was based on the town's Dudley Road, until around the 1840s when the operation appears to have out-grown its base there, and the move to the Willenhall Road site took place. This was the second operation in the town to adopt the 'Victoria' label. It appears he chose to relocate to Willlenhall Road after the company won a Government contract to supply horseshoes. But it was still primarily an edge-tool supplier for the mining industry and railways. William Edwards later became Mayor of Wolverhampton in 1874.

17) **The Beaver Iron and Steel Works** was founded by Isaac Jenks at Horseley Fields in 1857. This works possessed 3 sheet-mills and 14 puddling-furnaces and was distinctive with its 2 tall furnaces and 5 tall chimneys. The works produced of a wide variety of goods such as metal springs for railways, but all types of iron and steel products were made, as well as large amounts of sheet-metal. Jenks also owned the nearby Minerva Iron Works. After a period of inactivity, Messrs John Lysaght Ltd re-opened the works in 1891 when over 100 workers were initially taken on.

18) **The Britannia Boiler Tube Works and Patent Iron Tube Works** at Ettingshall, founded by Edwin Lewis and Sons in 1825, was a large operation specialising in the production of all types of iron tubes for a wide range of industrial and mechanical use, one of several firms specialising in this field of iron production. It possessed 13 puddling-furnaces, several other furnaces, and an iron-sheet-mill and a bar-mill.

19) **The Millfields Iron Works** was an early-1800s operation, that sometimes classed itself as a Bilston company and sometimes as a Wolverhampton company, as it was situated between the two towns but closer to Bilston. It registered as a Wolverhampton company with the Iron and Steel Institute in 1872. It contained 2 forges and 3 mills, including a rolling-mill that had around 20 puddling-furnaces and a large shingling-hammer. 28 people were killed here following a huge boiler explosion in 1862, due to a lack of maintenance of the old boiler by the new owner Thomas Rose, who re-opened the works with just 40 employees.

20) **The Priestfield Furnaces** were founded in 1811 by Samuel Fereday and were situated at Ward Street, Ettingshall. This was one of the earliest iron works in the district, that sometimes registered itself as a Bilston works, but usually as a Wolverhampton works, such as with the Iron and Steel

Institute in 1872. The works, like many in this region, were situated half way between Wolverhampton and Bilston in what was a continuous industrial zone. Around 1839 the works were taken over by William Ward and Sons when it possessed 3 blast-furnaces, producing nearly 10,000 tonnes of pig-iron per annum in 1839, making it one of the top dozen producing iron-works in the Black Country.

21) **The New Priestfield Furnaces** were built by William Ward and Sons who owned the original, nearby site. They constructed 2 new blast-furnaces further along Ward Street from the original Priestfield Furnaces, in the mid-1800s. Both works were in full operation for a period, meaning that the Company operated 5 blast-furnaces to produce primary pig-iron.

22) **The Capponfield Furnaces and Iron Works** were situated at Lanesfield, which is closer to Bilston, but the works usually classed itself as a Wolverhampton works. This was an early iron works in the area, dating back to the late-1700s. They were owned by Smith, Read and Co in 1805, but from 1839 owned by John Bagnall and Sons, before passing to the Chillington Company. 3 blast-furnaces were built in 1867, and the nearby works also contained 16 puddling-furnaces and rolling-mills. A variety of castings were made on site. The furnaces were demolished in the late-1920s after standing idle for many years.

23) **Chubb Lock Works** was founded by Charles and Jeremiah Chubb in 1820, originally based at Temple Street in central Wolverhampton. Chubbs of course is one of the most famous, household Wolverhampton names, but at the time they were simply a large manufacturer of locks. They moved to nearby St James Square in Horseley Fields in 1838, where they remained for many years, before moving to their famous, now preserved 'Chubbs Building' in the centre of town at Railway Street in 1889, where 700 workers were

employed making both locks and safes. They produced the locking-mechanism for the Country's first public post-box, and Charles' son John Chubb became 'official lock-maker' for the Queen.

24) **Chubb Safe Works** was the second large works the Company operated within the town, situated on the Wednesfield Road at Heath Town. Founded in the late-1800s, it employed several hundred workers and specialised in the production of cast-iron safes and strong rooms, but during the second world war it also produced armoured bren-gun carriers. The huge stamping-plates used to produce strong-rooms were obtained from the famous, obsolete battleship 'Dreadnought'.

25) **The Crane Foundry** at Horseley Fields was founded in 1827 as a small brass foundry initially called Atherton's Foundry, but it quickly produced iron as well. Co-founder Henry Crane purchased the works in his own name in 1830, and it thrived thereafter. The Crane Foundry initially had just 150 employees and produced iron-ware for industry, as well as iron and brass weights, but it then expanded taking over additional buildings including the adjacent Wolverhampton Chemical Works, to accommodate up to 600 workers, producing castings for motor-vehicles, as well as making locks, and especially quantities of hollow-ware.

26) **The Crown Iron Works (The Crown Galvanising Works)** was a well-established operation at Cross Street, off Stafford Road, just to the north of the town centre. It was founded in 1838 by the innovative Edward Davies, who claimed to have pioneered the galvanising process in the town, by preventing iron from rusting using a hot, zinc coating. As well as producing galvanised iron, the works also produced corrugated iron and hollow-ware, copper and tin, and galvanised steel-framed structures, notably agricultural farm

buildings. In 1891, he invented automatic machinery using rolls and a wire tramway that 'pickled' and galvanised sheet-iron before passing it to the packers, a creation that caused a sensation within the iron industry.

27) **The Cleveland Iron Works (later Beaconsfield Works)** was situated next to the New Griffon Works at Colliery Road, Lower Horseley Fields. Run by Messrs David North and Edwin Wright, owners of the Monmoor Rolling Mills, it operated with 9 puddling-furnaces and was concerned primarily in the manufacture of iron hoops and horse-shoes, but it closed in 1925 with the loss of 120 jobs as trade declined. By 1930, it was re-opened by Herbertson and Co, and then renamed the 'Beaconsfield Works'. One of its specialised products was cast-iron safes, but it was famous for the production and erection of large, fabricated, steel structures.

28) **The Moseley Hole Furnaces (later Moseley Iron and Steel Works)** operated 3 blast-furnaces producing pig-iron and were situated just to the south-east of the junction of Stowheath Lane and Willenhall Road. They were built by the Chillington Company at the eastern extreme of its coal-field, so the company had 7 blast-furnaces operating at its two eastern Wolverhampton works, at opposite ends of its colliery. By 1862 Moseley Hole Furnaces became redundant, due to the production of the narrow-gauge railways that transported coal to its main operation at Chillington Iron Works. But in 1868 a brand new high-pressure vertical blast-engine was acquired to power the blast-furnaces, and the iron-works was re-opened. The works continued to operate for some years thereafter, producing iron, and later steel.

29) **The Wolverhampton Furnaces** were one of Wolverhampton's first iron works, when a single blast-furnace was noted to be in operation around 1788. Situated on the northern side of Dixon Street in Monmore Green, off what was then

called 'Green Lanes', and just one-hundred yards from the Birmingham canal, operations were expanded firstly under the ownership of Messrs Dixon and Hill, then under the ownership of Edward Poole until 1859, then finally under the ownership of Isaiah Aston. Operating with 3 blast-furnaces that were rebuilt around 1826, the works was situated very close to the southern end of Victoria Iron Works, employing 130 hands. They were powered by 6 boilers and engines, and there was also a casting-shop and blacksmith's shop. It is unclear if Bayliss, Jones, and Bayliss took over control of the blast-furnaces for a period, or whether they simply worked in conjunction with them. In March 1864 one of the 3 blast-furnaces collapsed upon itself, due to a coal-shaft mined underneath, burning two workers. The remaining 2 furnaces finally ceased operations around 1880.

30) **The Rough Hills Furnaces and Iron Works** were in existence in the late-1700s, and they were one of the town's first iron-works. The 3 blast-furnaces were believed to be no longer in use by the late-1840s. They were offered for sale along with the adjoining Rough Hills Colliery in 1824, when the 3 blast-furnaces, said to be in good working order, were using 500 tonnes of iron-stone per week. At this point the buildings were said to be situated by the banks of the Birmingham canal, possibly at the eastern end of Rough Hills Road, though it was unclear who was selling the operation, though William Fereday and William Firmstone appear to have had some interest. Industrialist John Neve was also said to have some involvement with the iron works, for a period at least. Other maps suggest the furnaces were situated at what is now Cheviot Road, towards its southern end, close to the site of the Wolverhampton Furnaces (see above), which must have been within a few hundred metres of this operation. It is unclear whether they were one and the

same? Nevertheless, their specific locations were set a few hundred metres apart according to official Wolverhampton City Archives plans.

31) **The Manor Sheet Iron and Steel Works** was a large operation based at Ettingshall, Wolverhampton. Founded in the 1878 the works was originally a tin-plate and sheet works owned by Stephen Thompson and Co, that included forge and forge-train, 4 rolling-mills, and heating and annealing-furnaces. The works covered an area of 17 acres. It was taken over in 1910 by Joseph Sankey and Sons. It was a large, busy operation set in the heart of the Wolverhampton-Bilston iron and steel-making district. John Lysaght took a controlling interest in 1919.

32) **The Wolverhampton Corrugated Iron Company** was a large operation based at Church Lane and Nelson Street, Graiseley, founded in 1857 by John and Joseph Jones. The demand for corrugated iron, especially for corrugated roofing, quickly increased so in 1885 the Company led by Earnest Farnworth took over the southern half of the famous but then empty Shrubbery Iron Works in Horseley Fields, vacated by George Thorneycroft and Company, who had ceased operations in 1877. By 1896, they were operating 6 or 7 sheet-mills. However, in 1905, a decision was made to relocate the Company to the more favourable coastal location of Ellesmere Port, and after an appeal for labour, census records show that 300 workers and their families moved from Wolverhampton, Bilston, and other Black Country towns, many of whom would have previously worked for the company at Shrubbery.

33) **The Ettingshall Iron Works** was a fairly-large works founded in 1825, owned by father and son William and Thomas Banks. It was situated half way between Wolverhampton and Bilston, close to Mars Iron Works, and it contained a large mill and forge, and 21 puddling-furnaces, as well as a range of different forge trains, and cutting and drilling lathes. The

works produced all kind of merchant iron, strip and hoop-iron, and boiler-plates and sheets. In the late-1800s the works were purchased by Thomas Holcroft, who employed 400 workers and produced all sorts of iron and brass hollow-ware from their three-storey building.

34) **Wolverhampton Railway Works** was founded in 1858, based at the famous Stafford Road site to the north of the town centre, and for long periods they were considered the 'workshop of the north division' of the Great Western Railway (GWR). Managed enthusiastically by Joseph Armstrong for many years, during their one-hundred years of production, they built around 800 locomotives, mainly in standard gauge. These trains were largely made of iron and steel, and hence are included here.

35) **The Crown Nail Works (later the Crown Nail and Stamping Company) was** founded in 1850 by Welshman John Lloyd, and the works was situated on Commercial Road in Horseley Fields. It evolved from a small nail workshop into one of the biggest producers and most highly-respected exporters of machine cut-nails, and later blue- tacks, in the Country. In its earlier days, it also produced some iron products, notably frying-pans and shovels. It eventually ceased trading in 2001, after boldly making a comeback in 1986.

36) **The Culwell Foundry** was founded by Joseph Evans and Sons in 1810. This foundry was situated between the railway station and the town centre, off Little's Lane and Southampton Street in the heart of the impoverished slum area of 'Caribee Island'. As well as being a general iron-founder, it produced early pumps for the mining industry, but moved to larger premises in the late-1800s as it became more specialised in that field and needed space to expand. The foundry produced castings for building and machinery, as well as pumps, boilers, and hot-water heating apparatus.

37) **The Culwell Works** relocated to Woden Road, Heath Town in the late-1800s. This move enabled Joseph Evans and Sons to expand operations. The works specialised in engineering, especially in the production of all types and sizes of mechanical-pumps ranging from small to large, for use in a range of situations, for example to pump water out of mines and out of trenches in WW1, to beer-pumps. At their peak, the works employed almost 1,000 workers.

38) **The Fort Works and Tower Works (also The Ashes Works)** were first opened in the late-1800s, at Pelham Street, Graiseley, situated on opposite sides of the road. The buildings were originally known as The Ashes Works, which were founded in 1820 by the Country's leading gun-lock maker Joseph Brazier. These productive works were extended around 1890. William Thrustans and Co took over the Tower Works for a period, specialising in tin-plate and japanning, as well as papier-mache.

39) **Bushbury Engineering Works** was owned by The Electric Construction Company - E.C.C. This innovative, huge operation, covering 28 acres, was situated off Showell Road, Bushbury, at the northern end of town, operating between 1892 and 1927, and employing 2,000 workers at its height. Prior to that it had operated as a smaller iron-producing operation from around 1840. It produced power-systems for railways, tram-ways, collieries, and iron works. Some of the factory buildings are still in use today. Everything was powered by electricity, including huge plate-lathes. It had its own iron and brass foundry with a steam-hammer. Castings from the foundry weighted up to ten tonnes in weight. There was also a blacksmiths shop, a heavy tools and erecting shop, and heavy-tools bay. It possessed many electrically-powered machines and presses, as well as the largest armature-winding shop in the UK.

40) **The Phoenix Works** at Neachells Lane, Wednesfield was founded in 1882 by Jenks (A.E.) and Cattell, and at their industrial peak they employed 850 workers. The Jenks family have been involved in some form of agricultural metalwork in the town, using the 'James Gibbons' format, since the 1670s according to the sign outside their factory today. They specialised in production of agricultural equipment and produced all types of metal pressings such as washers, all types of wire-work, as well as garden spades, forks, and shovels. They also specialised in engineering, and continue to thrive today, though the 'Phoenix' name is seldom used.

41) **St John's Works** was founded in 1750, owned by James Gibbons and based at Church Lane, Graiseley. They were a general brass-founder that also created locks and keys, often for prisons, as well as ornamental work of every description in iron and brass. It opened branches in London, Dublin, Liverpool, and Manchester. They expanded and prospered, employing 900 workers at their mid-1900s peak.

42) **The Merridale Iron Works,** owned by The Henry Loveridge and Co, was founded around 1850 and was based at Merridale Street, Graiseley, which at the time was on the edge of Wolverhampton with green fields on one side. The works employed around 800 workers at its peak, working with iron, brass, copper, and tin-plate, but they were nationally renowned for their japanned-ware and papier-mache which was said to be of extremely high quality. They also specialised in making iron tea-trays. It was later owned by Messrs Shoolbred, Loveridge, and Shoolbred.

43) **The Niphon Iron Works** was another well-established and substantial operation founded in 1865 by Robert Stroud and Co, and later jointly owned by Bullivant and Stroud Bros, and based in an impressive four-storey building at Lower Villiers Street, Blakenhall. It produced a range of steel, tin-plate and

hollow-ware, and was a renowned japanning manufacturer. They employed more than 300 workers.

44) **The Imperial Iron Tube Works** was founded by John Brotherton in 1861, and it was situated off Cable Street, Monmore Green, close to the giant Victoria Iron Works and Monmore Green Rolling Mills. The works employed 400 workers and was a successful operation with a high-quality reputation in relation to its production of all sorts and types of tubes.

45) **The Vulcan Iron Works** was one of the busiest iron works in the Graiseley area of town, situated off both sides of Graiseley Row. The works was founded in 1860 by S.J and E. Fellows. The works had its own foundry, and it specialised in the production of a number of finished items such as milk-churns, coal-skuttles, and blank-trays, as well as iron-braziery. The works employed around 350 workers.

46) **The Atlas Iron Works** at Horseley Fields, founded by John Whitehouse in the early-1800s, specialised in the production of both iron parts for ship-building, and agricultural implements. The works also produced metal hinges, garden tools, and a whole range of other wrought-iron products. At some point, they moved from the heart of Horseley Fields, to a factory at nearby Bilston Road.

47) **The Eagle Foundry and Galvanising Works (later the British Edge-Tool Works),** often simply referred to as 'The Eagle Works', was another mid-sized operation close to the town centre at Bilston Street, Monmore Green. It was founded by John Parsons in the early-1800s, before William Rose took over the works around 1850. As well as galvanising metal products, they produced light and heavy edge-tools in great quantity, as well as specialising in the production of heavy steel toys. The foundry was attached to the galvanising works. Between the mid-1800s and 1865 it is believed that under the ownership of John Gibbons, the works were re-named 'The British Edge-Tool Works'.

48) **The Eagle Works** was another fairly-substantial operation again using the 'Eagle' name, at Graiseley, based at the junction of Great Brickkiln Street and Alexandra Street. The factory buildings have been used for a variety of purposes, originally as a brass foundry, then for gun-making, and then as a cycle works. It is believed they were co-owned, until 1858 at least, by Messrs Farmer, Underhill, Kendrick, and Manby.

49) **The Bridge Iron Foundry and Engine Works** was founded in 1845 by Thomas Bridges and Sons. This was a well-established operation at Horseley Fields, producing castings for machinery as well as steam-engines, agricultural engines, and cranes. It was also a tool and lathe manufacturer, and it also produced hydraulic presses and carried out any general brass and iron-work.

50) **The Albion Iron Works and Foundry** was founded in 1830 by John Hill and Sons, and it was set in factories either side of Willenhall Road at Horseley Fields, close to the town centre. It had a foundry using iron and brass, a machine shop, and a pattern shop. The works produced fixed and portable steam-engines, hydraulic presses, lifting cranes, and shearing machines.

51) **Spring Vale Foundry (also known as Thomas Sheldon and Company)** was a medium-sized foundry and works at Ettingshall that opened around 1853. The works was situated in a smoky and industrial part of town. Their most famous product was cast-iron flat-irons, which were stamped with the wording "T. Sheldon Wolverhampton". By 1878 they had 200 employees.

52) **The Moxley Foundry (later known as the Star Works)** was based at Frederick Street in Graiseley and founded in 1852 as a bicycle manufacturing works by Edward Lisle. It was used as a foundry by the late-1800s. The foundry

produced parts for vehicle manufacturers, including the Star Motor Company, and later Guy Motors. The building remains as a Grade-Two listed-building.

53) **The Star Iron Works** was founded by Elijah Banner in the 1830s and was situated off Grove Street, Heath Town. The works produced small squares and rounds, and any fancy type of iron work, and the works consisted of a guide-mill, blacksmith's shop, rolling-lathe, and forge with 7 puddling-furnaces and 2 heating-furnaces.

54) **The Mitre Iron Works** was founded around 1850, set in Monmore Green just off the Bilston Road, founded by Francis Clerk. They produced wire products, galvanised roofing, and all types of corrugated metal products. At its height, the works employed at least 200 workers. It specialised in galvanising many of its metal products.

55) **Lanesfield Iron Works** was another works slightly nearer Bilston, but which advertised itself as a Wolverhampton company. Owned by William G Merriman, this large works operated with 19 puddling-furnaces, and created sheet-iron bars, rounds, squares, and hoops, and it produced boilers, tanks, and gasometer-plates.

56) **Pelham Street Works** at Graiseley was used for various metal production purposes, and it also produced engines, carburetors, and gear-boxes, and was later puchased by Clyno Engineering who incorporated the buildings with the adjacent Fort Works.

57) **The Castle Iron and Machine Works (Daniel Smith Pressings)**, was situated at Raglan Street, Graiseley, and was founded around 1880, producing specialised and innovative items such as section rolling-machines, edge-tool rolling machines, cutting- out presses, shearing machines, and tube-rolling mills. It was noted to be dangerously crowded with equipment.

58) **The Brunswick Iron Works and Foundry** was situated on the border of Horseley Fields and Monmore Green, close to the Bilston Road. Founded in the early-1800s by William Hayward and Sons, they also specialised in the production of palisading, wrought-iron railings, fences, girders, gates, as well as metal bed-steads, brewing-boilers, water tanks, and all sorts of general iron-work. The works possessed a double-sided lathe, drilling-machine, 2 cupola-furnaces, smith's bellows, crane, and a steam- engine. It later became a chemical works. George Fletcher ran the works from 1860.

59) **The Excelsior Works (New Brotherton Tubes)** was founded by John Brotherton in 1897 and situated at the corner of Commercial Road and Lower Walsall Street, Horseley Fields. They specialised in the production of weldless steel-tubes for gas, steam, and water. John Brotherton also ran the Imperial Iron Tube Works a little further down the Bilston Road.

60) **MacFarlane and Robinson Ltd** was a Scottish-owned company based on Stafford Street and founded around 1882. They produced metal trays, steel signs, gas plates, and hollow-ware products. Situated where the Elephant and Castle Public house used to stand at the top of Cannock Road, their factory was fairly-substantial.

61) **The Cleveland Safe and Lock Works** was founded in the early-1850s by George Price, who became renowned in this field. As the name suggests, it was based at Cleveland Street near the town centre. Despite his excellent reputation, the works never employed more than 50 workers. Lock-making and filing was notably an occupation that led to a chronic back condition.

62) **The Vulcan Iron Works** was founded in 1860 by William Hayward and Sons. This was the second company in the town to utilise this name. They were situated close to the Willenhall Road at Lower Horseley Fields, and they produced wrought-iron gates, girders, railings, gates, and fences.

63) **John Smith and Co Village Foundry** at 'Three Hammers', Coven, just outside Wolverhampton, was founded in the 1830s and the works produced boilers, machine and traction engines, and most famously of all, steam engines specifically for iron works and collieries including four built for Chillington Colliery.

64) **The Elephant Works** was founded by Mr B.F. Williams and it specialised in all sorts of enameling and nickel-plating, as well as being general iron and brass-founders. It is believed the works was founded in the late-1800s, but it is unclear exactly whereabouts in the town it was, but probably around Bell Street near the town centre.

65) **Tonks Bell and Brass Foundry** was situated at St John's Square, Snow Hill, close to the town centre. They specialised in the production of large and small brass bells, along with other small products. They were founded in the 1800s by James Tonks and Sons.

66) **The Patent Tip and Horseshoe Company** was founded by Paul Elwell and Thomas Parker in 1881, and based at Commercial Road, Horseley Fields. They produced cut-nails, horse-shoes, and belatedly specialised in electric lighting. They had around 100 employees, but later up to 400 employees when they specialised in lighting.

67) **Hemingsley's Nail and Tip Manufactory** on Little's Lane employed 70 or so boys and young men aged 9-18, who were employed in a dilapidated three-storey factory amidst notoriously crowded, dangerous equipment. Many of the children here were beaten and were missing finger-tips or even entire fingers due to accidents, and a boy was killed and several others injured when part of a floor simply collapsed.

68) **The Wellington Brass Foundry** was situated at North Street, by Molineux, and founded in the late-1800s. Albert Marston purchased the works in 1924, producing car parts for local vehicle manufacturers like Clyno and Star, as well

as producing locks. They produced the famous Wellington 5-lever lock in 1928.

69) **The Vulcan Iron Works** was a third operation to adopt this name. Owned by R.L. Jones and Son, they were a general iron and brass-founder as well as engineers, specialising in the production of girders and boilers. They were based at Monmore Green.

70) **The Monmore Green Iron Works** specialised in the production of agricultural implements, and all types of iron work. They were founded in the 1850s by John Perks and situated on the opposite side of the Bilston Road to the great Victoria Iron Works and Monmore Green Rolling Mills.

71) **Wednesfield Heath Chain Works** was at Wednesfield Heath, by Heath Town, owned by Messrs Wood Brothers. Founded around 1850, it employed around 300 hands, and produced around 50 tonnes of heavy-chain per week. The company had another works producing smaller chains at Stourbridge, and one near Chester.

72) **St Peter's Iron Works** at Chapel Ash in central Wolverhampton was owned by Henry Denton. This company specialised in the manufacture of agricultural implements such as chaff-cutters, chain-harrows, and iron hurdles.

73) **The Scarboro Works** was founded around 1820 by Joseph Bates. Based at Temple Street near the town centre, they were a brass-founders with 250 workers, who specialised in nickel-plating. Locks were also produced in quantity.

74) **The Junction Iron Works** was an early-1800s operation founded by Joseph Walker. Based at Little's Lane close to the north-eastern part of the town centre, the works produced cut-nails and horse-shoes in its rolling mill.

75) **The Railway Iron Works** was situated near the town centre and founded by Francis Pope and Co. They specialised in the production of patent compressed railway spikes, bolts, screws, and rivets, for the railways, as well as iron fencing.

76) **E.P. and W. Baldwin Tin-plate Works** was founded around 1850, and situated at Horseley Fields, where they operated with 3 puddling-furnaces. They moved operations to the Wilden Works, Stourport in 1885.

77) **The Alexandra Foundry and Bolt Works** was based at Great Brickkiln Street, Graiseley. They were general brass-founders and lock-makers employing up to 200 staff.

78) **C. and B. Smith Iron-founders** were a late-1800s operation based at Stewart Street, Graiseley, who produced high-duty castings, especially cylinder-heads and blocks for automobiles.

79) **The Britannia Safe and Lock Works** was founded by Cyrus Price in 1840, and situated adjacent to the Lincoln Iron Works, at Lincoln Street, Heath Town. They specialised in producing fire-retardant safes.

80) **The Staffordshire Safe Works** was founded by Thomas Skidmore, based at Stewart Street. They specialised in the manufacture of safes at the heavier-end of the security market.

81) **The Union Iron Works** was founded in the early-1800s by John Neve. This was a mid-sized works at Horseley Fields producing cut-nails. It later became a varnishing shop.

82) **The Cannock Road Works** was founded in the early-1800s by G.R. Smithson and Co. They produced a wide variety of pressings for railway and vehicle manufacturers, as well as manufacturing chains.

83) **The Bell Works** was based at Bell Street near the town centre, founded in the 1880s by iron-monger J.H. Butler, making iron-stoves, tools, and farm equipment. He claimed to have made the first thief-proof cash-till.

84) **The Bloomsbury Foundry** was founded by William Lea and Co around 1850, producing locks and all sorts of iron and brass fittings from its base at Pool Street, Graiseley. It was one of the town's busiest foundries.

85) **The Bloomsbury Steel Toy Works** was also based at Pool Street, Graiseley, and was founded by W. and J. Plant. They were one of the most established manufacturers of steel toys in the Country.
86) **The Old Hall Street Works** based near the town centre produced iron hollow-ware and tin-plate. Founded by the Jones Brothers, they were also skilled japanners. They later moved to larger premises.
87) **The Priestfield Chain Works** was a busy operation founded by Joseph Instone, creating all sorts of chains for industry and mining, as well as for shipping. It ceased trading when he died in the early-1850s.
88) **The Blakenhall Works** was founded in 1864 at Upper Villiers Street by Edmund Bullivant, and they were reputed to be highly-skilled in japanning and in creating all sorts of tin and brass hollow-ware.
89) **Evans and Cartwright Steel Toy factory** was founded by John Evans and Sidney Cartwright in 1816 at Dudley Road, and at their height they employed 160 workers, many of them notably well-cared-for-children.
90) **The Pontypool Works** (later renamed the Pheonix Works) was founded in the early-1800s by Henry Fearncombe, as a tin plate and japanning works. They were based at Dudley Road near All Saints.
91) **The Pheonix Works** was based at Great Brickkiln Street, Graiseley founded by Jim Evans around 1840, and they created safes including miniature safes. This was the third works in the town to adopt this name.
92) **The Temple Street Brass Foundry** was set in the heart of Wolverhampton, owned by William Bowen. The works possessed 3 casting-shops, 4 pot-furnaces, and a warehouse.
93) **The Guardian Works** was a brass foundry as well as lock and gun-maker based on Great Hampton Street, Whitmore

Reans, owned by John Badger, Cookson and Co, and later by Charles Aubin. It had 3 furnaces.

94) **The Eagle Works** was an animal-trap maker at Hickman Street in Wednesfield. Founded by Henry Lane in 1844, they were one of the first trap-makers in the area, and the third company to use the 'Eagle' name.

95) **The Alexandra Works** was founded by William Elkington, based at Monmore Green. They produced machine chains, cut nails, bolts, screws, nuts, and all sorts of pressed washers.

96) **The Wellington Foundry** was a small works founded by Edward Fenn, situated in the heart of the Horseley Fields iron-making district. They were a general iron-founder undertaking all sorts of work.

97) **The Atlas Works** was a second operation in the town to adopt this name. Founded by Richard Cooper and Son, they were primarily a lock manufacturer at Church Lane, Graiseley, but undertook general iron-work.

98) **The Horseley Fields Bridge Foundry** was jointly owned by James Atherton and Henry Crane, but the partnership was dissolved in 1843 due to debts of the latter, who still owned the Crane Foundry nearby.

99) **The Monmore Green Galvanising and Tinning Works** was a small operation founded and co-run by Messrs Bishton and Toovey. As the name implies, they primarily concentrated in galvanising and tin plate.

100) **The Stour-Valley Works** at Monmore Green was owned by Brookes, Miller and Company. Having moved to the town, they specialised in the production of iron gates, hurdles, wheelbarrows, and bar or wire fencing.

101) **The Snow Hill Mill Works** was founded in 1800 by William Corns and Son. The Corns family gained a reputation for producing all sorts of grinders, including coffee- grinders.

102) **Benjamin Evans (junior)** founded a small works making flat-irons at Walsall Street, Horseley Fields, that gained fame in 1857 when a boiler explosion killed 3 men (including himself), and 2 children playing outside.
103) **The Old Hall Works** was founded by Frederick Walton and Co. They specialised in working with tin-plate, and they were also skilled japanners. They were based at the grand old home of the Leveson family.
104) **J. and J. Harriman** was a small iron works founded in 1808, based at Charles Street near Molineux, and they produced hollow-ware in the main, but also galvanised iron products.
105) **The Temple Street Iron and Tin-plate Works** was a small operation close to the town centre founded by George Hughes. It specialised in producing ships tackle such as hooks and hinges, and it was official contractor to the H.M. Board of Admiralty.
106) **The James Henry Iron Works** was founded in the early-1800s, near the town centre at the top end of Horseley Fields. They were one of Wolverhampton's earlier iron works.
107) **The Horseley Fields Iron Foundry** was owned by William Perry. It contained a single smelting furnace, large cupola furnace, eight large iron-vices, presses, shears, annealing pots and ovens, and other equipment.
108) **David Bate Company** was a small operation established in 1809 at Corn Hill, Horseley Fields, that produced all sorts of locks, specialising in those for use on ships, as well as brass-cabinet sliding-doors.
109) **Messrs Bentley and Young's Iron Works** at Horseley Fields was on offer in 1841, including iron-rolls, powerful stamp, drilling lathes, steam-cylinder and boiler, iron vices, smith's bellows, and powerful winding-crane.
110) **The Salopian Works** was a small works based at Cleveland Road, All Saints, founded by O.S. Walsh, and later run by

Chas Matthews. They produced galvanised fencing, gates, fencing, bedsteads, and wheel-barrows, as well as wrought-iron kettles.

111) **The Melbourne Works** was listed as producing galvanised and corrugated iron near the town centre at Frederick Street, Graiseley, founded and run by Messrs Pinson and Evans.

112) **W. and F. Perks** operated a small foundry and works at Moseley Street, off Stafford Road. They specialised in the production of cast-iron box-irons and were also general iron-founders.

113) **The Victoria Iron Works** was situated east of Stafford Road at 'Five Ways', close to Foxes Lane. This was a third but smaller operation using this name, run by the Perks family.

114) **The British Iron Company** operated a small iron works at Wednesfield Heath, close to Heath Town. It was a large company, but this Wolverhampton branch was a relatively small operation.

115) **The Jeddo Works** at Paul Street, Graiseley was one of Wolverhampton's earliest japanning and tin-plate works founded in 1790 by Edward Perry, Richard Perry, Son and Co. It was made famous by a prolonged strike of up to 100 workers.

116) **Messrs William Evans and Sons** was a small iron-braziers and galvanisers at Melbourne Street in the heart of Wolverhampton, made famous by a horrendous fire that killed three young workers.

117) **Gladstone Tin-plate and Japan Works** was a small works owned by G.H. Allcock and based on Stafford Street, that specialised in all sorts of finishing including papier mache.

118) **Bilston Street Brass Foundry** was established in 1811 by Messers Thacker, Sirdefield and Co, then taken over by Ready and Meynell in 1848. They produced mechanical-pumps, stop-cocks, valves, and brass-weights.

119) **Meynell Valves** opened a works in Pipers Row in 1798, under the ownership of Ready and Meynell. They were a general brass-founders who also specialised in the manufacture of pumps and water fittings, as well as coach fittings.

120) **Meynell and Inman** formed a partnership at Montrose Street from 1873, continuing to produce a range of brass fittings for water, tools, and whistles, allegedly including the one fitted on 'Stephenson's Rocket'.

121) **Meynell and Son** emerged around 1887, based on Little's Lane. They specialised in the production of mechanical-pumps, garden-engines, and wrought-iron tubes for water, steam, or gas, and later-on in chandeliers and lamps.

122) **The Rex Foundry** was founded at Charles Street by the Meynell family in the late-1890s, chiefly to supply iron for its thriving large cast-iron pump business. It also built small cast-iron bridges, until it closed in 1915.

123) **The Bilston Street Iron Works** at Monmore Green was owned by Messrs Fletcher, Matthews and Co. They produced iron and brass bedsteads, gates, fencing, wheel-barrows, and bolts.

124) **Snow Hill Galvanising Works** was Edward Davies's second operation in the town, not as large as his prominent works to the north of the town centre. It was founded around 1857.

125) **The Cleveland Works** was a small brass-founder that also undertook locks work, situated at Little's Lane, founded in 1848 by T.J. Cooke. It was taken over by James Meynell and Sons.

126) **Stork Nail and Washer Works** was based at Horseley Fields owned by W. Ashcroft, producing cut-nails and washers. The works possessed a lathe, 6 powerful punch-presses, and nail-cutting machines.

127) **Horseley Fields Tube Works** produced gas-tube fittings and was situated directly opposite the Shakespeare Foundry. Owned by Mr H. Thompson, it contained 2 smith's bellows, lathe, and anvils and vices.

128) **The Victoria Works** at Paul Street, Heath Town, owned by Mr Baraclough, had powerful cutting-machines, a large lathe, rivet and nail machines, anvils and vices, bellows, screw-presses, and grinders. This was the fourth to use the 'Victoria' name.

129) **The Phoenix Foundry** was a town centre works founded by W. Rocke that specialised in making machinery from pig and wrought iron. There were other works at Wednesfield and Blakenhall that used this name.

130) **White Hill Iron Works** was a small specialist iron works at Compton owned by T. Baker. He found a specific niche in the market by specialising in the production of liquid-manure carts.

131) **The Graiseley Foundry** was an operation based at Hallet's Row which operated with a cupola, 3 annealing ovens, lathes, anvils, grinders, screwing-machines, moulding-machines, and 50 bellows.

132) **The Tempest Works** was a small iron works with a forge, based at Tempest Street, also near the town centre. Founded in the early-1800s, they were also run by Joseph Bates.

133) **The Gothic Iron Works** was founded in the 1890s by Herbert H. Green, based at Herrick Street. They specialised in the production of locks and fancy gothic thumb- latches and wrought-iron iron coat and hat-hooks.

134) **The Wolverhampton Iron Works** was a foundry based at Dixon Street, Graiseley, Wolverhampton. A large chimney was situated at this industrious small operation.

135) **The Victoria File Works** was founded in 1860, based at Merridale Street, Graiseley. They made files, rasps, vices, steel-hammers, and other general hardware. This was the fifth works in the town using this name.

136) **The Elgin Works** was a medium-sized works at Great Brickkiln Street, Graiseley, founded by Orme Evans and Co in 1899, producing iron and tin-plate products.

137) **The Cleveland Street Galvanising and Tin-plate Works** was a busy operation at All Saints close to the centre of town, owned by Messrs Beckett and Beckett.
138) **The Colonial Works** was based at Amos Lane, Wednesfield, owned by John Mattox and Sons. In the early days, they created 'toasting-forks', as well as locks.
139) **The Albion Works** was another animal-trap-maker based at Wednesfield, founded in 1876 by John Marshall, but trading as S. Griffiths and Sons by 1892.
140) **The Pountney-Pool Works** was founded in 1860 by W. Vaughan and Sons, producing cast-steel hammers and files. It was also a reputed gun-maker and japanner.
141) **The St James Brass Foundry** was a brass foundry founded and owned by John Fell and Co, situated between Snow Hill and Graiseley, close to the town centre.
142) **The Lion Steel Mill Works** was based at Pountney Street between Graiseley and Snow Hill. Founded by Henry Corns, they produced all types of steel-grinders.
143) **S. Cassin-Pritchard & Co Iron and Steel Merchants** was a small company at Horseley Fields producing hammers, picks, hatchets, shovels, and other workers tools.
144) **The James Henry Brass Foundry** was a separate operation to the iron works of the same name, also based at Horseley Fields close to the town centre.
145) **The Britannia Foundry** was a small works based in Bell Street, close to the town centre, founded and run by W. Tolmans. They made all sorts of small iron products.
146) **The Paul Street Works** was a small iron and tin-plate works owned by John Marston, that also undertook specialised japanning and papier mache processes.
147) **The Clyde Works** was a small Heath Town operation owned by Knowles and Co. specialising in japanning, as well as working with tin-plate, iron, copper, and zinc.

148) **The Nursery Iron Foundry** was owned by J. Attwood and situated at North Street, off Nursery Walk, close to Molineux. It was a small works and general iron-founder.

149) **The Midland Iron Works** was owned by Thomas Pearson and Company, and they created corrugated corn-rick stands and covers for agricultural purposes.

150) **The Monmore Green Tube Works** was an early-1800s works that specialised in the production of gas and water-tubes, founded and run by Cornelius Whitehouse.

151) **The Jenner Street Tool Works** at Monmore Green was founded by Francis Lewis. The works produced cast-iron stop cocks, valves, taps, and hand-held tools.

152) **The Graiseley Works** on Ablow Street was an early foundry taken over by the Jones Brothers, to cater for their increasing japanning and tin-plate business.

153) **The Great Brickkiln Street Iron Foundry** was situated in the heart of Graiseley, serving 'Sunbeam', as well as the Tower, Fort, and Pelham Works in the same area.

154) **Richmond Iron Works** was founded in the early-1800s, and situated at Horseley Fields on the Bilston Road, at the junction with Commercial Road.

155) **The Galvanising Works** at Graiseley served vehicle manufacturers, notably Sunbeam, as well as the Fort, Tower, and Pelham Works in Penn Fields.

156) **The Hollies Works** was a small operation based at Heath Town, off the main Wednesfield Road. They specialised in the production of hooks and hinges.

157) **H. Gillman and Co** was a small works based at Cleveland Road, All Saints, who specialised in the manufacture of weighing-machines.

158) **The Anchor Iron Company** was a small iron works based in central Wolverhampton, owned and run by Frederick Lewis.

159) **St Paul's Works** was a locks manufacturer in Graiseley founded by John Cooper. They also made brass-cabinets.
160) **St Mary's Works** was another producer of locks and other items based on Little's Lane, founded by Thomas Bigford.
161) **The Hope Foundry** was a small works and general iron-founder situated near the town centre, founded and owned by Benjamin Nicholls.
162) **The Art Street Brass Foundry** was a small operation founded and run by J. Osborne, situated in the heart of Wolverhampton.
163) **The Grove Works** was a small operation at Heath Town owned by John Lewis that produced steel-trunks and 'deeds-cases'.
164) **The Midland Iron Works** based at Church Lane, was owned by Messrs Collegde and Bridgen, and they produced high-class builder's iron-mongery, including locks.
165) **Titus Neve's Shoe-tip Works** was small operation producing metal shoe-tips, based in the heart of Horseley Fields.
166) **The Corrugated Iron Works** was a fairly-large operation at Graiseley, situated off Nelson Street and Church Lane.
167) **The Excelsior Plating Works** owned by F.G. Walton, was an electro-plating and polishing works at Herrick Street, founded in the 1890s.
168) **The Princess Street Works** owned by T. Johnson, was a small tin-plate works that also produced steel-trunks.
169) **The Cut Nail Works** at Horseley Fields was a small operation owned by Messrs Danks, Walker and Company, for additional space from their Junction Works.
170) **The Union Foundry** was a small works situated on Bilston Road, near Monmore Green owned by George Fletcher.
171) **Harry F Thomas and Company** was based at Walsall Street, Horseley Fields, producing iron gates.

172) **Hall and Pickles Ltd** was a small iron works, but chiefly an iron stock-holder and merchant based at Lichfield Street.
173) **The Showell Road Works (Manley and Regulus Brass Foundry**) was an 1880s foundry and hot brass-pressings business.
174) **Benjamin Whitmore and John Edwards Junior Chain Works** at Monmore Green was a small enterprise producing round and flat-chains.
175) **William Meller's Brass Foundry** was a small family firm in Wolverhampton that ceased trading in 1850.
176) **Messrs Skidmore and Langman Wrought Iron Fire-proof Safe-makers** was a specialist safe-maker based at Bilston Street.
177) **The John Cassere Works** at Snow Hill found a niche in producing wrought-iron brewing-furnaces.
178) **The Penn Forge** was a small blacksmith operation on the Penn Road, run by Henry Roden.
179) **William H. Williams** was a small company based in Stewart Street producing aluminium dinner-carriers.
180) **The Derry Street Foundry** was a small operation at Blakenhall owned by Messrs Arnold and Large.
181) **The Adelphi Works** was another small iron works in the Graiseley area producing iron rod and tube.
182) **The Talbot Works** was a small operation at Stewart Street, producing iron and tin-plate.
183) **The Pountney Place Works** was a small operation in Graiseley that created zinc products.
184) **The Graisley Steel-trap Works** owned by William Sidebotham, was based at Rookery Street, Wednesfield, producing man-traps and animal-traps from 1830-1930.
185) **The Albert and Ionian Works** was another small operation based in Church Lane, Graiseley.
186) **The Green Lane Foundry** was based at All Saints near the centre of Wolverhampton

187) **The Cleveland Works** at Raby Street, All Saints produced brass door-lock furniture and lock-plates.
188) **Church Lane Engineering Works** was a Graiseley machine tool-maker, but little else is known.
189) **The Thornley Street Iron Works** was an operation in the heart of Caribee Island, near the town centre.
190) **The Reliance Brass Foundry** was a small works situated close to the Fibbersley Bridge at Wednesfield.
191) **Commercial Road Tank Works** was a works producing copper tanks in the heart of Horseley Fields.
192) **The Raglan Works** was a small works based between Chapel Ash and Graiseley, producing springs.
193) **The Stanhope Foundry** was a small works on Moseley Street, north of the town centre.
194) **The Old Monmore Works** was a small foundry based at Monmore Green, close to the Bilston Road.
195) **The Heath Town Works** were situated close to the old Wednesfield Heath train station, but little else is known.
196) **The Peel Works,** or '**The Wolverhampton Electro-Plate Company**' produced silver-plated ware.
197) **The Jenner Street Foundry** was founded in the 1850s and situated off Bilston Road at Monmore Green. It produced iron and brass products.
198) **The Brunswick Street Foundry** comprised a casting-shop, two blacksmith's shops, and warehouses.
199) **The Lear Works** was a small tin-plate works at Fern Road, Graiseley, on the south-western outskirts of town.
200) **Bilston Street Gas Fitting and Plumbers Brass Foundry** was a small works situated in Monmore Green, close to the town centre.
201) **The North Street Iron Works** specialised in the production of galvanised sheep- netting.
202) **The Albert Works** was a small operation very close to or even part of the Albion Works at Horseley Fields, founded in the 1800s.

203) **The Albert Iron Plate Works** was a small operation based on Stewart Street in the heart of the industrial Graiseley district.
204) **The Lincoln Iron Works** was a small but thriving operation at Lincoln Street, Heath Town.
205) **The Walsall Street Works** was founded in the 1800s located in the heart of Horseley Fields.
206) **E.P. Jenks** started off as a small operation in 1873, producing small pressings at Jenner Street, Monmore Green, but they expanded considerably in the 1900s.
207) **The Bell and Brass Foundry** was a small works thought to be in the Graiseley area.
208) **Lever Street Foundry** was a small late-1800s foundry run by F. Newman and Co.
209) **The Upper Zoar Street Foundry** was a small, light-metal foundry run by W. Moseley.
210) **Stevens Screw Company** was a small operation founded in 1874, producing screws, nuts and bolts. They were based at Retreat Street.
211) **Messrs Whitmore and Edwards Chain-manufacturers** were a small company producing round and flat-chains at Monmore Green.
212) **Bears, Pinchbeck and Co** were a small galvanising operation who also worked with iron-plate.
213) **Hills Foundry** was situated just north of the town centre by the canal wharf.
214) **The Forward Iron Works** was based at Monmore Green, producing iron tubes.
215) **The Lion Iron Works** was a busy iron and brass works based in Graiseley.
216) **The Drayton Iron Works** was yet another operation based in Graiseley.
217) **The Raglan Street Foundry** was a small foundry on Raglan Street, Graiseley.

218) **The Globe Tank and Foundry Company** was based at Green Lane, Blakenhall.
219) **The Raglan Street Foundry** was a small foundry on Raglan Street, Graiseley.
220) **Wolverhampton Gauge and Tool Company** was based at Sutherland Avenue.
221) **The Continental Iron Works** was based in All Saints, a fairly-small operation.
222) **Evans School Street Brass Foundry** was a small works near the centre of town.
223) **The Overland Works** was another small operation based in Graiseley.
224) **The Alexander Works** was a specialist lock works based at Heath Town.
225) **Ready and Son** ran a small foundry in Bilston Street from around 1870.
226) **The Commercial Road Works** was a cut-nail producer based in Horseley Fields.
227) **The Causeway Lake Works** takes final place in Wolverhampton's list of iron works of the 1800s Industrial Revolution period, as its owner Mr F.W. Gerhard claimed to have discovered a way of creating sulphur-free coke and ironstone without the need of a furnace in 1866 and claimed to have devised a simple and inexpensive process to charge fuel with double its ordinary combustible power, so as to decrease the weight of coal carried by a steamer by one half. This claim was highlighted in the Birmingham Daily Post on 20 October 1866. Ten years earlier he had patented a way of producing aluminium by exposing it to hydrogen at a red heat.

Iron-based works 1900-1970s (Major works only)

228) GKN-Sankey purchased Bayliss, Jones, and Bayliss huge Victoria Works and Monmore Green Rolling Mills in 1911. They had other large factories in the area. Nevertheless, despite the takeover, the works continued to be run by, and under the name of Bayliss, Jones, and Bayliss. Thereafter its most famous product included cast-iron and wrought-iron fencing, palisades, gates, railings, mining roof supports, components for the motor and railway industry. At its height, the works employed over 1,500 workers, and by the 1950s it produced up to 50,000 tonnes of high quality steel per annum. The works was at the cutting edge of technology, producing the world's most-advanced, heavy-plate mill, which was the biggest of its kind in the Country, capable of delivering up to 8,000 tonnes of standard quality steel plate per week. Huge lathes, presses, and high specification machine-tools were produced and utilised. GKN finally closed the works in the late-1970s, though the Victoria factory buildings continue to be used for a variety of purposes to this day.

229) The Monmore Green Rolling Mills Company (Cable Street Rolling Mills) was created in 1924, and it continued to prosper, later becoming Cable Street Rolling Mills. With a large new blast-furnace, and new puddling-furnaces, the works continued to produce sheet-iron and steel in quantity for a number of years.

230) The Chillington Tool Company was founded in 1919 by John Hunt, and he adapted the old iron-works site, with the Company concentrating on the production of edge-tools, with its brands gaining worldwide repute. 800 hands were employed as it prospered. Eventually the Company relocated to nearby Willenhall.

231) **Wolverhampton Steel and Iron Company (later Wolverhampton and Birchley Rolling Mills, British Steel, and Corus)** was formed in 1935 when it purchased Osier Bed Iron Works, which had stood empty for some years. The takeover was led by two Welsh industrialists. Through its increasingly productive sheet-mills, it was producing an impressive 100,000 tons of sheet-steel per annum by the 1950s. In the mid-1950s it operated under the name of the Wolverhampton and Birchley Rolling Mills, was then used by 'British Steel' as its 'tubes division', and then finally by 'Corus' as a steel distribution centre until it closed with 520 job losses in 1995. The works have had a long and industrious history.

232) **Alfred Hickman (later Stewarts and Lloyds)** was also known simply as Bilston Steel Works, and later Stewarts and Lloyds. Hickman had earlier amalgamated the Spring Vale Furnaces and the Staffordshire Steel and Ingot Works in the late-1800s, overseeing significant expansion as the 1900s progressed, with the works clearly became the prominent metal works in the Wolverhampton area. The renowned 'Elizabeth Furnace' replaced the smaller furnaces in 1954, and it was capable of producing 275,000 tonnes of steel per annum. Stewarts and Lloyds took over the works, but 2,500 employees were laid off when Spring Vale finally closed in 1979 amidst great controversy as it was claimed that it was capable of still running at a profit.

233) **Qualcast** opened an operation in Wolverhampton in 1945 when the company purchased the Crane Foundry, and in 1953 the empty Swan Garden Iron Works was also purchased, and the works continued as a foundry in some format until 2001. Qualcast produced all sorts of light grey-castings, such as lawn-mowers, sewing-machines, parts for washing-machines and cookers, and with the purchase of Swan Garden larger parts were manufactured for the vehicle industry.

234) **John Thompson Boiler Works** took over the Britannia Boiler Tube Works factory at Ettingshall in 1919. They expanded the works and opened different plants across the Black Country and indeed across the U.K. This plant specialised in steam-boiler production and erection. Large 'John Thompson Ltd, Wolverhampton' titles were painted on the factory roof, and clearly viewable in aerial photographs.

235) **The Wolverhampton Metal Works** was founded in 1903 and was situated off Rookery Street, Wednesfield. They originally evolved as The James Iron Works, but this was a small operation. When it was taken over and developed, the works specialised in smelting down scraps of lead, iron, and zinc using huge 160-tonne, coke-fired furnaces.

236) **The Weldless Steel Tube Company** first opened in 1901, owned by Francis Henry Lloyd. It became a substantial works in Wednesfield situated on Neachells Lane, producing all types of steel-tubes made to specification for power plants for aircraft and racing cars. 1,500 workers were employed here at its peak.

237) **E.P. Jenks** originated from small-time beginnings in the late-1800s, but they purchased a larger factory from John Brotherton on nearby Bilston Road in 1923 and became a major manufacturer of hot brass fittings and copper tubes, specialising in the production of water fittings. In the 1900s, they expanded with a workforce of 750 employees, creating all sorts of welded components for railways, shipping, aviation, and general trades products such as garden tools. They also undertook galvanising, nickel-plating, and tin, copper, and bronze-plating.

238) **H.M. Munitions Factory** was a specialist, 'phosperous-primed', munitions factory based at Old Heath Road near Heath Town, founded in 1916 by Wilson Lovatt Company. They had 26 electric-charged furnaces and 6 mud-based furnaces. Metal

was inevitably involved in some of its processes, for example with the casings of the munitions. When the operation closed, Manders Paints took over part of the site.

239) **Midland Metal Spinning Company** was formed in 1919 when the Fort Works were taken over by the 'Midland Metal Spinning Company' who produced all sorts of finished iron-ware including domestic utensils especially non-stick pans, but also pressure-cookers and singing-kettles under its 'presto' range. This company were owned by George Cadman, and they employed over 700 workers at its peak in 1942.

240) **The Owen Road Works (Britool Ltd)** was founded in 1915 by the Jenks brothers, based at their large factory at Penn Fields. They went on to become one of the main manufacturers of engineer's tools in the Country, with their innovative products. Their wrenches were of national fame. They moved to a new factory in Bushbury later in the 1900s.

241) **John Shaw and Sons** took over Britool from the Jenks Brothers in the 1900s, though Jenks seemed to have some continued involvement in the company. They shared a large, new factory at Bushbury, which contained around twenty separate bays, and they continued to produce all sorts of high-quality, metal-work tools.

242) **The Patent Axle Box Company and Foundry** was founded around 1904 by Cecil Crosskey, and this expanded to become one of the largest works in the Wednesfield area. Situated at the junction of Well Lane and Hall Street, they employed up to 400 workers, before closing around 1935. They utilised the 'Bessemer' process to create steel.

243) **The Alfred Herbert Steel Works** was situated on a green-field site by what is now Humphries Road, Low Hill. This was a later operation that started in the early-1900s. They supplied steel for machine parts. Their main factory was in Coventry, some thirty miles away.

244) **The Hollies - The Wolverhampton Die Casting Company** was founded in 1919, and based first at Great Hampton Street, Whitmore Reans, and then at 'The Hollies' at Graiseley Hill. They produced zinc and aluminium-alloy, pressure-die castings, where precise castings were produced. Another operation in the town also used the 'Hollies' name.

245) **Courtaulds Ltd** was a huge textiles factory situated at Dunstall on the less industrial north-western side of Wolverhampton. It was opened in the early-1900s, producing yarn and rayon. But in 1926 the works were extended and produced steel armoured vehicles for Guy Motors, and therefore are included here. At its height it, this huge factory employed 1,300 workers, mainly women.

246) **Alustar (Star Aluminium Company)** were a large company founded in the early-to-mid-1900s, and based at Marston Road, Blakenhall. It became a major national supplier of aluminium-foil, employing 700 workers at its peak. It eventually closed in the late-1900s.

247) **Wednesfield Steel Works** was a small company initially employing just 50 men, based on Neachell's Lane, and formed in 1919. It increased in size over the next few decades.

248) **The Beaconsfield Works** was based at Colliery Road at Lower Horseley Fields, the site of the Cleveland Iron Works. Founded by Herbertson and Co around 1930, they became renowned for the production and fabrication of large steel structures, and they also produced cast-iron safes.

249) **Fawdry Street Works** was founded in 1909 and situated initially at Whitmore Reans, but it is thought they moved to Plascom Road by Lower Horseley Fields, close to Chillington Colliery. The works was owned by the son of iron-master and colliery proprietor Henry Fowler, but although it undertook some galvanising of metal products, it mainly produced sewage-tank linings and road-surfacing materials, along with plasma.

250) **Sunbeam Car Company** are a famous company owned and managed by John Marston who first specialised in cycles, then cars and motorbikes, and even racing cars. Based at Blakenhall, they were founded in 1888, and worked in conjunction with Villiers Engineering, but the Sunbeam Car Company was only founded in 1905, when the operation really expanded. Their vehicles went on become famous throughout the world and are worthy of an entire chapter.

251) **Villiers Engineering** were founded around 1900 and run by John Marston's son Charles Marston. They patented the 'free-wheel' for bicycles, and being the sole producer, they evolved on a massive scale, and thereafter became a renowned manufacturer of engines. They were based at Blakenhall.

252) **Steelway** were founded in 1928 by C.W. Goodyear, and they were based at the Queensgate Works site, Monmore Green. They were famous for producing the first pedestrian guard-rails, and thereafter they constructed crowd-control barriers and during the war, steel stretchers to carry men. They are still in operation today, based in Wolverhampton and West Bromwich.

253) **A.J.S. (A.J. Stevens and Company)** were a famous manufacturer of cars and motor-bikes. Founded in 1909, they went on to hold 117 motor-cycle records. Their factory was based in Horseley Fields, upon part of the site of the old Shrubbery Iron Works. They were sold in 1931, when the company moved out of Wolverhampton.

254) **Clyno Engineering Company** were another well-known manufacturer of bicycles and cars, and they were based in the town from 1910-1929. They acquired a factory at Pelham Street, Pennfields, which was the old Fort Works.

255) **Star Motor Company** were initially manufacturers of bicycles, and then cars between 1898-1932. They were the 6th biggest manufacturer of vehicles in the UK at its

peak. Their factory was situated at Stewart Street, near to the town centre, at the famous 'Star Works' site.

256) **Guy Motors** were famous manufacturers of trolley-buses, lorries, and buses, and the company were based in the town from 1914-1982, at Fallings Park.

257) **Boulton-Paul Ltd** were originally a Norwich company who moved operations to Pendeford, Wolverhampton in 1934. They famously produced the WW2 night-fighter 'Defiant'.

258) **H.M. Hobson (Lucas Aerospace)** were originally a London company making carburettors, but they moved to Wolverhampton in 1911, basing themselves at the 'Accuracy Works' in Blakenhall. They initially supplied carburettors to De Havilland and other aircraft manufacturers. Their Stafford Road site opened in 1952, specialising in all sorts of aviation power-systems and hydraulics. They were taken over by Lucas Aerospace in 1972 and remain at the cutting edge of aviation technology, designing and supplying complex power systems for civil and military aircraft.

259) **Kieft Cars** were founded in 1947 and they produced sports cars and racing cars from their base at the Reliance Works at Derry Street, Blakenhall. Co-owned by racing driver Stirling Moss, the company also produced scooters, but they moved to Birmingham in 1956, before closing five years later.

260) **Frisky Cars** were a small Wolverhampton firm based at Fallings Park, founded and owned by Henry Meadows in 1957. The company made engines and gear-boxes, and then the fuel-efficient 'Frisky' car, for which the company was famed. The company moved south, but before closing in 1961.

Two more large-scale industrial operations in Wolverhampton are worthy of mention, though they did not create metal products, they definitely worked with them.

261) **Goodyear Tyres** were of course a famous American company who opened a tyre-manufacturing base in Wolverhampton in 1927, only finally closing in 2016. At one point 5,500 workers were employed at this giant plant. Of course, rubber tyres have nothing to do with metal production, but they obviously played a major role in the automobile industry which had a major base in Wolverhampton. Much of their equipment and machinery was inevitably metal, using heavy-metal presses and also furnaces.

262) **Tarmac Construction** were founded in 1903, when they were purchased by Sir Alfred Hickman in 1905, when headquarters moved to Wolverhampton, at Ettingshall. They were essentially a buildings-material company, supplying concrete, cement, and lime for road-building and other purposes. They inevitably utilised iron and steel and worked closely with iron producers. The company were taken over by Carillion, that went into liquidation in 2018.

Additionally, in the 1700s and 1800s, hundreds of small family-run businesses were involved in some form of metallurgy, mainly locks, nailing, and gun-making.

There were over 430 gun-makers in Wolverhampton, many specialising in making gun-locks. The nationally-acclaimed Joseph Brazier has already been included above, but John Stanton was another Wolverhampton gun-lock maker of national repute.

There were at least 400 small locksmiths, at least 40 small brass-founders, as well as smaller numbers of edge-tool makers, file makers, corkscrew makers, tin-plate makers, steel-toy makers, fire-iron makers, vice makers, trap makers, agricultural machine makers, and general blacksmiths all working from their homes.

Cycle manufacture was another thriving industry in Wolverhampton, by 1900 there were 59 cycle works in the town.

Virtually every iron product was made by somebody in the town.

D) Dangerous places of work

There was a general lack of regard for health and safety in the iron industry, in the early stages of the Industrial Revolution, and 14-hour days were the norm in the early-1800s.

Furthermore, many people raised great concern about the smoky atmosphere that hung constantly and grimly over Wolverhampton. This was demonstrated by an article in the Wolverhampton Chronicle on the 18 October 1865 highlighting a re-application under the 'Smoke Prevention Act', by the 'Local Health Boards' that possessed the power to apply such acts, and to exempt certain trades from the Act.

In subsequent argument, local iron-master Mr E.J. Gibbs argued: -

"The coke hills of a large iron-works made more smoke than the whole town of Wolverhampton. No doubt some of the manufacturers in this town, in certain processes, can consume their smoke, but an iron-master or iron-founder cannot."

In relation to the outcome of the Local Board application, Gibbs continued: -

"If they succeeded the Town Council would certainly appear in a most undignified position. If smoke was abolished, our friends the iron-masters and iron-founders would be compelled to migrate to the more genial atmosphere of Yorkshire or South Wales. Alderman Simkiss's swallows would build their nests in the deserted and ivy-covered stacks of the Shrubbery and Swan Garden works, and Wolverhampton, once the 'metropolis of South Staffordshire', would be renowned for the purity of its air, the exclusiveness of its society, and perhaps its medicinal waters and excellent ginger beer. I trust that the manufacturers and working people of this town will see it to their interest to unite for their common good, and oppose a measure calculated so seriously to injure the trade of the Borough. A measure the effect of which the promoters themselves scarcely realise."

The application was thrown out, with financial consideration inevitably taking priority over health.

Iron works themselves, of course, could be extremely dangerous places to work, with so much noisy and heavy equipment operating in extreme temperatures. Many men received horrendous burn injuries, and a number suffered quite horrific deaths whilst at work. Those in the foundries and rolling mills, such as the puddlers, were often prematurely worn out through sheer hard, hot work. Brass foundries were particularly dangerous places to work, and many workers, including young boys, died prematurely because a quantity of oxide of zinc was 'thrown-off' in pouring the metal into the moulds, and thereafter a white powder would hang around the shop to be subsequently inhaled by workers. Wolverhampton had many foundries specialising in brass, or at least in both brass and iron.

The processes of galvanising, enamelling, and jappaning were also prejudicial to health as they contained acids and lead, which inevitably were repeatedly inhaled.

Filing and cutting in the Locksmiths shops and factories, led to deformities because of the stance the workers would always take in their work. Wolverhampton and its parish town of Willenhall were the centres of the lock industry, and the latter town was often rather cruelly nick-named 'Umpshire' because of the hump-backed appearance of many of its residents, caused by long hours spent in the same standing position at the lathe.

If these issues did not make metal manufacture perilous enough, then those working in hot, cramped foundries were more likely to contract cholera when outbreaks occurred.

In August 1866, at the height of the Industrial Revolution, the Birmingham Daily Gazette highlighted the dangerous occupational reality of working in one of the town's huge iron works: -

"The great iron works of Wolverhampton, where iron is smelted, and cast into 'pigs', or manufactured into plates, rods, bars, and other large articles, require but brief notice. The works are generally surrounded

by much dense smoke, which renders the air very impure, and a most unpleasant, suffocating exhalation arises from the heaps of incinerating iron or near the blast-furnaces. The puddlers especially, are exposed to intense heat, and the men are said to be not unhealthy, but to become prematurely worn-out by-reason-of hard work. Sundays only excepted, the works are in active operation night and day throughout the week, one set of men relieving another at set times. Besides this larger kind of iron manufacture, there exists at Wolverhampton, several foundries and factories where iron vessels and implements of various kind are manufactured. The men employed in some of the casting-shops are exposed to the danger of inhaling dust arising from the sand and powdered charcoal used in making moulds for casting. The oldest man found at work as a caster, was under fifty years of age, and the impression among the casters is that they die early".

Indeed, it was recorded that puddlers died at an average age of thirty-seven.

Even in the 1960s, working in rolling-mills was extremely tough, as one worker at Wolverhampton and Birchley Rolling Mills, also known as Osier Bed Rolling Mills, named Stephen Fieldhouse explained: -

"After a while I got a job on the rolls and one of my first jobs was on the 'guides'; this could be a killer of a job especially if we were producing one-inch rounds off the roller. Mr Cox had to tighten the guides and you had to pinch the bars in and many times your hands would be close to bleeding; the rollers' cure was to run to the toilet and urinate on them. I asked the roller, Mr Cox, if I could have a light job for a couple of weeks, he started laughing and said a light job didn't exist and I had to work topside, this involved dragging a billet of up to two hundredweight from the first set to the third set and by the end of the shift I could hardly walk. I stuck it out for a number of months and was gradually getting worse."

It was a tough, rough occupation that ruined the health of many workers, and even in the 1960s it was one that took a huge toll on the physical well-being of men.

CHAPTER SIX

Accidents were common-place within iron works throughout the Black Country, and indeed throughout the Country. Examples can easily be found in reports from the 'Wolverhampton Chronicle'. There are simply too many to choose from.

The first of these highlighted here, was reported through an inquest held on 21 November 1835, where a thirteen-year-old boy named John Crawford was badly injured at Shakespeare Foundry, when an eighteen-year-old girl threw some spirits of tar into a fire near to which he was standing, resulting in explosion and appalling burns for the young man all over his arms, head and face, with his hair being melted into his scalp. After several agonising days of pain, he died in his bed at home.

In March 1841, 14-year-old 'nail-cutter' Peter McDermott was killed at the notorious Hemmingsley's Nail and Tip factory at Little's Lane, when one of the ramshackle floors simply collapsed under the weight of overloaded iron, crushing the unfortunate young boy and injuring several others.

In March 1842, a young boy only known as 'Borley' was killed at Mr Henderson's Tin factory in the town, when he foolishly placed a piece of iron against a revolving wheel. The boy must have slipped and been pulled into it and his head and arm were instantly severed from his body.

On the 22 August 1849, a 15-year-old boy called Edward Skitt was badly injured at Wolverhampton's Swan Garden Iron Works. A witness stated the following: -

"He was assisting in changing one of the rolls and was in the act of lowering the roll by a windlass, when, the weight being too great for his strength, the handle of the windlass was suddenly forced out of his hands, and revolved at a great speed, coming-in-contact with the boys' forehead and knocking him down. His forehead was completely stripped of the scalp, which hung over his face. The blow also produced two fractures of his forehead and likewise of the bones of his nose."

On 16 October 1850, a seventeen-year-old by the name of Joseph Hadley suffered a horrible injury when he was attempting to draw a piece of iron over one of the rolls at Swan Garden Iron Works, when his left foot slipped, it was drawn in between the rolls and was severed from the leg, to which it only remained attached by a piece of skin, the bones being completely smashed, with excessive lacerations of the muscles of the leg and knee-joint.

On 5 December 1850, a seventeen-year-old by the name of James Davis was found dead on the floor 'upon some riddled ashes' outside Swan Garden Iron works. It was unclear how he died but the previous night he had been ordered out of the works after being found 'skulking behind a stack'.

On 12 August 1854, a boy named Edward Richards, whilst picking up some iron shearings at Chillington Iron Works, fell backwards upon two massive cog-wheels, and being drawn between them was instantly crushed to death.

On 14 May 1855, twenty-one-year-old William Bartram was working as a labourer at Shrubbery Iron Works, and in the process of removing some iron rails, he slipped back in to a fly-wheel, resulting in his head and leg being cut off. Instantaneous death occurred.

Another horrific incident occurred at Swan Garden Iron Works on 30 October 1855, when a young man by the name of John Griffiths was acting as an assistant shingler to his brother, preparing to cast a slab of red-hot iron weighing 150 lbs between the rolls, when he stumbled backwards into a pit containing the cam-wheel, which worked huge pieces of iron weighing five tons. This possessed large cogs that lifted the helve (or long hammer) and raised it from the anvil so that it could fall upon the slabs of hot iron placed beneath it. Griffiths appeared to get caught on one of the cogs, and after just half a rotation, he was thrown out the opposite side of the pit in what was described as a 'frightfully mangled corpse'.

In 1857, five workers were killed at Millfield Iron Works, when a blast-furnace exploded after a 'tuyere' developed a fault. The works were owned by William Riley and Sons. The poor men suffered the most appalling injuries and were barely recognisable as body parts were littered all around, and the heat was said to have 'reduced their bodies to the consistency of coke', and their bodies had 'shrivelled and shrunk under the influence of the intense heat'. Those deceased were named as Thomas Davies, Samuel Thomas, Joseph Fletcher, John Marr, and a boy named Thomas Fletcher. At least four other men were said to have been badly burned and possibly unlikely to survive.

On 13 October 1862, part of the Monmore Green Chain Works floor, which belonged to Bayliss, Jones, and Bayliss, suddenly gave way. The works were surrounded by old pit-banks, and five young boys were working where the chains were forged, when the floor suddenly gave way with the bellows, the anvil, the 'bosh', and a quantity of iron chain and other heavy equipment falling thirty feet into the old mine shaft. A young lad named only as Ridgeway died quickly in hospital, crushed by the weight of the equipment, and another boy was thought unlikely to survive.

On 11 July 1867, the 'tuyere' of one of the blast-furnaces at the Parkfield Furnaces burst, resulting in molten iron and scalding cinders being 'belched out' by the force of the steam. Three men working by the 'tapping-hole' of the furnace were terribly burnt. Named as John Higginson, Henry Allman, and John Evans, all were taken to hospital with dreadful burns all over their bodies. Two of the men died that same night, and the life of the third man was said to lie in a 'precarious state'. A small hole in the hose of the tuyere was said to be the cause, and both men, lying in terrible pain in hospital, stressed to distraught relatives that 'they understood the dangers of their job' and that 'it was an accident, and no one was to blame', before they expired that night.

Three workers were burnt to death and six others seriously injured when a horrific fire occurred at the small Wolverhampton japanning works of Messrs William Evans and Sons, on 1 November

1869. Some spirits leaked from a barrel and ignited and spread to two of the workshops, one above the other. The two deceased girls were aged just fourteen and nineteen, one of whom was watched 'burning to death in the middle of the spirits'. The second young woman apparently 'leapt into the middle of the burning stuff' in the utter confusion of the moment, and a sixteen-year-old boy also suffocated after crawling into the japanning stove to escape the fire, but this became his tomb as it heated up and cooked him to an oven temperature.

On 1 February 1871, a newly-fitted tuyere on a blast-furnace suddenly burst at Osier Bed Iron Works, badly burning three men. John Payne, William Owens, and John Tudor were sprayed with red hot ashes and molten iron. Protective clothing reduced the amount of injury for two of the men who thankfully only suffered burnt feet, but Payne suffered awful disfiguring burns to his face and head.

On 12 April 1871, a fourteen-year-old boy named Joseph Bonald had his left eye burnt out by a piece of red-hot iron at the Minerva Iron Works.

On 15 May 1872, the death of a fourteen-year-old boy named Thomas Batten, the previous day at Chillington Iron Works was reported. During an interval in the work of the rollers, he foolishly climbed up onto an iron sheet to oil a small wheel. The iron plate was enclosed by what are called 'the boxers' that contained mechanical wheels moving at great speed. Unfortunately, his foot slipped, and his clothes caught on the boxers, and he was dragged through the wheels, the result being that 'the top part of his skull was torn off and his brain scattered about the place', resulting in instantaneous death.

On 25 July 1872, the inquest was held into the death of eighteen-year-old Frederick Arthur Smith who was killed at Stafford Road Railway Works four days earlier, when he operated the ratchet-jack too quickly to lower a locomotive that was being worked on. The engine, as a result, came down too quickly and 'jammed off his head, which rolled some yards from his body'. The victim was identified by his distraught father, who was also employed there.

On 25 November 1874, the inquest was held into the death of eleven-year-old William Cornall, who accidentally fell into a pot of molten metal at a small works in Church Lane, Graiseley.

On 3 July 1875, sixteen-year-old Elizabeth Michesre was killed at the Shakespeare Foundry when a chain hoisting a lift she had just stacked, suddenly snapped and landed on top of her, resulting in her instantaneous death.

On 18 September 1875, 4 men were killed when a blast-furnace belonging to the Spring Vale Furnaces experienced an escape of steam after a 'tuyere' burst. So dreadful were the injuries inflicted that skin and flesh peeled off the unfortunate victims, and one was said to have been 'dismembered'. Enoch Lewis was the man killed instantly, whilst William Egglestone, William Cooksey, and Thomas Howard all died in hospital. Cooksey had suffered appalling injuries, having been 'flayed' with scalding steam and hot ashes. All lived in the Wolverhampton area, and they left fifteen children as orphans.

On 25 February 1876, fourteen-year-old Samuel Roberts was dragged into the gears working the rolls at Star Iron Works. He suffered horrendous injuries, with his left leg virtually detached from his body, and his abdomen torn open. He suffered many broken bones. Thankfully, death was more-or-less instantaneous.

On 17 October 1876, fourteen-year-old Elizabeth Bowskin was very badly injured and deemed unlikely to survive, after her hair caught in machinery whilst 'worming some screws' at the Victoria Iron Works. She was then dragged into the machinery, sustaining dreadful cuts around her head, though the quick actions of a worker prevented immediate death. She was quickly taken to hospital but not expected to survive.

On 20 April 1882, an argument between two young men at Swan Garden Iron Works resulted in stones being thrown at Alfred Hammond by a youth named Matthew Reynolds. In response Hammond threw a red-hot piece of iron at Reynolds, killing him instantly.

On 31 December 1886, a John Maiden was 'oiling the engine' at Cleveland Iron Works when he got caught on some revolving machinery and whirled around the shafting at great speed, producing a quite mangled corpse after some fifty rotations.

Boiler Explosions

Furthermore, boiler explosions claimed the lives of a number of iron foundry workers in Wolverhampton, and indeed elsewhere. Around seventy men, too many to name here, were killed by boiler explosions in the Wolverhampton area. Most iron works relied on what could at the time be described as 'egg-shaped boilers', into which the flues of the puddling furnaces were run. But it was critical that they were maintained, serviced, and constantly managed by qualified and capable engineers. And that is where the problems often started.

In 1845, a man was killed, and sixteen others seriously injured at Shrubbery Iron Works in central Wolverhampton, including its reputed owner and town mayor George Thorneycroft who was present to oversee installation of a new pumping-engine. This incident occurred due to a faulty valve. He recovered from serious burns but eventually died in 1851, having never fully recovered from his injuries.

That same year, 1845, an engineer was killed when a boiler exploded at Parkfield Iron Works, when he tried to 'bodge' a repair to a leaking boiler, which all too inevitably failed.

At the same works, an unnamed worker was killed when a boiler exploded in 1854, when against the advice of an engineer, he screwed down the stop valve.

An explosion of the boiler at Swan Garden Iron Works also killed an unnamed man in 1855.

In 1857, six were killed when a boiler exploded at a small iron works in Walsall Street in central Wolverhampton, owned by Benjamin Mason junior. Three men, including Mason, were blown into pieces and thrown a hundred yards, after attempting to cool the boiler by naively pouring cold water into it. Mason was found minus his arms and part of his head, and another was found naked in the street with scalds all over his body and many broken bones, and he died quickly. Edwin Bradley suffered a fractured skull, but with his brain protruding, he died a few days later. Sadly, two small children William Turner aged five, and Isabella Hall aged twelve, who were playing outside, were also killed, the latter whom was simply passing having been sent on an errand by her distraught father who cradled her lifeless body in his arms. Ten other people were injured. A man was also arrested for picking pockets of the deceased.

By far the worst accident occurred at Millfields Iron Works, which had been vacant for over four years, after the earlier dreadful incident when a tuyere to the blast-furnace exploded in 1857, but it was purchased and re-opened in 1862 by a Thomas Rose who employed forty men working in the two forges and three mills, working the twenty puddling-furnaces. Unfortunately, upon the re-commissioning of the works, he failed to overhaul the two boilers after this four-year period of inactivity. One of the two boilers exploded, hurling it 300 yards away, and the building was totally-destroyed. This horrific explosion instantly killed fourteen workers whose bodies were mutilated, with limbs being found scattered all around. A number of others were injured, three of who died quickly in hospital, and another man died on his way home. Three more on a canal boat nearby were killed by falling debris, and eventually the total deaths stood at twenty-eight. The Mayor of Wolverhampton started an appeal for public donations for the families of the bereaved.

In May 1860, a serious boiler explosion occurred at Chillington Iron Works. One of five 'twenty-foot-high' boilers that had recently been serviced and was said to be of a good make, suddenly and unexpectedly exploded, resulting in the 'scattering of iron and brickwork with a terrible force in every direction'. The greater part of the boiler fell through the roof of the guide mill and a large pipe fell through the roof of the hoop mill. The watchman's wife and two children were buried beneath the chimney of their house but fortunately saved. Incredibly just one man died though another ten people were seriously injured.

On 29 January 1861, a boiler exploded near the Cockshutts Colliery, 'spreading ruin around' and killing the engineman and another man. The Inspector observed that: -

"*some of the appliances were of the most primitive nature and dangerous character, and the men who had the engines in charge were lamentably ignorant of the duties they had undertaken to perform*".

The situation with boiler explosions was becoming so worrying that in January 1864 the heads of Wolverhampton's main iron works called a 'Meeting of Forgemen' from Shrubbery, Swan Garden, Minerva, Monmore Green, Horseley Fields (Osier Bed), and Chillington Iron Works, to propose regular inspections by a Safety Board. This Wolverhampton Boiler Safety Board inspected boilers that were used for a variety of purposes. That same year a total of 770 boilers were inspected, of which 71 were for colliery-engines for pumping and 327 for colliery-engines for winding, 109 for blast-furnaces, 269 in rolling-mills and forges, 41 for pumping-engines at canals and water works, 21 for lathe-engines, 18 for clay-mills, and 14 for other purposes such as saw- mills.

Although the situation improved somewhat thereafter, dreadful incidents still occurred. In October 1868, six men were killed when a boiler exploded at Moseley Iron and Steel Works, with the inquest yet again laying the blame at quality of boiler. Nevertheless, a verdict of accidental death was returned.

In December 1869, eight men were killed after a boiler exploded at the Britannia Iron Works in Bradley. A few died instantly, but the others died hours or even days later, due to the horrific nature of their burns.

In June 1870, two men were killed and several badly injured when a boiler exploded at Lanesfield Iron Works.

In September 1872, a man and three boys were badly scalded following the explosion of a twelve-year old boiler at Chillington Iron Works. The three fifteen-year-old boys were burnt all over the body and one also on his head, when boiling water escaped from one of the six boilers. Fifteen-year-old John Manning died several days later.

In July 1874, two men named as William Owen and William Hunt were sleeping next to a boiler at Chillington Works, and were 'scalded to death by an escape of steam and boiling hot water'.

In July 1875, the engineer of Star Iron Works in Heath Town was killed when a boiler exploded. Six others were reported as being very badly injured and not expected to survive.

In 1883, three more workers were killed after a boiler explosion at Spring Vale Iron Works, and finally in 1903 another four were killed at an iron works at nearby Bradley.

Working close to the boilers in the iron works was clearly very hazardous. Child-labour was a key feature of both the mining and iron industries of the Black Country, and children formed much of the workforce, especially in nailing shops and factories, often living and working long hours in dreadful conditions. This was especially the case at small household locksmiths who could barely afford to pay them, never mind feed them, and many working children experienced a squalid existence.

The Union Works, and Hemingsley's Nail and Tip Factory both in central Wolverhampton both relied heavily on child labour. The latter was renowned locally for being a dangerous place to work. The ramshackle-building was set over three-storeys, and had previously partly-collapsed, and subsequently been literallly propped back up. Children reported seeing through the gaps in the floor. Dangerous power-driven equipment was notably crowded, leaving children to work in confined places. The 1841 report on child-labour, remarked that a number of children at 'Hemingsley's' were noted to be missing finger-tips or even fingers, and a young boy died at these works when part of floor which was so rotten, simply collapsed.

Iron manufacture, in whatever form, was a tough, physically-draining, demanding, and very dangerous occupation.

We now move on to look at Black Country iron industry statistics.

3) BLACK COUNTRY AND NATIONAL IRON INDUSTRY STATISTICS

G.C Allen in his 1928 work 'The Industrial Development of Birmingham and the Black Country 1860-1914' in the mid-1800s, highlighted that 6,000 workers were employed in the 'primary pig-iron-producing' industry, and 17,000 workers were employed in the 'finished iron industry'. The figures would have peaked around 1860-1870.

Wolverhampton and Bilston, along with most Black Country towns, were prominent in the production of both pig iron that created cast iron products, as well as 'finished-iron' products through the rolling mills, forges, and foundries.

Three sets of figures demonstrate the significance of Wolverhampton's iron industry - the number of blast-furnaces along with production output, the number of puddling- furnaces usually in the rolling-mills, and finally the number of iron works overall.

A) Blast-Furnaces (producing primary pig-iron)

The average blast-furnace at the peak of the Industrial Revolution gave employment to an average of 150-200 men. In 1790 there were just 21 small, 'charcoal or coke-fueled' furnaces in the Black Country, 15 of which were in Wolverhampton parish, 5 in Stourbridge, and 1 in Tipton.

CHAPTER SIX

The first blast-furnace in the Black Country was at West Bromwich. The Wolverhampton Civic and Historical Society website highlights that there were over 100 furnaces in regular action in the Wolverhampton area by the mid-19th Century, at the peak of the Industrial Revolution. Furthermore, official figures from 1839 reveal that only 12 Black Country iron works with blast-furnaces were producing more than 10,000 tonnes of iron per annum. 4 of these were in Wolverhampton, 1 in Bilston, 5 in the wider Dudley area, 1 in Wednesbury, and 1 in West Bromwich.

At the head of this list was Chillington Iron Works in east Wolverhampton, producing 16,600 tonnes per annum, followed by Golds Green Iron Works in West Bromwich which along with 2 works in Dudley each produced up to 13,500 tonnes per annum, followed then by Stow Heath Iron Works in east Wolverhampton that produced 12,750 tonnes per annum. So, the two works at what is now known as the East Park area of Wolverhampton produced nearly 30,000 tonnes of iron per annum at this point. Both Priestfield Iron Works, and Parkfield Iron Works in Wolverhampton, produced around 10,000 tonnes per annum, and were in the top dozen.

An informative on-line map produced by 'Distinctly Black Country' (Figure 30) shows 'Blast-Furnaces at Work 1823-1830', and this again highlights or emphasises Wolverhampton's significant iron producing industry.

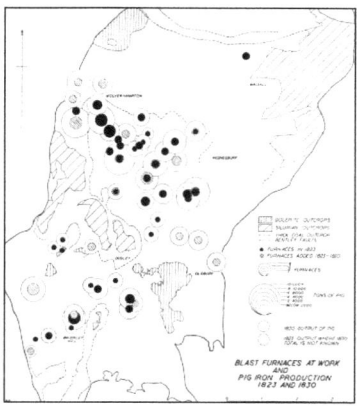

Figure 30 – Blast-furnaces at work 1823-30 by 'Distinctly Black Country'

In 1842, this being around the time the term 'Black Country' was first recorded, nine iron works with blast-furnaces in the Black Country region were producing 200 tonnes or more of iron per week, six of which were in the Wolverhampton area. These were: -

1) Stow Heath Furnaces, Wolverhampton producing 350 tonnes per week
2) Chillington Iron Works, Wolverhampton producing 270 tonnes per week.
3) Capponfield Furnaces, near Wolverhampton producing 270 tonnes per week.
4) Parkfield Furnaces, Wolverhampton producing 240 tonnes per week.
5) George Jones's Furnaces, Bilston producing 240 tonnes per week.
6) The Lays Furnaces in Dudley producing 240 tonnes per week.
7) Millfields Furnaces in Bilston producing 200 tonnes per week.
8) The Oldbury Furnaces producing 200 tonnes per week.
9) Shutt End Furnaces, Dudley producing 200 tonnes per week.

As time passed, blast-furnaces became more efficient, with some works in Wolverhampton and elsewhere in the Black Country producing around 1,000 tonnes of iron per week, or 50,000 tonnes per annum by the 1870s. Most Black Country blast-furnaces operated with cold-blast.

In 1860, at the region's industrial height, 191 blast-furnaces were listed at iron works in the Black Country area. 181 of these can be found at www.newmanlocalhistory.org – released by The Iron and Steel Institute - they are listed as being 39 in Wolverhampton (27 Bilston, 18 in Wolverhampton), 33 in West Bromwich (21 in West Bromwich, 12 in Wednesbury), 30 in Tipton, 17 in Dudley, 8 in Walsall, 7 in Stourbridge, 5 in Brierley Hill, 4 in Oldbury, 3 in Smethwick, and 2 each in Darlaston, Willenhall, Moxley, Bloxwich, and 2 even in Birmingham.

Twelve years later, in 1872, The Iron and Steel Institute released figures highlighting that Wolverhampton had 52 blast-furnaces (28 blast-furnaces in Wolverhampton and 24 in Bilston), Tipton had 23, West Bromwich had 14, whilst the wider Dudley / Brierley Hill area had 38 blast furnaces. Overall 166 blast-furnaces were registered at that point in time, in the Black Country area.

To provide perspective nationally in 1872, in contrast to the Black Country's 166 blast- furnaces, figures highlight that there were a total of 945 blast-furnaces in the whole Country at this point in time, of which 188 were spread around South Wales, 154 were in Scotland of which 80 were in the Clyde / Glasgow area, 94 were in Cleveland of which 76 were around Middlesborough, 51 were in Derbyshire of which 23 were in Chesterfield, and 46 were in North Staffordshire of which around 20 were in Stoke. Sheffield had just 7 blast-furnaces at this point.

Wolverhampton iron works with known blast-furnaces at some point included Chillington Iron Works with 4 initially but later 5, Parkfield Iron Works with 5, Stow Heath Iron Works with 5, Osier Bed Iron Works with 4, Mars Iron Works with 3, Rough Hills Furnaces with 3, Moseley Hole Furnaces with 3, The Wolverhampton Furnaces with 3, Ettingshall Furnaces with 3, Priestfield Furnaces with 3, and later Monmoor Rolling Mills with 1. This gives a total of 38, and additionally the 3 at Millfields Furnaces and 5 at Spring Vale often registered themselves as Wolverhampton works - so a total of 46 blast-furnaces existed at works using a Wolverhampton postal address. By 1890, many of the works had ceased operations, or reduced significantly, and Alfred Hickman's Spring Vale Works became the biggest and most productive in the borough.

B) Puddling-Furnaces, in Rolling-mills and Forges (producing finished wrought-iron)

Figures should be treated with caution at times, for instance, included in an 1871 list of 438 puddling-furnaces for West Bromwich were 63 at Corngreaves Iron Works, Brierley Hill, and 26 at Stow Heath Iron Works, Wolverhampton. In contrast, it is understandable that some furnaces mid-way between the two-to-three-mile industrial belt between Wolverhampton and Bilston centres, were sometimes counted as lying in each others district because they lay mid-way between both.

The 'Iron and Steel Institute', released figures for 1872, that show that the Wolverhampton area had 409 puddling-furnaces (216 in Wolverhampton, 193 in Bilston), the West Bromwich area had 390 puddling-furnaces, Tipton had 280, Brierley Hill 246, Wednesbury 202, Walsall 109, Stourbridge 104, Dudley 102, Smethwick 86, and Oldbury 35.

An article from the Staffordshire Advertiser on 21 September 1919 highlights the impressive statistics of the Black Country Iron industry, stating that 'in its hey-day', as well as possessing over 170 blast-furnaces, the key Black Country towns could claim the following figures: -

"Wolverhampton had 290 puddling-furnaces and 39 mills and forges.
Bilston had 238 puddling-furnaces and 47 mills and forges.
Wednesbury had 210 puddling-furnaces and 28 mills and forges.
Tipton had 172 puddling-furnaces and 47 mills and forges.
Walsall had 137 puddling-furnaces and 68 mills and forges.
Dudley had 131 puddling-furnaces and 13 mills and forges.
Willenhall had 15 puddling-furnaces and 3 mills and forges".

These puddling-furnaces, which were initially sometimes referred to as air, ball, mill, annealing, heating, or reverberatory-furnaces created immense fire and smoke over the district. The three-mile stretch between the centres of Wolverhampton and Bilston must have formed an incredible site at that time, with around 530 puddling-furnaces, 86 mills and forges, along with at least the 50 blast-furnaces already highlighted.

By 1896 it was recorded that John Lysaght was operating some 24 rolling-mills at his Wolverhampton works of Osier Bed and Swan Garden, and both the Shrubbery and Mars Iron Works were operating 6 or 7 rolling-mills. These were virtually all what were called 'black-sheet' mills.

Again, according to figures produced by the Iron and Steel Institute in 1872, there were 2049 puddling-furnaces registered at iron works in South Staffordshire (the Black Country), 1990 in Cleveland, 1338 in South Wales, 565 in Scotland, and 444 in North Staffordshire.

The highest number at any one plant included 190 at Darlington, 165 at Newport, 160 at Merthyr Tydvil, 151 at Consett, 120 at Middlesborough (Redcar), 109 at Hartlepool, 101 at Bishop Auckland, 100 at Middlesborough, 91 at Newport, 90 at Stoke (Shelton). These were purpose-built 'super-plants'.

The Black Country was characterised by many mid-sized works due to the way they evolved close to each other, largely beside the canal. Chillington operated 95 puddling-furnaces, 56 of these were at Chillington Iron Works in east Wolverhampton, the remaining were at their works at the nearby Capponfield Furnaces in Bilston, or at their works at Bradley and Darlaston.

According to figures released in the Staffordshire Advertiser on 3 October 1857, seventeen iron works or foundries in the Black Country operated '30-or-more' puddling- furnaces. In order, these were: -

Chillington Iron Works, Wolverhampton	56
Bloomfield Iron Works, Tipton	56
Corngreaves Iron Works, Kingswinford	56

Albion Works, West Bromwich	50
Patent Shaft Company, Wednesbury	48
Round Oak Iron Works, Brierley Hill	45
Shrubbery Iron Works, Wolverhampton	44
Corbyn's Hall Iron Works, Kingswinford	40
Oak Farm, Kingswinford	38
Brierley Works, Brierley Hill	38
Shutt End, Dudley	34
Bradley Iron Works, Bilston	33
Wednesbury Oak Iron Works	32
Gold's Hill, West Bromwich	31
Swan Garden Iron Works, Wolverhampton	30
Hart's Hill Iron Works, Brierley Hill	30.

But by the late-1870s, as highlighted, Shrubbery Iron Works operated at least 80 puddling-type furnaces, Spring Vale Iron Works operated 68, and Round Oak operated 65.

Other Wolverhampton Iron Works with less than 30 puddling-furnaces included Stow Heath Iron Works with 26, Horseley Fields Iron Works (Osier Bed) with 26, Minerva Iron Works with 21, Ettingshall Iron Works with 21, Capponfield Iron Works with 16, Beaver Iron Works with 14, Monmore Rolling Mills with 11, Star Iron Works with 9, Cleveland Iron Works with 9, and E.P. and W. Baldwin's Tin-plate works with just 3.

So, by the end of the Industrial Revolution, around 1880, the number of puddling- furnaces operating in Wolverhampton Iron Works reached a staggering total of 333, a figure that roughly tallies with the Staffordshire Advertiser total of 290 above.

Other substantial works not included in the above lists also had some types of heating, annealing, pot, ball, or reverberatory-furnaces, which in effect were types of puddling-furnaces specifically used for creating nails or tubes for instance, and others had mini-blast furnaces called foundry-cupolas. The Shakespeare Foundry,

The Griffon Iron Works, and particularly the vast Victoria Iron Works must have had large numbers of some type of furnace.

In summary, although the Black Country possessed more puddling-furnaces overall than any other district of the Country, they were spread across a much higher number of iron works than other key areas because of the natural way the industry developed and evolved in the area.

C) Iron Works of the Black Country

Samuel Griffiths highlighted that in 1871, the Black Country had 53 out of 160 'substantially-sized' iron works in England, approximately one-third.

The following register shows most of the main Black Country Iron Works around 1860, those with blast-furnaces, puddling-furnaces, or rolling-mills, noting the town which they gave as their home address: -

Wolverhampton (24) - Wolverhampton Iron Works, Chillington Iron Works, Moseley Hole Furnaces, Minerva Iron Works, Ettingshall Furnaces, Spring Vale Iron Works, Osier Bed Furnaces, Parkfield Furnaces, Roughwood Furnaces, Horseley Fields / Osier Bed Iron Works, Stow Heath Furnaces, Shrubbery Iron Works, Swan Garden Iron Works, Priestfield Iron Works, Wolverhampton Furnaces, Victoria Iron Works, Monmore Iron Works, Cleveland Iron Works, New Griffon Iron Works, Mars Iron Works, Star Iron Works, Beaver Iron and Steel Works, Shakespeare Foundry and Iron Works.

Bilston (25) - Capponfield Iron Works, Ettingshall Iron Works, Millfields Iron Works, Deepfield Iron Works, Millfields Furnaces, Prior Field Furnaces, Bankfield Furnaces, Bovereux Furnaces, Barbersfield Furnaces, Bilston New Furnace, Bradley Iron Works, Moxley Iron Works, Albert Iron Works, Hall Fields Furnace, Britannia Iron Works, Bilston Brook Furnaces, Stonefield Iron Works, Bridge Iron Works,

Herbert's Park Iron Works, Highfields Iron Works, Regent Iron Works, Batman's Hill Iron Works, Bradley Field Iron Works, Bradley New Iron Works, Coseley Furnaces, Ebenezer Iron Works.

Tipton (23) - Leabrook Furnaces, Toll End Iron Works, Bloomfield Furnaces, Factory Iron Works, Tipton Green Iron Works, Horseley Furnaces, Tipton Iron Works, Tipton Green Furnaces, Dudley Port Field Furnaces, Willingsworth Furnaces, Groveland Iron Works, Dudley Port Furnaces, Summer Hill Iron Works, Park Lane Furnaces, Dudley Port Iron Works, Stour Valley Furnaces, Great Bridge Iron Works, Tividale Iron Works, Gospel Oak Iron Works, Old Church Iron Works, Coneygie Iron Works, Union Furnaces, Albion Iron Works.

West Bromwich (18) - Golds Hill Furnaces, Golds Green Iron Works, Waterloo Iron Works, Atlas Iron Works, Wellington Iron Works, Golds Hill New Iron Works, Bromford Iron Works, Eagle Greets Green Iron Works, Spon Lane Iron Works, Sheepwash Iron Works, Victoria Iron Works, Hall end Iron Works, Roway Iron Works, Providence Iron Works, Crookhay Furnaces, Ridgeacre Iron Works, Union Furnaces, Albion Iron Works.

Dudley (15) - Old Hill Furnaces, Russell's Hall Furnaces, Woodside Furnaces, Malleable Iron Company, Withymoor Furnaces, Parkhead Furnaces, Leys Furnaces, Corbyn's Hall New Furnaces, Corbyn's Hall Furnaces, Kettley Furnaces, Netherton Furnaces, Dixon's Green Furnaces, Netherton Iron Works, Oak Farm Furnaces, Windmill End Furnaces.

Wednesbury (6) - Imperial Iron Works, Waterloo Furnaces, Old Park Furnaces, Kings Hill Iron Works, Monway Field Iron Works, Brunswick and Victoria Iron Works.

Walsall (7) - Walsall Iron Works, Birchills Iron Works, Pelsall Iron Works, Wedges Mill Iron Works, Green Lane Furnaces, Birchills Furnaces, Bentley Furnaces.

Stourbridge / Brierley Hill / Cradley (10) - Stourbridge Iron Works, Leys Iron Works, Cradley Iron Works, Brettel Lane Iron Works,

Hyde Iron Works, Brockmoor Iron Works, Old Level Iron Works, Hartshill Iron Works, Nine Locks Iron Works, Level New Furnaces.

Oldbury (4) - Oldbury Furnaces, Britannia Iron Works, Ebenezer Iron Works, Brades Iron Works

Darlaston (3) - Rough Hay Furnaces, Eagle Iron Works, Darlaston Iron Works

Smethwick (3) - Anchor Iron Works, Crown Iron Works, Delet (?) Iron Works

Willenhall (1) - Moomer Lane Iron Works

Bloxwich (1) - Hatherton Iron Works

Additionally, as well as furnaces, iron works, and rolling-mills, there were other substantial operations in the Black Country producing iron goods, not listed above as they did not have furnaces or rolling mills.

In Wolverhampton, for instance, there was John Loveridge's Merridale Iron Works, Edwards Davies's Crown Iron Works, The Griffon Iron Works, the Niphon Iron Works, and the Vulcan Iron Works amongst others.

CONCLUSION - Wolverhampton's Iron Industry

These statistics, maps, and descriptions highlight the sheer scale of iron operations in the central area of the town, particularly on the eastern and southern side.

Wolverhampton, even without Bilston, clearly played a key role in the iron-producing industry of the Black Country. The concentrated district running for around two-three miles between the town centres of Wolverhampton and Bilston was arguably the most industrial area in terms of iron works, within the entire Black Country district, and the Wolverhampton area at its industrial peak around 1860-1870 was said to have produced nearly one-third of all iron in the Country.

Therefore, when one chooses to define or partly define the Black Country by the Iron industry or by the number of furnaces, by manpower statistics, or whether it be through 'primary-iron production' or 'finished-iron production' levels, Wolverhampton surely deserves considerable recognition as playing a key role in Black Country iron history.

Samuel Griffiths recognised Wolverhampton's immense significance, at the peak of the Industrial Revolution in the 1870s, when he referred to it as: -

"The Capital of the Iron Trade in the Black Country."

He should know, the iron industry was his specialist field after all.

As already alluded to in this work, perhaps Wolverhampton should alternatively adopt the title of 'Iron Country', as English journalist William Cobbett, as well as Queen Victoria defined the town and surrounding area. Or perhaps: -

"The Capital of the Iron Country".

It was after all, perceived widely as 'the centre of the iron trade', nicknamed in 1866 by the Manchester press as: -

"Ironopolis".

It would be a fitting title for Wolverhampton – and hence that nick-name has been adopted and incorporated into the title of this work.

CHAPTER SEVEN

Wolverhampton Social Conditions During the Industrial Revolution, and Later-on

CHAPTER BREAKDOWN

1) **Working Conditions during the Industrial Revolution**- Including: - A) Damning reports on Wolverhampton's working conditions and the employment of children. B) Politics, strikes, social disorder, and distress.
2) **Reports regards Housing Conditions in Wolverhampton** including: - A) A Chronological History from 1750. B) Fatal housing-related diseases and deathly statistics.
3) **Conclusion** - Housing and Working Conditions of Wolverhampton.

Although not directly relevant to the central question of whether Wolverhampton was part of the Black Country, the working and housing conditions form two separate, fascinating strands to investigate within this chapter. The evidence does perhaps dismiss the myth that it was the workers of the smaller central towns who suffered all the hardship.

Figure 31 – Slum housing, Skinner Street, Wolverhampton, early-1900s

The wonderful early-1900s photograph of slum housing in the centre of Wolverhampton, courtesy of Wolverhampton City Archives (Figure 31), portrays rather typical housing in the town. Slum-courts developed in a rather-haphazard manner in the town during the 1800s, with houses built in any available space seemingly devoid of any planning structure, rather than the clearly laid-out, long straight streets that were being widely constructed at that point in time.

Much of the following information was obtained from websites such as the historywebsite.co.uk, newmanlocalhistory.org, wolverhamptonhistory.org, and notably Britishnewspaperarchive.co.uk. Specifically, however, George Barnsby's work 'A history of Housing in Wolverhampton 1750-1975', as well as his excellently-researched 1990 book 'Social Conditions in The Black Country' were both particularly revealing. As was the excellent 2001 University of Leicester thesis by John Butland Smith for his PhD, titled 'The Governance of Wolverhampton 1848-1888'. More recently, I must give credit to Simon Briercliffe who has given lectures on the slums of the Black Country, and who researched Wolverhampton's Caribee Island for his PhD. Some of his notes can be found on his wonderful blog, Uptheossroad.com.

The extremely dirty, general environment of those living and working around Wolverhampton's central and eastern districts does convey an image that lends itself to one of incredible poverty and real hardship, in stark contrast to the experience of the minority of residents who were fortunate enough to reside within its far more prosperous but smaller western suburbs, or in what were then separate villages such as Tettenhall - the so-called 'green borderland'.

In 1849, the 'Morning Chronicle' set out to investigate working-class life in England and Wales. P.E. Razzell and R.W. Wainwright, in the 1973 publication 'The Victorian Working Class', edited these reports, one which highlighted in fairly, crude terms just how primitive housing conditions were for many of the colliers and iron-workers of the Wolverhampton and wider Black Country district: -

"Gardens are unknown in the coal and iron district of Staffordshire. Indeed, for mile after mile, nothing green will grow. Here and there an individual has attempted to form some sort of artificial garden, by bringing soil from a distance and lying it upon the coal refuse, but the constant smoke kills every bud and sprout. I have already alluded in general terms to the cracked and dilapidated state of immense numbers of the houses, owing to the continued sinking and shifting of earth. This is one of the worst features of the district. It makes great numbers of houses uncomfortable - almost uninhabitable - and not a few, absolutely-dangerous. A visitor to the western outskirts of Bilston, in the direction of the village of Ettingshall, might well imagine that he gazed upon a tract which had been recently convulsed by an earthquake."

Indeed, many colliers, such as those at Rough Hills in Wolverhampton, resided in primitive, 'tumbledown-shacks' close to the iron and coal mines. They needed to be close to their place of employment.

Wolverhampton had notorious concentrations of slum housing in its very-own 'east-end', and notably a central district 'delightfully' called 'Caribee Island' (or 'Cribby Island', as it was known locally) which was so bad that on 24 July 1866, the 'Dundee Courier' reported the following: -

"The Lancet has some horrible notes on the sanitary state of the Black Country. Wolverhampton and the neighbourhood appear to be as bad as Shanghai itself. Constant instances occur of one open, doorless water-closet for a whole row of cottages, nay, often a room, or even two, are built over the ash-heap. This is common in the delightful locality called Caribee Island."

Other writers rightly emphasised the great population boom as being the main cause of over-crowding. In 2005, the author John Smith, in chapter eight of the book 'Towns, Regions and Industries – Urban and Industrial Change in the Midlands 1700 –1840', titled his chapter 'Industrial and Social change – Wolverhampton Transformed 1700–1840', in which he highlighted Wolverhampton's incredibly rapid population growth to become the tenth largest population-centre in the Country. He stated: -

"By the middle of the Industrial Revolution, Wolverhampton was at the forefront of a new urban experience, truly a 'shock-city' of the Industrial Revolution. The downside of this manufacturing success was that the eastern district and some central districts of the town became desperately overcrowded, populated, and very unhealthy".

Manchester was widely considered to be the 'shock-city' of the Industrial Revolution, but it was used to describe very few other urban areas. This 'shock-city's' booming population relied far too heavily on the rapidly-expanding mining and iron-producing economy during the Industrial Revolution of the late-1700s and throughout the 1800s, and when economic down-turns occurred, desperation prevailed, with many relying on east Wolverhampton's huge workhouse, which housed up to a thousand, destitute residents.

Many of the poorest residents also relied on 'Common Lodging houses', of which there were several hundred in Wolverhampton, and at times of economic difficulty many depended on handouts from the Horseley Fields corn-flour mill to prevent starvation. During one particularly severe winter, 20,000 loaves of bread were handed out. Others who came to the town would simply sleep where they could, by furnaces and factories, canals, railways, and on the coal-field. Accidents were inevitable, especially in the dark. Many bodies would later be found down unguarded pit shafts.

Although we have not really touched on crime, Wolverhampton, like many towns of the Industrial Revolution, was a far-more violent place to live in than it is today. Poverty, disease, and hardship are inextricably linked to crime.

So, the first sub-section examines working conditions in Wolverhampton throughout the Industrial Revolution, with a strong emphasis on the working conditions for the children of the district. The reports undoubtedly make grim reading, but it should be remembered that we are concentrating on hardship, which although widespread, was of course not the experience for everyone.

1) WORKING CONDITIONS DURING THE INDUSTRIAL REVOLUTION

A) Damning reports on Wolverhampton's working conditions and the employment of children

'Ragged Schools' were introduced in the poorest towns and cities of the Country in the 1840s, in areas where children were found to be most destitute. Not only did these schools provide free education, they also tried to provide some free clothing and food. It was no surprise therefore that one was set up in Caribee Island, the worst slum area in Wolverhampton, in June 1848. Its creation was deemed to be as appropriate as could possibly be found anywhere, according to the editor of the 'Wolverhampton Chronicle and Staffordshire Advertiser', who remarked: -

"With great pleasure, we learn that a Ragged School has been recently established in Carribee Island, in Stafford Street, in this town. The well-known character of the neighbourhood - and a recent visit has added force to our impression - assures us that in no case can such an establishment be more beneficially operating. In this district, many hundreds, almost thousands of persons live, suffering, if they have families, the severest poverty. Do not their children, ragged though they are, present one of the strongest claims that can be advanced for charitable assistance? Their very rags plead for them."

Nearly twenty years later, by 1865, the Ragged school system was established, but the main Ragged School in Wolverhampton only had 120 boys and a similar number of girls turning up to receive an education early morning, before they started work, or for evening classes.

Increasingly through the mid-1800s, the spotlight was falling on the welfare of children, though it has to be said, not generally from those who employed them but through concerned, enlightened, and forward-thinking individuals. In fact, it was increasingly becoming a national issue, and as public opinion and momentum gathered, high-level Government intervention soon followed.

A body called the 'Children's Employment Commission' instigated an official Government Inquiry led by Messrs Thos Take, T. Southwood-Smith, Leonard Horner, and J. Saunders, who with a team of advisors carried out a most detailed and thorough investigation of the living and working conditions in towns and cities the length and breadth of the Country, with an emphasis on the welfare of children. Mr R.H. Horne Esquire was tasked to carry out investigations throughout the Midlands, in which he interviewed many young children as well as their employees throughout 1840-1841, culminating in the famous and lengthy, landmark 1843 'Hansard report' given to the House of Commons, on 'The Condition and Education of the Poor'.

Mr Horne was genuinely alarmed and moved to sincere sadness by the situation he found in Wolverhampton, at its locksmiths, galvanising works, nailing shops, japanning works, and foundries and mines. He highlighted that in many of the Country's towns and cities, children started working around the age of 12 or 13, but in the Wolverhampton and Birmingham area virtually all children of the working-class started working aged just 8, usually as part of an Apprenticeship system to which they would be tied to until they were older. According to the register at Wolverhampton's Monmore Green Work-house, which replaced the decrepit Horseley Fields Work-house in 1837, children as young as 8 were sent to the town's mines on 12-year-long apprenticeships, and furthermore, in Wolverhampton children would work a staggering and grinding 14 hours a day. Mr Horne noted that these children were generally in a terrible, malnourished condition, whilst the children of the nailers of Sedgley, who were often considered by local historians to sit right at the bottom of the Black Country social-class structure, were for comparison only noted to be 'nearly as bad'.

His solemn, detailed Wolverhampton report made many observations, some of which are highlighted below': -

"The children of Wolverhampton are semi-starved, poorly, stunted, and wretchedly-thin. I have observed that the character and habits of the numerous labouring poor are of the lowest order. There are many things of an extremely horrid description to be detailed concerning the physical condition of the children in these parts, but I forbear to touch them at present, being engaged only on their moral deficiency. They often worked 12-14 hours a day, and not a penny which they had for their own use, who were clothed in rags, who acknowledged that they often felt sick or ill and that they had not had enough to eat, who were sometimes beaten badly but who only felt it for a day or two, but who still replied that they liked their work and were well treated.

The physical condition of the children is poor, it is poor because of the diet, which is generally-speaking, not good, nor in sufficient quantity, and which they consume as they can during their work, and while noxious fumes or dust are flying about in the shops or manufactories – I allude to those who work in the casting shops of the foundries, and those who are apprenticed to locksmiths, screw-makers, and general forge or smith's work. Their physical condition is poor from other causes. They commence work at too tender an age, the nature of the work is bad, and they work too many hours in the day. Great numbers are very uncleany in their persons, seldom washing themselves above once or twice a week, and then generally only their hands and faces. In some parts of town, filthiness prevails to an alarming extent, and is attended by sickness and consumption. Great numbers are very badly clothed, and no difference is made in their summer or winter clothing. In external appearance, there are none of the children engaged in these works who are robust or well-formed. Some appear strong at their work, upon examination, but appear to have little general strength, many are very delicate, some sickly, many ill-formed, meagre and awry, some few badly deformed. Many have the blade-bones displaced and jutting out, especially the girls, so as to resemble the back of a grass-hopper, attributable directly to the nature and duration of their work. Boys and girls aged 14 and 15 continually present the external appearance of children aged 11, 12, and 13. In stature they are stunted, nearly all of them. All were alike. The only exceptions to the rule were young persons who had not come to work til they were 11 or 12 years of age, or they lived comfortably with respectable parents, or they were not natives to Wolverhampton. Young lads 15 and 16 are the size of ordinary English schoolboys aged 12 and 14, but not by any means as healthy and strong as the latter. Their long, melancholy faces and vacant stare seemed to be half-conscious of the progressive injury to nature whereby they earned their daily bread, but ignorant of the cause. Some had a look of hopelessness, as though they had once known what it was to hope. The great majority seemed reckless or totally indifferent. Amongst all the children and young persons I examined, I found with very few exceptions, that their minds were as stunted as their bodies; their moral feelings stagnant. The children and young persons possess but little sense of moral duty towards their parents and have little affection for them. One child believed that Pontius Pilate and Goliath were apostles; another, fourteen or fifteen years of age, did not know how many two and two made. In my evidence taken in this town alone, as many as five children and young persons had never heard even the name of Jesus Christ. You will find boys who have never heard of such a place as London, and of Willenhall, only three miles distant, who have never heard of the name of the Queen, or of such names as Wellington, Nelson, Bonaparte, or King George. Furthermore, most who said prayers before going to sleep only knew two words, "our father", but nothing else. They evidently knew of nothing else but to wake and go to work from day-to-day and to continue working until permitted to leave. Poignantly, such a question as "do you feel tired?" had never-before been asked of them, and they did not understand it."

If that was not sad enough, the treatment of children at work in the town was described as 'semi-barberous' at times. In Wolverhampton, Willenhall, and Sedgley, children were reported to be 'most cruelly beaten', whilst in Darlaston, Bilston, and especially Wednesbury, children were in-contrast, rarely beaten. It is unclear why these polar-opposite differences existed. The process of 'nailing the ear to the counter' was a famous punishment.

Mr Horne also noted that many children in Wolverhampton resided in quite awful housing conditions, describing the hovels in which many lived as: -

"*'wretchedly-dreadful', with Salop Street and its courts being the worst in the district, yet this western district is healthier than the other side of the town".*

Horne was also appalled by the slums of Caribee Island, of its eastern district, and by the ramshackle 'hut conditions' he found on the road from Wolverhampton to Sedgley and beyond. More of the housing conditions he encountered in due course.

Interestingly, one man interviewed by Mr Horne was also a local GP, Peter Bell Esquire, who had practised in Wolverhampton for many years, and he made the following interesting and somewhat surprising observation about the superior health of boys involved in mining in the town, compared to those working in the iron manufactories: -

"The colliers are so healthy that wounds are cured with a quite surprising rapidity. Compound fractures are cured with scarcely a troublesome symptom. As to formation, the collier, as he walks, rolls along, swinging at the hips as though he were double-jointed. The manufacturer creeps along as if his bones were all huddled together."

He also noted that: -

"the colliers always live on the best of everything, and their boys always fare the same as the men. It is notorious that on the first day of 'ducks and green peas', the colliers buy up all that are in the market".

Mr Horne also walked through Wolverhampton on a Sunday to discover what the population did on the Sabbath: -

"I first encountered a group of working men, clad in aprons and caps, with their arms begrimed and their faces smeared from their previous night's work. Their sleeves were rolled up, and they passed wearily, unconcerned by the fact that it was time for morning service. These might be idlers who had been off work earlier in the week and had stayed late at work on Saturday night to make up the time. I next observed small boys fighting in imitation of the prize-fighters. They cursed and swore as blood dripped from their faces. Idly watching them stood their mothers, each woman at the end of an entry or in front of a brown doorway, its doorstep already worn down during sixty-years it had been walked over. Further along, boys were sitting in a hole in the ground using pick-axes to play at mining, while some girls, in rags and without shoes, were playing in elementary dance routines or else just chasing each other. One better-dressed group of girls were

jumping from mounds of dirt, dung and rubbish and sprawling on the road, immediately picking themselves up and scuttling up the heaps of rubbish again. Soon a clock struck and a few seconds later the chapel doors opened to let out the Sunday school children. Some of them trotted primly down the steps, little black books under their arms, their clothes as neat as possible, if not always new. Others rolled out of chapel as wildly as the children playing on the rubbish heaps".

He also watched colliers empty from the town's pubs at midnight on pay-day, and happily engage themselves in numerous brawls, and he concluded that the people of Wolverhampton were: -

"semi-barbarous".

Overall, his chief impression of life in Wolverhampton was summarised by just four words: -

"dullness and vacuity, indifference and waste'".

Mr Horne's report went on to describe the situation he found in Wolverhampton's nearby parish towns: -

"I now go to Willenhall, and there it is said, a lower condition of morals cannot, I think, be found—they sink some degrees, if that be possible, below the worst classes of children and young persons in Wolverhampton; they do not display the remotest sign of comprehension as to what is meant by the term of morals. Next, of Wednesfield, it is said the population are much addicted to drinking; many besotted in the extreme; poor dejected men; with hardly a rag to their backs, are often seen drunk two or three days in the week, and even when they have large families. The same profligacy and ignorance at Darlaston, where we have the evidence of three parties, an overseer, a collector, and a relieving officer, to a very curious fact. I quote this to show the utter recklessness and intellectual apathy in which these people live, caring little but for existence, and the immediate physical wants of the passing hour; they state that there are as many as 100 men in Darlaston who do not know their own names, only their nicknames. But it is said that in Bilston things are much better. It is remarked that the moral condition of children and young persons on-the-whole, was very superior to that

in Wolverhampton. He excepts, however, the bank-girls, and those who work at the screw manufactories. Among them, 'great numbers of bastards', the bank-girls drive coal-carts, ride astride upon horses, drink, swear, fight, smoke, whistle, sing, and care for nobody. Here I must observe, if things are better in Bilston, it is owing to the dawn of education, to the great exertions of the Rev. Mr. Fletcher and the Rev. Mr. Owen in the church; and Mr. Robert Bew (chemist), and Mr. Dimmock (iron merchant), among the Dissenters. Next as to Sedgley, children and young persons, (says the rector), grow up in irreligion, immorality, and ignorance. The number of girls at nailing considerably exceeds that of the boys; it may be termed the district of female blacksmiths; constantly associating with depraved adults, and young persons of the opposite sex, they naturally fall into all their ways; and drink, smoke, swear, and become as bad as men. The men and boys are usually naked, except a pair of trousers; the women and girls have only a thin ragged petticoat, and an open shirt without sleeves. Throughout the long descent of the main roading, or rather the sludge-way of Lower Gornal, and throughout the very long, winding and straggling roadway of Coseley, I never saw one abode of a working family which had the least appearance of comfort or of wholesomeness, whilst the immense majority were of the most wretched and sty-like description".

In its final conclusions to Parliament, the Commission made a number of recommendations, but it singularly picked-out Wolverhampton from any other region in the Country, with an extremely damning and eye-catching statement: -

"The district which requires special notice, on-account of the general and almost incredible abuse of children, is that of Wolverhampton and the neighbourhood – in the nail and tip manufactories, in some of the foundries, and among the very numerous class of small masters generally, the punishments are harsh and cruel, and in some cases, they can only be classed as ferocious. Many of these poor children are so oppressed by the circumstances in which they are placed, that they are even sunk below the consciousness of the misery of their condition".

The now-famous work of German writer Friedrich Engels, titled 'The Condition of the Working Class in England' (1844), a subject matter that he clearly became besotted with, also emphasised the desperate situation of child-labourers. In one of his chapters, titled 'Single branches of Industry - Factory hands', he also highlighted just how grave working conditions were for children in the Black Country: -

"In the iron district of Staffordshire, the state of things is still worse. For the coarse wares made here neither much division of labour (with certain exceptions) nor steam-power or machinery can be applied. In Wolverhampton, Willenhall, Bilston, Sedgley, Wednesfield, Darlaston, Dudley, Walsall, Wednesbury, etc., there are, therefore, fewer factories, but chiefly single forges, where the small masters work alone, or with one or more apprentices, who serve them until reaching the twenty-first year. The small employers are in about the same situation as those of Birmingham; but the apprentices, as a rule, are much worse off. They get almost exclusively meat from diseased animals or such as have died a natural death, or tainted meat, or fish to eat, with veal from calves killed too young, and pork from swine smothered during transportation, and such food is furnished not by small employers only, but by large manufacturers, who employ from thirty to forty apprentices. The custom seems to be universal in Wolverhampton, and its natural consequence is frequent bowel complaints and other diseases. Moreover, the children usually do not get enough to eat, and have rarely other clothing than their working rags, for which reason, if for no other, they cannot go to Sunday school. The dwellings are bad and filthy, often so much so that they give rise to disease; and in-spite-of the not materially unhealthy work, the children are puny, weak, and, in many cases, severely crippled. In Willenhall, for instance, there are countless persons who have, from perpetually filing at the lathe, crooked backs and one leg crooked, "hind-leg" as they call it, so that the two legs have the form of a 'K', while it is said that more than one-third of the working-men there are ruptured. Here, as well as in Wolverhampton, numberless cases were found of

retarded puberty among girls, for girls too, work at the forges, as well as among boys, extending even to the nineteenth year. In Sedgley and its surrounding district, where nails form almost the sole product, the nailers live and work in the most wretched stable-like huts, which for filth can scarcely be equalled".

Three years later, in May 1847, Reverend J.B. Owen gave a lecture in Wolverhampton, 'On the habits and habitations of the Midland Manufacturing Districts'. In this lecture, he too made similar observations and conclusions about the residents of the town: -.

"In the manufactories of this town, I have sometimes been painfully struck with the pallid, unhealthy appearance of a large portion of the operatives, both children and adults".

Despite the far-reaching conclusions of the 'Hansard Report' of 1843, any misbehaving children still found themselves at the receiving end of brutal retribution at work, even from authority. An article from the 'Wolverhampton Chronicle' on 29 October 1862 highlighted that 'a boy was imprisoned for three days and whipped once', at the order of the Court, after he was said to have 'stolen a small chain and small wheel worth one shilling, from a skip at The Wolverhampton Colliery, Rough Hills'.

Further concern was expressed just over twenty years later, on 16 January 1865, when the 'Birmingham Daily Post' published a report issued by the Royal Commissioners on the 'Employment of women and children', which again looked closely at the situation in South Staffordshire. It quickly became clear that things had changed very little since the 'Hansard Report' of 1843. The Commission spoke to a number of prominent local individuals, including the Reverend B Walsh, vicar of St Matthews, Horseley Fields in central Wolverhampton, who said: -

"All the children in my district are in the mines and the iron works. They are all boys. There is little or no work for the girls here under fourteen or fifteen years of age, at this age they get work in the nail works."

The children employed in the thin seam mines that were prominent in Wolverhampton, were often required to crawl down narrow-tunnels as the thin seam was often more difficult to retrieve.

A Mr John Kenney, master of St George's National School in Wolverhampton, was also interviewed by the Commission, and he highlighted the long hours children often had to work, when he spoke of a 'church-going man with a steady wage' that he knew, who got paid to 'black iron hurdles' made at a foundry. He said: -

"He employs his own boys to do it. The father has worked these boys from four in the morning to twelve at night and had them at work again at four or five o'clock the next morning. He did this for two or three weeks together last summer, to get up an American order."

The Commission of 1865 also looked very closely at educational opportunity, expressing great concern about the lack of educational resource for children. It highlighted that the night-schools that had been introduced as a potential remedy, at least to provide a basic education for a few Black Country children, were not a great success at that point, as just 5% of children aged twelve or over attended day-school in the Black Country area. Figures varied from as high as 10% of children attending school in Corngreaves and Brockmoor in Brierley Hill, to just a pitiful 1% - 2% in Monmore Green in Wolverhampton, Ocker Hill in Tipton, and St James in Wednesbury. The main reason given was because they were employed at such an early age in the nail trade, in the locksmith trade, in the many iron works and foundries, and of course in the mines.

The Reverand H.R. Sandford, of the Inspector of National Schools, also expressed specific concern about the virtual absence of education for Wolverhampton school-children, as part of the 1865 Commission report: -

"My experience as School Inspector for the last twelve years in different parts of the Country, induces me to believe that the proportion of those who receive no proper education is greater in the coal and iron districts than in the textile manufacturing districts. A large

proportion of the lads and boys from the works and mines in South Staffordshire night-schools were unable to read even easy naratives – 50% of colliers, and 40%% of those from the works. It is evident then that in spite of the great work which Education has 'effected' in South Staffordshire, there is a large class whom it does not influence. Prison returns, reformatory returns, the amount of pauperism which exists, in spite of the wealth of the district, proves it. At the Saltley Reformatory for instance, out of forty-two boys now there for various crimes, there are twenty-three from the South Staffordshire iron and coal district, only three of whom could read when admitted. The master of the Reformatory routinely complains about much of the intractable nature of the Wolverhampton boys of this class".

Whilst the children of the region clearly received little if any education, there was perhaps a more pressing concern regards their welfare. A year after the Commission Report, the 'Birmingham Daily Gazette' issued a further statement on 24 May 1866, summarising the dire and depressing situation for children working in the Black Country, when its reporter wrote: -

"The Black Country is a casing point. Here the mines, forges, and workshops abound with children, many little more than infants, who, for a miserable pittance, are deforming their bodies, corrupting their minds, becoming lost in ignorance and crime. Few districts in the Country have furnished more revolting instances of juvenile depravity. The commercial progress of the district has also been to some extent retarded by the poor mental and physical condition of its work people."

It certainly seems that the 'Hansard Report' of 1843, and subsequent commission reports made little difference locally. Wolverhampton was certainly a grim place to grow-up in if you were a child. Overall, the working and living conditions for Black Country children was simply dreadful throughout the Industrial Revolution, taking a real physical and emotional toll on thousands of deprived youngsters, many of whom expired during childhood.

B) Politics, strikes, social disorder, and distress

To improve working conditions, pay, and over-crowded housing conditions too, politics and religion were increasingly seen as a pathway to a better life for residents of many British towns and cities throughout the Industrial Revolution.

In the 1700s the famous preacher John Wesley risked life and limb to preach his Methodism in the impoverished Black Country. He was nearly thrown into a fast-flowing river in Walsall, and when he came to Wolverhampton in 1761 he famously said: -

"Such a bunch of wild men I have seldom seen".

Civil unrest was always likely at times of economic strife, with employers and employees both struggling to make ends meet. In November 1815, 400 men employed at a Wolverhampton iron-works rioted, after being informed of the intention to reduce their wages. The Staffordshire Yeomanry Infantry tried to restore order as bricks and stones were thrown. The cavalry twice charged the group but only manged to arrest one of the rioters.

In 1819, tin-plate workers of Wolverhampton formed a union to try to bring better conditions, but it is little known that several ended up being arrested, tried, found guilty, and transported to Tasmania, this being before the infamous Tolpuddle Martyrs experienced the same outcome.

In May 1822, miners rioted at Monmore Green Colliery due to safety issues and pay, and as they gathered to attack those who still went in to work and ascended the pit, the military were called in, and a rioter named as John Robson was shot dead.

The iron industry saw the 'puddlers' strike in 1830 in relation to low pay, but it was a failure and subsequently resulted in a desperately hard winter for many of the workers.

At the end of 1831 the colliers strike occurred in the town, which was again a protest striving for better pay. Colliers received better pay levels than iron workers, probably because of the increased risk of injury or fatality. It was noted that coal-miners in Staffordshire had a higher death rate than any other county in the Country, and appalling injuries were frequently experienced by miners - death by explosion, choking, falling down the shaft due to snapping of the often illegal, single link-chains that suddenly broke through wear and tear without warning, and most commonly death by unstable coal or clod collapsing on top of them. As a result of the collier's strike, the army was brought in, and although it was comparatively peaceful, it ultimately resulted in only a slight increase in pay for the thick coal seam workers.

The 1830s were certainly an unsettled and turbulent period in the town. In 1835, political protests after a Wolverhampton election turned to stone-throwing. The 'Riot Act' was read out and the First Dragoon Guards brought in. They charged the crowd with sabres drawn which exacerbated the situation greatly, leading to persistent rioting and stone throwing from large baying mobs, especially around Queen Street with estimates of up to 2,000 people being involved. Eight people were shot, including one or two young boys, and one of the guard's horses was killed after being stabbed. Extra re-enforcements were called in. Many felt that it had been an over-reaction to read the 'Riot Act', but either way it led to considerable trouble, with peace only being restored late in the evening.

There were further colliers strikes and disturbances in the town in 1842 and 1845, with miners at Moseley Hole actively involved, and workers of the japanning trade were also to undertake strike action in the town within the following decade, as did impoverished workers of the town's large lock trade.

In June 1875, up to 1,000 men gathered at the local police station in Monmore Green, many of whom fought with a large body of police, after two men had been arrested. Trouble never seemed far away from the tough areas of Monmore Green, Horseley Fields, and of course Caribee Island, where poverty and hardship were rife.

1883 saw the worst wage-related rioting of all, when a total of 12,000 puddlers were said to have rioted at four Black Country iron works - one each in Tipton and Dudley, and two at Wolverhampton, where they invaded the great Chillington Iron Works. Non-strikers were prevented from gaining access and attacks on the puddling-furnaces were made. Just thirteen of the ring-leaders were eventually charged in November at Stafford Assizes, and the worst sentence was one-month's imprisonment.

But such desperate attempts to resolve wage issues usually resulted in little benefit for the workers, with the iron industry in gradual decline.

According to Richard Trainor in 'Black Country Elites – The Exercise of Authority in an Industrialised Area 1830-1900', the Black Country experienced large-scale strikes and widespread 'Chartist agitatiion'.

'Chartism' was a movement that sought to better the working and trade conditions for its workers, so this movement grew rapidly during the first half of the 19th-Century in the north and midlands particularly, with strongholds locally at Bilston and Dudley. The movement was also strong in Wolverhampton, amongst its miners and impoverished locksmiths and foundry workers.

Somewhat unusually however, it is fair to say that generally for long periods, Wolverhampton's iron workers enjoyed reasonably good working relations with the owners of its great works. When Shrubbery Iron Works owner George Thorneycroft died in 1851, 1,000 iron-foundry workers contributed towards a collection for a bronzed, cast-iron monument, in his recognition. Isaac Jenks also received a similar tribute from his employees, upon his death. Chartism reduced in popularity and influence during the latter half of the 1800s, when in fact many of the towns iron-workers may have been far more active due to trading and economic difficulties that were to follow as the latter half of the 1800s progressed.

But there was considerable sympathy for the plight of out-of-work iron workers, and the town's prominent people often did what they could to provide basic food rations.

Additionally, the role of 'Poor Law Unions' was becoming increasingly important across the Country, and the heavily-duressed Wolverhampton Poor Law Union was actively involved in helping to distribute food to the impoverished of Wolverhampton, Bilston, Wednesfield, and Willenhall for many years, especially as the mid-1800s progressed. From 1865, The Wolverhampton Trades Council, later to become The Wolverhampton, Bilston, and district Trades Union was also often involved in various disputes, representing its miners, iron workers, tin-plate workers, japanning trade workers, and locksmiths, especially at a time when workers had few rights due to the much despised 'Masters' and Servants Act', which was widely utilised, and arguably abused by employees in the region to carry out mass sackings. At the peak Industrial Revolution period of 1857-1867, Wolverhampton had a higher incidence of prosecutions under this act than anywhere else in the Country.

In the early-1870s, workers won the right to work a ten-hour day. Up to that time, fourteen-hour days had been the norm. But this period also saw the 'Great Depression' in the region as the iron and coal mining trades declined, and immense poverty, hardship, and even starvation routinely occurred, notably between 1870-1895. A sadly not untypical example of starvation was highlighted by a court case that was reported by the press during the recession of 1870, when a couple named as John Smith and Sarah Smith were accused of 'feloniously killing and slaying' five-year-old Sarah King from North Street, Wolverhampton, who was a daughter from his previous relationship. The hearing was reported by the 'Birmingham Daily Gazette' on 25 July 1870. Neighbours had seen the barefooted little girl put outside in winter, and heard her scream during beatings, but she eventually died of malnutrition, weighing barely half the weight expected of a child that age, and she had access only to dirty water. A lodger who lived with the family, told the Court that during the week leading to her death, he had only seen her eat one egg, a penny-worth of rice, and half-a-penny worth of milk. The biopsy revealed that she had no food in her intestines and just two teaspoonsful of blood in her body. The Court found the parents guilty, but they were only sentenced to six months imprisonment. Such was the lack of value on human life, or blame attached at such times of hardship.

Such a sad story was neither significant nor unusual during these difficult times of profound distress.

On 19 January 1885, the 'Birmingham Daily Post' reported the desperate poverty existing in 'Wolverhampton's East-End' in what was probably the Black Country's poorest parish, following the recent closure of Osier Bed and Chillington Iron Works: -

"The lowest rated houses in the borough are to be found in St Matthews parish, with a population of 7,600. The poverty that has greeted the vicar of the parish during the past week has been very conspicuous. He is besieged as he visits many portions of his parish, especially the Horsley Fields and Walsall Street portions, for tickets for bread, for oatmeal, and other necessaries of basic existence. The condition of the children in many streets is piteous, and cases are mentioned of children when on their way to school, stopping others of more fortunate parentage, and asking if they might go to the houses of the latter, as they could eat the crusts".

St James parish, according to the same report, also witnessed 'an abnormal amount of poverty, but it is by no means as bad as in St Matthews'. The 7,000 population of St James were said to be virtually entirely comprised of iron-workers and founders, edge-tool and horse-shoe makers, and other workers in metal.

It was to the credit of the 700 workers at Swan Garden Iron Works, that despite being on reduced wages, they arranged soup kitchens for fellow out-of-work iron-workers families. The iron-working community of east Wolverhampton was a closely-knit one. Those 'in work' appreciated that they could face the same appalling predicament at any point in time. But the hardship continued as the iron industry in the town continued to struggle.

In 1891, enquiries into the situation of Wolverhampton's 'east-end iron workers' revealed a dreadful state-of-affairs. The 'South Wales Daily News' highlighted the desperate situation on 24 January: -

"Visits paid yesterday to the homes of the iron workers discovered a most shocking state of things. Dwellings were furnitureless, grates empty, and the dwellers hungry and emaciated, and some dying".

Things did not get much better in the 20th-Century, as Wolverhampton's traditional iron industries declined still further. By 1921, with thousands of soldiers having returned from the 'Great War', 18,000 people were unemployed in Wolverhampton alone, and another 17,500 on 'short-hour labour', and local politicians urged the Government's Minister of Labour to award the town the dreaded status of a 'distressed area'. Emergency provisions were put in place to prevent starvation in the town, and serious riots occurred in both Wolverhampton and Bilston.

The Wolverhampton, Bilston, and district Trades Union continued to be highly active in various industrial disputes, right up to the late-1970s with the closure of Spring Vale Steel Works, and 2,300 job losses.

Clearly, like many industrial towns and cities, Wolverhampton has experienced a deeply troubled past, and there have been disturbances in the town in recent years.

2) REPORTS REGARDING HOUSING CONDITIONS IN WOLVERHAMPTON

A) A Chronological History from 1750

Local historian Harold Parsons summarised the situation in his 1986 book 'Black Country' where he stated: -

"Considerable study has been carried out on the state of housing in Wolverhampton during the 18th and 19th centuries, and it is not a pretty story. Not until the extensive council house boom of the 1920s-1930s was

the problem really tackled. Whilst the war interrupted slum clearance, the task was resumed in the 1950s, Wolverhampton claiming to be the first to submit a scheme when it became possible to do so".

During the Industrial Revolution, entrepreneurs and wealthy owners inevitably profiteered heavily, whilst the ordinary working man and woman earned a pittance. The homes within which the poor lived were often more prejudicial to health than their dangerous occupations in the coal-mines and iron works. Wolverhampton's housing conditions were notably desperately poor throughout the entire period of the Industrial Revolution.

There are a number of lengthy, detailed reports from throughout the 1800s especially, that highlighted its appalling housing situation. These were usually produced to emphasise the absence of any sanitation, resulting in very high death rates.

Of course, slum housing here was not unique. It was a feature of all big towns and cities during the Industrial Revolution, from London's sprawling east-end including its 'rookeries' and infamous slums such as The Old Nichol and St Giles, to Glasgow's notorious 'Gorbals', to the streets along Liverpool's Scotland Road, and to the back-streets of Manchester, Leeds, Sheffield, Birmingham, and Nottingham. But Wolverhampton, even by national standards, had notoriously bad areas of slum housing, especially in the 1800s and early-1900s. They were often regarded to be even worse than in neighbouring Birmingham.

It should however, be remembered that despite the appalling slum conditions that will be described by many clearly-concerned people in various reports over two-hundred years, Wolverhampton still possessed a handsome town centre of great antiquity and character, that partially retained a market-town appearance, and one that held beautiful houses and suburbs on its smaller western side. This continues to be the case.

But the condition of the homes of its artisans, miners, and iron-workers was generally abject. For instance, the condition of homes for Black Country miners compared to those of miners in the

North, was remarked upon by author John Rule in his 1986 book 'The Labouring classes in early industrial England 1750-1850': -

"Living conditions in the Midlands were if anything, worse. Only about half as good according to one view in 1849. Here the miners ate well in good times, but lived in poor detached cottages, or else in rows or clusters sprinkled amid the rubbish waste. Gardens were unknown because the constant smoke allowed nothing to grow for mile after mile. Shifting or sinking of the ground made the cracking of the house walls very noticeable."

Wolverhampton itself experienced severe deprivation even by the worst of British standards, and the reports are now investigated in chronological order, from as early as the 1700s, throughout the entire-1800s, and well into the 1900s. But even prior to these, William White first highlighted the impoverished reputation of the then-leafier, north-western section of pre-industrial Wolverhampton as far back as the 1500s, in his 1834 book 'History, Gazetteer, and Directory of Staffordshire' when he stated: -

"The now highly productive land called the Broad Meadows and Whitmore Reins was in the 16th-Century little better than a morass, and on-account of its poverty, distinguished by the name of 'Hungry leas'."

A hundred years on, in April 1654, two Protestant ministers at St Peter's complained about: -

"the state of this miserable town".

And yet another hundred years on, appalling housing conditions in Wolverhampton were noted in 1754 by the visiting Swedish Commissioner R.R. Angerstein, when he remarked: -

"Towards the evening I took a walk in the town. On the outskirts, where most artisans live, there are also many wretched hovels, which clearly show in this place the worker is left with the bones, whereas the merchant takes the meat for himself."

As early as 1788, a map of Wolverhampton was created by Godson, and he highlighted the desperate housing situation in the town at that 'early Industrial Revolution' point in time. Of its houses, he said: -

"Relatively few are back to backs, but new houses squeezed into gaps in the existing houses".

It is widely recorded that these so-called 'slum-courts' were to be the curse of Wolverhampton housing for hundreds of years. They were mainly built in the late-1700s and early-1800s and would be routinely built around a central courtyard and of course built to the highest possible density. The worst areas were Little's Lane, Stafford Street, Peel Street, Bilston Street, Walsall Street, Pountney's Fold, Horseley Fields, Monmore Green, Zoar Street, Little Brickkiln Street, Salop Street, and the area between Queen Square, Berry Street and Stafford Road - an area that became infamously known as 'Caribee Island', which according to Godson: -

"Comprised 846 houses, of which 408 were old and dilapidated, 54 in ruins".

Following the cholera outbreak in 1832, the Anglican curate appealed for the widespread demolition of Wolverhampton's courts, when he dramatically and uncomprisingly called for: -

"the rebuilding of those 'brick-graves' called courts, alleys and back-squares, where the poor are buried alive, amid the gloom, damp, and corruption, human scoria and every other attribute of the churchyard, except its sanctity and peace".

Two years later, in 1834, D.B.M. Duffer highlighted the continuing and rather damning housing situation in Wolverhampton, when he stated: -

"Half of the total houses in Wolverhampton were deliberately built to squalid specifications".

And then just six years after that, on 20 January 1840, the dire housing situation in the town was specifically highlighted in 'A report of Wolverhampton' by John Dehane (Esquire), as part of a wider Government 'Sanitary Enquiry of England' investigation, in which he stated: -

"It may with truth be asserted that few if any of the larger provincial towns in the UK have been suffered to continue in so

neglected a condition. The larger population is employed chiefly in the coal and ironstone mines in the neighbourhood, in the iron works, and in getting up, principally in their own residences, making a variety of articles in the iron brass and tin trades. The houses were more harmful to health than the occupations. The principal thoroughfares are narrow and what is worse, it is their immediate neighbourhood that close courts and alleys abound. A dense population is consequently congregated in these places, almost excluded from public view, and a stranger would pass through the town with little or no idea of the immense numbers by which these precincts are inhabited. Many of them have only one privy allocated for the use of several families. Dirt and disarrangement mark their interior, and it is only to the free consumption of coal to which their comparative healthiness can be attributed. Damp is excluded, and with it a train of disease".

Housing Inspector James Gates examined housing conditions around the central courts and houses at Horseley Fields at that time, and he also highlighted the occupation of most of the inhabitants, remarking: -

"The locality is chiefly occupied by miners".

This was relevant, because as highlighted, it meant that at least there was a wide availability of coal for domestic purposes, providing fundamental warmth during the colder months.

Yet local 'House Surgeon' Rowland Mason also talked about the same central areas of the town saying: -

"Nearly all of these places, for the last 5-6 months, have never been free from fever, more than half have a low typhoid character accompanied with catarrh and bronchitis, which I have not met with in drained and better ventilated parts of town".

That same year, 1840, a Mr Payne of the 'Wolverhampton Board of Guardians', highlighted what he described as the 'frightful dens of iniquity' that existed in the central areas of the town. He highlighted the words of Mr Castle, Superintendent of Police: -

"In one public house, I turned out fourteen women and thirty-six men at eleven o'clock at night, most of them drunk and very disorderly. There is now another, the 'Brown Bear' in Lichfield Street, the lower order of colliers and boatmen know these public houses and go to find the women at them. The low prostitutes are supported by miners and canal boatmen. From that one yard, Rollaston Yard, in what is called 'Cribby Island', or Caribbee Island, I have, with a man or two, and a good stick, driven out nearly one-hundred men on a Saturday night or Sunday morning. There are about eight brothels and about twenty prostitutes in the yard, and wives go there to seek their husbands. The wives have sometimes, dreadful fights with the girls."

Meanwhile, if they were not found lingering in or around the town's many public houses, the town's many-destitute relied heavily on the vast Horseley Fields Workhouse, whilst many of the town's poorest people, those who were ill, elderly, unable to find work or those thrown out-of-work, alternatively relied on the numerous 'common lodging houses' of the town. At a prestigious dinner held in Dudley, a Lord Ingestone summarised the scale of the siuation when he remarked: -

"If Wolverhampton did not strictly operate the common lodging houses act, one-thousand poor creatures – destitute itinerants - would sleep nightly in the streets".

And indeed, the appalling living conditions of its 'common lodging houses' were soon to be highlighted.

We now return to the detailed landmark report given to Government by Mr R.H. Horne (Esquire), who as we know was actively concerned in highlighting working and social conditions. Following his visit to the town in 1841-42, his report was submitted and considered in Parliament during 1842-43 as part of the nationwide 'Hansard report', on the conditions of the poor.

He described the slums of Wolverhampton town centre in detailed terms: -

"In the smaller and dirtier streets of the town, in which the poorest of the working-classes reside, there are narrow passages, at intervals of every 8 or 10 houses, and sometimes at every 3rd or 4th house. These passages are in a very few instances of the width of three yards, and about nine feet high, but the great majority are only three feet wide and six feet high, some of them are only two and a half feet wide and less than six feet high. These narrow passages are the general gutter, which is by no means always confined to one side, but often streaming all over the passage. Having made your way through the passage, you find yourself in a space varying in size with the number of houses, hutches, or hovels it contains. They are nearly all proportionately crowded. Out of this space there are other narrow passages sometimes leading to other similar hovels".

Horne highlighted exactly how these slum areas evolved: -

"The great majority of these yards contain only from two to four houses, one or two of which are workshops, or have room in them for a workshop. The passage that leads to them is long or short, according to the depth of the houses in the street from which they lead. They evidently originated with the small householders in the street retaining a 'right of way' along the side of their houses to go to their little workshops at the back. In the process of time, as the inhabitants increased in number, small rooms were raised over these workshops, and hovels also built wherever space could be found, and tenanted, first perhaps as workshops, and gradually by families also. These are the dwellings and workshops of the poorest of the working classes."

He then proceeded to describe the alarming lack of sanitary provision: -

"None of these houses and hovels in courts and alleys have any under-ground drainage, and very few of them have any privies. When there is a pump in these places their condition is not so very bad, but when there is no pump it is exceedingly dirty, often filthy and degraded. In front of some of the smaller houses there are

stagnant pools, containing all matter of filth, the effluvium from which, even in the depth of winter, is most offensive. There is often a dunghill at one end, or in one corner, where everything is cast. Some of the better sorts of courts have one privy in common. The slush in front of the doors is usually of the most disgusting kind. The interiors of the dwellings are extremely squalid, they contain little furniture, and are for the most part exceedingly dirty in every respect".

Finally, the report provided an explanation as to why these squalid, over-crowded slums simply built up and built up within the same enclosed district: -

"By these means the rapidly increasing population were lodged from year to year, while the circumference of the town remained almost the same for a long time, owing to the difficulty of obtaining land to build upon, as it was all private property or belonged to the Church. As soon as land was available to build upon, Stafford Street and Walsall Street were built for the working classes, two of the largest and most disgraceful streets in the town. The greater portion of Salop Street and Horseley Field, which is very long, is in the same condition".

So, the evident poverty, over-crowding, vice, crime, and hardship was created by the population boom that took place during the Industrial Revolution, with existing and new inhabitants having to be housed within the same tight geographical area, until permission was granted to build on private or church-owned land. Wolverhampton's population increased by 50% between 1831-1841, and the slum areas became even more over-crowded. With no or little sanitary provision. The following image of a Victoria Sreet slum court in the town centre, below, shows some of the oldest and most decrepit houses in the town-centre, courtesy of Wolverhampton City Archives (Figure 32). Broken windows were the norm in these back-streets and court-yards, though Victoria Street was by no means one of the worst areas in the town.

Figure 32 – A slum court at Victoria Street in central Wolverhampton, late-1890s

During the Industrial Revolution, many people thronged to the Country's great, evolving centres of industry. Irish families came to Wolverhampton in large numbers, which was already known as 'Little Rome' due to the prominence of Catholics in the town. By 1850, around 12% of the population was Irish – 6,000 of a 50,000 population. By 1871 17% of the town were Irish, one of the highest rates in the Country, though behind Liverpool with 25%. As has been highlighted, many of them lived in Wolverhampton's poorest area, a notorious slum regarded as the 'worst-of-the-worse' at the time, called 'Caribee Island' (sometimes spelt 'Carribee' and sometimes 'Caribbee', or even 'Carribbee'), which also had the nickname 'Cribby Island' as well as 'fever nest'. 2,071 of its near 4,000 residents at that time, comprising over 51% of its population, were either Irish-born, or of Irish heritage. One 1843 health report to the Commissioners set the scene by highlighting: -

"One man lived with his wife, child and donkey in one room with a common dung-hill at one end of the room".

Another Irish family at that time, wrote about their experience since moving to England. They noted that they first moved to Wolverhampton but managed to find alternative employment in Manchester, stating: -

"We managed to escape from the hell-hole that was Caribee Island".

Shropshire barrister and M.P. Robert Slaney released a now all-too-familiar, type of report regards Wolverhampton's housing in 1845, when he concluded: -

"Courts were in the most-filthy state, full of stagnant puddles of fetid water, neglected privies with open vaults, pigsties and heaps of manure on all sides."

Two years later, in May 1847, Reverend J.B. Owen gave a lecture in the town which he called 'On the habits and habitations of the Midland Manufacturing Districts'. He commented on the appalling, over-crowded housing, and drew specific attention to the town's 'common lodging houses': -

"As to the common lodging houses, the fevers, diseases, and deaths I have known as either caught in them or communicated to them by the wretched habits by the lowest class of mendicants, almost exceed belief."

Later that year, on 11 December 1847, the 'Staffordshire Advertiser' published the report of J Dehane from 'The Journal of Public Health', who again tried to draw attention to the dreadful experience of the impoverished residents within the appalling slum of Caribee Island: -

"In this district, a few hundred yards only removed from the Collegiate church, are huddled together many scores of miserable habitations totally destitute of any drainage, and where the filthy surface water is permitted to lay in pools until it becomes putrid, emitting very offensive and noxious exhalations, while the immediate neighbourhood generally presents a most disgusting accumulation of filth and rubbish, in the shape of dunghills, and unemptied privvies, frequently over-flowing with their foetid contents. It is almost needless to say that in such a locality little can be expected in the way of cleanliness,

either as respects the houses or their inhabitants, and such is indeed the fact. The buildings are of the most squalid description, containing a population of frequently ten or twelve in a room, without either beds or the commonest articles of furniture. Here are found a congregation of men, women, and children in every stage of rags and destitution. Even water, that commonest necessary of life, is wanting, there being scarcily a pump in the whole district."

It is no wonder that whilst it was noted that the properties in which they lived were in such a miserable state, that the residents would often remain out in the open air, standing on street corners, often in, or just outside a public house, depending on whether they had any money to buy a drink.

The obsession with Wolverhampton's slum housing continued. The year before the dreaded cholera visited Wolverhampton for a second time with such deadly effect in 1849, W.A. Lewis Esquire gave a lengthy lecture to prominent councillors regarding the 'Sanitary State of Wolverhampton'. The lecture was reported in the 'Wolverhampton Chronicle' on 26 January 1848 after he had undertaken a detailed study. He made some harrowing comments about the shocking situation he found, stating: -

"Wolverhampton suffers 225 murders every year, yet if a murderer escapes from gaol, great efforts would be made to capture him. Yet in relation to its sanitary condition, Wolverhampton should be up in arms".

In relation to the potential return of the cholera he stated: -

"To be fore-armed is to be fore-warned. As regards the courts, alleys, and narrow streets where the poorer classes are housed, the drainage for the most part is neglected or very indifferent. Many of the courts are in the most-filthy state, full of stagnant puddles of fetid water, pig-sties and heaps of manure on all sides. Many of the streets, as Walsall Street and Stafford Street, have courts and alleys leading off from them, to which the air finds admission only in small quantities at a time, passing sometimes through a long, narrow passage, scarcely wide enough for a person to walk through without touching both sides

of it, and with a quantity of dirty, green water and filth, draining certainly, through into the court, not out of it!"

He then described the deeply-shocking scenes that existed along the 'blind-alleys', out- of-sight to the general-public passing through: -

"When at length you have found your way into one of these courts, what a scene meets your eyes! Numerous houses of one-storey high, very often with the flooring of mud or broken tiles, at a lower level than an adjoining pig-sty, the fluids and exhalations from which filter through the thin wall that alone separates them. Directly under the windows, in front of the house, and often-times at the back as well, heaps of filth of all sorts, animal as well as vegetable, accumulating for days and weeks and often months, give off effluvia and gases that impregnate the atmosphere. The fluids that filter from these heaps are generally of a deep black or green colour, charged to saturation with noxious matters, find a resting place for themselves generally in a narrow gutter, midway between the two rows of houses. No language can describe the combination of colours presented to the senses".

He then asked the question: -

"But I hear you say, as these places are so very unwholesome, surely few people reside there?"

This was his answer: -

"On the contrary, no parts of town are so densely-populated. I have been repeatedly assured by the residents themselves that houses consisting of two bedrooms upstairs, and one on the ground floor, are let to persons who take in ten, twelve, fourteen lodgers, mostly Irish. It is a rare thing in these houses to see a window without many panes of glass broken, and an equally rare thing to see a fireplace where the smoke does not prefer making its exit through the room and out of the window or door, instead of up the chimney".

Mr Lewis implored people to go and witness such appalling squalor themselves, and he tried to describe the effect of the miserable existence on the poor residents: -

"*Your eyes will be met with the most revolting sights, and your nose with the most offensive smells. Some of these localities are so bad, and fever appears so thoroughly to have taken possession of them, that I am convinced that nothing short of complete demolition and razing them to the ground will purify them. Better ventilation, and the free use of whitewash, may do a little towards sweetening the atmosphere in some of the houses I allude to, but many of the worst are past all cure short of annihilation. Go examine, cross-examine, for it is only by these methods, that you will come to the real state of the health of these places. Most of them have had the fever more than once. Nearly all have lost relations from it. They themselves are old before their time, thin, sallow, with sunken eyes, and nearly all complaining of diarrhoea. And what are the characters and pursuits of those who inhabit the low courts and unswept alleys? Some few are labourers with large families, whose earnings will only allow them to choose the cheapest lodgings. Some are Irish navvies who seem to prefer dirt and filth even if they may have cleanliness for the same price. But many of them are people of the worst class, and the most forbidding characters and manners, and whose haunts and habits are only known to police*".

He went on to talk of Wolverhampton's general population, summarising the existence experienced by many of them: -

"*The hard and difficult labour that many thousands of the population are daily engaged in - colliers working half their lives underground, with their health previously debilitated from having commenced their labours as mere children, accidents met with in coal-pits and iron works - the greater exposure of human life in this town than in most others*".

But in terms of its natural location and situation in relation to sanitation, Lewis rather damningly said: -

"*I know of no town whose situation is more admirably adapted for efficient and thorough drainage than Wolverhampton. Situated on a hill of new red sandstone, with a fall and sharp incline in almost every direction from the market place, nature has done everything for it, man nothing! I have scarcely a doubt, that if it were not for the happy geological position of the town, the mortality would be very considerably higher than it is. I repeat that the first step towards the improvement of health of the inhabitants of the town is a good system of drainage. Need we wonder then, that under such obstacles, and with an atmosphere rarely free from soot and smoke, the poor of this town are more than usually remarkable for dirt. The only wonder I see, under the circumstances, is to find them as clean as they are. Such abominations as five, six, seven families in the houses of the courts and alleys, containing only two rooms and a kitchen must be put a stop to."*

Lewis went on to make several further recommendations, and he also pin-pointed the location of those slum areas that harboured the disease and were responsible for the extremely high mortality in the town. He identified them as: -

"The courts and alleys of Caribee Island, Cole's Croft, Walsall Street, Bilston Street, and the courts connecting Walsall and Bilston Street, Horseley Fields, Monmore Green, Salop Street and its courts and alleys such as Halletts Row, Brickkiln Lane, bottom of Merridale Street, the back-houses of Worcester Street, Pountney Street, and the houses in the neighbourhood of Pountney's Fold".

Finally, in relation to Wolverhampton's mortality rate, Mr Lewis questioned the officially- recorded level, stating: -

"1,661 deaths took place here in 1847. Now this is one in twenty-four, a mortality far higher than Bilston or Liverpool, which as you have seen, have the unenviable notoriety of being the two most unhealthy towns in the kingdom, and their rate is one in twenty-nine".

And just a year after Mr Lewis's detailed lecture, Robert Rawlinson, on behalf of the Governments Board of Health, compiled and released a detailed report in 1849 on the state of towns and cities, noting improvements in Birmingham for example, where: -

"the whole of the streets are regularly watered and cleaned with sweeping machines".

Indeed, the slums of Birmingham were noted to be 'better-planned, less-crowded, and so less-liable to breed disease' than those in Wolverhampton, and he confirmed this where he made the following comment about the latter town: -

"To the almost total absence of sanitation, is related the exceptionally low life expectancy which averages 19 years and 1 month".

A harrowing and alarming statistic, the third worst or lowest in the Country, with one in five children dying during their first year. It was widely suspected that this was exacerbated by a common practice in Wolverhampton where working mothers routinely left young children to look after babies all day, with the instruction to give them a unique but widely-available medicine containing a mixture of hot water and treacle combined with opium, that was said to make them sleep.

Walsall and West Bromwich's average life-expectancy age-levels were slightly higher, but Dudley possessed the 'lowest average life-expectancy age' in the Country 'at this point in time', at just 16 years and 7 months, an entirely staggering statistic. Epidemics were the key reason for these alarming rates, which affected young people and babies especially. These epidemics were caused chiefly by insanitary housing conditions rather than deaths caused by dangerous employment.

Rawlinson led the 'Inquiry into the sanitary state of Wolverhampton', which was then discussed in depth by a General Board of Health, with the intention of making a provisional order against Wolverhampton under the 'Public Health Act' 1848, as highlighted by a lengthy report published in the 'Wolverhampton Chronicle' on 7 February.

His report summarised the worst slums in and around Caribee Island as: -

"A collection of the most squalid-looking houses comprising an area of sixteen acres. Sewers ran through this loathsome neighbourhood."

The newspaper report discussed the inquiry by first setting the scene, describing the make-up of the population living in the town's slums: -

"Mr Rawlinson, Health inspector, first visited Caribee Island, where he found intolerable nuisances and nests for fever. It was stated that all the privvies that were put up were rendered useless by the filthy habits of the inhabitants in this locality. The Irish paid better than the English, and the reason for this was that the former took in so many lodgers that it could never be ascertained how many they would take into one house, that they slept on the floor, men, women and children being crowded together...............over twenty people residing in one house was not unremarkable".

Water Works engineer Mr Henry Marten, part of the Inquiry team, then went on to describe Caribee Island in quite familiar but gauling detail: -

"A passage of one-hundred yards in length and about three or four wide leads into the heart of this loathesome neighbourhood. The passage is topped at the farther end by a cross wall and collection of filth. I found that the roadway, footpaths being a luxury unknown, was more than ankle deep in mud. An open gutter passed down the passage between the houses, or rather the whole was an open gutter, for the line of demarcation between the houses was very inaccurately defined, and some of the houses being below the level of the street, had the benefit of the flush from the outside. The houses, with the exception of a few, have no back doors and generally consist of not more than two small rooms. At the bottom, before entering the sewer, a stagnant pool of putrid filth forms itself".

The inquiry-report next focused on other, poor Wolverhampton neighbourhoods near the town centre: -

"He next visited Stafford Street, North Street, Brook Street, Bell Street, and the Merridale district where Zoar Street was in a very stagnant and very filthy condition. Of the western side, the report noted that there were entries in Salop Street, which were filled with filth and nuisance. There were also courts in Worcester Street and Great Brickkiln Street in a very bad state. In one half of Zoar Street the mud was about twelve inches deep, the refuse which was swept

into this street from thirty or forty houses was daily accumulating. On the surface of this mud there was a green sort of filth which at times smelt most dreadfully".

It was ascertained, quite evidently, that the major problem was a lack of sanitation in the town. 4,000 houses, comprising two-thirds of the town, had no sewage system and hence people on a daily basis, 'were necessitated to retain their dirt and filth about them, either in their own houses or in their immediate neighbourhood'. 26 of Wolverhampton's 32 miles of roads had no sewerage sytem at all.

The Board of Inquiry were also taken aback by the abject poverty they found in many households in Wolverhampton, with many families sleeping on the bare floor, as they had no bed or furniture at all. Young children were found lying upon bare coals, with just a thin blanket covering them. In one tiny room in Caribee Island, barely seven-foot in length and six-foot in width, they found a family of seven trying to sleep, including the father who was being sick with cholera.

They also visited some of the estimated two-hundred 'Common lodging houses', whose abject conditions had been highlighted by Reverend J.B. Owen two years earlier, where some of the poorest Wolverhampton residents were housed. It was estimated that these were used by half a million people that year alone, 1848. The condition of those lodging houses visited in Salop Street and in Caribee Island even astounded the members of the Health Board, who were quite used to investigating Britain's slum areas. They described what they witnessed: -

"Between two to four beds would typically be found in each room, with up to four people sharing a bed. In one case, seven people were found in one bed, others were found lying on bare floorboards underneath the beds, sometimes the only place they could rest their weary limbs".

So, it was not unusual to find up to twenty to thirty people in a room, and therefore those lodging houses with five or more rooms sometimes accommodated over one-hundred people. Yet regards sanitation, it was remarked: -

"Some lodging houses had but one closet for the use of all these people, so it was not uncommon to find corners of a room used as a toilet".

Rawlinson summarised the appalling and upsetting situation: -

"We may go on to enumerate many other similar scenes, but nothing excepting a personal inspection could convey any adequate idea of the wretchedness and misery to be found in these houses".

In their summary, the inquiry report made clear, costed recommendations that included licensing of 'Common lodging houses', and of course sanitary and drainage improvements especially in the poorest areas which were 'fever nests' for diseases like cholera, which hit Wolverhampton and Bilston especially hard in 1849. It stated: -

"The excess of disease may be distinctly traced to close and confined courts, over-crowded tenements, want of sewers or drains, with want of privy conveniences, to a scarcity of good and wholesome water."

Rawlinson and the Board of Health did as much as they could to get necessary improvements instigated, but ultimately the cost would constitute an all too familiar barrier.

So unsurprisingly, investigations and reports regarding Wolverhampton's desperate, insanitary housing conditions continued to be published.

The official town census of 1851 revealed an average of 10.25 people living in each 'one-up, one-down', ten-foot square cottage with no water, in one Caribee Island street, and ten years later, in 1861, a Charity Commission Inspector described 'Townwell Fold' in the central area of Wolverhampton, as: -

"The vilest nest of iniquity in Wolverhampton, where there are ten or twelve brothels".

The respected publication 'The Builder' joined the seemingly endless list of official bodies or publications all-too-keen to highlight the scandalous condition of Caribee Island, but in its case, it left no stone unturned regards its condemnation of the Irish, something that the writers would undoubtedly struggle to get away with these days. Of course, only half the residents there were of Irish descent, but it did not stop such widespread generalisations. In its report titled 'The Condition of Wolverhampton', which was then published in the 'Birmingham Daily Post' on 29 January 1861, it controversially stated: -

"How comes it that the dirtiest, most tumble-down, vermin-haunted localities always shelter a settlement of Irish? Here in Wolverhampton, as everywhere else, the blackest shadows are cast by the Irish quarter - Caribbee Island. The narrow, irregular, imperfectly-paved alleys and courts, with their tattered fringes of miserable houses are known to the resident medical practitioners as fearful well-springs of fever. Would that St Patrick disentangle the meshes of this rotten network, and send order and cleanliness to its swarming population? Something short of a miracle would do it."

In 1862, the Government's Registrar General, in his report on 'The state of England and Wales' specifically drew attention to the 'continued insanitary state of Wolverhampton', noting its critical mortality rates that were significantly higher than would be expected. Whilst it reported on-going improvements in Liverpool, Manchester, and Birmingham, it reported: -

"In the district of Wolverhampton alone, 980 deaths occurred in 91 days, the mortality was high before and the health is every year getting worse. Several hundreds of the inhabitants are every year disabled by sickness, funerals are a staple trade, parents lose their children, wives their husbands, children their fathers, by the poison of the place, workmen and people in trade are cut down at all ages in alarming numbers."

In response to this 'rather damning' national report, 'The Times' national newspaper even rather-condescendingly 'urged' "Wolverhampton people to 'emulate the biblical leper Naaman': -

"to wash and be clean".

If only they could.

The arguments and counter arguments that took place at local level, regards the evidently necessary sanitary improvements, were highlighted by George Barnsby in his 1990 book 'Social Conditions in the Black Country'. Barnsby highlighted the somewhat surprising existence of an 'anti-sewerage party' in the town at that time, 1862, and that during heated debate Frank F. Fellows, one of those in favour of desperately-needed sanitary improvements, responded to the 'anti-sewerage party' by producing a piece including a sketch, called 'Fellowsiana' which began: -

"Smokery, chokery, stenchiness, slum,
How do you like your filthiness done?
Stagnant, preserved, or sent off with a run,
Electors of Caribee Island."

Fellows followed this with a speech made before the Town Council, in which he read out a poem as part of his argument: -

"There be thousands in our city
In noisome alleys pent,
Where every breath of air that comes,
Is foul and pestilent,
Where the narrow casements,
All that they can descry,
Are the reeking, rotten houses,
And a little square of sky.
There, crowded altogether,
To live as best they may,
Are children, men and maidens,
And mothers of yesterday.
There are thousands in our city
That drink from day to day,

The water in the stagnant butt,
All black with foul decay.
So, let us work together,
To win the happy time,
When our fair city shall be cleansed".

But this impassioned cry for sanitary improvements fell on deaf ears, with some councillors voting against the proposals for sanitary improvement on the grounds of cost, with the final vote in Council going to 21 for, but 24 against, as highlighted in the report in the 'Wolverhampton Chronicle' on 15 January 1862.

In his book, Barnsby highlighted some of the key reasons improvements were not sanctioned by the Council: -

Councillor Willock – "*Commercial depression*".

Councillor Wallace – "*Wait the working out of the mines at Monmore Green*".

Councillor Sidney – "*The matter should be decided by referendum*".

So, the status quo remained.

The 'Birmingham Daily Post' even sympathised with the plight of 'neighbouring Wolverhampton's slum-dwellers', by highlighting potential 'cholera hot-spots' in the town, in a report on 29 August 1865, which were initially brought to the attention of the newspaper by the obviously concerned Rector of Wolverhampton, Reverend J.H. Isles. The newspaper's reporter visited the town and described the slums in the centre of Wolverhampton in shocking but what was now becoming familiarly-revealing detail: -

"*Out of one of the principal streets in Wolverhampton, there are four courts, containing about eighty houses, three-quarters of which consist of one room on the ground floor, with a dark pantry behind it, and one bedroom above with a small closet, capable of containing one bed. These miserable hovels are entirely shut out from the purifying operation of fresh air. There are no back doors or windows, and consequently there is no through-ventilation. The houses appear to be simply closed* boxes, so arranged as to collect and retain all the fetid and dangerous gases that infect the neighbourhood".

In terms of sanitation, the reporter noted the following: -

"Each court contains one pump, and in two of the courts there are taps from the waterworks, but very few of the houses have the right of using the water from these taps. For some weeks, the water from one of the pumps - the only supply for forty houses - has been undrinkable. The water from another pump, when boiled, is found to be crusted over with a red-scum and is unfit for making tea. In both instances, it is believed, the sewage from the drains and the ash-pits finds its way into the wells. Furthermore, the refuse water from many of these houses is thrown out into the badly-paved gutters, often remaining in deep, stagnant gutters, soaking into the frontage, and only partially reaching the drain. Some of these houses are wretchedly damp, or that there are cellars with twelve to eighteen inches of fetid water standing in them. But wretched as it is already, even these touches do not quite complete the picture. There are groups of privies built round open cess-pools, blocking up the narrow open spaces, and in summer scenting the neighbourhood. Then again, there is the usual compliment of horses, donkeys, pigs, and poultry, with their attendant smells. It only needs one additional touch, this carefully organised cholera-nest ought to be called 'Paradise Place', and then the grim satire upon modern sanitary arrangements would be complete".

The report summarised the effect such conditions had on its 'miserable residents': -

"It is this living in close unventilated houses, where to open the door is only to let in a more powerful smell, which settles on the walls and on the ceiling, and hungrily makes for the bedroom...........it is this utter despair of cleanliness and sweetness, settling down into a consistent neglect of the person and the house."

Finally, the report warned of the likelihood of further visits of cholera, almost pleading for Authority to address the issues: -

"Our Wolverhampton neighbours suffer a perfect cholera nest to be established in the very middle of their town, houses packed by dozens

into close, evil-smelling courts. If cholera or fever does break out in this wretched nest of courts - and it will be a miracle if it does not break out - no power will suffice to hinder it from spreading to districts inhabited by the better classes. On former occasions, like other towns of the Black Country, Wolverhampton has suffered fearfully from cholera. The only way to prevent this is to enforce the strictest regulations against uncleanliness, to provide an ample supply of clean water, to cleanse and ventilate the dwellings of the poor, and to sweep away bodily such nuisances. And yet not withstanding the wide diffusion of sanitary knowledge, despite the lessons of experience - in their case terribly bitter. ".

It is no wonder that in that same year, 1865, another health report, this time commenting on the open operations of a manure and hazardous waste operation at New Cross, Wednesfield ironically noted: -

"After all, he, the owner Mr Bradburn, was an employer of many men, most of whom it has to be said, came from the stinking slums of Wolverhampton and who wouldn't have noticed much of the bad smell anyway".

It certainly seems that at this point, that Wolverhampton's slum housing was becoming as renowned and notorious as any of the worst in the Country. A report from the 'South London Chronicle' on 18 November 1865 drew attention to the slum housing in its own neighbourhood, but it commented: -

"Kent Street is as unpoetical and dirty as the veriest slum in Glasgow or Wolverhampton."

We are all aware that the name 'Glasgow' was synonymous with slum housing, but it is somewhat revealing and even startling to see Wolverhampton highlighted in the same breath. Poignantly, it highlights just how desperate the housing situation was at that time considered to be in the town.

Unsurprisingly perhaps then, the Registrar Generals report in 1866 on the 'Sanitary Condition of the Country's towns' revealed that Wolverhampton had the highest mortality rate in the Kingdom, at nearly 31 per thousand people. This was the year Queen Victoria famously visited the town, and her travel diaries highlighted just how she was struck by the poverty as she travelled along Peel Street in the town centre.

That same year, on 4 June 1866, stimulated by its report a year previously, the 'Birmingham Daily Post' undertook and published a major and significant report, through a series of detailed descriptions titled a 'Sanitary Report of the Black Country', with a view not to create panic, but to highlight 'potential asiatic-cholera spots'. It first centred on Wolverhampton and described what it called 'some shocking spots' in the town, and in later editions it revealed the existence of equally appalling conditions in the overcrowded courts of nearby Bilston, which it described as: -

"the blackest, the most dismal, dilapidated, and desolate town in the Black Country".

Dreadful slum conditions were also described during its series of reports in Willenhall, Darlaston, Dudley, Gornal, and Oldbury, but the investigators found better conditions somewhat surprisingly perhaps, in Tipton and Wednesbury which were noted to have had better sanitation levels. Tipton was noted to have few of the close courts and narrow streets that the other towns possessed. The Local Health Boards were also noted to be very effective in these two towns. Interestingly, it was also stressed that all the Black Country towns lay on relatively high ground, and should therefore have had an advantageous, natural situation when it came to sanitation.

The extensive report highlighted the 'ten-year death rates' between 1851-1860 of each town in its 'Black Country research area', with Wolverhampton despite having a wealthy western suburb, having the highest death rate at 30.88 per 1,000 population, very closely followed by Bilston at 30.53, Darlaston at 30.34, West Bromwich at 27.28, Oldbury at 27.06, Tipton at 26.73, Willenhall at 26.58, Dudley at 26.52, Walsall 26.01, and Wednesbury at 25.53. It did point out however, that the larger towns were not all bad, such as Wolverhampton and Dudley, which had notorious slum areas like 'Caribee Island' (Wolverhampton), and 'The Mambles' (Dudley), which clearly elevated mortality levels.

The newspaper's detailed investigation over a number of weeks, commenced by first publishing a report in intricate detail, of the dismal, over-crowded slum court system of central Wolverhampton and its adjacent eastern districts of Horseley Fields and Monmore Green. Inevitably, it condemned the central 'Caribee Island' slum in quite compelling but by now familiarly-harrowing detail, which it described as a 'fever-nest'. Their description of this notorious 19th-Century slum with its tiny houses is perhaps the best-known of all: -

"The evil condition of the place arises largely from construction. It is a labyrinth of narrow, tortuous courts, in which every scrap of space has been built on. There is no single passage through it for the free circulation of air, its alleys are as intricate as the wards of some gigantic key. Even where there has been a spare corner for an ash heap, privy, or what not, some wretched building has been run up and let out for a small consideration weekly. Some of the houses have one room upstairs as well as one down - each room being six or seven square feet - the upper one reached by a kind of ladder, often out of repair. Others have one floor only, and that not partitioned, excepting by a curtain. In one place, a couple of houses have come down, and the place has been used as a refuse heap, urinal, and filth receptacle generally for two or three courts. Here the drains are ill-made and out of repair, while the houses are damp and odorous with the urinary deposits made near them. The only effective improvement that can be made to Caribee Island is to pull it all down".

In relation to other central parts of Wolverhampton, the report was particularly damning of the habit of keeping pig-sties for instance at North Road, off Dudley street, and off the Horsefair in the centre of town. The situation was particularly acute near Caribee Island, at Little's Lane where many Irish lived, as the report highlighted: -

"There are other courts near this, in Stafford Street, which although

not quite as bad as Caribee Island, are still very unhealthy. Some of the courts in Little's Lane - the whole district here is chiefly inhabited by the Irish - are in a very bad condition. In Court number 10 for instance, there are four houses and two privies close to them, and three pigs".

The report also pin-pointed and described several other slum areas of the town: -

"In Pountney's Fold, a series of narrow passages, there are forty houses with not a single drop of wholesome water for any of them".

"Salop Street is also a densely-inhabited thoroughfare, with courts running out of it right and left, presenting the usual condition of impure atmosphere rising from bad ventilation, bad drainage, and exposed fecal matter. Salop Street, and streets running off it such as Skinner Street, especially at the lower end, consisted of very small, ill-constructed tenements, often very filthy, and occupied by the very lowest of the people, together with vagrants, mendicants, and other characters of a similar description".

"At Great and Little Brickkiln Streets there is a good deal of small houses with no back outlets and densely crowded courts, closely packed together".

"A road opens out of the Market Place, through Lichfield Street into Berry Street and Canal Street, and so on to the Lower Level Station. We would remove several places that are morally objectionable and sanitarily offensive".

Skinner Street, set just off Salop Street is again portrayed in the photograph below (figure 33), showing the rather desperately-poor conditions even on the west side of town.

If people thought that the dreadful, stinking, slums were restricted to courts and alleys around the town centre, the extensive report hadn't finished with Wolverhampton just yet, as it arguably saved its most damning description and verdict until last, describing Horseley Fields and Monmore Green in Wolverhampton's 'east end' as follows: -

Figure 33 – Skinner Street, Wolverhampton.

"By far the most dangerous part of the town however, is that comprised in Bilston Street, Walsall Street, and the mass of byeways that lie between them, spreading right away to Monmore Green on the one hand, and to that part of the Willenhall Road where the turnpike used to stand on the other. All along these streets are close courts and blind alleys - some with high walls in front of houses almost blocking out light, others with ash-pits and privy soil mingling together. Further along there are houses lying a good six feet below the road level, and in rainy weather they are of course, flooded. Further out things grow worse not better - ill-paved courts with broken drains, offensive piggeries, open privies and ash-pits, privies flush with the street, and drainage lying bubbling with poisonous gases between the backs of thickly inhabited rows of cottages - these are some of the sights that are to be seen in the district leading up to and ending with Monmore Green. Along the road to Willenhall, there are one-floor houses with low roofs, lying below the level of the road, and built almost flush up with the pit-banks at the back of them."

This important 1866 report made a worrying observation: -

"In all the streets and places above described, cholera raged 'more-or-less furiously' either in 1832, or 1849, or both. In most of them, there has been no improvement since - in many there has been absolute deterioration".

So, it clearly concluded that the areas of the town that had been ravaged by cholera in 1832 and 1849 were in a worse condition now, in 1866, than even at those points in time, and to re-emphasise the desperate severity of the towns problems, it stated the following: -

"Wolverhampton's death rate stands at nearly 31 in the thousand. This death rate surpasses that even of Liverpool (30.0), notoriously the most unhealthily situated of any large town in the country. This is due to the surface drainage at such localities as Caribee Island and Pountney's Fold, and by the terrible district stretching away from the bifurcation formed by Bilston and Walsall Streets to Monmore Green on the one hand, and to the old Willenhall tollgate on the other."

This 'Sanitary Report of the Black Country' report then moved on to its adjoining neighbour and eastern district of Bilston, which was equally as problematic as eastern Wolverhampton. Similar courts as those in central Wolverhampton were found in its central areas, though on a smaller scale, as described by the report: -

"There are alleys so narrow that the occupants on the one side can almost reach out of their own broken windows into the broken windows of the occupants on the other side. Privies so dilapidated that that no one can wonder to find empty tenements, and even exposed corners to use their stead. Ash and filth pits so full that their contents, piled high above the walls, pour down into the drain gratings that serve merely to gather the sewage into noisome puddles. The whole place is a filthy dilapidation, pestilential as the valley of death."

Dudley, the other large Black Country town with appalling problems, was also described in a report within the series released by the newspaper. Despite its terribly low 'life expectancy level', the reporter offered some hope: -

"Dudley stands even more favourably, naturally, than Wolverhampton, and it has no district like that lying between Bilston

and Walsall Streets, in that town. Furthermore, it has got rid of its pigs. It stands on the highest ground of all, open to the winds from heaven in all directions."

Nevertheless, the narrow, over-crowded, alleyway slums of 'The Mambles' in Dudley, a smaller but concentrated slum containing just 65 houses housing 300 residents, was very-similar to the much larger slum of Caribee Island in Wolverhampton containing 850 houses and housing 4,000 residents, and it was undoubtedly amongst the worst of districts in the Black Country, as the report highlighted: -.

"The houses are for the most part ruinous and tumbledown, the drains broken and filthy, the privies doorless, roofless. Many of the alleys and passages are but three or four-foot wide, so closely are the buildings packed together that privies, ash-heaps, and worse, run up close to the houses and taint the very atmosphere of the food cupboards and dwelling rooms."

Another report in this series summarised the situation in the other large Black Country towns of West Bromwich and Tipton: -

"West Bromwich ought to be one of the healthiest towns in the Black Country, it has so few courts, and Tipton is the model village of the Black Country".

Nevertheless, even West Bromwich was noted to have some poor areas of housing to the north of its centre at Hill Top and Golds Green, where cholera had struck previously.

Regards Walsall, the report highlighted the following: -

"Walsall, as the writer has been given to understand, indignantly refuses to consider itself as belonging, either wholly or in part, to the Black Country, but it tolerates pigs and is over-run with ill-drained courts".

Willenhall, and Darlaston were also noted to be in a terrible general condition, with the former 'full of pigs', but 'perhaps less crowded and with some spaces', in contrast to the dense slum areas of the larger towns. Portobello, on the road from Willenhall to Wolverhampton, was a notably squalid collection of miner's cottages.

Overall, the 'Birmingham Daily Post's' 'Sanitary Report of the Black Country' highlighted continued, appalling housing conditions, devoid of proper if any sanitation, and it emphasised and specified in no uncertain terms, those districts deemed at high risk of a return of the 'dreaded cholera'.

Yet some ten years after the highly-critical Home Office Registrar General's report of 1862, and despite this detailed and much-publicised 'Birmingham Daily Post' report in 1866, Wolverhampton again came under the spotlight in 1872 through a number of reports, demonstrating that little or no progress had been made in relation to desperately-needed sanitary improvements.

Again, we refer to the work of Frank Mason. In his 1979 book 'The story of an Industrial Town – Wolverhampton'. He highlighted an 1872 report that stated: -

"Two-thirds of the townsfolk lived in houses with no sewers or drains".

At this point in time, 1872, the Medical Officer of Health for the town, Mr John Henry Love, reminded people of the scale of the situation, when he highlighted that 'the population had increased to 68,000 contained within 12,000 houses, 210 streets, and some 600 courts' - the latter being the scurge of Wolverhampton housing.

But incredibly the town's elders continued to disregard any reports or recommendations made for sanitary improvements, probably because improvements cost money. A Councillor Barker had responded to such repeatedly-highlighted concern by saying: -

"Wolverhampton is one of the healthiest towns in the kingdom and if it is dirty, why, the people must thrive on dirt".

With such a mentality Mason highlighted that it was no wonder that a total of 670 people, mainly children, died of small pox or scarlet fever in Wolverhampton that very same year, 1872.

Another 1872 report in the respected-publication 'The Builder' uncompromisingly described Wolverhampton as having: -

"The most odious court system, countless courts of the most unhealthy and objectionable character, with middens full, stinking and confined,

and deadly. In Peel Street and its neighbourhood, and in what is called 'Caribee Island', the condition of things is frightful. If the latter were really the settlement of a tribe of wild Indians, it would be an object of wonder to the civilised upper classes of Wolverhampton."

The 'Birmingham Daily Mail' newspaper even described the Caribee Island slum area in simple terms, as: -

"Evil".

Just two years later, a significant, twenty-eight-page report on the 'Sanitary Condition of Wolverhampton' was published in July 1874 by Local Government Board Inspector Dr Edward Ballard, on behalf of the highly-respected publication 'The Lancet' and he made a number of harrowing observations that were by now entirely predictable, regards its lack of sanitation and appalling housing conditions. He said: -

"I have never-before inspected a town in which the dwellings of the poor and labouring classes were so generally unwholesome from the causes I have stated............there are a very huge number of such unwholesome places. Many are residences in which no human being should be lodged".

Of Caribee Island he stated: -

"Nothing but the systematic destruction and re-arrangement of the whole area could make it fit for healthy habitation."

Ballard also highlighted that: -

"There were less than 500 water closets among 13,000 houses in the town and the great majority of dwellings used noisome privies and ash-pits which were emptied at long intervals when they became full. As quickly as practicable, privy cesspits and midden privies should be abolished throughout the town".

The lack of sanitation he referred to continued to be highlighted as the primary cause of so many of the infectious diseases that had so profoundly affected the population for many years.

Ballard also drew attention to a different type of slum in Wolverhampton, albeit on the Wolverhampton coal-field at

Rough Hills, where he noted ramshackle huts belonging to miners. He said: -

"Upon this irregular coal mining land, a few blocks of houses are erected, but in addition there are numerous huts, isolated or two or three together, each with its little irregular plot of garden ground. These huts mostly belong to the occupiers, who are generally colliers who pay a few shillings annually as an acknowledgement for the use of the land".

All in all, this at last was to become a life-changing report and perhaps the most impacting one, for finally the authorities felt obliged to address the appalling problems that the poor of Wolverhampton had tolerated for around 200 years.

But overall, he concluded that things had in some ways improved since Mr Rawlinson's 1849 report, and over-crowding was 'somewhat reduced'. But in relation to raw sewerage, he noted that piles of effluence had all too often simply built-up to the point that it was piled up against the walls of many houses, resulting in much damp condensation on inside walls, a direct consequence of the presence of those liquids and substances. The startling absence of sanitation was the critical concern for Ballard.

It was certainly the case that since Queen Victoria's famous 1866 visit, Wolverhampton was more and more in the national spotlight, and its ruling-classes perhaps felt increasingly-compelled to act in the face of ever-increasing criticism. Indeed, as highlighted by D.M. Palliser in his book 'The Staffordshire Landscape' (1976), such appalling conditions were increasingly being discussed, and conversely improvements were increasingly being recommended. He said: -

"From the mid-nineteenth Century, considerations of hygiene began to have a belated effect on housing policy. Terraced streets were laid out which, if often unattractive to modern eyes, were at least much more sanitary than the crowded courts".

This early-1900s photograph of industrial and desolate Horseley Fields perhaps shows the haphazard manner that remaing slum houses were squeezed into any space in the town, so that workers could be close to their factories (Figure 34).

Figure 34 – Aerial view of Horseley Fields, Wolverhampton, early-1900s

Nevertheless, inaction in Wolverhampton was still perceived by many outsiders. Ten years later, on 8 April 1876, the 'Midland Times and Examiner' criticised, belittled, and mocked Wolverhampton's seemingly unconcerned and unresponsive politicians: -

"But while other towns are showing by their action that they are alive to questions of imperial importance, 'hum-drum Wolverhampton' sleeps on its way, or is only awake to the tremendous importance of the life and death question, "Fair or no fair?", or "Where shall we hold it? In Queen's Square or St James's Square?" We would suggest Caribee Island. There are a number of houses there that might be fittingly used for wild beast shows, and the inhabitants of the district would not be likely to vote it a nuisance."

Quite a damning inditement not only on the inactive local politicians, but also on the condition of the housing and the lifestyle of the inhabitants of this famous slum, an area that many people including police would often not risk entering, and an area that many people had no inkling even existed as it was mostly out of view.

That same year, in May 1876, collier William Carey was arrested at his Caribee Island home after police were called to a domestic quarrel. The remains of two of his sixteen children were found, along with three living children in the house. His wife could account for all but five of them, so police had to fully search the house, that had two bedrooms and a cellar half full of water. The medical officer condemned the house as being unfit for human habitation, and the police were unable to conduct a thorough search of the house for a week whilst it was cleared, such was the appalling condition of the property.

Some of the slums at that time were so dilapidated that in 1876 several houses in central Wolverhampton collapsed like a deck of cards on Walsall Street, Horseley Fields, sadly killing a young boy.

It was high time that such issues were addressed, and it was incidents such as the above combined with the routinely-damning reports that finally forced politicians to confront the dreadful conditions. In truth, politicians had been debating the sanitation issue throughout the 1860s and 1870s, and perhaps of greater significance, discussed at great length just how to fund the necessary improvements.

It was to the Council's belated-credit that with new powers, they eventually acted in 1877. Proposals were at last made to pull down a large part of the eastern centre of town, from Queen Square to what is now the ring road, in a segment bounded by Queen Street and Stafford Street including most of the notorious 'Caribee Island', which apparently housed 3,385 occupants at that point in time.

The detailed report leading up to the demolition, highlighted in the 'Midland Examiner and Times' on 28 April 1877, made distinct comments about the dilapidated condition of the district. A valuer named as Mr Barnett stated: -

"Of over 700 houses in this area, 632 were inhabited, 72 uninhabited. 408 were dilapidated and in ruins, and 54 condemned. There were only 39 water closets in the area, and 366 privvies. Houses with no back doors or windows 249, and houses situated in courts more-or-less dense 274. It was absolutely necessary to sweep away all these buildings".

Cole's Croft, at the edge of Caribee Island, is seen below, photographed in the late-1880s (Figure 35), not long before these final streets of the district were swept away for ever. But even then, there was no drainage or sanitation in some streets, so cess-pits routinely gathered at the front or back of houses, and the narrow streets were ankle-deep in revolting effluent. The worst slums in Caribee Island were set off streets like Cole's Croft, along narrow alleyways just 2-3 feet wide, and too dark and dingy for photographers to do their work and reveal the worst slums.

Figure 35 – Cole's Croft, on the edge of Caribee Island, Wolverhampton, late-1880s

Medical officer Mr John Henry Love highlighted that Wolverhampton's death rate for one year in the past decade had reached over 40 per thousand, and that: -

"Two-thirds of the whole area were dilapidated buildings incapable of repair".

The Council planned to build housing for up to 2,000 displaced residents on land that it had acquired at Springfield, just to the north-east of the town centre. Most of these residents would be from Caribee Island.

Dr Malet released his 'Sanitary Condition of Wolverhampton' report in 1894, published by the 'Birmingham Daily Post' on 14 October 1895, and this highlighted that the situation was still fairly-desperate despite the worst central slums at Caribee Island having been cleared: -

"The death rate of 21.66 for Wolverhampton was above the average of the thirty-three towns, at 19.59............There was an excess of deaths in the east end of the town, especially from respiratory diseases."

Regards its 'poor rate' he said: -

"He had not been able to get the poor rate of ten of the large towns, but of the other twenty-three, Wolverhampton was first with 2s, 1d. Erroneous notions about feeding and cooking (especially child-feeding), and ignorance of ventilation and the value of poor air, sunlight, and cleanliness, were all, no doubt, answerable for much needless suffering and death among the poor. Much of the insanitary condition of the borough was due to poverty, such as over-crowding, living in ill-ventilated or damp or draughty houses, or in houses in close unhealthy situations, or dirtiness in respect of yards, drains, or ashpits. There was in Wolverhampton an enormous number of houses not strictly fit for habitation, and a considerable number quite unfit. The latter must be closed by degrees, the former eventually. But there was no point in doing so if there was no place for the poor to go - none at least, that they could afford to pay for".

But critically his report remarked: -

"*There was no doubt however, that on the whole the condition of the town was decidedly improving*".

Thankfully, from the early-1900s, death rates in the town started to fall as demolition-work continued at some pace. The worst housing was being cleared, and the dire sanitation issues were finally being addressed.

However, despite the wholesale demolition of the worst over-crowded alley slums, of the 20,000 houses standing in Wolverhampton in 1900, half were built before 1850 when building regulations were non-existent, and of these one-quarter were built in the 1830s around the over-crowded town centre, and it was here that the festering slums were still to be found.

In 1901, a survey revealed that out of a population of 94,000, 5,422 people still lived in the remaining squalid, town-centre courts, and despite the on-going slum-clearance programme, in 1908 local reporter Tom Fletcher felt compelled to write of some of the worst housing, which he reported in the local paper as 'Our Black Stain'.

Some of the worst houses in the Wolverhampton area were described as 'simple, brick-box graves', such as the tiny, windowless property seen below (Figure 36). These properties lacked any sanitation and usually contained a single small room downstairs with a washing tub and table, with a ladder of some sort leading to upstairs where if people were lucky, they would be able to sleep on a bed, but more often families would simply sleep on rags or some sort of blanket, and huddle together for warmth.

In another central area of the town, the tiny 'one-up, one-down' houses at Crooked Lane (figure 37), were photographed around 1900, below. There were 3 outside toilets serving every 10 houses there. Again, tables, chairs, and washing-tubs were downstairs and a bed upstairs. Imagine rows of these tiny houses facing each other with no back doors and separated by an alleyway just 2-3 feet wide and covered in revolting effluent, and you have impression of Caribee Island.

CHAPTER SEVEN

Figure 36 – Typical Wolverhampton box-house, early-1900s

Figure 37 – Crooked Lane, Wolverhampton, early-1900s

From a national perspective, many of the Country's worst areas of housing were progressively being cleared under slum-clearance programmes. Up to 1900, it was noted that the largest single site cleared was a 15-acre site at Bethnal Green in East London at a cost of £280,000, which involved rehousing more than 5,000 residents.

London had inevitably spent more than any other authority on slum clearance, rehousing over 50,000 people and costing over £10 million, whilst the other notably high-spending authority was predictably Glasgow that spent £2 million on its slum clearance programme. Other high spending authorities included Birmingham that spent £550,000, Liverpool £500,000, and Wolverhampton £250,000. But when you consider that Wolverhampton was less than a quarter of the size of the other named major cities outside London, it puts the scale of the town's problems into perspective. Only a dozen cities and towns outside London received considerable financial support to address housing problems, Wolverhampton being one of them.

In 1903, Dr Malet, the Medical Officer for Health in the town, specifically drew attention to the squalid condition of the remaining slum courts, stated: -

"A gipsy in a ragged tent in the open is more healthily housed, even in winter, than the occupants of some of the houses in the slums of Wolverhampton."

Then, in 1910, the reporter for the 'Sheffield Daily Telegraph' inadvertently highlighted just how bad Wolverhampton was still perceived to be even at that time. In passing reference to the town, he talked of 'beautifying his home city', highlighting that visitors had to negotiate some of the worst slums 'en-route' from the railway station to the town's high streets.

He said: -

"You have in Sheffield a great opportunity awaiting you in the approach to your main thoroughfares from the stations. You have there a lot of valuable sites covered with slum property, through which everyone who goes to the town passes before they come into contact

with the buildings upon which you spend your money. I always quote Sheffield and Wolverhampton as the two towns in the Country which have the worst approaches."

In August 1913, local councillors debated the condition of the remaining slum housing in the town at a council meeting, and the medical officer rather dramatically declared that: -

"In its insanitary conditions and slums, Wolverhampton equalled, if not exceeded, anything in absolute degradation and filth to be found outside of it."

Clearly, there was still undoubtedly much to do to bring Wolverhampton's housing conditions up to the standard of many other industrial towns and cities. One of those improvements was to provide lighting. The wonderfully atmospheric photograph, below, of a typical Wolverhampton court, taken in the early-1900s, shows 'Old Gas Yard' in Horseley Fields, courtesy of Bev Parker's excellent Wolverhampton History Website (Figure 38). This was a landmark occasion, as it was one of the first courts in Wolverhampton to receive gas-lighting. Residents, including children, are decked-out in their best clothing for the occasion.

Figure 38 – Old Gas Yard, Horseley Fields, Wolverhampton –
a typical court early-1900s

Lawyer's Field, in central Wolverhampton, below, also photographed in the early-1900s courtesy of Wolverhampton City Archives (Figure 39), depicts a fairly-typically grim, back-street setting, with a mud-baked road surface that would churn up in bad weather, and worn-out dilapidated pavements.

Figure 39 – Lawyer's Field, central Wolverhampton, early-1900s

And in 1914, local political paper 'The Wolverhampton Worker' highlighted the bleak experience of some of its residents, when it stated: -

"Workers in the east-end lived in a different world, a world of back-to-back houses, in long, tedious, dreary rows, often unhealthily close to a factory, close to the drink shop, with nothing to induce a healthy state of mind or develop strength of character. Consider the chances of children born in such surroundings - it sees dirt, disease, drunkenness, and ugliness in all its worst forms around it. Its moral outlook is blighted, its conscience stunted, its intelligence dwarfed in its infancy. Can we be surprised at its failings, then, compared to a child of the west-end? I do not expect roses out of cellars, nor do I expect a healthy working class out of the slums."

1919 was a landmark year, due to Lloyd George's Housing Act, called the 'Addison Act'. Subsidies were given to Local Authorities to build social-housing estates, with thousands of men returning from the Great War. Between 1920-1950, the older slum housing was cleared, and eventually an incredible 62,000 council properties were built in the town, which constituted one of the highest proportions of council-owned properties of any town or city in the U.K. Yet in 1930, some sixty years after the damning Government and high-profile press reports detailing the town's appalling slum housing, a further report condemned its continuing terrible housing conditions: -

"The great scandal of Wolverhampton housing was the indiscriminate building of courts and alleys, facing each other and squeezed into any space, built so that neither air nor light could penetrate their noisome depths. These courts were tucked away from site in such a way that the Medical Officer of Health could opine that many people had no idea of the maize of courts or streets lying behind the main thoroughfares into the borough".

Such slum conditions prevailed in several areas including Stafford Street, Peel Street, and Little's Lane, and what still remained around the fringes of Caribee Island, and also at Horseley Fields, Monmore Green, Heath Town, and Graiseley. As the courts were gradually cleared during the late-1800s and early-1900s, rows of new terraced housing were built all around the centre of Wolverhampton. These new houses were built at Springfield, Park Village, Graiseley, Merridale, and All Saints. These mean-looking back-to-back streets replaced squalid courts and ramshackle miner's huts and cottages in the neighbourhood and were a great improvement at the time. Dartmouth Street in the All Saints area is seen below courtesy of Wolverhampton City Archives, an area that chiefly housed iron workers and a few remaining miners (Figure 40).

Figure 40 – Dartmouth Street, All Saints, Wolverhampton, mid-1900s

For the upper-working-classes, rows of purpose-built terraced houses were constructed including many with gardens, and an unknown luxury - individual outside toilets. Whitmore Reans, built as a new town and originally called 'New Hampton', sat to the north-west of the town centre and was a community built to house such residents. Blakenhall to the south, was similar. Most of these long, straight streets had small, front paddocks and large back gardens, and the streets were generally wide.

Perhaps the worst area of Wolverhampton in the mid-1900s was the central district of Graiseley, also known as Merridale, especially around Dale Street, Little Brickkiln Street, and Zoar Street, which contained the oldest houses over one-hundred years old and crammed so closely together that they were devoid of light and adequate ventilation. These included 459 houses of which 80% had no water supply, 72% no sink, and 61% no lavatory. They were in a decomposing state and the vast-majority were infested with vermin. Elsewhere in the town, some ramshackle miner's cottages remained around the south-eastern side of the town, and quite a lot of older slum housing still existed around central Wolverhampton, some of which was only cleared as recently as the 1960s. The photograph of Grove Street at Heath Town, below, courtesy of Wolverhampton City Archives, portrays a typical Wolverhampton court and a fairly-desolate scene, with some of the houses semi-derelict (Figure 41). These houses shared a communal water pump and toilets.

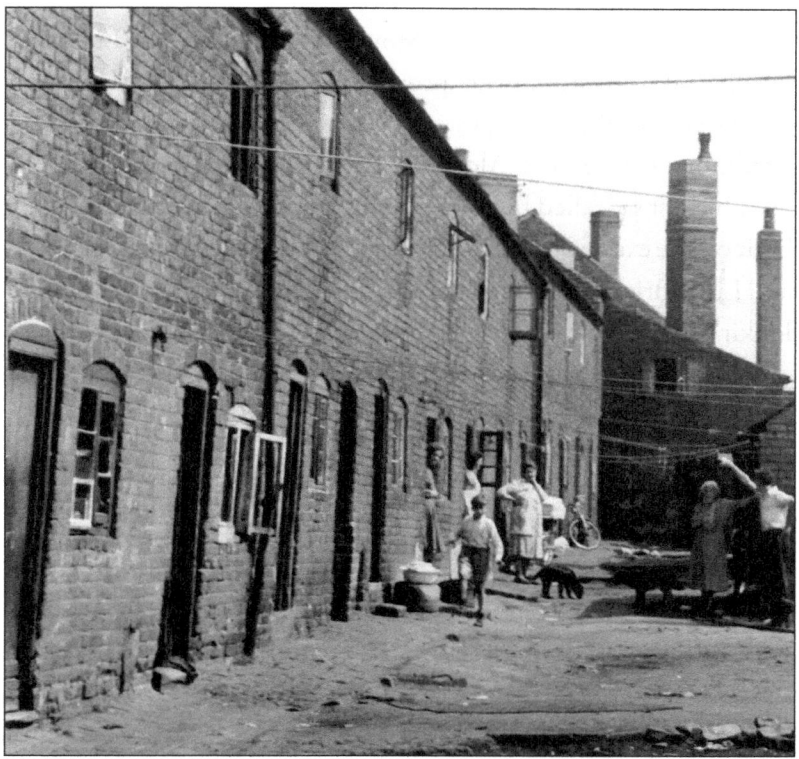

Figure 41 – Slum housing at Grove Street,
Heath Town, Wolverhampton, early-1960s

As older housing was cleared away for ever, sprawling, new Local Authority family-housing estates were built on green-field sites, that expanded the boundary of the town. To the north-east, the vast and adjoining Low Hill, Scotlands, and Bushbury estates were constructed – comprising over 5,000 houses – the size of a small town. Nearby, Three Tuns and St Annes estates were constructed to the north. At Wednesfield, large estates were built at Ashmore Park, Long Knowle, Moathouse, and Perry Hall. To the immediate east of the town and close to expired mining land, estates were constructed at Eastfield, Deansfield, East Park, and at Portobello. To the south of the town centre, large new estates emerged at Parkfield, Rough Hills, and around Ettingshall, whilst similar scale schemes were constructed to the south-east at Stowlawn, St Chads, The Lunt, and Bradley all in Bilston. Even 'prosperous western Wolverhampton' saw large social housing estates built at Warstones, Finchfield, Bradmore, Castlecroft, Aldersley, and Tettenhall Wood.

The first so-called high-rise council flats sprung up at Graiseley, built on the exact spot where the Zoar Street, Dale Street, and Great and Little Brickkiln Street slums once stood. The two rather-austere looking blocks on the Graiseley estate, photographed below (Figure 42), have themselves been demolished in recent years.

Figure 42 – Graiseley Estate, Wolverhampton in the 1970s

But with the social isolation that building upon peripheral green-field sites created, combined with extremely high levels of unemployment and low-income levels, some of these new council estates started to experience severe problems and associated stigma's. Parts of these estates sometimes became ravaged by anti-social behaviour and crime, resulting in selective demolition where the environment had simply become too run-down. Even as far back as 1952, local author Phil Drabble in his book 'Black Country' aptly described the effect of the construction of the Low Hill, Scotlands, and Bushbury estates on this once peaceful rural tranquility: -

"When I think of Bushbury Hill I always think of hares. Old men of the district will tell you that there have always been an abnormal number of hares there. But now they should have gone. The place is becoming a 'dormitory' for Wolverhampton. A huge building estate, with all the noise and concrete roads and wild dogs and wilder children has appeared. Grotesque pre-fabricated houses sprang up like fungi overnight".

And during the 1970s, 1980s, and 1990s, sections of these post-war council estates at Low Hill, Bushbury, and the Scotlands symbolised everything that was wrong with out-of-town, social housing experiments. In some cases, it was simply a case of moving people out of the town-centre slums and giving them new houses with gardens – it did not always end well. The 1970s photograph below (Figure 43), shows the run-down condition of the Scotlands estate, courtesy of student George Foster. This image shows the typically-unkempt condition of the back gardens at Keats Road. Sections of this estate, including part of Keats Road, Barrie Crescent, and Tennyson Road were demolished in the 1980s. Similarly, Purcel Road and Stanley Road at Bushbury, part of Kipling Road at Three Tuns, and Humphries Road, part of Broome Road, and part of Fourth and Fifth Avenue's at Low Hill were demolished in the early-2000s. All had become very run-down and unpopular, with most of the houses in these roads in a dreadful state and many semi-derelict.

Figure 43 – Keats Road, The Scotlands, Wolverhampton, 1970s.

Even as recently as 2012, 'Low Hill South' ranked as 3rd poorest in terms of child poverty out of over 34,000 'Super Output Areas' (districts smaller than wards) in England and Wales. An indicator of the poverty levels there. Today, Low Hill is a far better place, and as is always the case most of its residents are good, hard-working people. I know that from having lived and worked there. But such infamous estates always have a quarter which creates an unfair reputation for everyone.

Additionally, high-rise and low-rise housing estates sprung up following slum clearance, such as the Heath Town estate erected on the east side of town. This famous estate was the one that most characterised 1960s high-rise estates – a mixture of 4 high-rise towers, 5 mid-rise blocks, and 21 blocks of 'rabbit-run' maisonettes. Parts of it were demolished in the 1990s, after some sections became deeply unpopular. The scale of this huge estate can be seen in the 1960s image below, from an unknown source (Figure 44). But it was well-constructed and although improvements and renovation are still ongoing, the bulk of it still stands today.

Figure 44 – Heath Town, Wolverhampton, 1960s

Wolverhampton built over 50 tower blocks as part of its slum-clearance rehousing scheme. Another large estate, named 'Blakenhall Gardens' comprised six huge tower blocks, which were demolished in recent years, as were the Mayfields and Rydal Green estates. Elsewhere, low-rise blocks of flats were constructed across the city, and in the 1970s the sprawling new Pendeford-Dovecotes estate was constructed on its western fringe, comprising family-houses and low-rise flats.

Older housing around the centre and on its eastern side remains somewhat problematic in parts, though much money has been spent bringing areas up to standard, and housing conditions are considerably improved compared to the desperately poor ones of the Industrial Revolution, and even of the mid-to-late-1900s.

You would find it difficult to tour any part of Wolverhampton these days, and find such scenes of deprivation, which is credit to the local authority and to central Government. An important point to remember. Though pockets of deprivation inevitably still exist. Concurrently, for balance, Wolverhampton possesses some charming, leafy suburbs, as it always has done. Poverty is always relative.

Fatal housing-related diseases and deathly statistics

Fatal housing-related diseases

Abject poverty and appalling insanitary housing conditions as those described, were directly associated with fatal diseases such as cholera, typhoid, typhus, small-pox, and scarlet fever.

Up to a dozen cramped, over-crowded houses often shared a single communal privy in Wolverhampton's slums, and some even contained adjoining pig-sties. Open sewers built-up as stagnant cess-pits, and festering detriment trickled along the narrow alleyways leading through the slums. In the worse cases, heaps of human and animal waste would be dumped at one end of a room, or more often immediately outside the house where there was space to do so, and stagnant, fetid pools of water stood all around. Inevitably, water-borne and air-borne diseases struck where the conditions were worst.

Cholera outbreaks of 1832, 1848-49, and 1854

The dreaded cholera hit Wolverhampton three times - in 1832, 1848-49, and 1854. It initially always appeared in the over-crowded slum areas, where sanitation was worse.

Caribee Island and its network of over-crowded, narrow alleys and courts, Stafford Street, Bilston Street, Walsall Street, Zoar Street, Brickkiln Street, Salop Street and its courts, Pountney's Fold, Monmore Green, Horsley Fields, Portobello, Rough Hills, Ettingshall, and Catchem's Corner, and also the courts of Bilston were usually affected. These were where the worst housing conditions were to be found in Wolverhampton.

1) 1832 Cholera outbreak

In the 1832 cholera outbreak, nearly 1,000 people died in the Wolverhampton area. 193 died in Wolverhampton itself, but 742 perished in nearby Bilston, which constituted the highest ratio per head in the entire country. To put this into perspective, 3,000 died of cholera at this time in the entire Scottish city of Glasgow, a huge industrial city notorious for its slum housing.

It is easy to find information relating to the cholera outbreaks in the smaller Black Country towns on local history websites. 277 perished in Dudley, 404 in Tipton, and 290 in Sedgley, during the 1832 cholera epidemic, and it is also easy to find information regarding the relatively smaller number of 193 deaths during the same outbreak in 'larger Wolverhampton', or just 85 deaths in 'larger Walsall', or just 62 deaths in 'larger West Bromwich' - figures which are frequently used for comparison.

2) 1848-1849 Cholera outbreak

As cholera broke out in earnest in September 1849, killing 350 in central and east Wolverhampton during that terrible month alone, the local priest of St George's made the brave decision to 'stay put' whilst many from the rich, including doctor's, simply fled the town to safer and healthier countryside districts. Tents were erected at Graiseley Hill and at Goldthorn Hill, on the outskirts, to house the affected residents.

He described the scene as follows: -

"Thousands of sick and dying men, women, and children were confined to quarantine wards in the Union workhouse or carted out to tents erected on a hill a couple of miles out of town. Within a year more than 500 people perished. Many were laid to rest in a vast, unmarked pit in a graveyard at St George's Church".

Indeed, September 1849 saw a peak of this dreadful epidemic in Wolverhampton. 'Quarterly figures' released later, show that the 'total number of recorded deaths' in the Wolverhampton Borough, or union area, during the 'third-quarter' of 1849 alone, were three times higher than usual, standing at 1,897, so it was possible to deduce that the extra 1,200 deaths were likely caused by cholera-related disease (English or Asiatic Cholera, along with fever or diarrhoea which were cholera-related). This tallies with 'quarterly' cholera-death figures released for the borough of Wolverhampton, that included 485 in Wolverhampton, 560 in Bilston, and 243 in Willenhall. Elsewhere in the Black Country, 'third-quarter' figures revealed that only Wednesbury suffered to similar degrees, with around 300 succumbing to cholera-related illness, whilst around 80 died of cholera-related illness in Tipton during this outbreak, 61 in Dudley, 42 in Stourbridge, 34 in Darlaston, 34 in Walsall, and just 9 in West Bromwich. This third-quarter accounted for three-quarters of the final figures as that was when it was at its most virulent.

It is much harder to find 'final, overall figures' for this second cholera outbreak during the 1848-49 epidemic, but it is very-rarely highlighted that 720 eventually died in Wolverhampton itself, along with around the same number again in Bilston which was hit extremely hard for a second time, whilst 281 also succumbed in Willenhall. So, these figures for the three Wolverhampton-parish towns roughly correlate with final figure of 1,608 cholera-related deaths in the 'Borough of Wolverhampton' highlighted above, which at the time included Wolverhampton town with a population of around 50,000, Bilston 20,000, Willenhall 9,000, and Wednesfield around 4,000.

But even that total may have been an under-estimate.

Dr Farr's report to the Registrar General highlighted that 3,275 people eventually died of cholera-related disease during the 1848-49 outbreak in what it called 'The Woverhampton cholera field', far more than the 1,608 quoted, though this included a 12 square-mile sweep of Wolverhampton, and so included the whole Black Country.

On top of the 1,608 who 'officially' died in the borough of Wolverhampton, around 400 eventually succumbed in Wednesbury, 100 in Tipton, 80 in Dudley, 50 in Stourbridge, 40 in Darlaston, and a dozen in West Bromwich.

Elsewhere, 828 succumbed to cholera in Manchester, over 1,000 in both Hull and Merthyr Tydfil, 1,154 in Bristol, 2,323 in Leeds, and 14,590 in London. It clearly affected many major cities. The disease struck where housing conditions were worst.

Central and east Wolverhampton, and Bilston were the areas of the Black Country affected most of all during this 1849 outbreak as the worst housing conditions were to be found there.

3) 1854 Cholera outbreak

Cholera unfortunately struck for a third time in Wolverhampton in 1854, when 392 people died from cholera or suspected cholera-related illness, usually diarrhoea.

4) Other Housing and Social Condition related diseases - Typhus, Typhoid, Small Pox, Scarlet Fever

In relation to other deadly diseases, they typically appeared in the same insanitary slum areas highlighted. Diarrhoea and scarlet fever were common-place.

The solicitor and Alderman H.H. Fowler highlighted that in the 1850s, Wolverhampton had a higher rate of typhoid annually than London, Manchester, Leeds, or Birmingham, but along with typhus it was relatively uncommon compared to some other diseases.

There were a few outbreaks of small-pox in the town during the 1860s, and then in 1872 another 670 died in Wolverhampton. 224 perished due to scarlet fever, and according to Frank Mason, 446 people also died of small-pox in the town. Many of the victims were young children.

These deaths were undoubtedly caused by its continued insanitary housing conditions.

Further deathly statistics

In discussing the medical history of Wolverhampton, the locally-reputed Dr Wilkes made comment in the Wolverhampton Chronicle on 27 April 1864 that: -

"*Disease and crime rest upon the same bases, that one cannot exist without the other, and that to remove one is to remove both. The diseases, the mortality, the population, and the meteorology of the district being known, deduce from these facts the amount of crime perpetuated by the said population*".

No wonder perhaps then, that just fifteen years earlier, it was randomly remarked by W.A Lewis Esquire in his report of 'The Sanitary Condition of Wolverhampton' that there had been 225 murders in Wolverhampton the previous year (1847), which amounted to between a staggering 4 to 5 murders each week, a notably high level compared to modern times. And Wolverhampton is now 4 times larger than it was then, and it only suffers around 3-10 murders per year.

That same year, 1847, The Registrar General's official report compared mortality levels for large provincial towns with populations of around 40-50,000 in the Midlands and South, using 'summer-quarter' figures from 1845 and 1846. Worryingly they possessed death rates higher than the largest cities in the Country. Nottingham lost 285 and 469 persons respectively over the summer quarters of these two years, Coventry 188 and 200, Plymouth 191 and 279, Northampton 182 and 221, Oxford 89 and 194, Brighton 219 and 372, Ipswich 119 and 240, and Norwich 300 and 451. In the Black Country, Walsall lost 158 and 288, whilst the two worst towns overall were predictably Wolverhampton with 429 and 687, and Dudley with 457 and 744. These two towns arguably had the worst sanitation issues in the kingdom, at that time.

It all too predictably summarised: -

"The high mortality of towns has been traced to crowded lodgings - personal uncleanliness - the concentration of unhealthy emanations from narrow streets, without fresh air, water, or sewerage. The rapidity of decomposition, and the facility with which all kinds of animal matter become tainted, and run into putrefaction, enable us to understand how, in a summer like the past, in which the temperature was unusually high, the diseases referable to impure atmosphere should be so prevalent and fatal."

John Butland Smith, within his comprehensive thesis at University of Leicester titled 'The Governance of Wolverhampton 1848-1888' highlighted that the average death rate in East Wolverhampton during this period was 31 per thousand, compared to 21 per thousand in more prosperous West Wolverhampton. During the most extreme year of that period, the east side experienced a death rate of 44 per thousand, compared to just 17 per thousand on the west side. He also highlighted that in 1889 the east side of town had a death-rate from Tuberculosis (TB) twelve times that of the west side of town.

For contrast, the average death rate for this period was 25 per thousand for the Black Country as a whole, and 22 per thousand for the whole Country. In 1850, Dudley was noted to have the highest death rate in the Country, at 28 per thousand, though Wolverhampton had a death rate of more than 30 per thousand at one point during that period.

More alarmingly, in 1852, the 'average age of death' in Dudley was just 16 years and 7 months, the lowest average age in the Country, quite a shocking statistic. Second worse was Merthyr Tydfil at 18 years and 2 months, followed in third place by Wolverhampton, despite the inclusion of its distinctly more prosperous western side, at 19 years and 1 month. Walsall and West Bromwich were only marginally better. Next on the list were Liverpool, Sheffield, Manchester, and Birmingham with the 'average age of death' ranging between 20 years and 5 months, to 23 years and 9 months. The fact that around 1 in 5 youngsters died in their first year in these cities, did affect these figures, though they are still alarming. Furthermore, figures from that year reveal that 1,436 'under-5-year-old's' died in Dudley, 1,314 in Wolverhampton, 727 in West Bromwich, 619 in Stourbridge, and 505 in Walsall. Further evidence of where the main concentrations of real hardship existed.

In 1864, Wolverhampton had the 4th highest annual mortality rate in the Country, just behind Manchester, St Georges in East London, and Leeds, at 28 per thousand, and the mortality rate for children 'under five years of age' was alarmingly high. A large number of children in Wolverhampton died in the home, as many under-8's were often left to their own devices whilst their parents were at work. Many such accidents were recorded where their clothing caught fire as they simply stood too close to the stove for warmth. Unable to raise alarm or get out, many died a horrible burning death. Other children died by drinking scalding hot kettle water, again left alone but unable to differentiate between the hot water of the kettle on the stove, and the cold water they collected from the communal water-tap, using the same implement. The frequency of these two type of accidents involving children in the town was alarming.

Things had not improved much by 1866, when the 'Birmingham Daily Post' undertook its detailed study, as already highlighted, of the worst, insanitary slum areas of the Black Country, and for the ten-year period of 1851-1860 Wolverhampton again had the highest mortality rate, higher even than Liverpool, at 31 per thousand.

George Barnsby in his 1990 book 'Social Conditions in the Black Country' examined the issue further by examining death rates at the peak of the Industrial Revolution between 1840-1870. He stated: -

"The table gives death rates for 18 Black Country towns beginning with the unhealthiest. The worst was always East Wolverhampton."

However, he suggested the reason for this was that Wolverhampton's figures were split between east and west, and that if this had been done for other Black Country towns, their 'east-side' rates might be similar or worse.

But this stance does not seem to hold water, except perhaps for in the case of the substantial town of Walsall, which might be similar. Virtually the entire populations of smaller Black Country towns in the central area of the region did not really develop an eastern or a poorer side, and certainly not a wealthier western side like Wolverhampton, as this 1848 description of Bilston by solicitor George Robinson highlights: -

"There are two thousand, four-hundred and fifty houses in Bilston - eight-tenths of the land is covered with heaps of mineral rubbish and five-sixths of the houses are of the poorest description. With the exception of a few good houses on the principal street, the whole of this township is a scene of desolation, except for mining purposes".

The entire reason Wolverhampton's figures were split was to highlight the unusual, polar-opposite existence of the two parts of it population, firstly of its smaller but more affluent 'green borderland' western side, and secondly of its heavily-industrial, smoke-begrimed eastern 'Black Country' side. There were no such distinctive, polar-opposite social conditions between east and west, anywhere else in the Black Country.

To further contradict Barnsby's theory, figures for another substantially-sized town, West Bromwich, were also geographically split, this time between its poorer and more industrial North-east, and its more affluent South-west. As expected, the heavily industrial North-eastern side of West Bromwich continuously though-out that thirty- year period 1840-1870, had a higher death rate than its wealthier South-western side, yet North-east West Bromwich still had a death rate up to one-third lower than that of East Wolverhampton.

Over the entire thirty-year study period 1840-1870, several conclusions can be drawn in relation to Wolverhampton East: -

* It consistently had the highest death rates per 1,000 population in the Black Country.

* It had the highest 'single-year death rate' at 44 per 1,000 population.

* It had the highest average death rate over the thirty-year period.

* It had the highest 'average ten-year period death rate' in the Black Country, at 33 per 1,000 population

In terms of this final measure, adjoining Bilston was just behind Wolverhampton East, followed in order by Walsall, Darlaston, Dudley, Wednesbury, Willenhall, Tipton, West Bromwich north-east, Sedgley, Oldbury, and Kingswinford, which all had an 'average ten-year death rate' of over 25 per 1,000 population.

In contrast, the slightly better or more prosperous Black Country areas of Stourbridge, Rowley Regis, West Bromwich South-west, Wolverhampton West, Halesowen, and Bloxwich each had an 'average ten-year death rate' between 20-25 per 1,000 population between 1840-1870.

The Registrar General's returns for December 1871 revealed that Wolverhampton's insanitary conditions continued to account for its exceptionally high death rate. In terms of death rate per thousand, Wolverhampton's latest figures stood at an alarming 56, whilst in contrast the UK's other large towns returned the following figures – Sunderland 45, Nottingham 44, Norwich 42, Salford 36, Manchester 35, Edinburgh 33, Newcastle 32, Leeds, Glasgow, Leicester, Portsmouth each 31, Liverpool 30, Sheffield 29, Bristol 28, Bradford 26, Hull 24, Dublin 24, and Birmingham 20.

But statistics can only partly paint a picture. Although death rates do indeed reflect 'true 'levels of hardship', there is no doubt that the smaller Black Country towns of Bilston, Sedgley, Gornal, Wednesbury, Rowley Regis, Quarry Bank, and Oldbury suffered appalling levels of hardship, overcrowding, and poverty, with ramshackle, dilapidated dwellings, whilst the larger towns like Wolverhampton, Dudley, Walsall, and to some degree West Bromwich had larger and denser slum areas which suffered incredible over-crowding and lack of sanitation. Many of these deaths were indeed primarily caused by the insanitary housing conditions, but you will not find much, if any detail of these poverty-related Wolverhampton deaths on many Black Country-related websites.

And to be fair, Wolverhampton's own history-writers have primarily concentrated on the finer aspects that the town undoubtedly possessed.

3) CONCLUSION- Housing and Working Conditions of Wolverhampton

Wolverhampton was certainly a town of extreme contrast, being situated on the edge of the Black Country, and the wealthier section of its population on the smaller but beautiful western suburbs certainly tried to distance itself from the gloom, abject poverty, and hardship experienced by the unfortunate residents living and working in its Black Country central and eastern districts. It should again be highlighted that there are some lovely residential areas within the city, all around its western side at Tettenhall, Finchfield, Compton, Penn, but also in Wednesfield on the eatern fringes too.

The working conditions in its collieries and iron and brass works were notably perilous and tough, and children were forced into slave labour-like conditions where they were employed by locksmiths and nailers. There was no Health and Safety in those days. Conditions were somewhat better in its japanning and other skilled 'finishing' factories though even they still had distinct hazards.

In terms of its housing conditions, they were simply dreadful. 'Caribee Island', spread over some sixteen acres of land, was arguably the largest and worst slum area of the Black Country and possibly the entire midlands, for many years. It was an area that police were very wary of entering, for instance an officer was killed when two burly police officers tried to quell a feud between two families, being battered to death by a group. On another documented occasion, several officers pursued someone into the slum area and were pelted with bricks, and a police officer was struck over the head with a hand-held, half-brick. But this was not untypical of many disturbances due to the general drunkenness and disorder that occurred. The maize of alleys in Caribee Island especially, constituted a dangerous place to enter, and hence it is no wonder that there are few if any photographic records of anywhere but its fringe areas. But the slums were not restricted to Caribee Island, they were also situated elsewhere around the town centre, at Salop Street, Peel Street, Walsall Street, Bilston Street, and Stafford Street, and at what were then the town's suburbs at Horseley Fields, Monmore Green, Graiseley, and Merridale.

These homes were often even more prejudicial to health than their occupant's places of work, and it was only due to the free abundance and availability of coal that much more disease did not occur. Sanitation was non-existent, and it took authority in the town a long time to address what was a fundamental health issue.

Wolverhampton was a true 'shock-city' of the Industrial Revolution, for the most part, with a typical Black Country environment, and it is fair to say that the degree of sheer deprivation experienced by so many

Wolverhampton people in the home or at work, has never before been accurately expressed and fully highlighted in any history book.

Wolverhampton was undoubtedly a wonderful place to live if you were rich during the Industrial Revolution, but if you were an ordinary hard-working artisan or a child tied into an apprenticeship it was more than likely a wretched place to live and work in, and if you were out-of-work or destitute......words could not attempt to describe the abject misery that lay ahead during what would very likely be a fairly short life.

CHAPTER EIGHT

Other Considerations Regards the Black Country- Myths and Modern-day Arguments

CHAPTER BREAKDOWN

1) **Coat of Arms and Motto**
2) **The Football Argument**
3) **Modern Stereotypical Views**
4) **Poignant Concluding Words**

In this short chapter, I examine some less important facts and issues that are much discussed in modern times, some relevant to the wider discussion, and some that are fairly, arbitrary.

In-essence, a light-hearted look at popular mythology and viewpoints that seem to be prominently aired when the 'Black Country issue' is discussed these days.

These discussions are not really determining points of view, they do not contribute much to the earlier discussion or to the main subject matter, but nevertheless it is worth highlighting them in my opinion because in a modern context, these views reflect some of the generalised views of the current population.

CHAPTER EIGHT

1) Coat of Arms and Motto

Firstly, it may be argued that Wolverhampton's Coat of Arms demonstrates its Black Country past. The crest on the Wolverhampton coat of arms has a brazier that is said to stand for the Black Country for which Wolverhampton is part.

According to Frank Mason in 'The Book of Wolverhampton' (1979), the first mayor George Thorneycroft, owner of Shrubbery Iron works, gave a mace to the town. A coat of arms was needed, and designed to represent everything about Wolverhampton, starting with 'a churchyard pillar, a beacon filled with burning coals was added to give reference to the worship of the Britons, the beacon of the Saxons, and the colliers of the present'.

As we know, when Queen Victoria visited Wolverhampton, an arch was created comprising shovels, picks, iron bars, and huge chunks of coal, arguably a true representation of Wolverhampton during the Industrial Revolution, and proof of the importance of coal to Wolverhampton.

Wolverhampton's motto 'Out of Darkness Cometh Light' is said by many to represent the flickering furnaces, black coal, and general mirk that represented east Wolverhampton, and then also the light and fresh air of its prosperous western side, with beautiful, green countryside just beyond.

2) The Football Argument

An article in the Lancashire Evening Post on the 9 February 1901 sadly summarised the state of football in the district, where it hypothesised: -

"The Black Country seems to me strangely typical of the football played within its busy borders. Rough, and devoid of even remotest claims to be picturesque, its dismal pit banks and blazing foundries yet

bespeak the very soul of business. So does its football. Catch the famous old Wolves..............there is no reminiscence of the perfect precision in passing characteristic say of the old North Enders, no individual excellence of the Corinthian order. There is however, in overflowing measure full-flavoured dash, unquenchable determination, and never-wearying persistence".

Has much changed in recent times? Certainly not for The Wolves, not until very recent exciting times.

These days, fans of both major Black Country clubs tend to exaggerate each other's lack of belonging to the Black Country. As the song goes: -

"The Black Country's 'ours'......"

West Bromwich Albion fans suggest that their club represents the Black Country solely as they propose that West Bromwich is the only Black Country town. The name 'Baggies' is said to be symbolic of miner's clothing. They highlight somewhat light-heartedly that Wolves were based in a 'market town lying in Staffordshire'.

Wolves fans argue that Albion (the club at least) are situated more-or-less in Birmingham, certainly outside the Black Country, and light-heartedly that they have a Birmingham postcode and telephone number, as well as highlighting that 'Bromwich' is a corruption of the name 'Brummagem'. They occasionally point out that the club nickname 'Throstles' highlights an agricultural or rural origin and that the nickname was given to the club due to the heath and greenery present at the time.

Wolves colours of gold and black are often said to be symbolic of the Black Country contrast of the black of the smoky atmosphere, the slag heaps and the coal, and the gold or orange of the flame of the furnace. Or alternatively, due to the light of its western side, the gold reflects the light when emerging from its dark, smoky industrial side. 'Out of Darkness Cometh Light' is therefore said to be a reflection of its Black Country history.

Clearly, the Black Country heartlands lie between both club's actual locations, with neither club's current ground being quite within it. Fans of both clubs lie within the core areas in more-or-less equal measure.

Wolves first true ground, on Dudley Road between 1877-1897, where they were founded, lay a stone's throw from many collieries with some the thickest coal and iron-ore seams in the Black Country, this coinciding with the end of the Industrial Revolution. Molineux has always sat just outside the Black Country border. WBA's Hawthorns home also lay outside the 'original Black Country', it was surrounded by fields until 1876 when Sandwell Park Colliery at Smethwick was first mined, but even then, that was a deeper operation not scarring the surface in the same way. Albion moved there in 1900. Earlier Albion grounds were located a little nearer the town centre of West Bromwich at Dartmouth Park, at Coopers Hill, Four Acres, and Stoney Lane, which are debatably on the edge of the Black Country.

In truth, both clubs are arguably now situated fractionally outside the Black Country, but the towns and areas they represent are of course core Black Country areas.

3) **Modern stereotypical views**

In modern times, the definition of The Black Country for some seems to be based on where you can still get 'faggots and pays', or where the accent is perceived to still be the strongest. This has already been demonstrated by the recent, highlighted work of Esther Asprey, who has shown that perceptions regarding which geographical areas should be classed as the 'Black Country' is now somewhat fragmented.

But such modern perceptions were not what defined the Black Country at the time it was so-named back in the 1840s. So that arguably has little relevance unless historical context and information is fully considered.

Clearly, so much has changed over the centuries, since the Black Country was really with us.

It seems very unlikely that a definition of the Black Country is ever likely to be agreed by everyone, and the Black Country Society definition is certainly controversial, and it has arguably divided opinion due to its reliance on the thick coal seam.

Therefore, the arguments and counter-arguments in modern times will rumble on and on, based on fact or fiction, and will continue to be largely based on where exactly one lives within the Black Country, with Dudley folk adopting the 'thick seam' definition, and Wolverhampton folk adopting the 'iron' definition.

4) Poignant Concluding Words

I will finish this chapter, by highlighting the rather beautiful words of my favourite local author Phil Drabble from his 1952 book 'Black Country': -

"Do not be misled too much by the popular novelists and modern planners. They will emphasise the Black in our name. They will pick out stories of children in our mines and women toiling at heavy work. They will tell sad sagas of how the merchants preyed on the workers. And all they will say will probably be true. But during the time when the country in a circle round Bilston really was black, when blast furnaces were as common as thistles and chimney-stacks like stubble, and when the sun shone only on Sundays – the day the smoke pall rolled aside – during all this time the standards of living had improved beyond recognition. It had improved all over the country, of course. But it had mainly improved because of events in this district, because of the developments in technique that had taken place in this black spot."

And Wolverhampton, so clearly and proudly considered a Black Country town throughout the 1800s and even its 'Capital' or 'Metropolis' for most of that time, today has to vie for its place in Black Country history due to the reinterpretation, or misinterpretation of the 1960s by the Black Country Society.

But the so-called experts aside, and perhaps of far greater significance is the fact that a substantial 2015 survey in the local newspaper revealed that Wolverhampton residents demonstrated the highest level of pride of their Black Country legacy of the 4 Black Country boroughs.

Perhaps they rightly feel that 'The Black Country is Ours'.

CHAPTER NINE

Wolverhampton and the Black Country – Ten Overall Conclusions

CONCLUSION ONE

The first written descriptions of the 'original Black Country' in the 1840s refer to it as an area of South Staffordshire, and quite clearly did not initially include Dudley which lay in an enclave of Worcestershire, though evidently the term incorporated the Worcestershire section of the region including Dudley as well, by the 1850s. It is evident that the 'original Black Country' referred to the mineral plateau running from central Wolverhampton to Bilston and Willenhall, through to Darlaston, Tipton, Wednesbury, and northern West Bromwich, but not Dudley.

CONCLUSION TWO

In geographical and geological terms, there is no evidence that the 'original Black Country' was thought to have been solely-represented by those areas where only the thick coal seam was found, nor in fact 'solely' defined by the visual effect of coal-mining on the landscape. And if one still chooses to adopt that theory, the Black Country landscape most damaged by mining was often noted to be the shallow thin seam tract lying between the centres of Wolverhampton, Bilston, and Willenhall, described as 'mile upon mile of heaps of black rubbish'. But coal-mining had taken place in the region for 500 years before the term 'Black Country' evolved, strongly suggesting that the area was so-named due to additional or other factors.

CONCLUSION THREE

Mining of the deeper, concealed coal seam, that came later-on at the end of the 1800s, certainly played no role in defining the Black Country and these newer operations only constituted a continuation of the mining industry around and just outside the borders of the 'original Black Country'.

CONCLUSION FOUR

The industrial development of the Black Country was at least equally due to the existence of the iron-stone tract of the Black Country coal-field, and also due to the thin seam of coal that was often better suited than the thick coal for use in the iron works and furnaces. Much of the thick coal seam was only suitable for domestic household use, yet the Black Country Society choose to define the area solely by the existence of this mineral, whilst wrongly excluding those districts where the best iron-ore and thin seams of coal existed.

CONCLUSION FIVE

It is evident that the 'original Black Country' was defined by iron-ore and the iron industry as much as by coal, this clearly reflecting the views throughout the 1800s Industrial Revolution. Critically, only once the iron industry became firmly established did the term 'Black Country' emerge to describe the region, and this was largely due to the constant emission of black smoke from the iron industry's furnaces and chimneys that stifled any growth of vegetation and turned the atmosphere, and everything and everyone underneath it sooty-black. Whilst it is true that without coal the process of smelting iron-ore would not have been possible on such a large scale, 'timeframe evidence' shows us that the Black Country evolved both 'in name' and 'as a mighty industrial entity' only once iron production began to take place on a large scale. During the Industrial Revolution, the Black Country was the leading national producer of iron and iron products, but it was not the leading district extracting coal, so iron should always play a pivotal role in any definition of the Black Country.

CONCLUSION SIX

The location of the great iron industry was dictated particularly by the location of the iron-ore tract of the coal-field as well as by the presence of thinner seams of coal, but critically also by the location of the canal system due to the initial reliance on water, at least as much as the location of the thick coal seam.

CONCLUSION SEVEN

Wolverhampton was clearly perceived as a Black Country town throughout the entire Industrial Revolution, and quite widely perceived as 'The Metropolis or Capital of The Black Country' throughout that period. Wolverhampton became the main administrative trade centre for the coal and iron industry in the

Black Country during the Industrial Revolution. Wolverhampton also has a mining legacy of its own, even excluding Bilston. Its coal-field covered much of Wolverhampton's eastern and southern side, and at the time the term 'Black Country' first appeared in writing in the early-1840s, it had more miners than any Black Country town except Bilston. As its western and northern suburbs expanded on green belt land, it was then first suggested during the late-1930s that it was 'Of the Black Country', if not 'in it', due to its geographical position on the edge of the region. These newer suburbs certainly lay outside the original Black Country, which always confuses and compounds the discussion somewhat. But the rest of Wolverhampton lay firmly in the Black Country.

CONCLUSION EIGHT

Wolverhampton could adopt either of the alternative labels of 'The Capital of the Iron Country', or 'Capital of the Iron Trade in the Black Country' due to its prominent role in the Black Country Iron Industry during the Industrial Revolution. In simple terms Wolverhampton was perceived as 'the centre of the iron trade' during the peak of the Industrial Revolution due to its great iron-producing industry. 'Ironopolis' was a fitting accolade bestowed upon it by the Manchester press.

CONCLUSION NINE

The Black Country Society and many Dudley-based 20th-Century historians maintain the concept of a 'core Black Country area' lying around Cradley and Rowley Regis, with Dudley often now perceived as the undisputed 'Capital of the Black Country'. During the Industrial Revolution, the Black Country was noted to be at its blackest where the greatest concentration of iron works lay within the central mineral-producing plateau district of South Staffordshire, and this area stretched from central Wolverhampton, continuing south-eastward through Bilston, Darlaston, Tipton, and Wednesbury to northern West Bromwich. A second core-zone existed west of Dudley around Brierley Hill and Cradley, which although also heavily industrial was comparatively smoke-free as it lay on rolling hills. Today, a perception exists that a 'core area of the Black Country' exists around Cradley Heath, perhaps because that area most typically continued to represent the Black Country and its traditions throughout the 1900s, and even to some degree today.

CONCLUSION TEN

The Black Country Society definition based solely on the thick coal seam is arguably idealistic, contrived, and based on a lack of evidence. The adoption of this definition was quite possibly used in a way to demean Wolverhampton's Black Country history, and with it, its long-standing stature as 'Capital or Metropolis of the Black Country'. It is arguable that in 're-defining the Black Country' in the 1960s, the Black Country Society have re-written history with some disregard to historic fact and evidence. At worse, it might be surmised that inadvertently, through its 1960s definition, they have stolen the Black Country identity and legacy from Wolverhampton and Walsall and dismissed their contribution. One might ask, 'how can one steal something that is already yours?' If it was once jointly-owned, you can.

CHAPTER NINE

The CORRECT DEFINITION OF THE ORIGINAL BLACK COUNTRY

"The original Black Country was defined by those areas of South Staffordshire where the 'shallow seams' of thick or thin coal and iron-ore were mined, which gave the general landscape a pitted appearance, and it was defined at least equally by the adjoining districts where the great iron and brass-manufacturing industries developed with their resultant piles of furnace-slag, spoil, scrap metal, and cinder ash, and with their numerous furnaces and chimneys constantly spewing out dense clouds of smoke that blackened the general atmosphere and everything underneath it".

CHAPTER TEN

A New Development and Partial Acknowledgement

During 2017, I was in contact with Mike Pearson, Chief Editor and Website Administrator of the Black Country Society, and to his credit they have allowed me to express my views in some length in a four-page article in the summer edition of 'The Black Countryman', which shows an openness of thought. I am deeply indebted to Mike, for allowing me to express views which arguably contradict their definition.

Regards the boundary of the Black Country, Mike stressed that many people held different views which he felt was good as it encouraged and stimulated debate, but he also told me that at a personal level he agreed with the concept of 'a wider border'.

I do hope he doesn't mind me revealing that. I doubt that he will, as he made comment himself in the following magazine edition, explaining why he thought Wolverhampton was a Black Country town, whilst acknowledging the sensitivity to many people.

And critically, I am pleased to see some official recognition for Wolverhampton at last, as a few simple lines have been added on the 'Black Country Society' web-page, in the sub-section 'About', and then 'What or Where is the Black Country?' For some time, it has totally ommitted Wolverhampton, simply stating: -

"The Black Country is defined by geology. The coal lies beneath Wednesbury, Darlaston, Wednesfield, Bilston, Coseley, Tipton, Dudley,

Brierley Hill, and Halesowen, together with their nearby smaller townships, and at a greater depth beneath West Bromwich, Oldbury, and Smethwick."

But it is highly significant that a few simple but very important lines have been added to this paragraph, in October 2017: -

"A recently reprinted 1836 map of the extent of the seam includes much of Wolverhampton, and also parts of Walsall. More modern thinking should include most, if not all, of the four modern boroughs that cover the Black Country region. i.e Dudley, Sandwell, Walsall, and Wolverhampton".

I had also sent in the draft version of the chapter of this work covering coal-mining, though perhaps I over-emphasise the influence of that. I never received a response, but if they looked at it, it would hopefully only have helped the case.

So, this new acceptance of Wolverhampton, to some degree, negates the key strands of argument throughout this work. Nevertheless, their website is still rather confusing and contradictory, as after at last including Wolverhampton, it then states: -

"The Black Country Society believes the 'original Black Country' to be that area of South Staffordshire and North Worcestershire that was on the famous thirty-foot seam of coal."

So, although the Black Country Society have at least come around to acknowledge Wolverhampton's coal-mining legacy, perhaps after much persuasion, which in itself is undoubtedly a significantly-progressive step, their final statement regards 'the original Black Country' is still open to much debate, as it still inevitably disregards those key areas where iron-stone and thinner seams of coal were utilised, or where the iron industry was concentrated. They ignore the fact that the 'original Black Country' evidently excluded the Worcestershire section of the region – including Dudley.

Nevertheless, it is pleasing that some within the Black Country Society accept a wider Black Country definition, with Wolverhampton's inclusion, certainly at least in part.

It does seem to be the case that although many continue to support the somewhat-romantic notion of an 'original Back Country' based on the thick coal seam alone, knowledgeable people who thoroughly study its history, agree with the conclusions of this work – that it was quite clearly based on a combination of coal and iron.

Some people appear in awe of and afraid of contradicting Dr Fletcher's 1967 views and his definition, despite the findings and conclusions of so many other people during the Industrial revolution and subsequently.

The thick coal seam theory is undoubtedly one that serves Dudley well, and one that in the view of the findings of this investigative project, has created a false sense of ownership there.

CHAPTER ELEVEN

Wolverhampton and Black Country Quiz

Q1) When was the term Black Country first recorded?

A1) A recently discovered 1841 article in the Staffordshire Advertiser described going "into the Black Country in Staffordshire…..Wolverhampton, Bilston, Tipton". This is currently the first known written record of the Black Country. The term may well have been in local use from the 1820s or 1830s, but this cannot be substantiated.

Q2) William Gresley was previously accredited with the first official written reference of the Black Country in his 1846 book ' Colton Green - a tale of the Black Country'. How long, in mileage, did he describe the Black Country as being, and which County did this, and the quote in Q1, restrict the 'original Black Country' to?

A2) Twenty miles, which would inevitably have included Wolverhampton at one end. This is totally at odds with the 1967 Black Country Society geographical definition of the area. Both early records only referred to the Black Country as being an area of South Staffordshire, which at that time did not include Dudley. Though within a few years the term 'Black Country' undoubtedly did include a wider area of South Staffordshire and East Worcestershire.

Q3) Was the Black Country so-named due to the effects of coal-mining, iron production, or a combination of both?

A3) The Black Country Society suggest that it was so-named solely because of the existence of the thick coal seam, and they subsequently define its exact borders as being solely based on its existence, but the thick coal seam was first mined 500 years prior to the name 'Black Country' emerging. In fact, the Black Country was so-named at a point (1830-1840) when iron production utilising coal for fuel and steam-power for energy, dominated the entire district, so it seems sensible to conclude that it was a combination of both iron and coal industries which were inextricably linked, that truly defined the Black Country. Quite clearly, based on so much evidence, it was never coal in isolation.

Q4) The thick coal seam was unique to the Black Country, but the iron-ore and thinner coal seams were arguably even more important for the developing iron industry. Which were the key mining areas of the Black Country?

A4) Although the much-celebrated thick coal seam was mined extensively throughout Wednesbury, Bilston, and Brierley Hill, it was also mined as far north as just a mile from the centre of Wolverhampton, at Monmore Green and Chillington for instance. Additionally, however, the Wolverhampton coal-field was notably the finest in the district for iron-ore. The famed Birmingham geologist Joseph Beete Jukes confirmed that the vast Black Country iron industry predominantly evolved where the iron-stone tract of the coal-field lay. The thin coal seam of much of the Wolverhampton field was also generally better suited for use in the iron works, whilst much of the thick seam, especially east of Dudley, was only suitable for domestic household use. Finally, the shallow, thin seam district around Wolverhampton was arguably that tract of land most damaged by mining operations.

Q5) In 1841, when the Black Country became first named as such, which two town parishes had most miners in the Black Country region, according to official census records?

A5) Bilston, then Wolverhampton.

Q6) At the same time, around 1840, twelve firms in the Black Country were producing 10,000 tonnes of iron per annum? How many of these were from Wolverhampton?

A6) 4, as well as a 5th from Bilston. Heading the list was Chillington Iron Company in east Wolverhampton. Wolverhampton alone had 260 firms specialising in some form of metal manufacture during the Industrial Revolution.

Q7) Before the term 'Black Country' emerged, what was the area frequently referred to as?

A7) 'The Iron Country', with Wolverhampton often referred to as the 'centre of the iron trade' nationally, as evidenced by regular 'state of trade' reports in various regional and national newspapers, from the 'Wolverhampton correspondant'. Wolverhampton was also labelled 'Ironopolis' by members of the press.

Q8) When viewed from the elevated position of Dudley Castle, or from the rail journey across the region, which section of the Black Country was frequently observed to have had the thickest industrial smog or smoke lying over it?

A8) A number of authors and visitors, such as Walter White, Samuel Sidney, Elihu Burritt often described the Wolverhampton and Bilston area as being that where the thickest smoke lay. Wolverhampton's 240 towering chimneys were a distinctive feature of its landscape in the 1800s, drawn famously by the artistic editor of a major London Newspaper reporting Queen Victoria's 1866 visit. The Lancet publication described the residents and homes of Monmore Green and Horseley Fields as being covered in coal-dust. Writers described Wolverhampton's landscape and atmosphere in vivid detail, including Friedrich von Raumer, Charles Darwin, Charles Dickens, and J.B Priestley.

Q9) Which town was widely considered to have been the 'Capital' or 'Metropolis of the Black Country' during the 1800s and early 1900s?

A9) Although Dudley is now fairly-widely promoted as the 'Capital of the Black Country', there is a significant amount of evidence that proves that Wolverhampton was considered as such throughout the Industrial Revolution of the 1800s and early-1900s. This may have been because Wolverhampton and the majority of towns lay in Staffordshire, whilst the town of Dudley lay in a Worcestershire enclave. Local iron-industry expert, Bilston-born Samuel Griffiths, amongst others, confirmed in the 1870s that 'Wolverhampton was considered 'Capital of the Black Country', and 'Capital of the Iron Trade in the Black Country'. A local man primed with local knowledge. Other writers confirmed this aswell.

Q10) Despite the views of Dr Fletcher in 1967, representing the then newly-formed Black Country Society, who were themselves conceived from the remnants of the Dudley Canal Tunnel Closure Group, out of seventeen historians and writers who wrote about the Black Country in the 1800s and 1900s, how many of them considered Wolverhampton - at least in part, to be within the Black Country?

A10) 16 out of 17. Only H Rees in 1946 seems to have definitively excluded Wolverhampton entirely from the Black Country, whilst other 1900s writers such as Walter Allen, Frank Dribble, WKV Gale, Harold Parsons, Edward Chitham, George

Barnsby, John Ogden, Alec Brew, and the Black Country Muse web-host all consider at least part of Wolverhampton, even excluding the Bilston part, to be very much part of the Black Country. This aligns with the stance of virtually all 1800s writers including William Gresley, William White, Samuel Sidney, Elihu Burritt, Joseph Beete Jukes, Samuel Griffiths, and John Bartholomew, who all considered Wolverhampton to be a very important, if not 'the' major Black Country town.

REFERENCES

Allen G.C 1928 "The Industrial Development of Birmingham and the Black Country 1860-1914" (University of Birmingham)

Allen W 1946 "Black Country". (London. Paul Elek publishers).

Angerstein RR 2001 "Illustrated Travel Diary - Industry in England 1753-55" (London. The Science Museum)

Asprey E (Doctor of Philosophy) 2007 "Black Country English and Black Country Identity". (University of Leeds, School of English).

Barnsby G "A History of Housing in Wolverhampton 1750-1975" (available at www.distinctlyblackcountry.co.uk)

Barnsby G 1990 "Social Conditions in the Black Country" (Wolverhampton. Integrated Publishing Services)

Bartholomew J 1887 "Gazetteer of the British Isles" (London. Bartholomew & son)

Betjemen J 1997 "Coming Home: An anthology of his prose 1920-1977" (London. Candida Lycett Green)

Black Country Historic Landscape Characterisation Survey, on behalf of the Archaeological Service "Two-hundred years in twenty seconds" at www.distinctlyblackcountry.org.uk/.../two-hundred-years-in-twenty-seconds

Black Country History Organisation at www.blackcountryhistory.org

Black Country Muse at www.blackcountrymuse.com

Brew A 1999 "Monmore Green and Ettingshall" (Tempus)

Britain From Above at www.britainfromabove.org.uk

British Newspaper Archive at www.britishnewspaperarchive.co.uk

Burritt E 1868 "Walks in the Black Country and its green borderland" (Birmingham. S Law, son & Marston)

Chapman N 2011 "The South Staffordshire Coalfield through time". (Stroud. Amberley Publishing)

Chitham E 1972 "The Black Country" (London. Longman)

Clare D 2005 "Wolverhampton - Photographic Memories" (Salisbury. Teffont)

Coal Mining Website at www.cmhrc.co.uk

Cobbett W 1893 "Rural Rides 1830" (Volume Two) (London. Dent)

Cooper T 1872 "The Life of Thomas Cooper – an Autobiography" (London. Hodder & Stoughton)

Crouzet F 1982 "The Victorian Economy" (London and New York. Routledge)

Darwin C 1835 "Voyaging – A Biography, Volume One" (London. J Browne)

Dean R 2008 "The Canals of Birmingham and the Black Country" (Stoke-on-Trent. Cartographics)

Derby H.C. 1973 "A New Historical Geography of England after 1600" (Cambridge. Derby)

Dickens C 1838 "Old curiosity shop" (London. Wordsworth)

Distinctly Black Country Organisation at www.distinctlyblackcountry.org

Drabble P 1952 "Black Country" (London. R Hale)

Engels F 1844 "The Condition of the Working-class in England in 1844" (Gutenberg)

Farley K "A History of Wolverhampton 985-1985" (Article from website)

Fordyce W 1860 "A History of Coal, Coke, Coalfields, and Iron Manufacture in Northern England" (Newcastle. Frank Graham)

Gale W 1966 "The Black Country Iron Industry – A technical history" (London. The Iron and Steel Institute)

Gresley W (Rev) 1846 "Colton Green, a tale of the Black Country". (London. Masters).

Griffiths S 1872 "Griffiths Guide to the Iron Trade of Great Britain" (London. Griffiths)

Guillou M Le 1972 "Development of the Iron and Steel Industry 1850-1913" (Thesis)

Howe W - Lost Wolverhampton – www.lostwolverhampton.co.uk

Iron and Steel Institute (via www.gracesguide.co.uk)

Jones J 1904 "Tettenhall – The bright, green borderland" (Wolverhampton Journal)

Jones P (Professor) 2009 "Industrial Enlightenment – Science, technology and culture of Birmingham and the West Midlands". (Manchester. University Press)

Jones W.H. 1903 "The Municipal Life of Wolverhampton" (London. Alexander and Shepheard)

Jukes J.B 1859 "The South Staffordshire Coalfield" (2nd edition) (London. Longman, Green, Longman, and Roberts)

Keir J 1793 "The Mineralogy of the south-west part of Staffordshire" (Memoir)

King P.W. 2007. "Black Country mining before the Industrial Revolution" (The Bulletin of the Peak District Mines Historical Society. Volume 16, No.6, winter 2007)

King W.W. 1916 Plexographic map of the thick coal of South Staffordshire (University of Birmingham. Lapworth Museum Archives, Wickham King Collection)

Lawrence J 1998 "Speaking for the People – Party, Language and Popular Politics in England 1867-1914" (Liverpool. Cambridge University Press)

Mason F 1979 – "The story of an Industrial Town, Wolverhampton" (Buckingham, Barracuda Books)

Millward R and Robinson A – "The Black Country" (London. MacMillan)

Murchison R 1839 "Silurian system based on geological searches" (London. Murray)

Newman Local History Organisation at www.newmanlocalhistory.org

Ogden D 1998 "Defining the Black Country" (from Black Country website and pages)

Palliser D.M. 1976 "The Staffordshire Landscape" (London. Hodder and Stoughton)

Parker B 'Wolverhampton History Website' www.historywebsite.co.uk

Parsons H 1986 "The Black Country" (London. Hale).

Pelling H 1967 "Social Geography of British Elections 1885-1910" (London).

Phelps J.G. 1897 "Illustrated Towns of England - Wolverhampton, a Business Review" (Birmingham. Industrial publishing Company).

Pitt W 1817 "A Topographical history of Staffordshire" (Newcastle-Under-Lyme. Smith)

Plot R 1686 "Natural History of Staffordshire" (Oxford. Printed at the Theatre).

Priestley J.B. 1934 "English Journal" (Re-printed 2009 Great Northern Books)

Queen Victoria's Journals - Available On-line at www.queenvictoriasjournals.org

Quigley P 2009-10 "Black Country Historic Landscape Characterisation" (University of York)

Rana S 2009 "New evidence supporting Wolverhampton as the location of the first working Newcomen engine". (Article) (International Journal For the history of English and Tech. Vol 79, No.2 July 2009)

Razzell P.E. and Wainwright R.W. 1973 "The Victorian Working Class" (a selection of letters to the Morning Chronicle) (Abingdon, Oxon. Routledge)

Rees H 1946 "Birmingham and The Black Country" (in Economic Geography 222)

Rule J 1986 "The Labouring classes in early Industrial England 1750-1850" (London. Routledge)

Russell S 2011 "The Relationship between Agricultural development and Industrial growth 1660-1880 – A case study of the Black Country" (University of Birmingham)

Sidney S 1851 "Rides on Railways" (Re-printed 2009 Dodo press) (Also available as Audiobook on www.youtube.com)

Smith J 2005 "Industrial and Social Change – Wolverhampton transformed 1700-1840" (From Chapter Eight of "Towns, Regions and Industries – Urban and Industrial Change in the Midlands 1700 – 1840" (Edited by John Stobart and Neil Raven) (Manchester. Manchester University Press.)

Smith J B 2001 "The Governance of Wolverhampton 1848-1888" (thesis, PhD University of Leicester)

Staffordshire Advertiser 1841 'A report on Leading Liberal Reformers Meeting at the Guildhall, Lichfield on 24 November 1841'. Available at Thebritishnewspaperarchive.co.uk

Tamie E at www.dickens-jp/archive/ocs/ocs-tamai.pdf

Tancred T 1843 "Midland Mining Commission Report" (Government Paper)

Thorneycroft-Fowler E 1899 "A Double Thread" (London. Hutchinson and Co).

Timmins S 1866 "Birmingham and Midland Hardware District" (Oxford. Routledge)

Trainor R 1993 "Black Country Elites – The Exercise of Authority in an Industrialised Area 1830-1900 (Oxford. Clarendon Press)

Von Raumer F 1835 "Series of letters" (Memoirs translated by S Austin. H.E. Lloyd)

White W (William) 1834 "History, Gazetteer, and Directory of Staffordshire" (Sheffield. White)

White W (Walter) 1860 "All Around The Wrekin" (London. Chapman and Hall).

Wikipedia.org.uk at www.wikepedia.org.uk (Wolverhampton history page)

Wolverhampton City Archives

Wolverhampton Civic and Historical Society at www.cityofwolverhampton.com

Wolverhampton History Organisation at www.wolverhamptonhistory.org.uk

Young F.B.   1927 "A Portrait of Clare" (Heinemann)
             1934 "This Little World" (Heinemann)
             1940 "Mr Lucton's Freedom" (Heinemann)